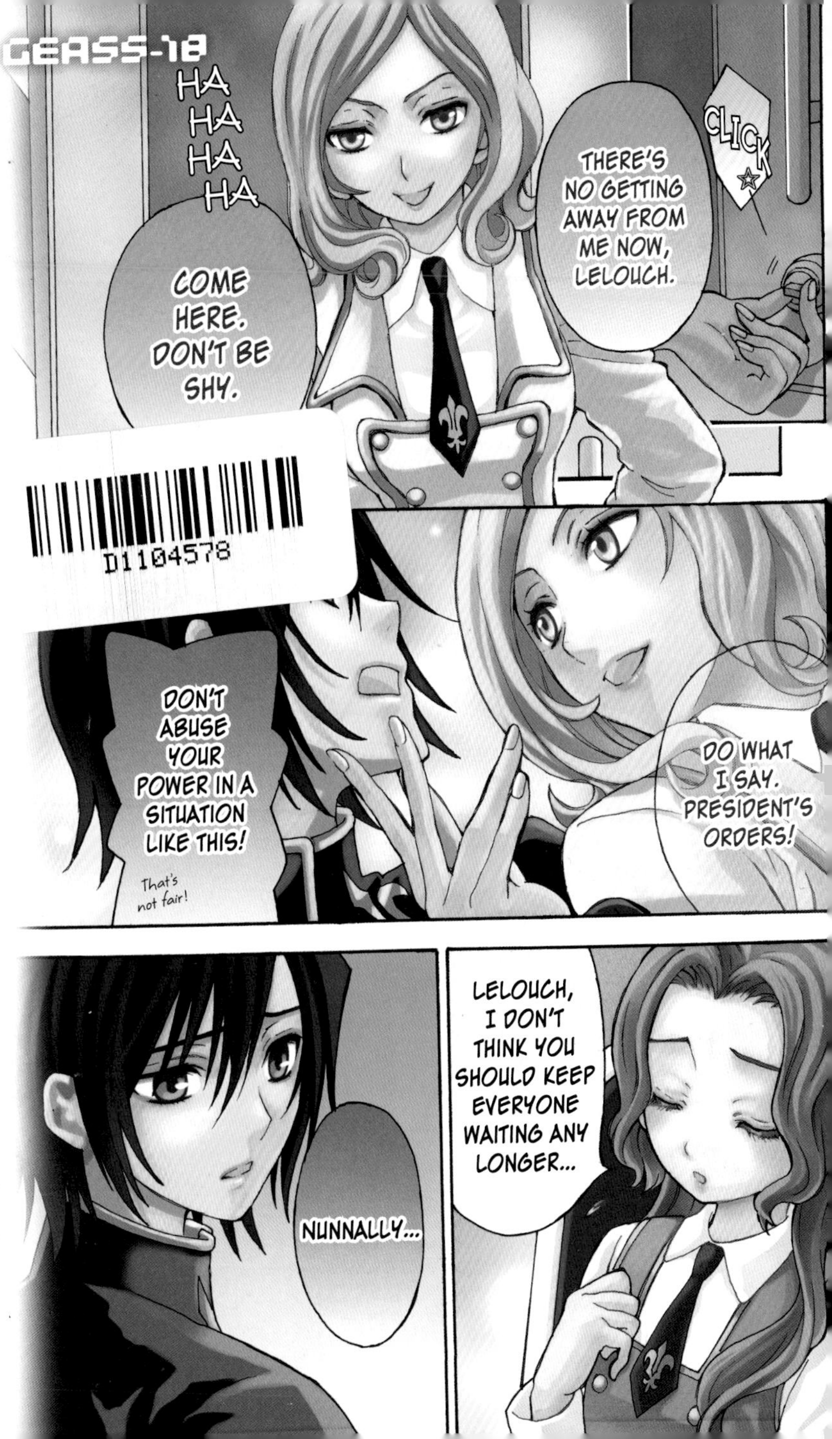
GEASS-18
CLICK
THERE'S NO GETTING AWAY FROM ME NOW, LELOUCH.
HA HA HA HA
COME HERE. DON'T BE SHY.
DO WHAT I SAY. PRESIDENT'S ORDERS!
DON'T ABUSE YOUR POWER IN A SITUATION LIKE THIS!
That's not fair!
LELOUCH, I DON'T THINK YOU SHOULD KEEP EVERYONE WAITING ANY LONGER...
NUNNALLY...

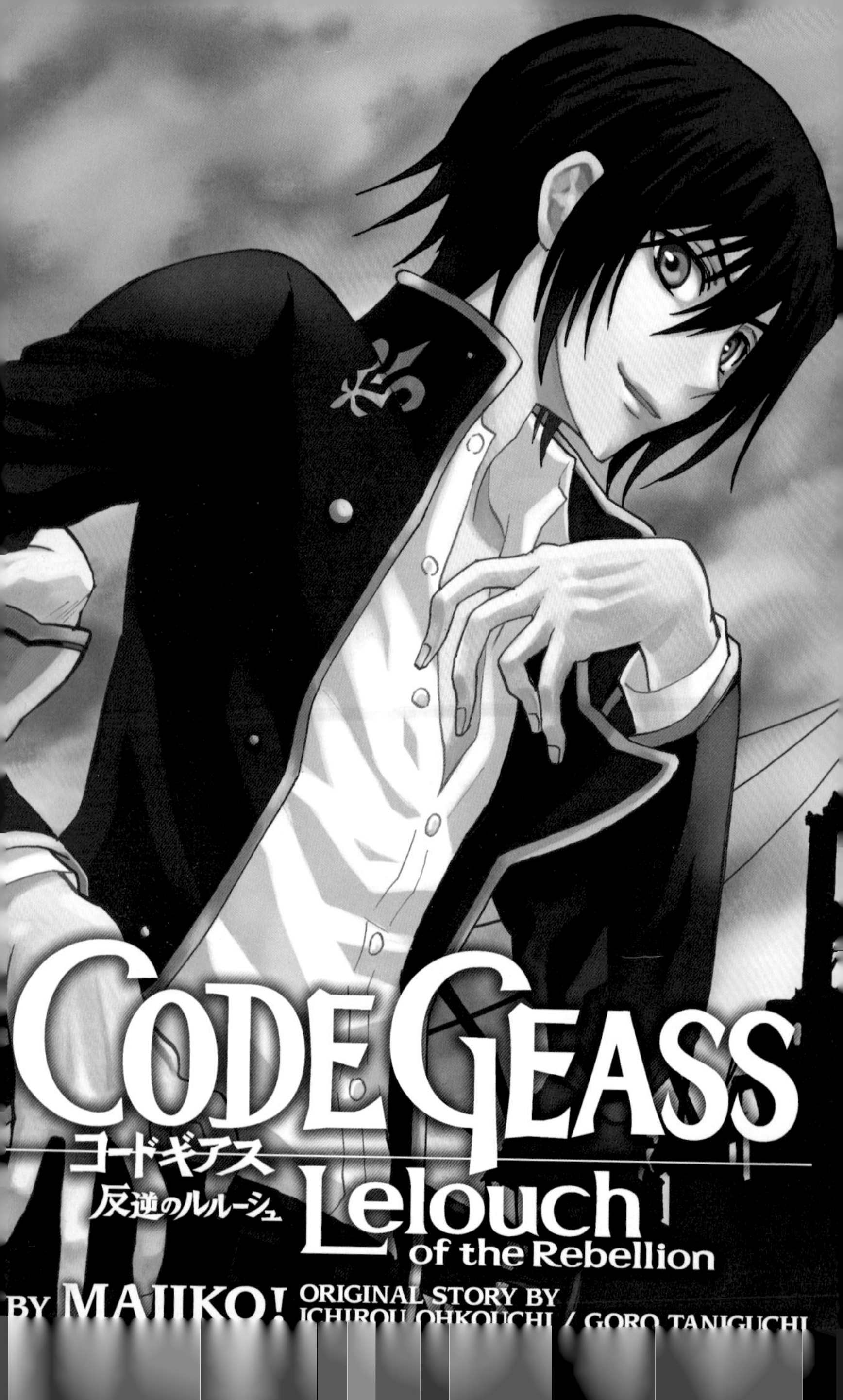
CODE GEASS
コードギアス
反逆のルルーシュ
Lelouch of the Rebellion
BY MAJIKO!
ORIGINAL STORY BY
ICHIROU OHKOUCHI / GORO TANIGUCHI

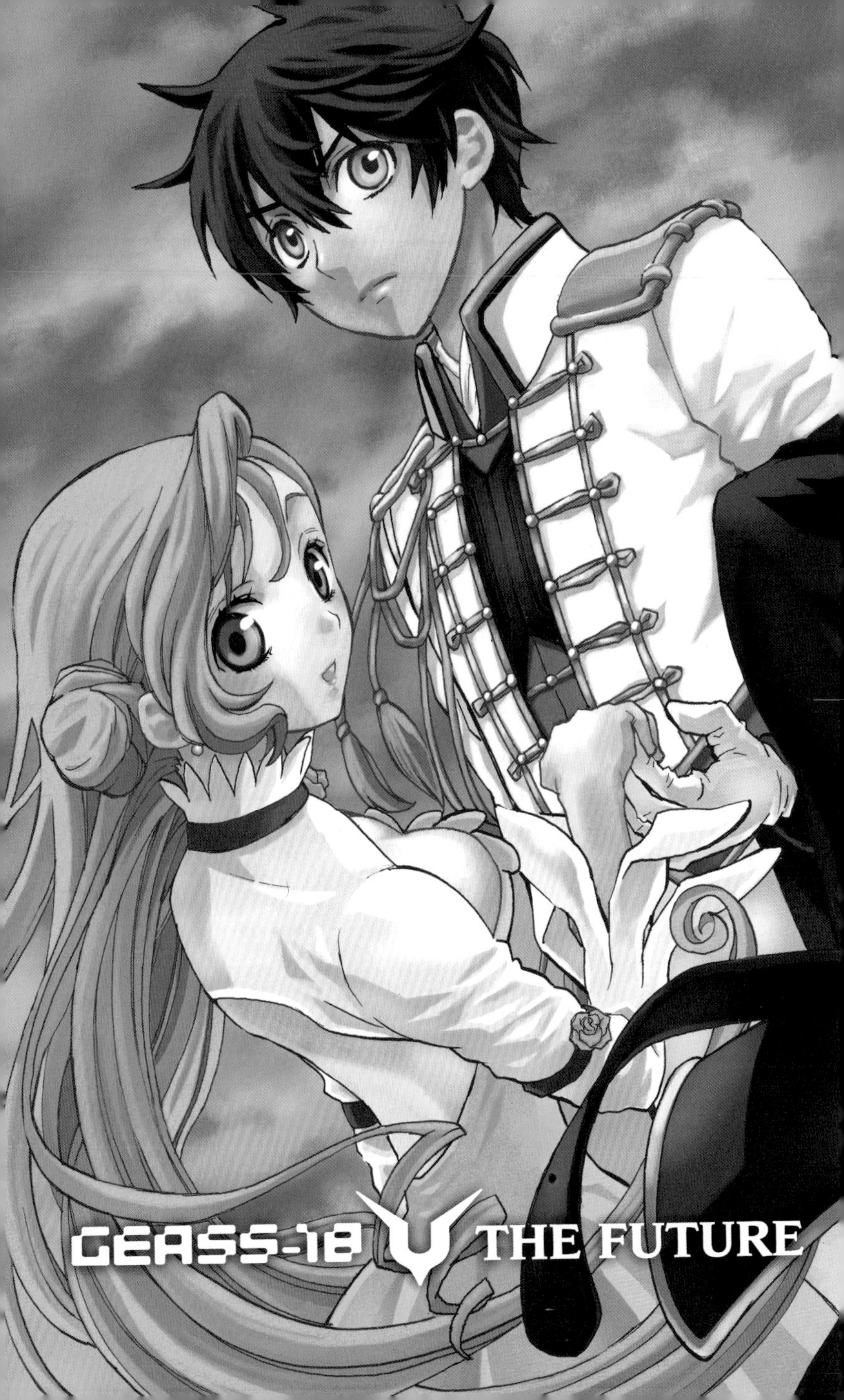
GEASS-18 THE FUTURE

GEASS-18 THE FUTURE...................3

GEASS-19 THE SPECIALLY
ADMINISTRATED ZONE
OF JAPAN.....................49

GEASS-20 SEPARATION...............97

GEASS-21 THE CACOPHONY OF
COLLAPSE..............125

THAT VOICE, THAT
SUMMER.............171

Afterword......193

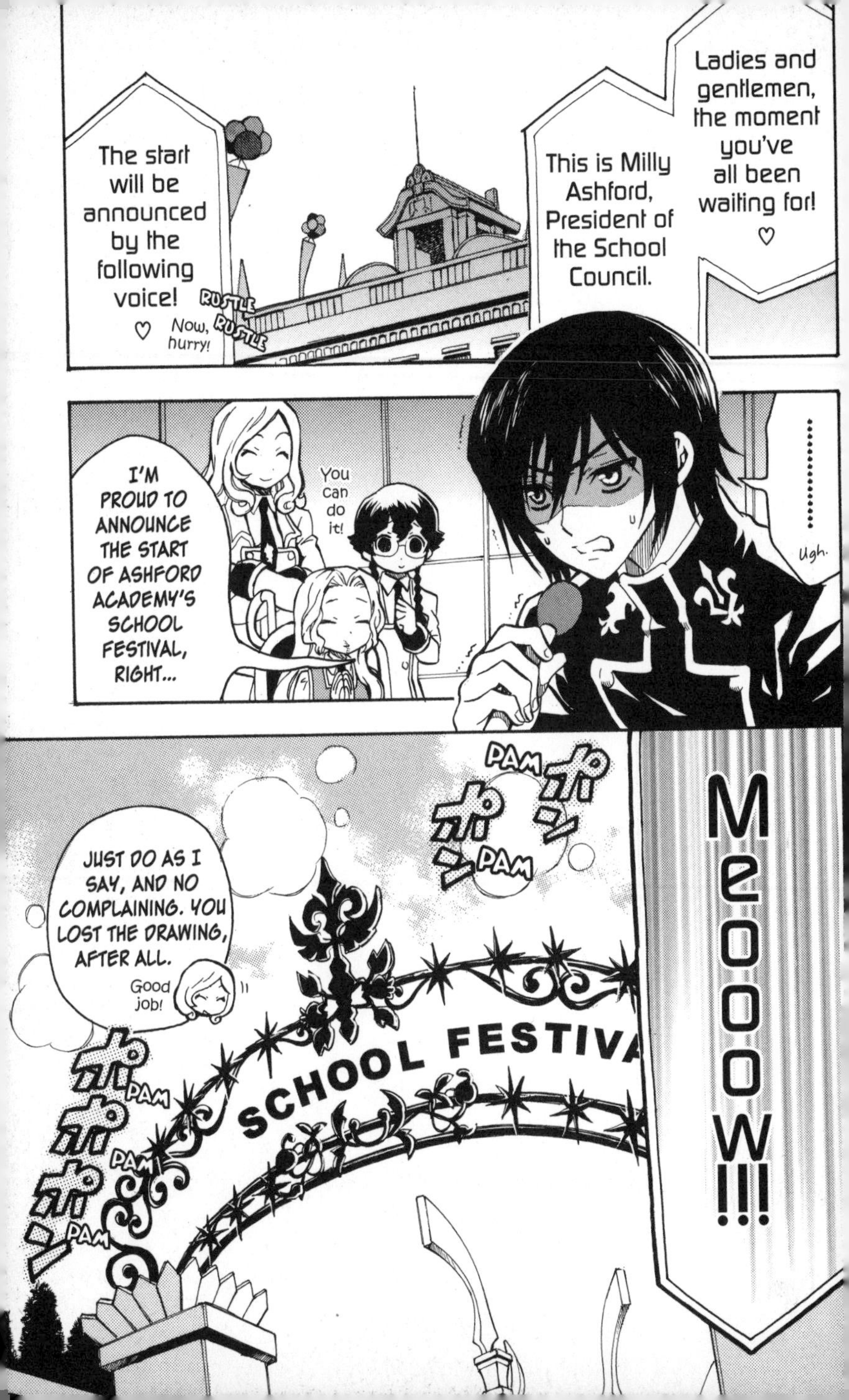

Ladies and gentlemen, the moment you've all been waiting for! ♡
This is Milly Ashford, President of the School Council.
The start will be announced by the following voice! ♡
RUSTLE RUSTLE
Now, hurry!
....
Ugh.
You can do it!
I'M PROUD TO ANNOUNCE THE START OF ASHFORD ACADEMY'S SCHOOL FESTIVAL, RIGHT...
MEOOOW!!!
ポン PAM
ポン PAM
JUST DO AS I SAY, AND NO COMPLAINING. YOU LOST THE DRAWING, AFTER ALL.
Good job!
SCHOOL FESTIVA
ポ PAM
ポ PAM
ポン PAM

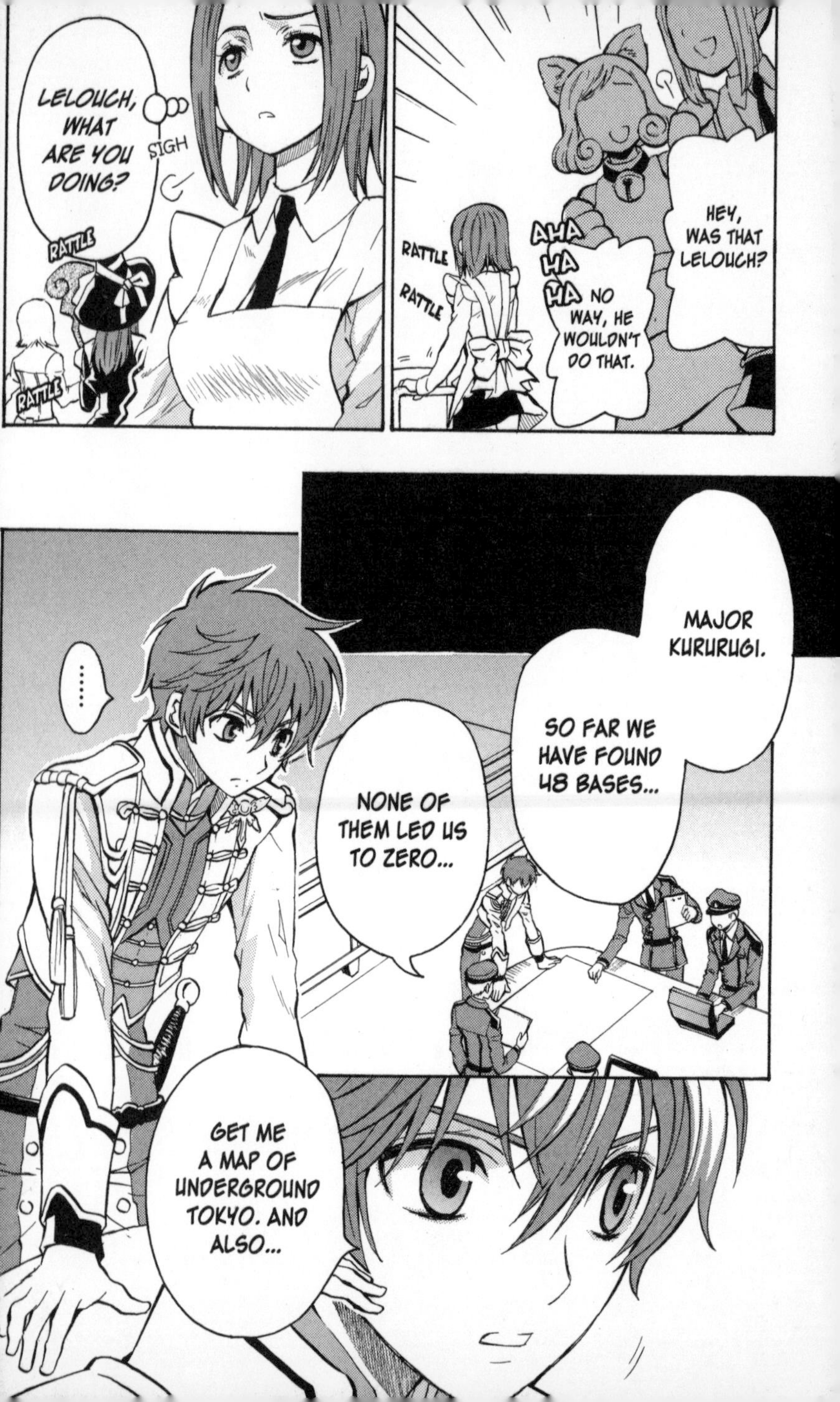
HEY, WAS THAT LELOUCH?
AHA HA HA
NO WAY, HE WOULDN'T DO THAT.
RATTLE
RATTLE
SIGH
LELOUCH, WHAT ARE YOU DOING?
RATTLE
RATTLE
MAJOR KURURUGI.
SO FAR WE HAVE FOUND 48 BASES...
NONE OF THEM LED US TO ZERO...
......
GET ME A MAP OF UNDERGROUND TOKYO. AND ALSO...

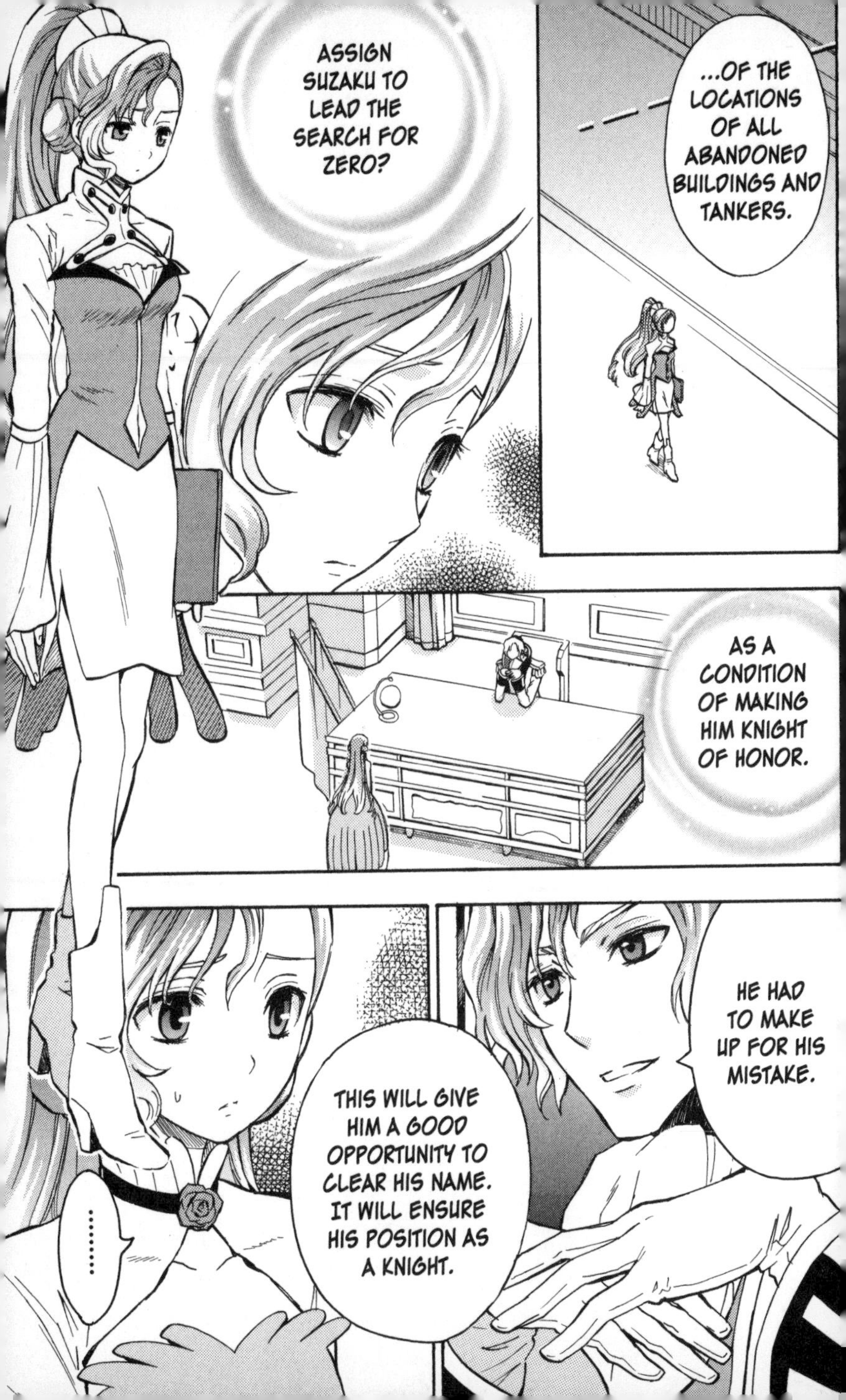
...OF THE LOCATIONS OF ALL ABANDONED BUILDINGS AND TANKERS.
ASSIGN SUZAKU TO LEAD THE SEARCH FOR ZERO?
AS A CONDITION OF MAKING HIM KNIGHT OF HONOR.
HE HAD TO MAKE UP FOR HIS MISTAKE.
THIS WILL GIVE HIM A GOOD OPPORTUNITY TO CLEAR HIS NAME. IT WILL ENSURE HIS POSITION AS A KNIGHT.
....

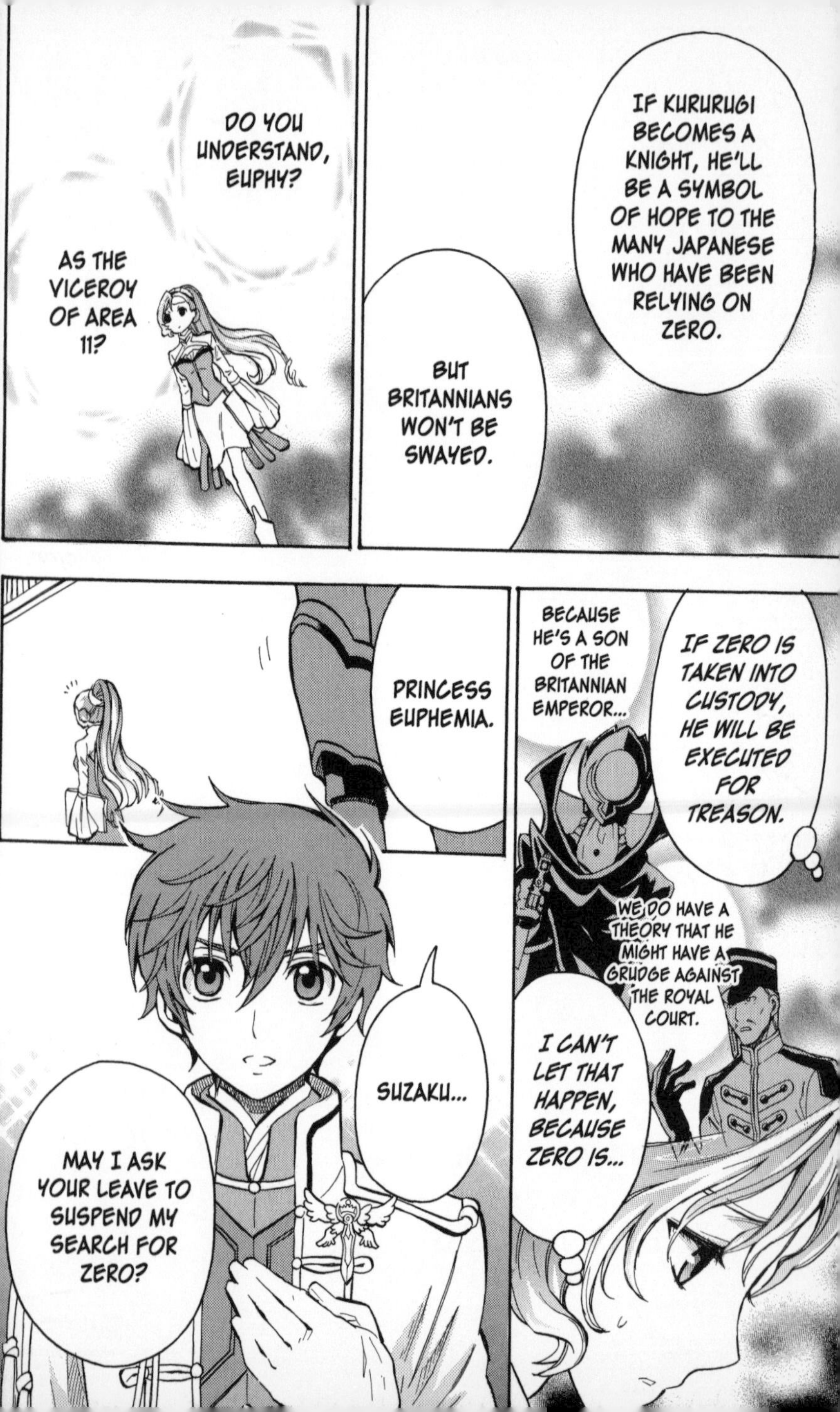
IF KURURUGI BECOMES A KNIGHT, HE'LL BE A SYMBOL OF HOPE TO THE MANY JAPANESE WHO HAVE BEEN RELYING ON ZERO.
BUT BRITANNIANS WON'T BE SWAYED.
DO YOU UNDERSTAND, EUPHY?
AS THE VICEROY OF AREA 11?
IF ZERO IS TAKEN INTO CUSTODY, HE WILL BE EXECUTED FOR TREASON.
BECAUSE HE'S A SON OF THE BRITANNIAN EMPEROR...
WE DO HAVE A THEORY THAT HE MIGHT HAVE A GRUDGE AGAINST THE ROYAL COURT.
I CAN'T LET THAT HAPPEN, BECAUSE ZERO IS...
PRINCESS EUPHEMIA.
SUZAKU...
MAY I ASK YOUR LEAVE TO SUSPEND MY SEARCH FOR ZERO?

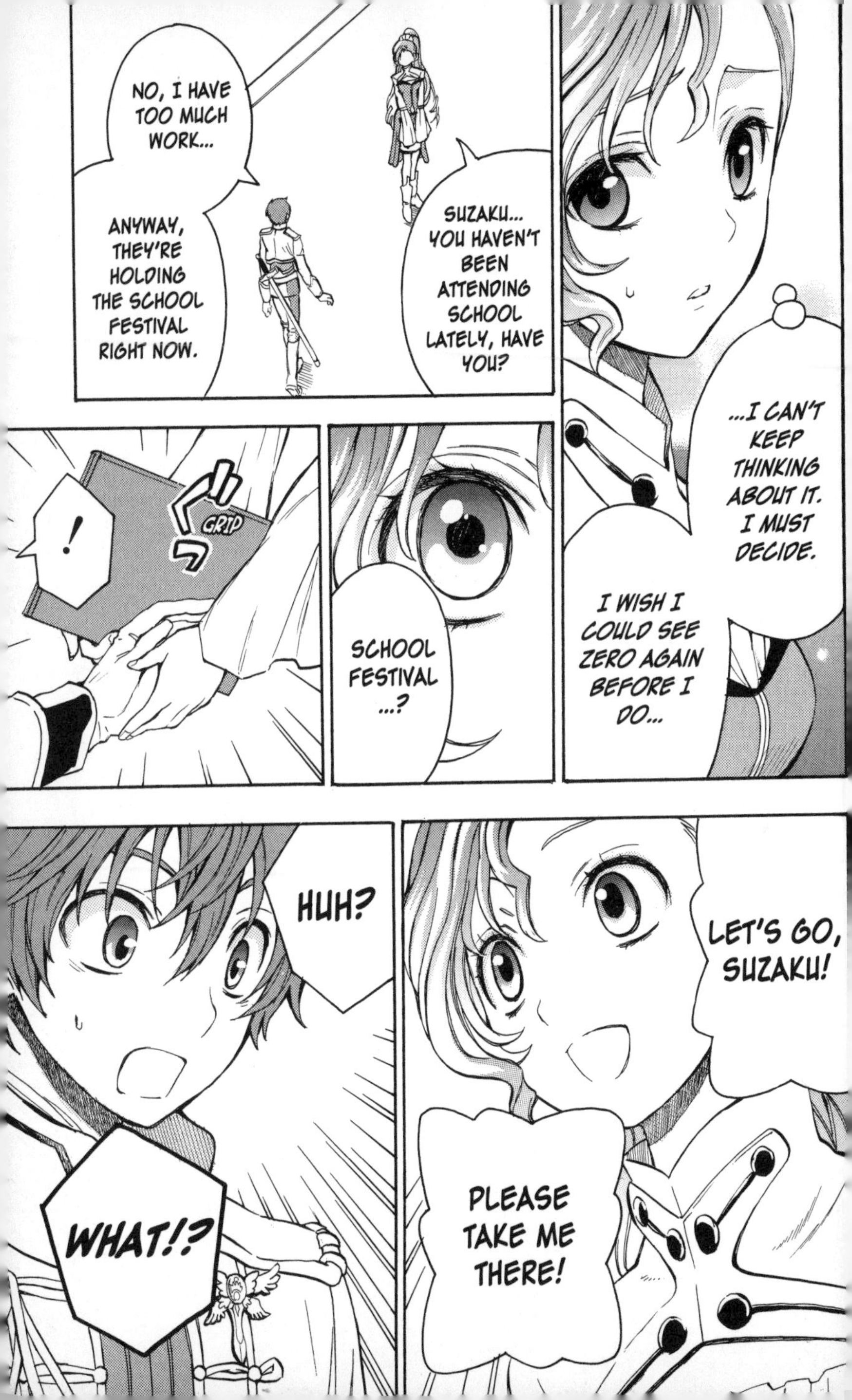

...I CAN'T KEEP THINKING ABOUT IT. I MUST DECIDE.
I WISH I COULD SEE ZERO AGAIN BEFORE I DO...
SUZAKU... YOU HAVEN'T BEEN ATTENDING SCHOOL LATELY, HAVE YOU?
NO, I HAVE TOO MUCH WORK...
ANYWAY, THEY'RE HOLDING THE SCHOOL FESTIVAL RIGHT NOW.
SCHOOL FESTIVAL ...?
GRIP
!
LET'S GO, SUZAKU!
PLEASE TAKE ME THERE!
HUH?
WHAT!?

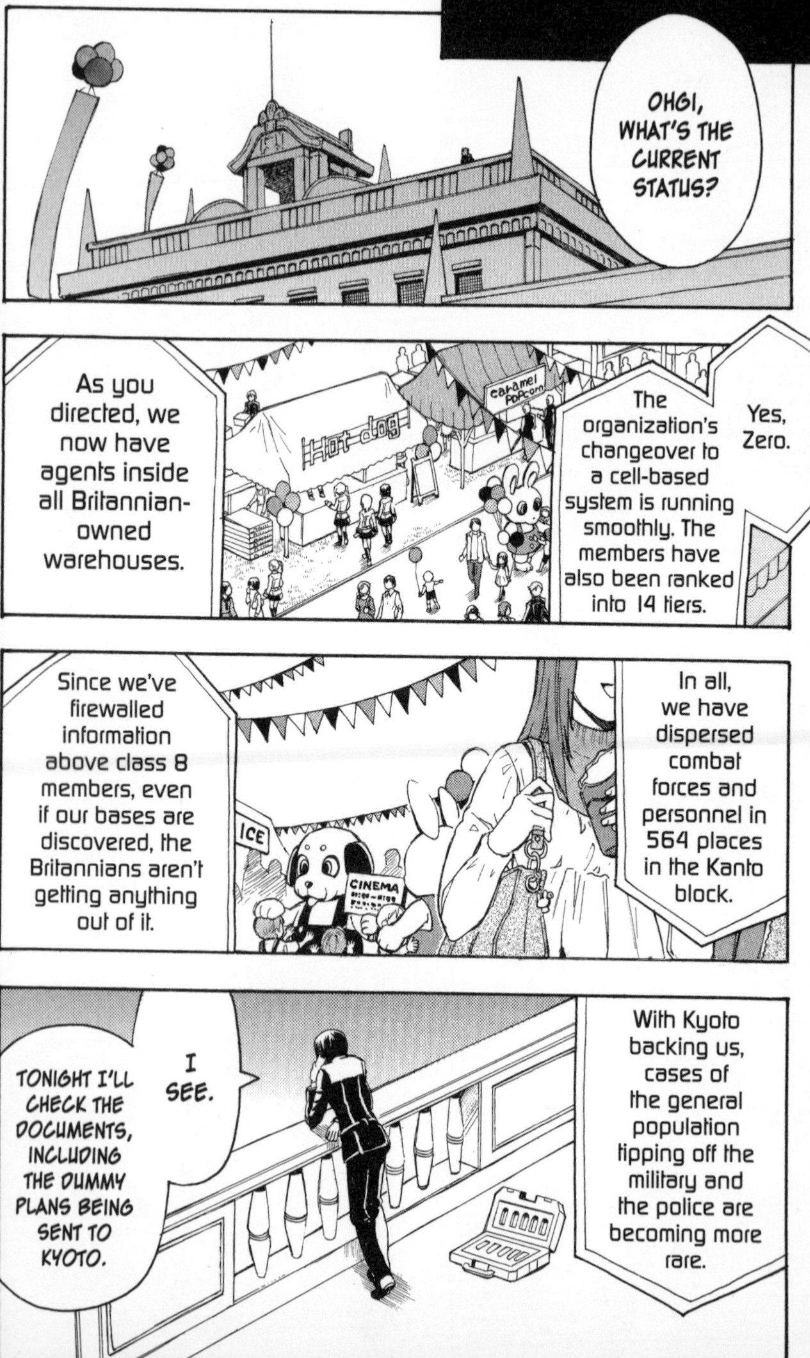
OHGI, WHAT'S THE CURRENT STATUS?
Yes, Zero.
The organization's changeover to a cell-based system is running smoothly. The members have also been ranked into 14 tiers.
caramel popcorn
Hot dog
As you directed, we now have agents inside all Britannian-owned warehouses.
In all, we have dispersed combat forces and personnel in 564 places in the Kanto block.
CINEMA
ICE
Since we've firewalled information above class 8 members, even if our bases are discovered, the Britannians aren't getting anything out of it.
With Kyoto backing us, cases of the general population tipping off the military and the police are becoming more rare.
I SEE.
TONIGHT I'LL CHECK THE DOCUMENTS, INCLUDING THE DUMMY PLANS BEING SENT TO KYOTO.

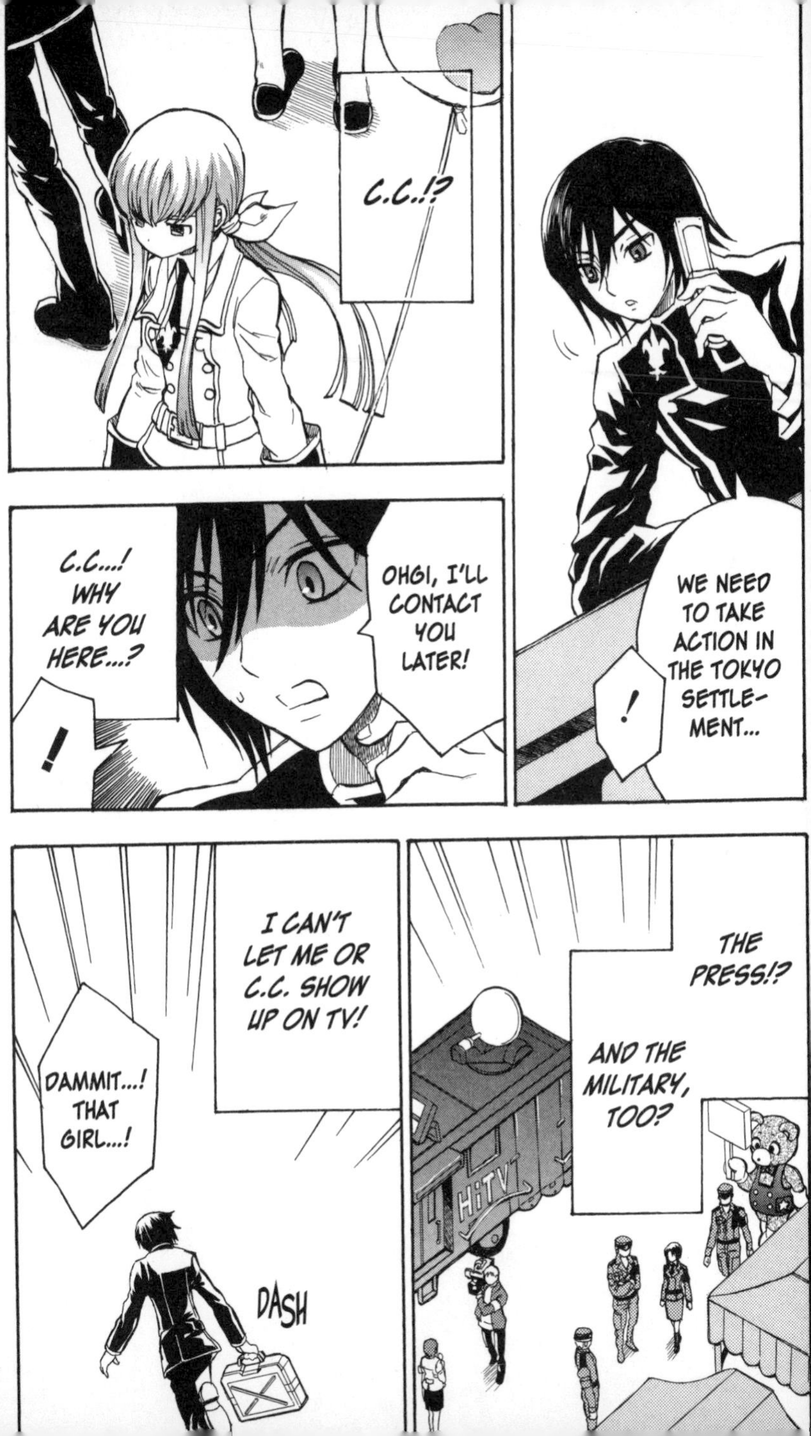
WE NEED TO TAKE ACTION IN THE TOKYO SETTLEMENT...
!
C.C..!?
OHGI, I'LL CONTACT YOU LATER!
C.C...! WHY ARE YOU HERE...?
!
THE PRESS!?
AND THE MILITARY, TOO?
HiTV
I CAN'T LET ME OR C.C. SHOW UP ON TV!
DAMMIT...! THAT GIRL...!
DASH

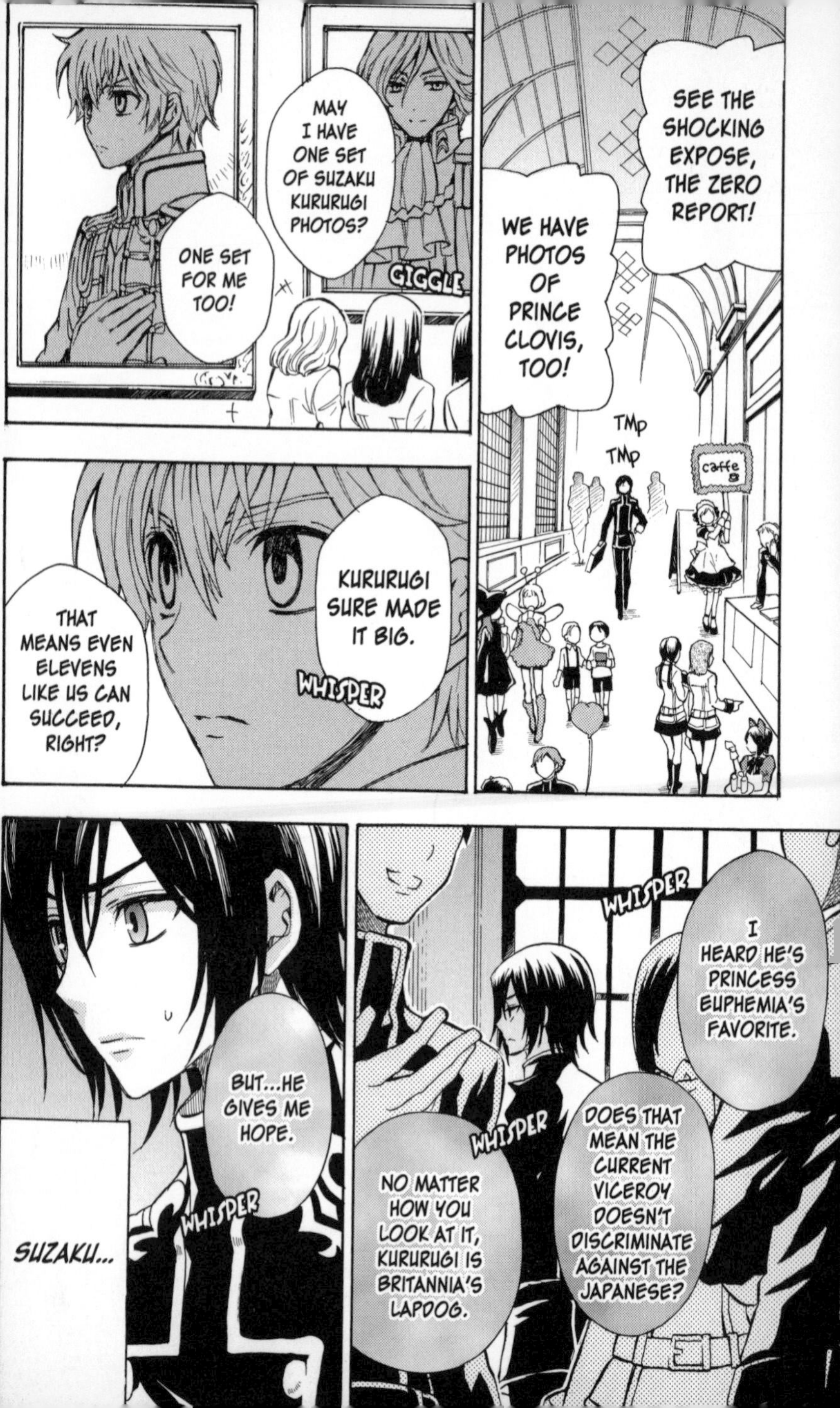
SEE THE SHOCKING EXPOSE, THE ZERO REPORT!
WE HAVE PHOTOS OF PRINCE CLOVIS, TOO!
TMP TMP
caffe
MAY I HAVE ONE SET OF SUZAKU KURURUGI PHOTOS?
GIGGLE
ONE SET FOR ME TOO!
KURURUGI SURE MADE IT BIG.
WHISPER
THAT MEANS EVEN ELEVENS LIKE US CAN SUCCEED, RIGHT?
WHISPER
I HEARD HE'S PRINCESS EUPHEMIA'S FAVORITE.
DOES THAT MEAN THE CURRENT VICEROY DOESN'T DISCRIMINATE AGAINST THE JAPANESE?
WHISPER
NO MATTER HOW YOU LOOK AT IT, KURURUGI IS BRITANNIA'S LAPDOG.
BUT...HE GIVES ME HOPE.
WHISPER
SUZAKU...

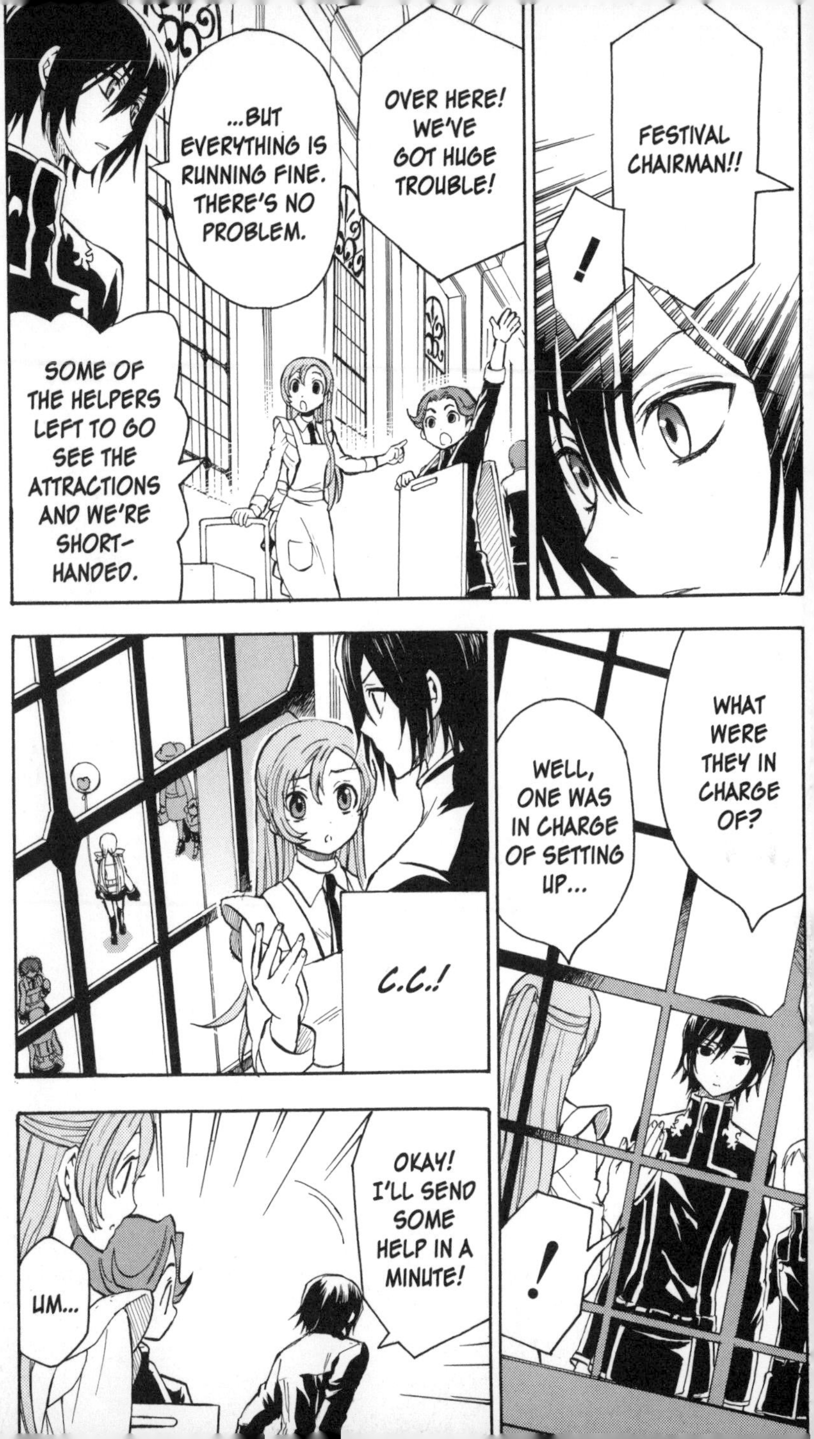
FESTIVAL CHAIRMAN!!
!
OVER HERE! WE'VE GOT HUGE TROUBLE!
...BUT EVERYTHING IS RUNNING FINE. THERE'S NO PROBLEM.
SOME OF THE HELPERS LEFT TO GO SEE THE ATTRACTIONS AND WE'RE SHORT-HANDED.
WHAT WERE THEY IN CHARGE OF?
WELL, ONE WAS IN CHARGE OF SETTING UP...
!
C.C.!
OKAY! I'LL SEND SOME HELP IN A MINUTE!
UM...

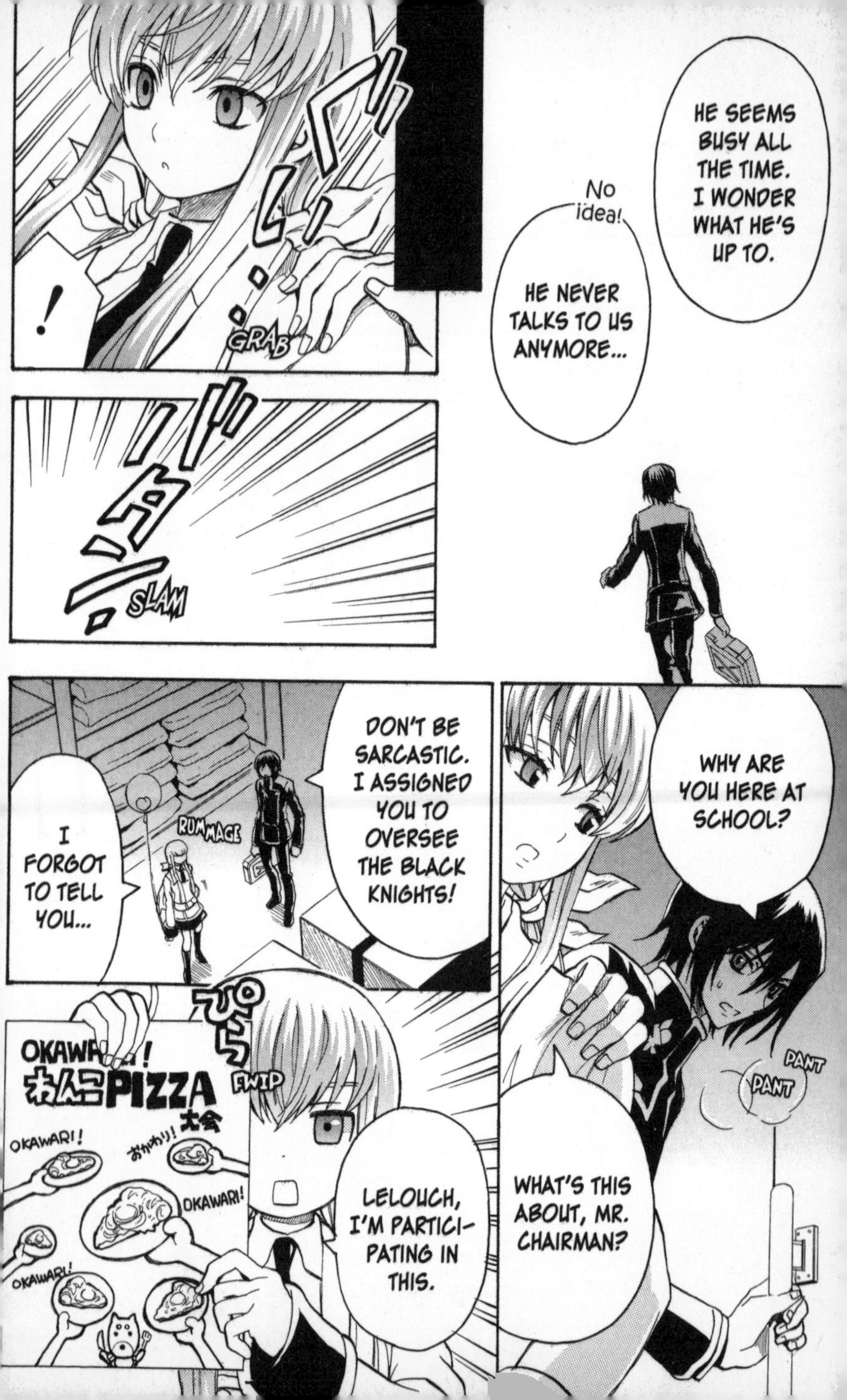
HE SEEMS BUSY ALL THE TIME. I WONDER WHAT HE'S UP TO.
No idea!
HE NEVER TALKS TO US ANYMORE...
!
GRAB
SLAM
WHY ARE YOU HERE AT SCHOOL?
PANT
PANT
WHAT'S THIS ABOUT, MR. CHAIRMAN?
DON'T BE SARCASTIC. I ASSIGNED YOU TO OVERSEE THE BLACK KNIGHTS!
RUMMAGE
I FORGOT TO TELL YOU...
ぴら
FWIP
LELOUCH, I'M PARTICI-PATING IN THIS.
OKAWA !
おんこPIZZA
大会
OKAWARI!
おかわり!
OKAWARI!
OKAWARI!

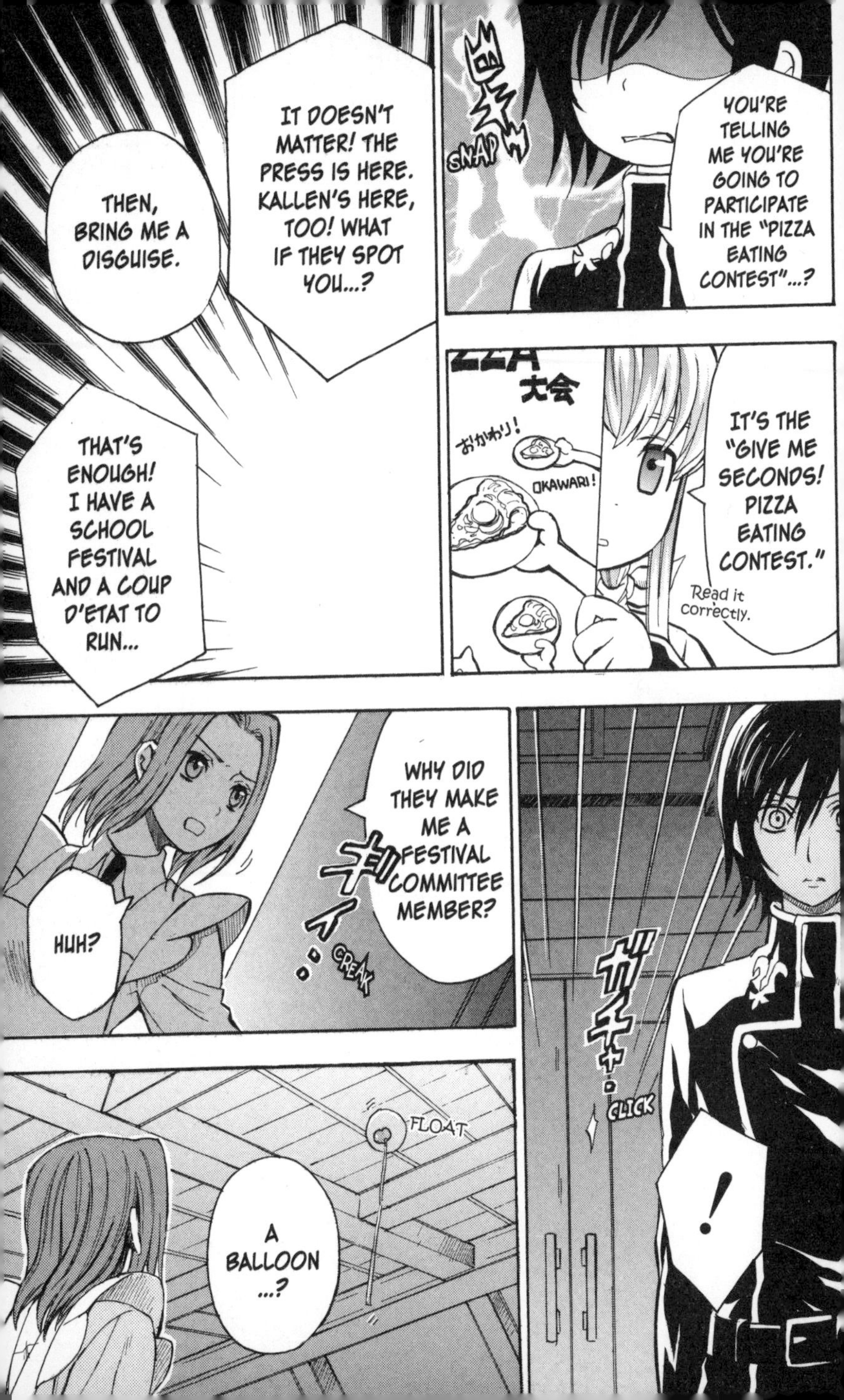
SNAP
YOU'RE TELLING ME YOU'RE GOING TO PARTICIPATE IN THE "PIZZA EATING CONTEST"...?
ZZA 大会
おかわり!
OKAWARI!
IT'S THE "GIVE ME SECONDS! PIZZA EATING CONTEST."
Read it correctly.
IT DOESN'T MATTER! THE PRESS IS HERE. KALLEN'S HERE, TOO! WHAT IF THEY SPOT YOU...?
THEN, BRING ME A DISGUISE.
THAT'S ENOUGH! I HAVE A SCHOOL FESTIVAL AND A COUP D'ETAT TO RUN...
CLICK
!
WHY DID THEY MAKE ME A FESTIVAL COMMITTEE MEMBER?
CREAK
HUH?
FLOAT
A BALLOON ...?

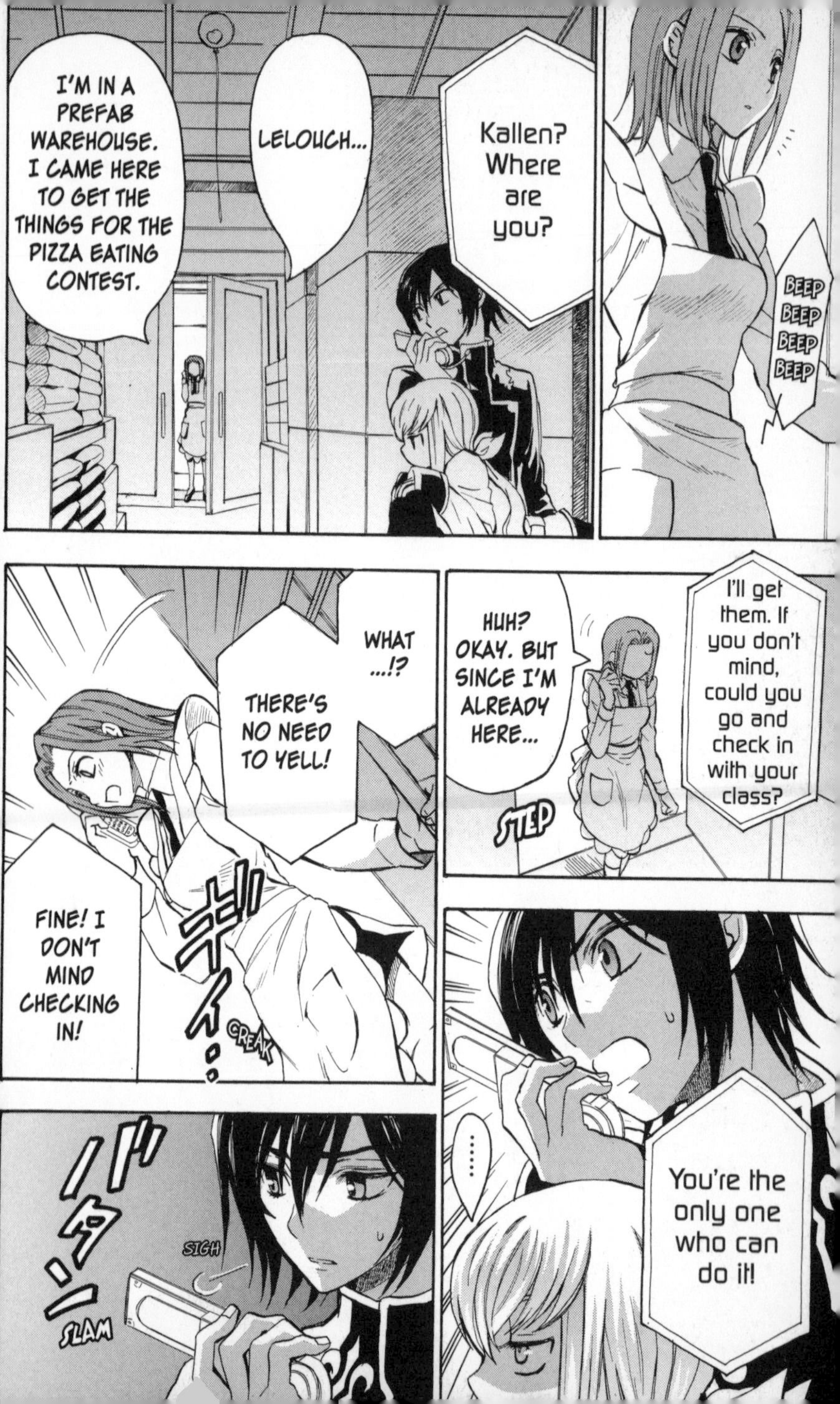

BEEP
BEEP
BEEP
BEEP
Kallen? Where are you?
LELOUCH...
I'M IN A PREFAB WAREHOUSE. I CAME HERE TO GET THE THINGS FOR THE PIZZA EATING CONTEST.
I'll get them. If you don't mind, could you go and check in with your class?
HUH? OKAY. BUT SINCE I'M ALREADY HERE...
STEP
WHAT ...!?
THERE'S NO NEED TO YELL!
FINE! I DON'T MIND CHECKING IN!
CREAK
......
You're the only one who can do it!
SIGH
SLAM

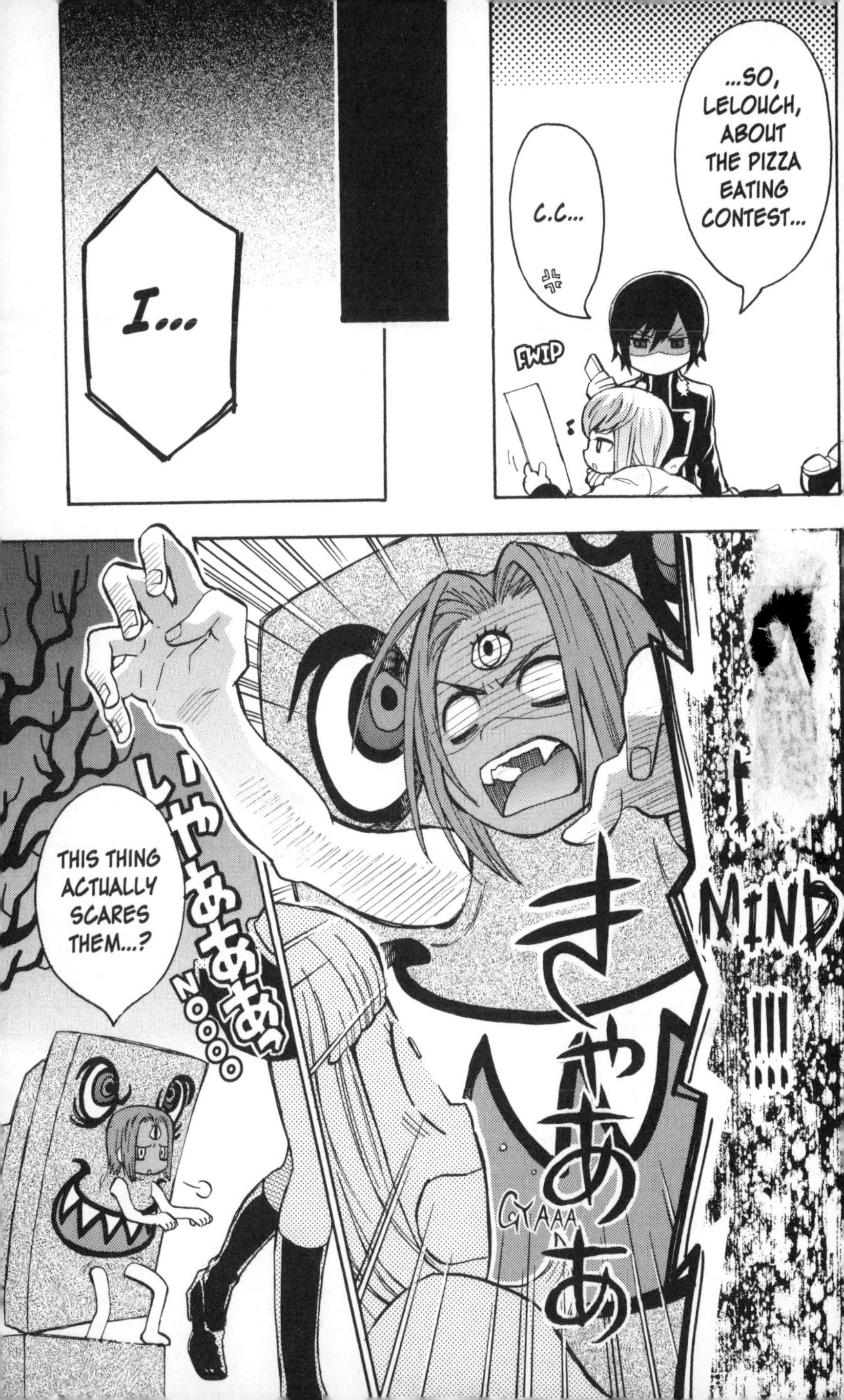
...SO, LELOUCH, ABOUT THE PIZZA EATING CONTEST...
C.C...
FWIP
I...
I MIND!!!
きゃあああ
GYAAAN
いやあああ
NOOOOO
THIS THING ACTUALLY SCARES THEM...?

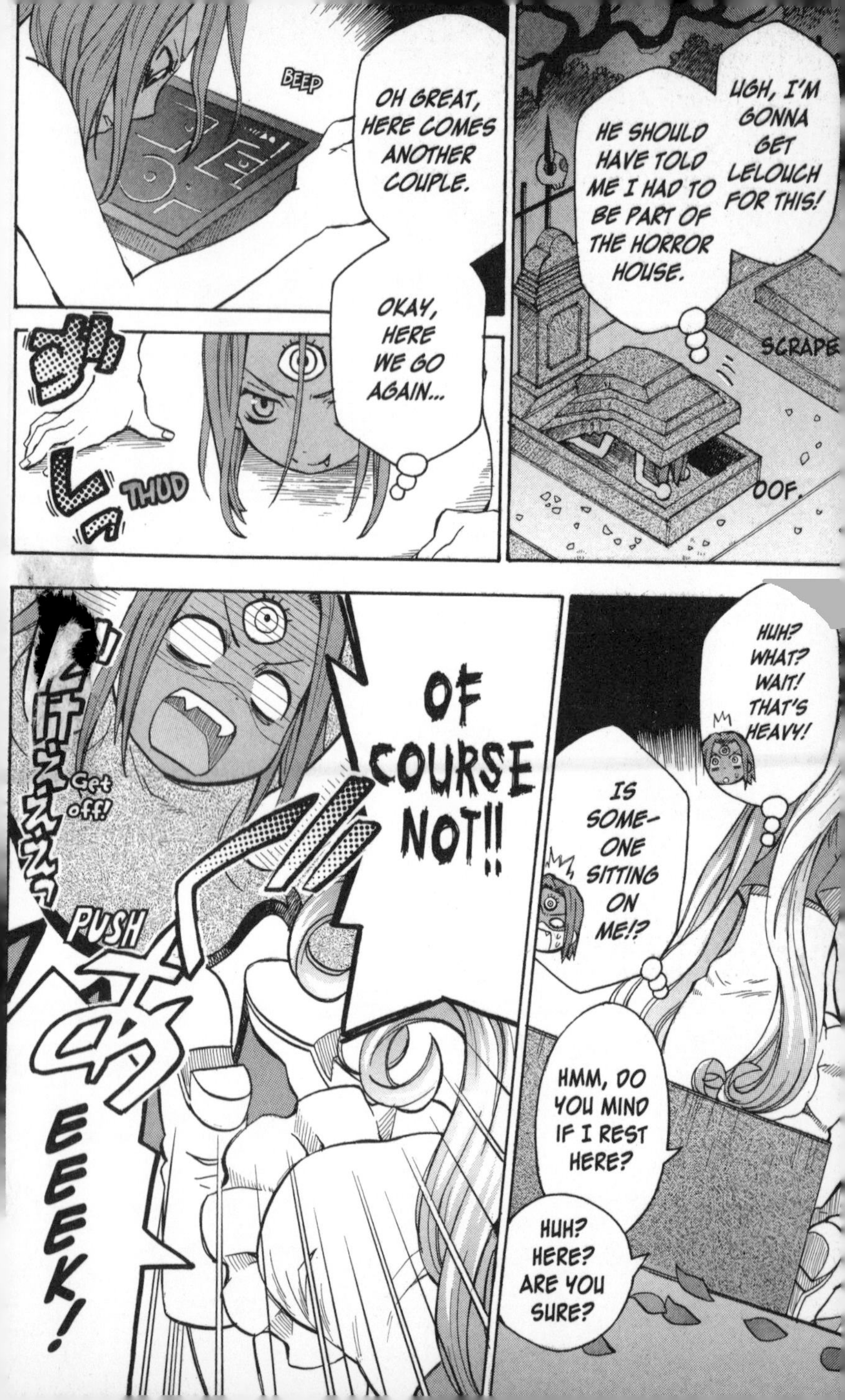
UGH, I'M GONNA GET LELOUCH FOR THIS!
HE SHOULD HAVE TOLD ME I HAD TO BE PART OF THE HORROR HOUSE.
SCRAPE
OOF.
BEEP
OH GREAT, HERE COMES ANOTHER COUPLE.
OKAY, HERE WE GO AGAIN...
THUD
HUH? WHAT? WAIT! THAT'S HEAVY!
IS SOME-ONE SITTING ON ME!?
HMM, DO YOU MIND IF I REST HERE?
HUH? HERE? ARE YOU SURE?
OF COURSE NOT!!
Get off!
PUSH
EEEEK!

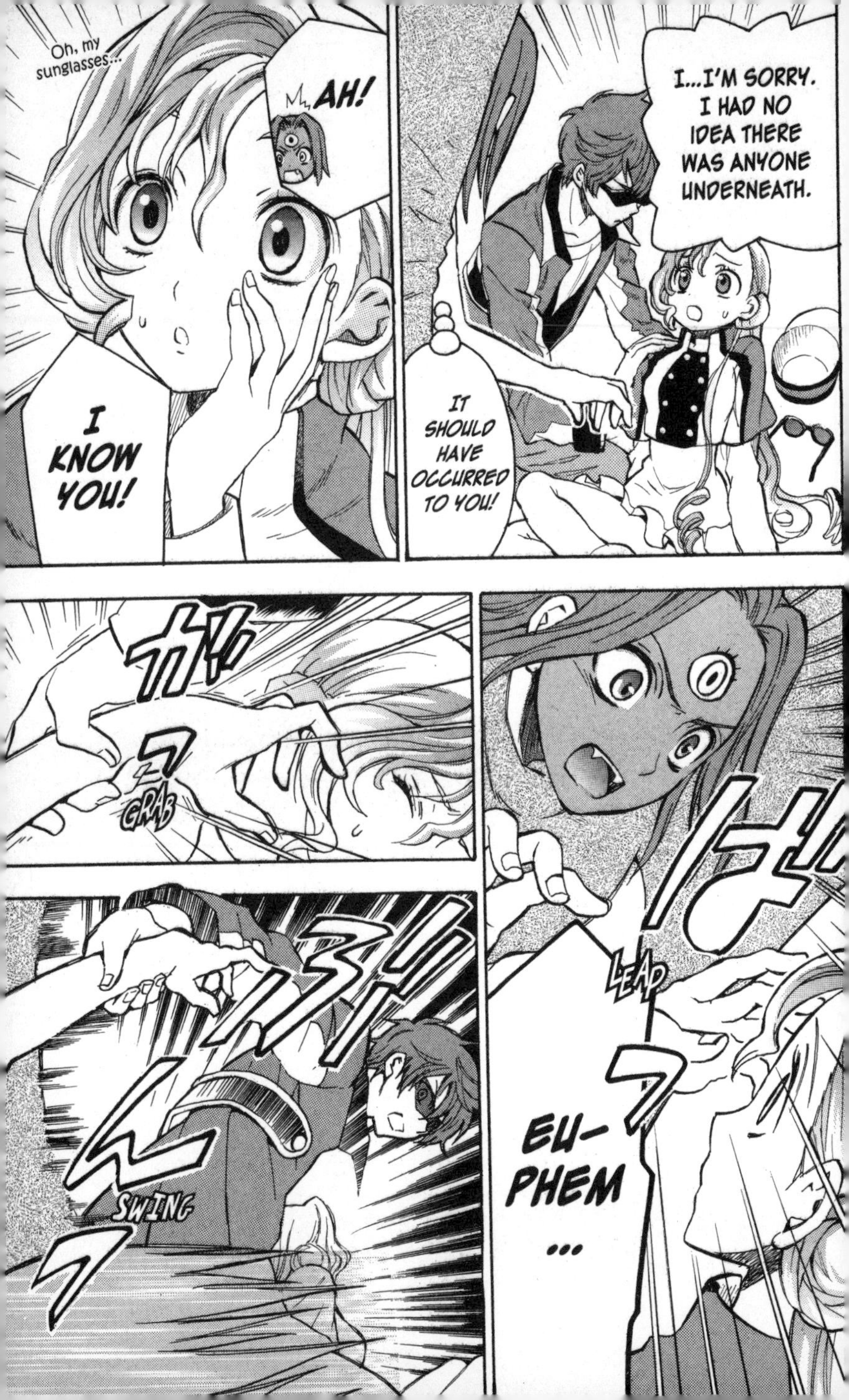
I...I'M SORRY. I HAD NO IDEA THERE WAS ANYONE UNDERNEATH.
IT SHOULD HAVE OCCURRED TO YOU!
Oh, my sunglasses...
AH!
I KNOW YOU!
LEAP
EU-PHEM...
GRAB
SWING

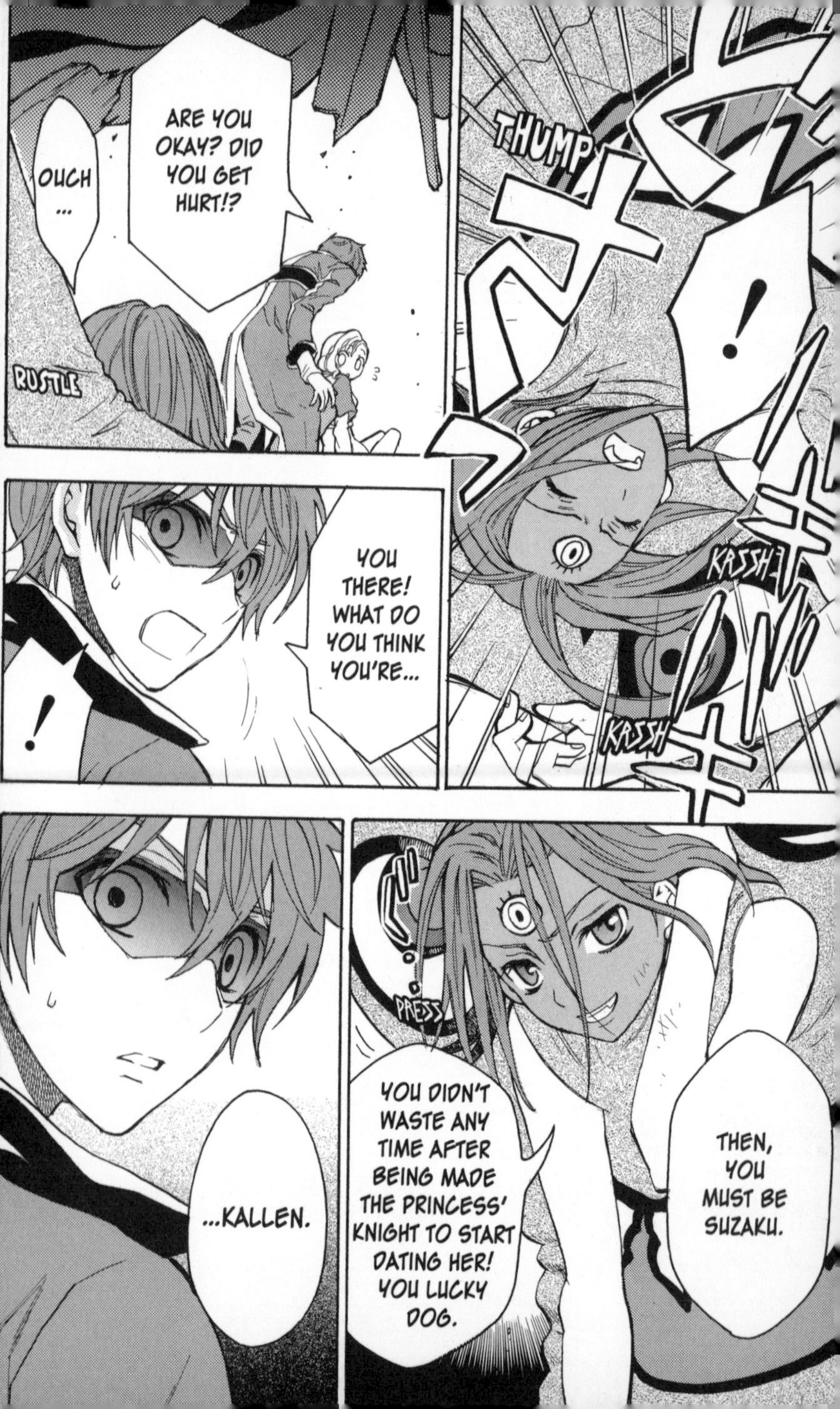
THUMP
!
KRSSH
KRSSH
ARE YOU OKAY? DID YOU GET HURT!?
OUCH ...
RUSTLE
YOU THERE! WHAT DO YOU THINK YOU'RE...
!
THEN, YOU MUST BE SUZAKU.
PRESS
YOU DIDN'T WASTE ANY TIME AFTER BEING MADE THE PRINCESS' KNIGHT TO START DATING HER! YOU LUCKY DOG.
...KALLEN.

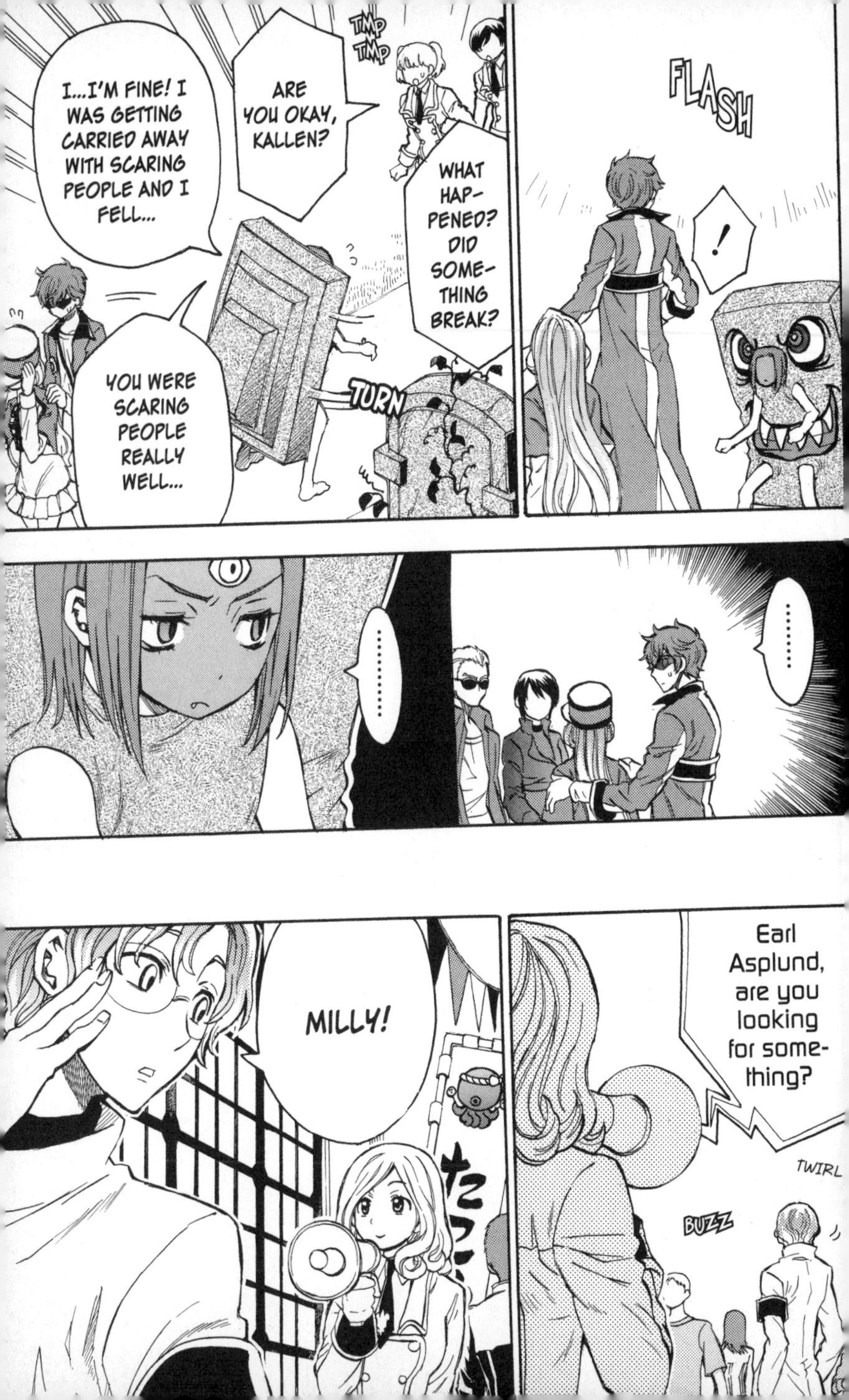
FLASH
!
TMP TMP
ARE YOU OKAY, KALLEN?
WHAT HAPPENED? DID SOMETHING BREAK?
I...I'M FINE! I WAS GETTING CARRIED AWAY WITH SCARING PEOPLE AND I FELL...
TURN
YOU WERE SCARING PEOPLE REALLY WELL...
....
....
Earl Asplund, are you looking for some-thing?
TWIRL
BUZZ
MILLY!

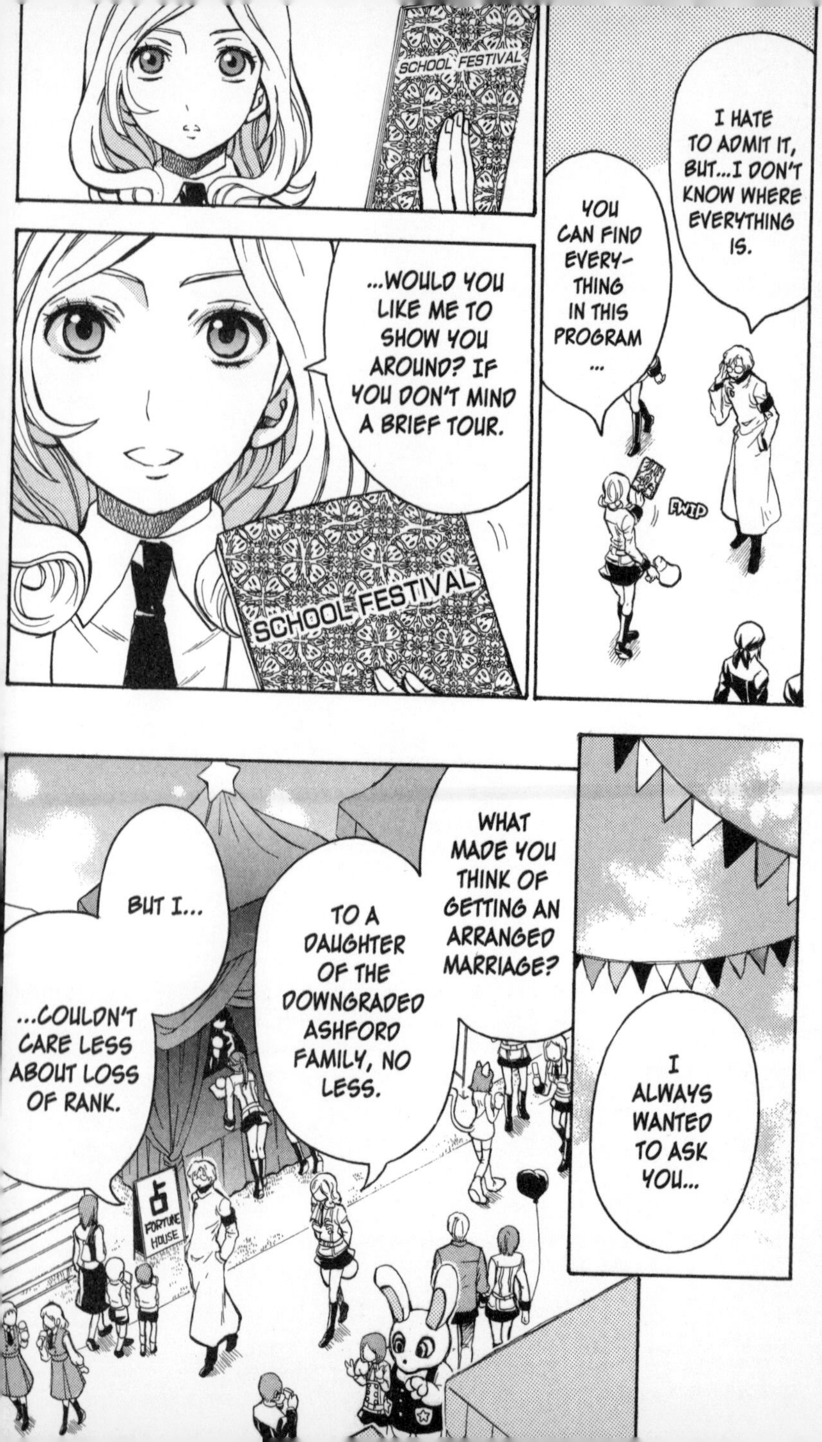
I HATE TO ADMIT IT, BUT...I DON'T KNOW WHERE EVERYTHING IS.
YOU CAN FIND EVERY-THING IN THIS PROGRAM...
FWIP
SCHOOL FESTIVAL
...WOULD YOU LIKE ME TO SHOW YOU AROUND? IF YOU DON'T MIND A BRIEF TOUR.
SCHOOL FESTIVAL
I ALWAYS WANTED TO ASK YOU...
WHAT MADE YOU THINK OF GETTING AN ARRANGED MARRIAGE?
TO A DAUGHTER OF THE DOWNGRADED ASHFORD FAMILY, NO LESS.
BUT I...
...COULDN'T CARE LESS ABOUT LOSS OF RANK.
占 FORTUNE HOUSE

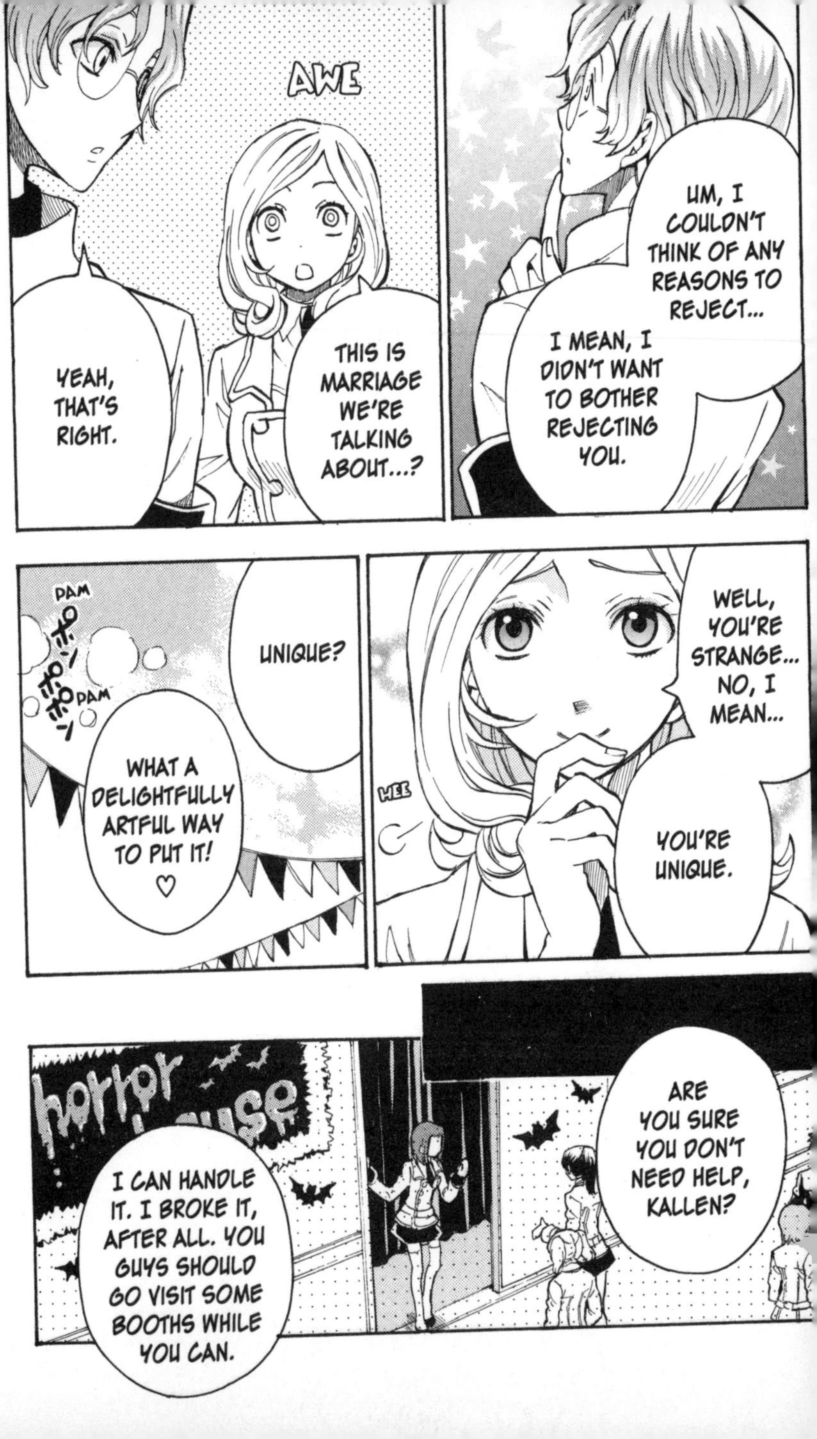
UM, I COULDN'T THINK OF ANY REASONS TO REJECT...
I MEAN, I DIDN'T WANT TO BOTHER REJECTING YOU.
AWE
THIS IS MARRIAGE WE'RE TALKING ABOUT...?
YEAH, THAT'S RIGHT.
WELL, YOU'RE STRANGE... NO, I MEAN...
HEE
YOU'RE UNIQUE.
UNIQUE?
PAM
PAM
WHAT A DELIGHTFULLY ARTFUL WAY TO PUT IT! ♡
ARE YOU SURE YOU DON'T NEED HELP, KALLEN?
horror house
I CAN HANDLE IT. I BROKE IT, AFTER ALL. YOU GUYS SHOULD GO VISIT SOME BOOTHS WHILE YOU CAN.

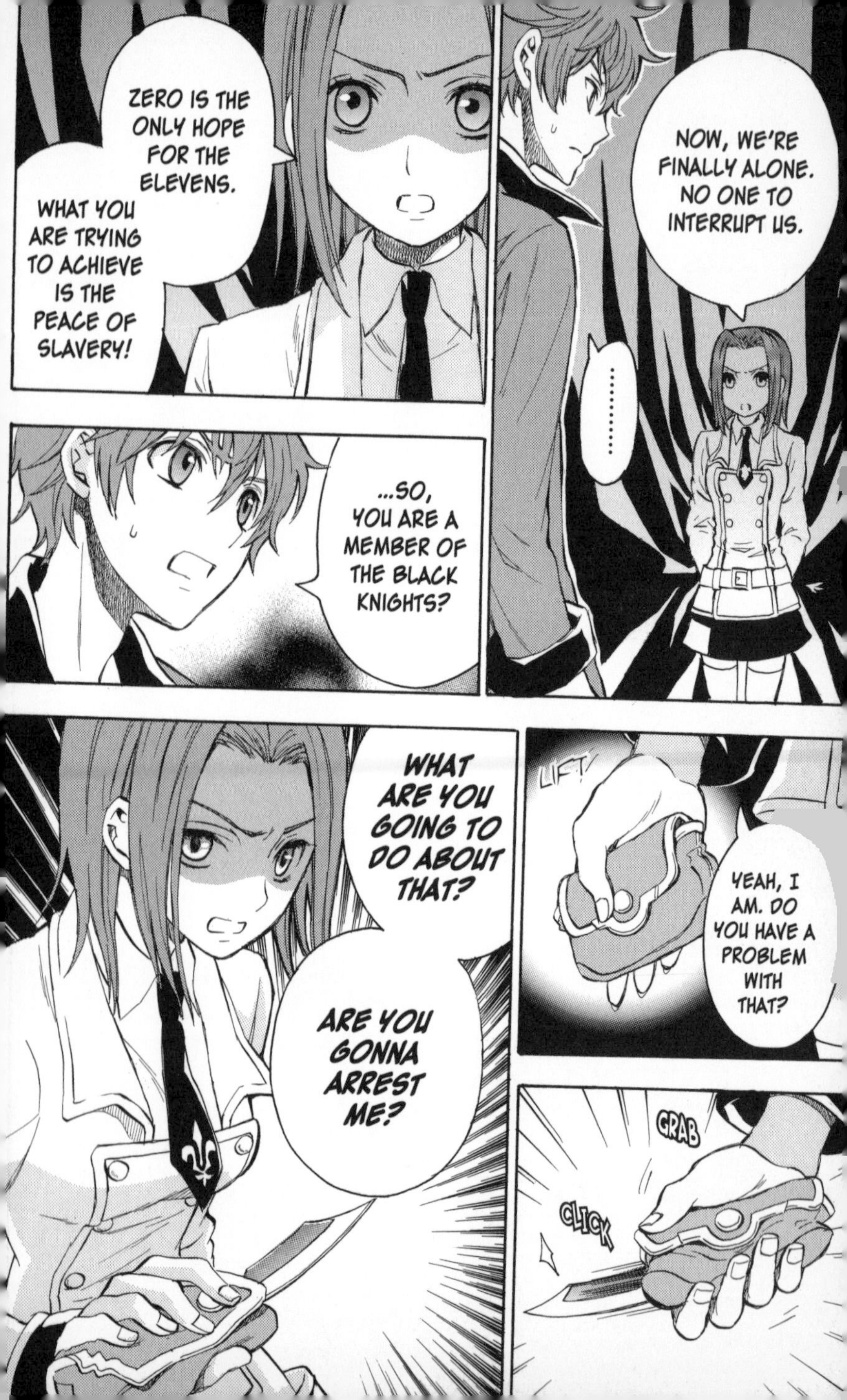
NOW, WE'RE FINALLY ALONE. NO ONE TO INTERRUPT US.
......
ZERO IS THE ONLY HOPE FOR THE ELEVENS.
WHAT YOU ARE TRYING TO ACHIEVE IS THE PEACE OF SLAVERY!
...SO, YOU ARE A MEMBER OF THE BLACK KNIGHTS?
LIFT
YEAH, I AM. DO YOU HAVE A PROBLEM WITH THAT?
GRAB
CLICK
WHAT ARE YOU GOING TO DO ABOUT THAT?
ARE YOU GONNA ARREST ME?

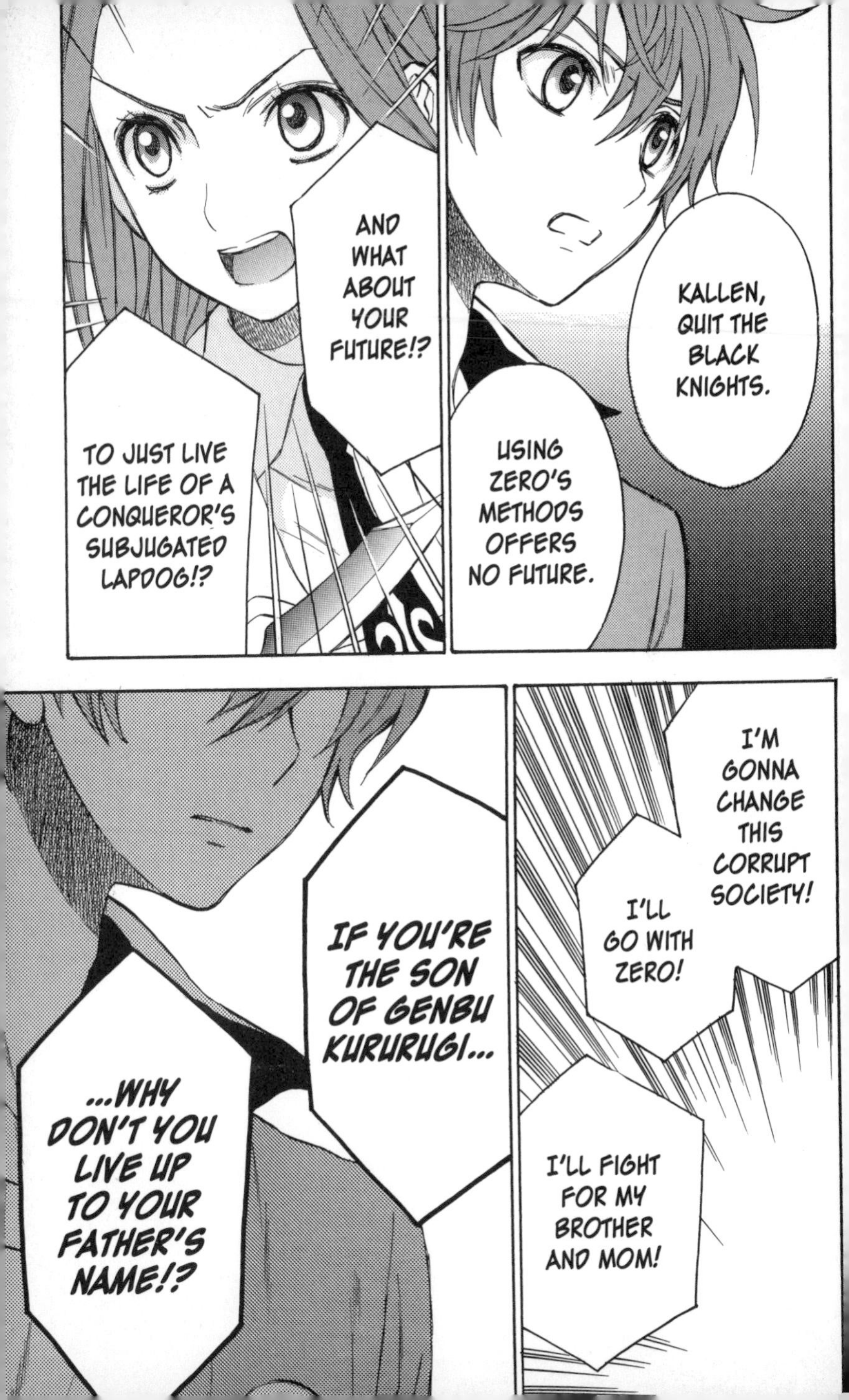
KALLEN, QUIT THE BLACK KNIGHTS.
USING ZERO'S METHODS OFFERS NO FUTURE.
AND WHAT ABOUT YOUR FUTURE!?
TO JUST LIVE THE LIFE OF A CONQUEROR'S SUBJUGATED LAPDOG!?
I'M GONNA CHANGE THIS CORRUPT SOCIETY!
I'LL GO WITH ZERO!
I'LL FIGHT FOR MY BROTHER AND MOM!
IF YOU'RE THE SON OF GENBU KURURUGI...
...WHY DON'T YOU LIVE UP TO YOUR FATHER'S NAME!?

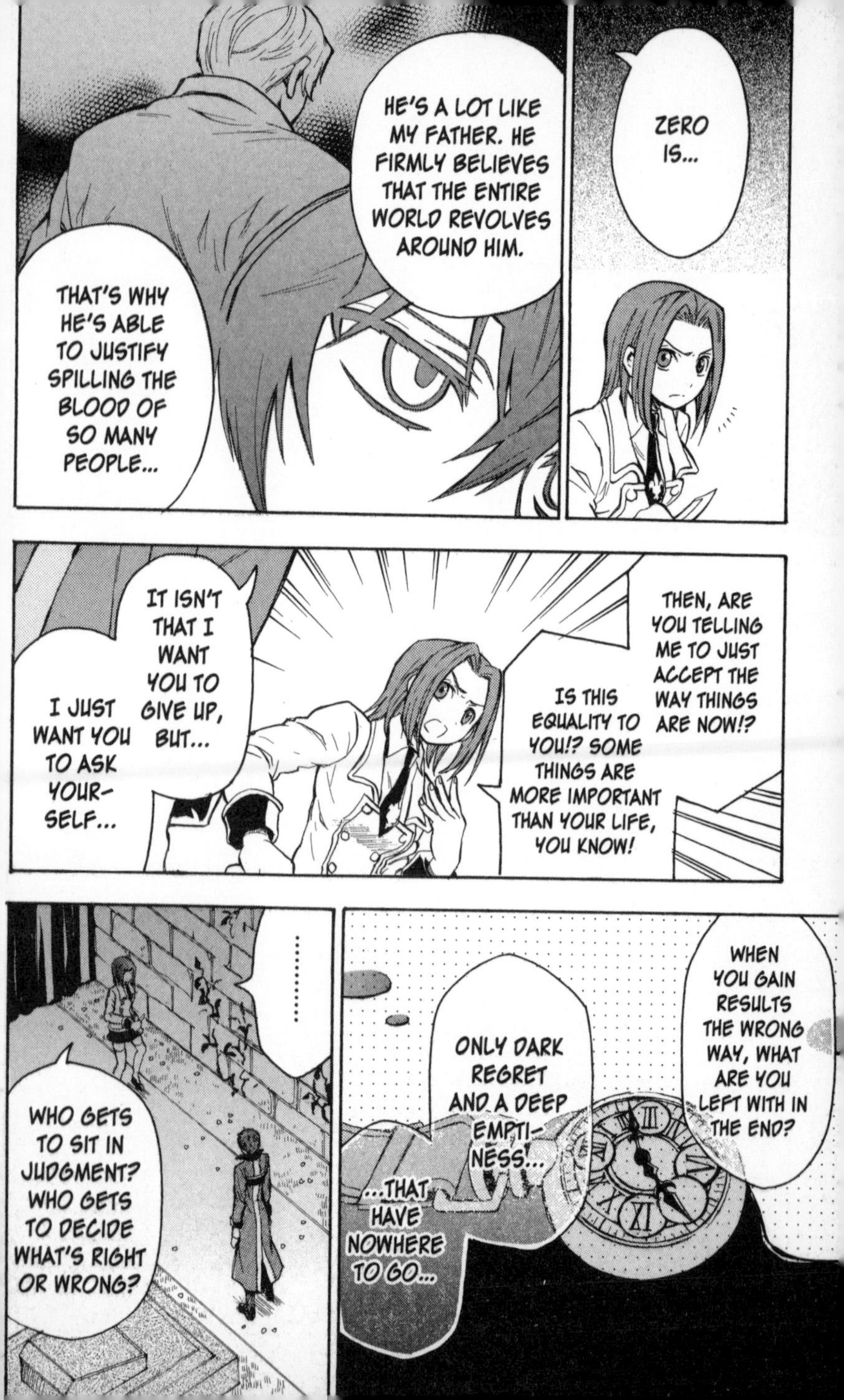
ZERO IS...
HE'S A LOT LIKE MY FATHER. HE FIRMLY BELIEVES THAT THE ENTIRE WORLD REVOLVES AROUND HIM.
THAT'S WHY HE'S ABLE TO JUSTIFY SPILLING THE BLOOD OF SO MANY PEOPLE...
THEN, ARE YOU TELLING ME TO JUST ACCEPT THE WAY THINGS ARE NOW!?
IS THIS EQUALITY TO YOU!? SOME THINGS ARE MORE IMPORTANT THAN YOUR LIFE, YOU KNOW!
IT ISN'T THAT I WANT YOU TO GIVE UP, BUT...
I JUST WANT YOU TO ASK YOUR-SELF...
WHEN YOU GAIN RESULTS THE WRONG WAY, WHAT ARE YOU LEFT WITH IN THE END?
ONLY DARK REGRET AND A DEEP EMPTI-NESS...
...THAT HAVE NOWHERE TO GO...
......
WHO GETS TO SIT IN JUDGMENT? WHO GETS TO DECIDE WHAT'S RIGHT OR WRONG?

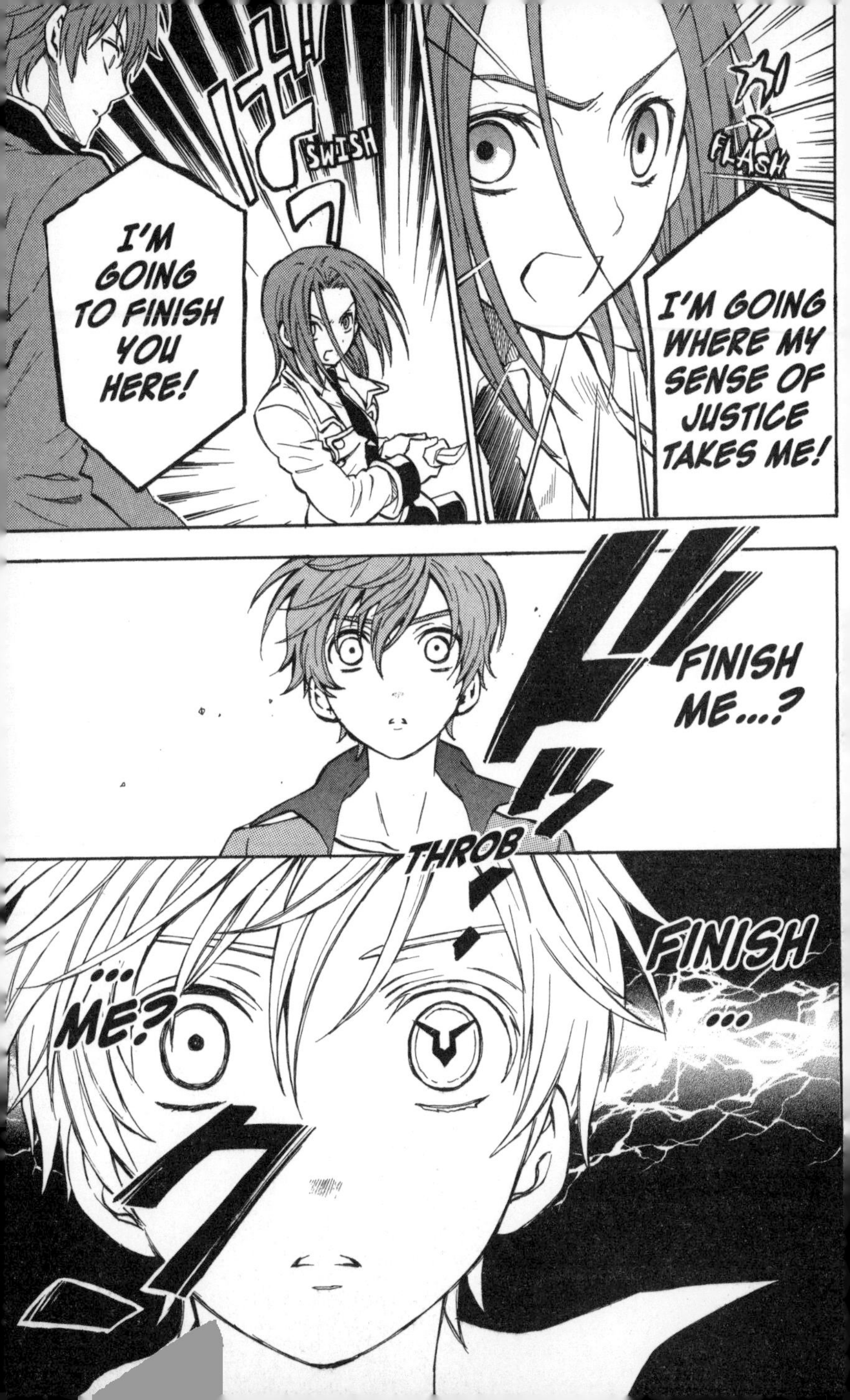
FLASH
I'M GOING WHERE MY SENSE OF JUSTICE TAKES ME!
SWISH
I'M GOING TO FINISH YOU HERE!
FINISH ME...?
THROB
FINISH ...
...ME?

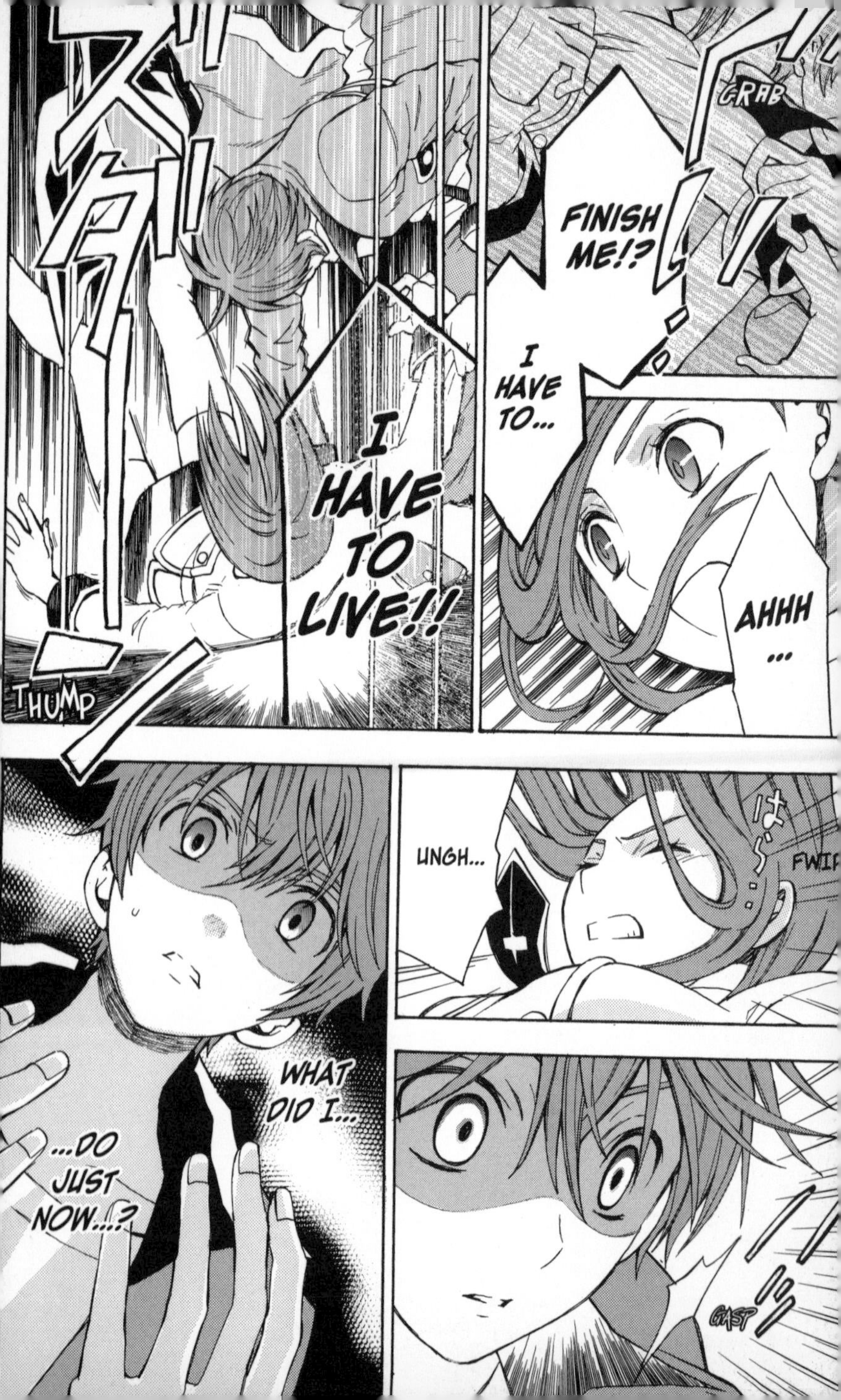

GRAB
FINISH ME!?
I HAVE TO...
AHHH...
I HAVE TO LIVE!!
THUMP
UNGH...
FWIP
GASP
WHAT DID I...
...DO JUST NOW...?

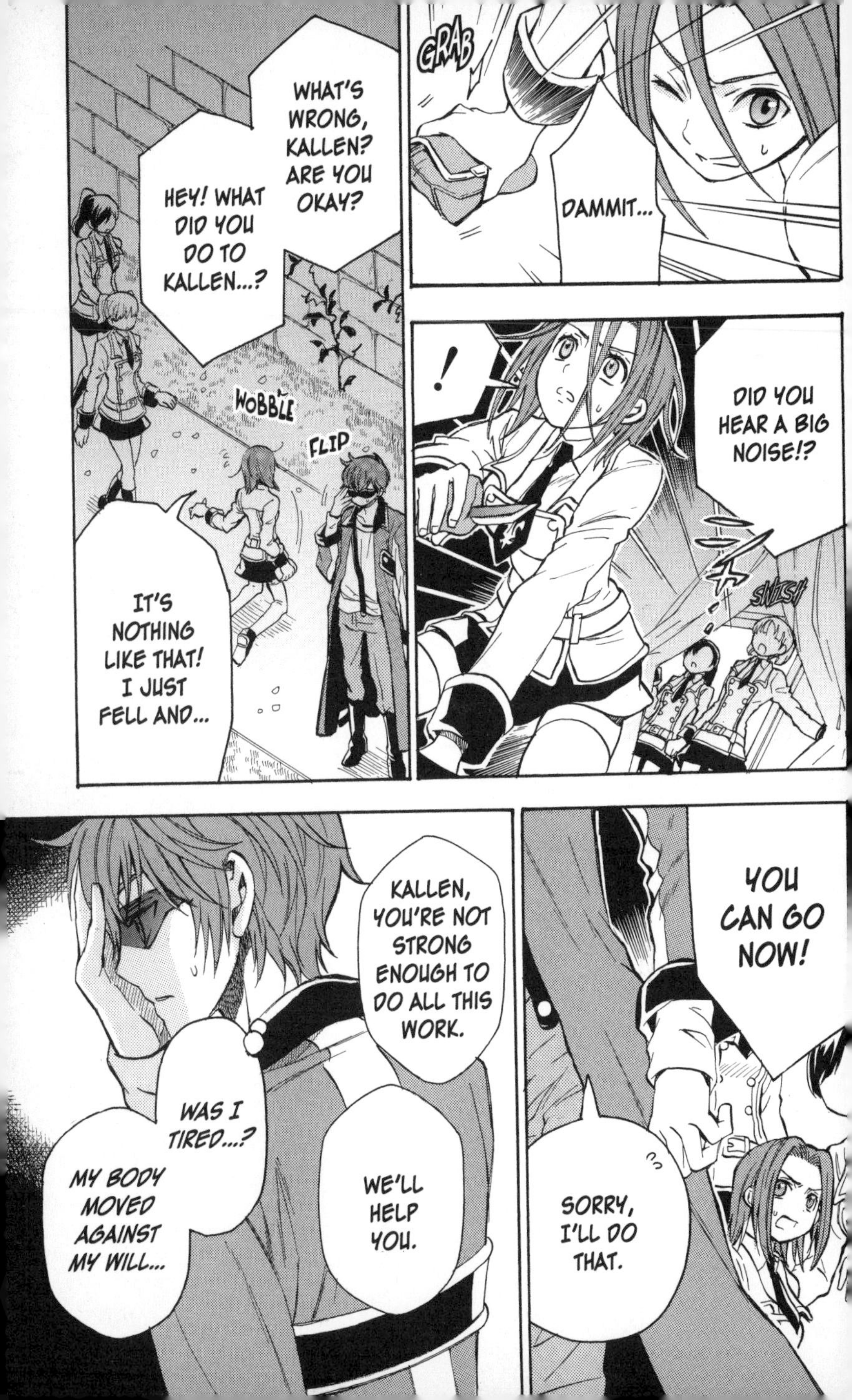
GRAB
DAMMIT...
!
DID YOU HEAR A BIG NOISE!?
SWISH
WHAT'S WRONG, KALLEN? ARE YOU OKAY?
HEY! WHAT DID YOU DO TO KALLEN...?
WOBBLE
FLIP
IT'S NOTHING LIKE THAT! I JUST FELL AND...
YOU CAN GO NOW!
SORRY, I'LL DO THAT.
KALLEN, YOU'RE NOT STRONG ENOUGH TO DO ALL THIS WORK.
WE'LL HELP YOU.
WAS I TIRED...?
MY BODY MOVED AGAINST MY WILL...

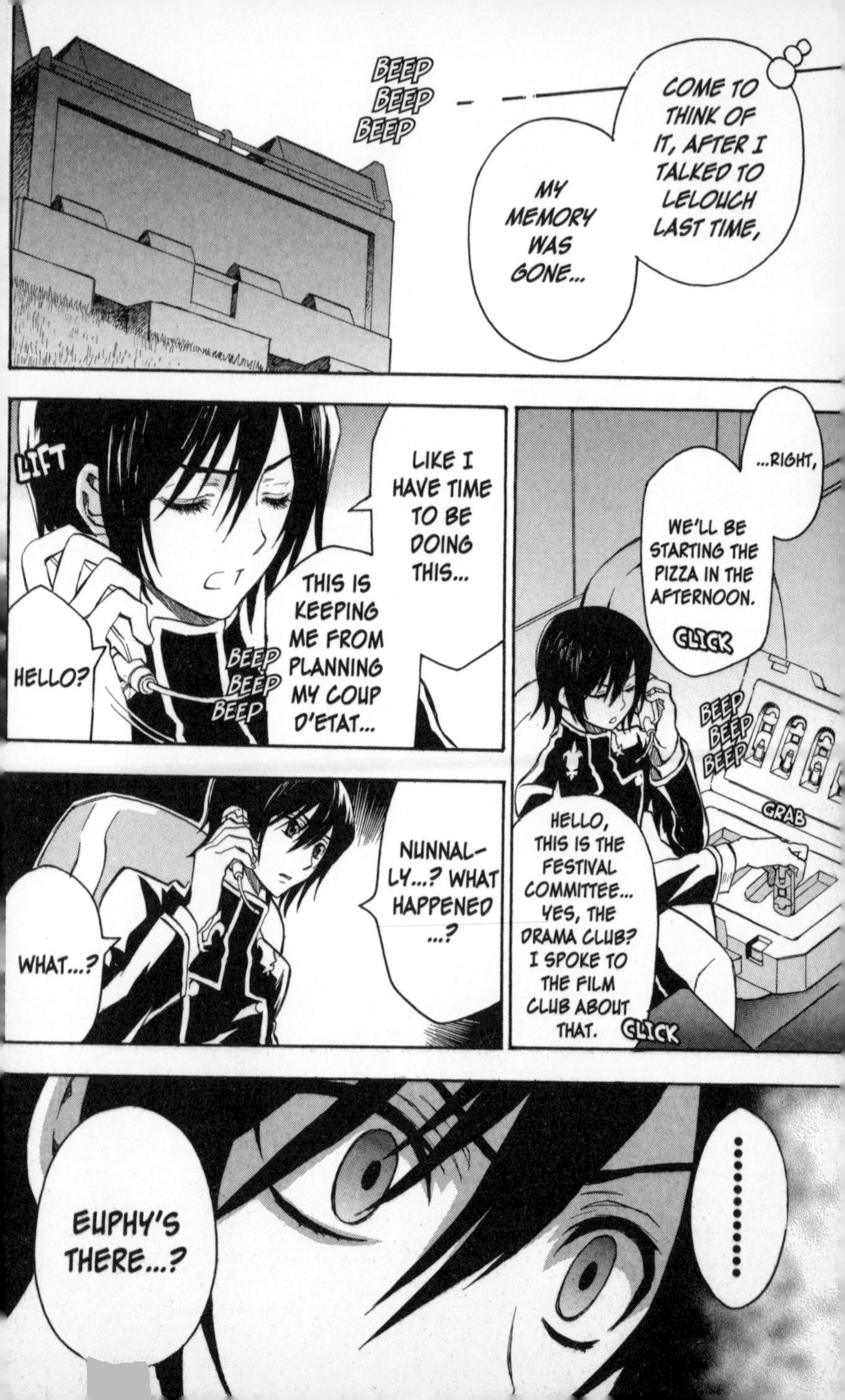

COME TO THINK OF IT, AFTER I TALKED TO LELOUCH LAST TIME,
BEEP BEEP BEEP
MY MEMORY WAS GONE...
...RIGHT,
WE'LL BE STARTING THE PIZZA IN THE AFTERNOON.
CLICK
BEEP BEEP BEEP
GRAB
HELLO, THIS IS THE FESTIVAL COMMITTEE... YES, THE DRAMA CLUB? I SPOKE TO THE FILM CLUB ABOUT THAT.
CLICK
LIKE I HAVE TIME TO BE DOING THIS...
LIFT
THIS IS KEEPING ME FROM PLANNING MY COUP D'ETAT...
BEEP BEEP BEEP
HELLO?
NUNNAL-LY...? WHAT HAPPENED ...?
WHAT...?
....
EUPHY'S THERE...?

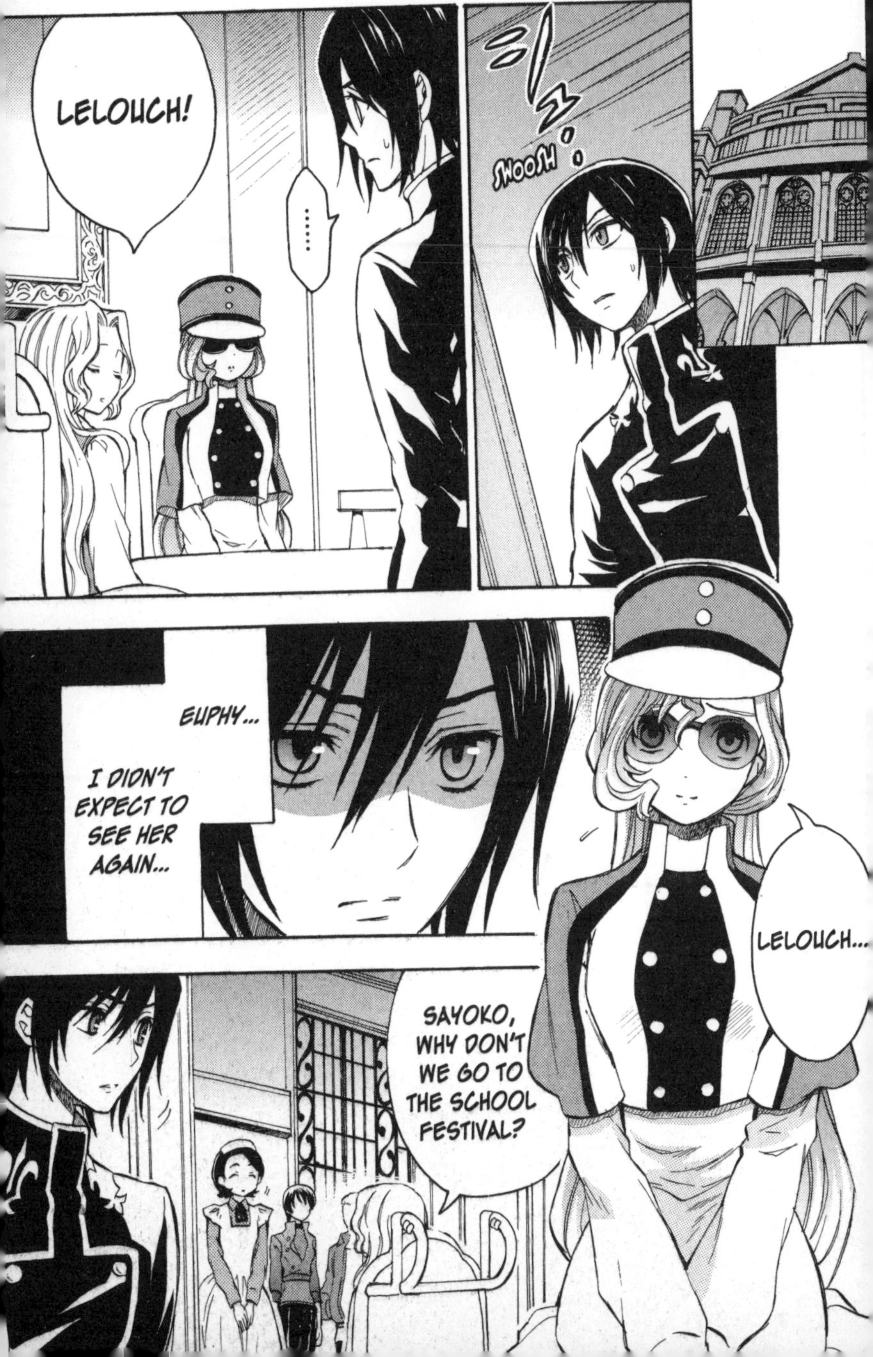
SWOOSH
......
LELOUCH!
EUPHY...
I DIDN'T EXPECT TO SEE HER AGAIN...
LELOUCH...
SAYOKO, WHY DON'T WE GO TO THE SCHOOL FESTIVAL?

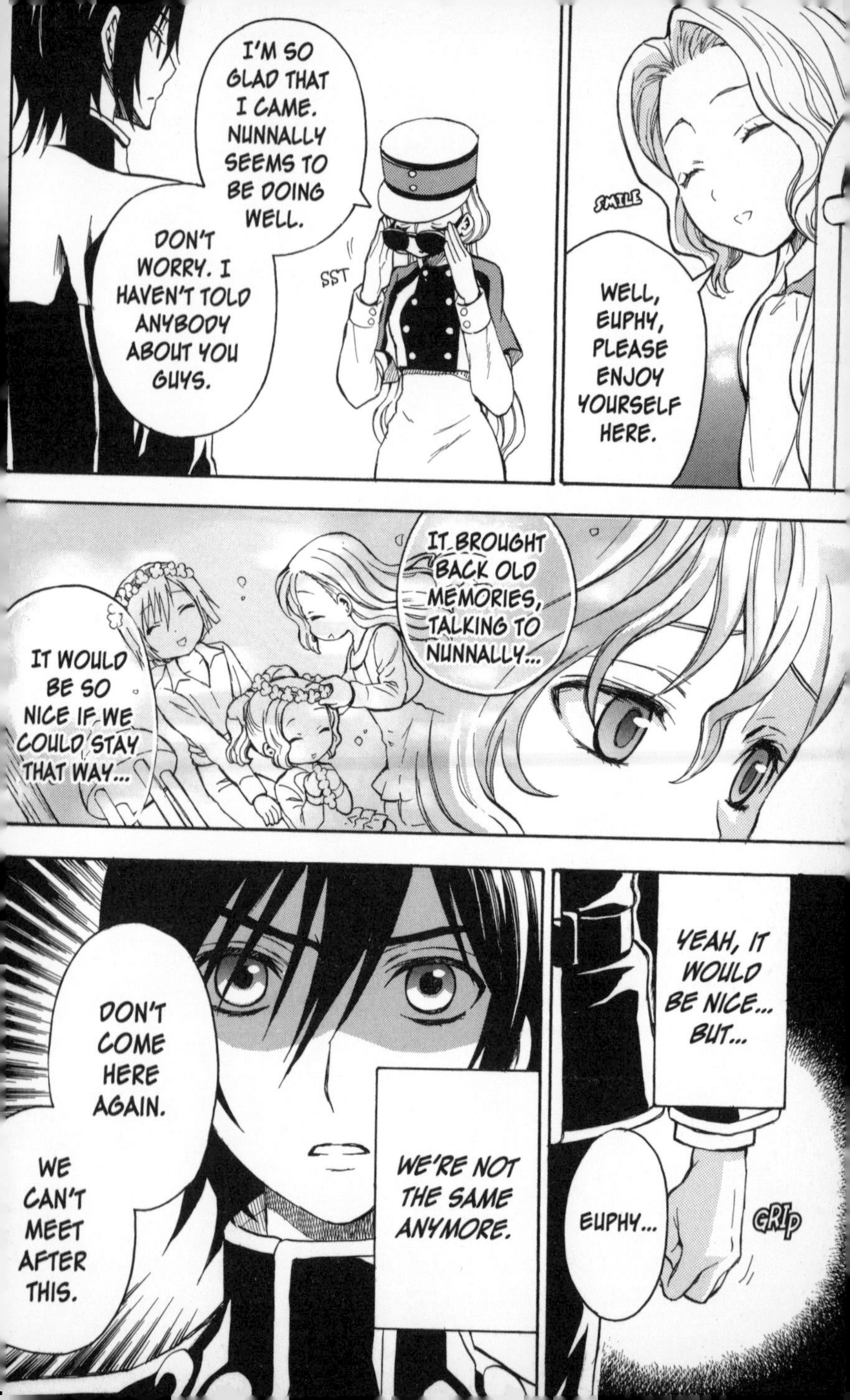
SMILE
WELL, EUPHY, PLEASE ENJOY YOURSELF HERE.
I'M SO GLAD THAT I CAME. NUNNALLY SEEMS TO BE DOING WELL.
SST
DON'T WORRY. I HAVEN'T TOLD ANYBODY ABOUT YOU GUYS.
IT BROUGHT BACK OLD MEMORIES, TALKING TO NUNNALLY...
IT WOULD BE SO NICE IF WE COULD STAY THAT WAY...
YEAH, IT WOULD BE NICE... BUT...
EUPHY...
GRIP
WE'RE NOT THE SAME ANYMORE.
DON'T COME HERE AGAIN.
WE CAN'T MEET AFTER THIS.

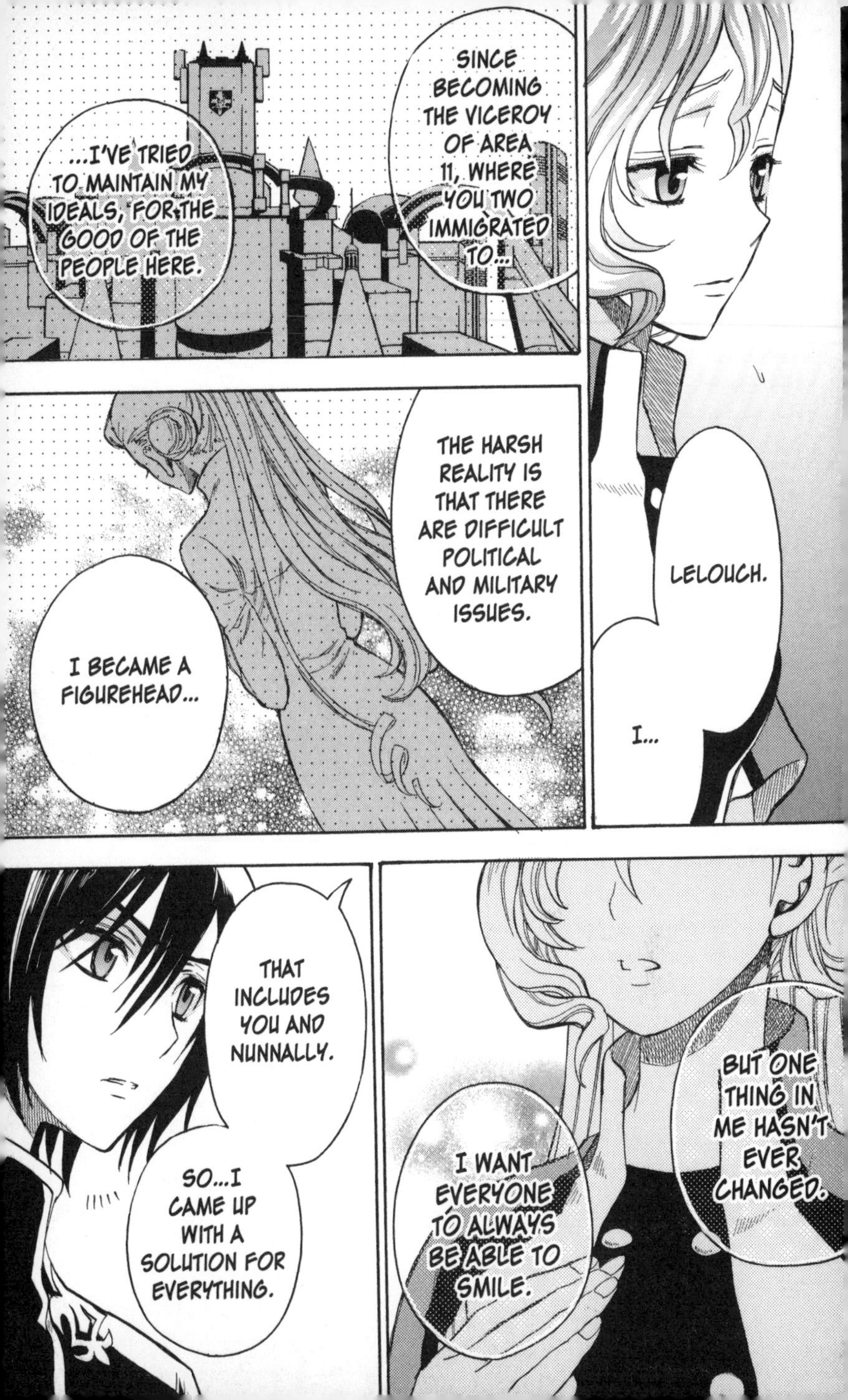
LELOUCH.
I...
SINCE BECOMING THE VICEROY OF AREA 11, WHERE YOU TWO IMMIGRATED TO...
...I'VE TRIED TO MAINTAIN MY IDEALS, FOR THE GOOD OF THE PEOPLE HERE.
THE HARSH REALITY IS THAT THERE ARE DIFFICULT POLITICAL AND MILITARY ISSUES.
I BECAME A FIGUREHEAD...
BUT ONE THING IN ME HASN'T EVER CHANGED.
I WANT EVERYONE TO ALWAYS BE ABLE TO SMILE.
THAT INCLUDES YOU AND NUNNALLY.
SO...I CAME UP WITH A SOLUTION FOR EVERYTHING.

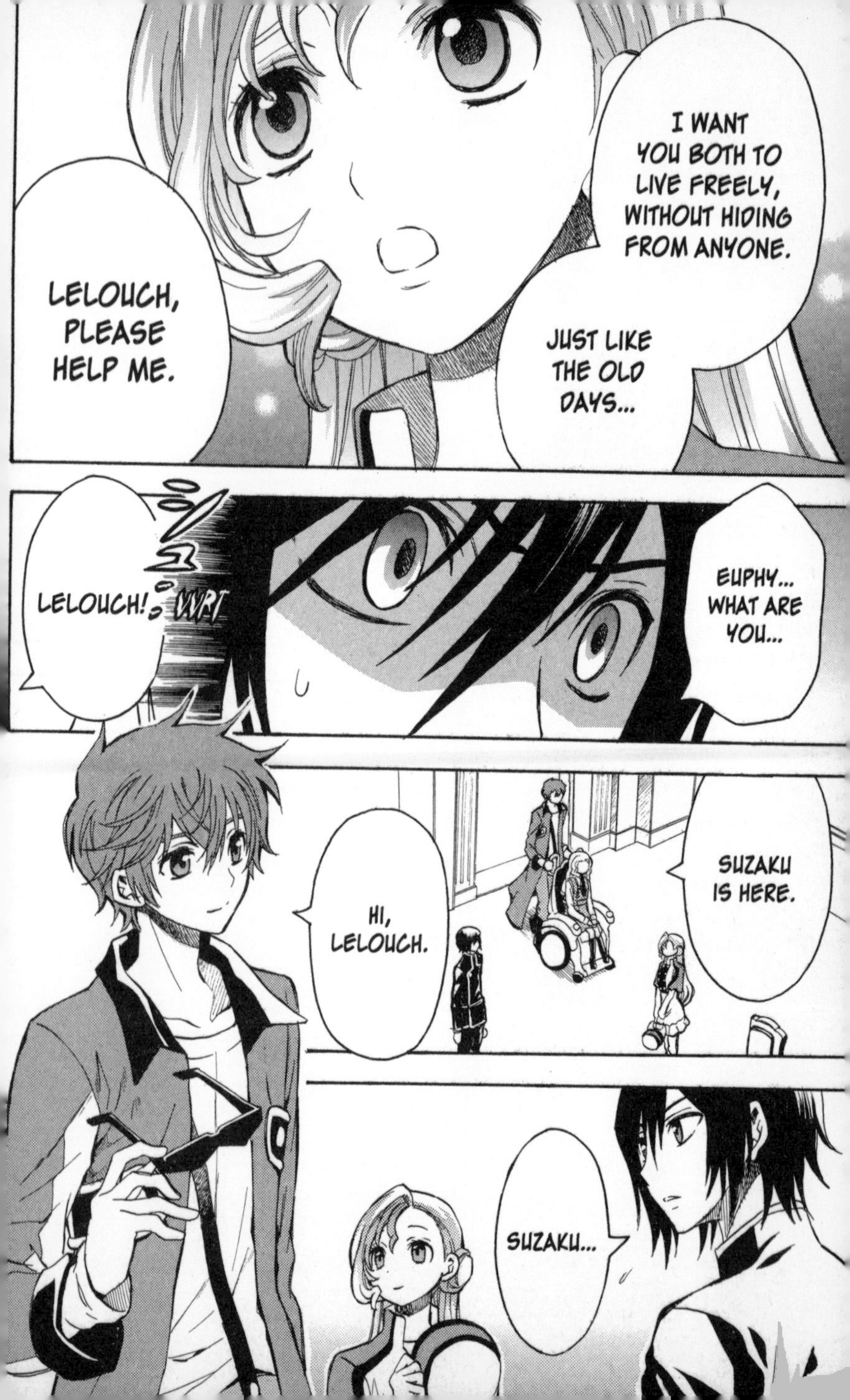
I WANT YOU BOTH TO LIVE FREELY, WITHOUT HIDING FROM ANYONE.
JUST LIKE THE OLD DAYS...
LELOUCH, PLEASE HELP ME.
EUPHY... WHAT ARE YOU...
VVRT
LELOUCH!
SUZAKU IS HERE.
HI, LELOUCH.
SUZAKU...

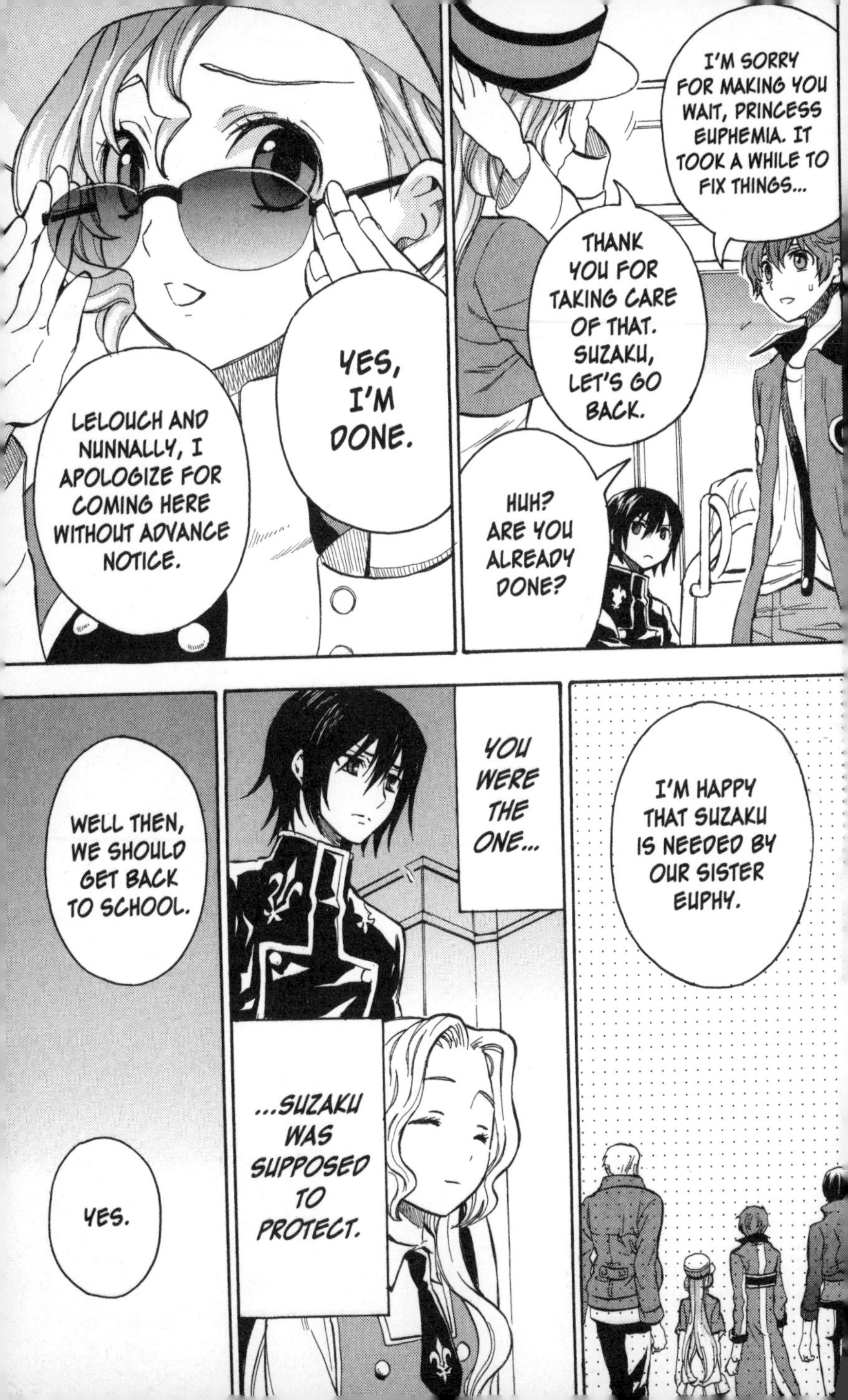
I'M SORRY FOR MAKING YOU WAIT, PRINCESS EUPHEMIA. IT TOOK A WHILE TO FIX THINGS...
THANK YOU FOR TAKING CARE OF THAT. SUZAKU, LET'S GO BACK.
HUH? ARE YOU ALREADY DONE?
YES, I'M DONE.
LELOUCH AND NUNNALLY, I APOLOGIZE FOR COMING HERE WITHOUT ADVANCE NOTICE.
I'M HAPPY THAT SUZAKU IS NEEDED BY OUR SISTER EUPHY.
YOU WERE THE ONE...
...SUZAKU WAS SUPPOSED TO PROTECT.
WELL THEN, WE SHOULD GET BACK TO SCHOOL.
YES.

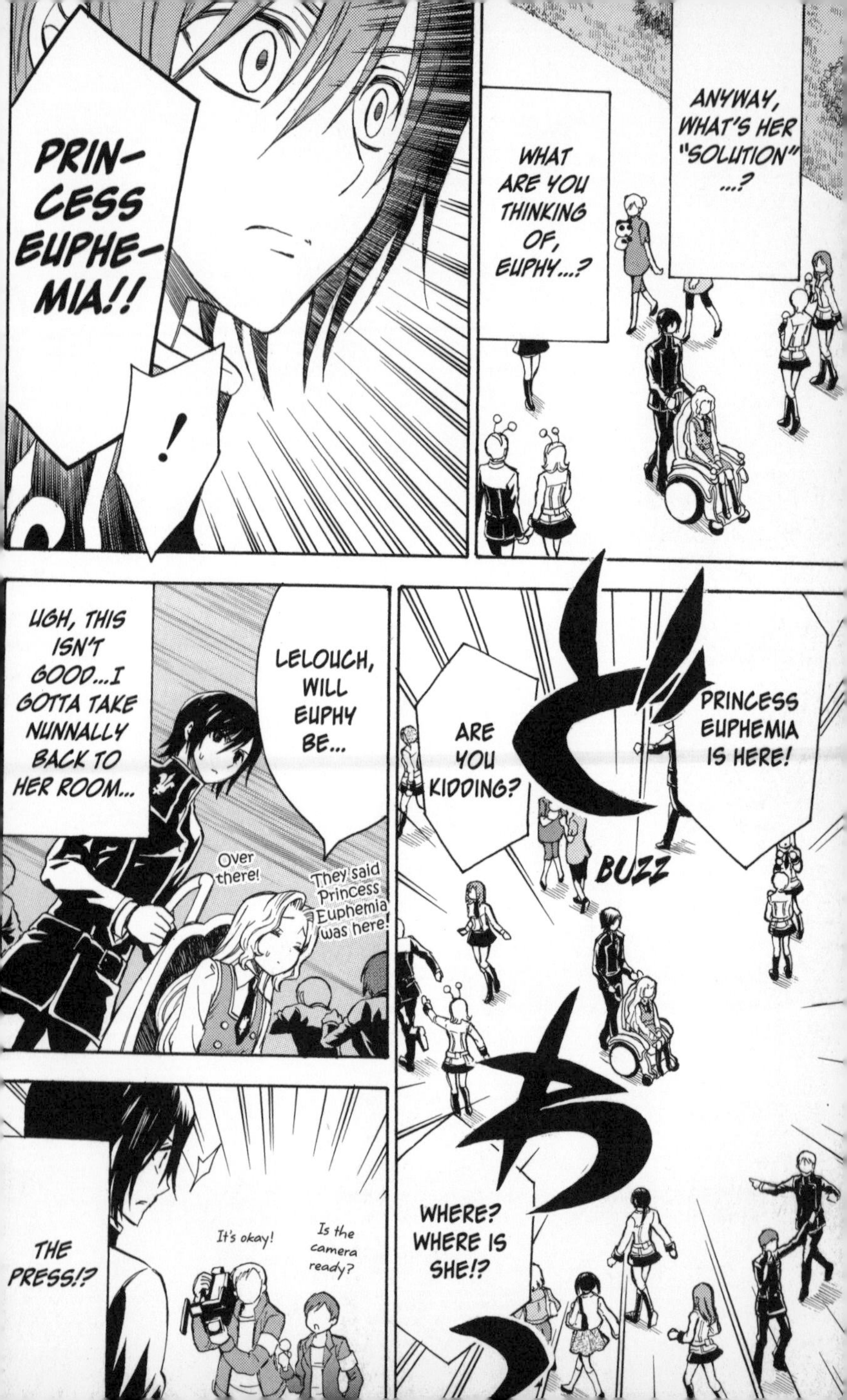
ANYWAY, WHAT'S HER "SOLUTION" ...?
WHAT ARE YOU THINKING OF, EUPHY...?
PRIN-CESS EUPHE-MIA!!
!
PRINCESS EUPHEMIA IS HERE!
ARE YOU KIDDING?
BUZZ
WHERE? WHERE IS SHE!?
LELOUCH, WILL EUPHY BE...
UGH, THIS ISN'T GOOD...I GOTTA TAKE NUNNALLY BACK TO HER ROOM...
They said Princess Euphemia was here!
Over there!
Is the camera ready?
It's okay!
THE PRESS!?

わあわあ BUZZ

きゃあ BUZZ BUZZ

きゃあ

Princess Euphemia!

わあ BUZZ わあ

DAMMIT....!

TURN

SOMEONE, TAKE MY OTHER GUN!

I can't take much more!

What delicate slim legs! What a face!

THIS IS A SCHOOL!

EVERY-ONE, STOP!

I'm sorry. I'm sorry.

DON'T PUSH. DON'T PUSH!

Look at me!

One question! Just one question!

IT'S NOT SAFE. STAY BACK...

EEK

PUSH

PUSH

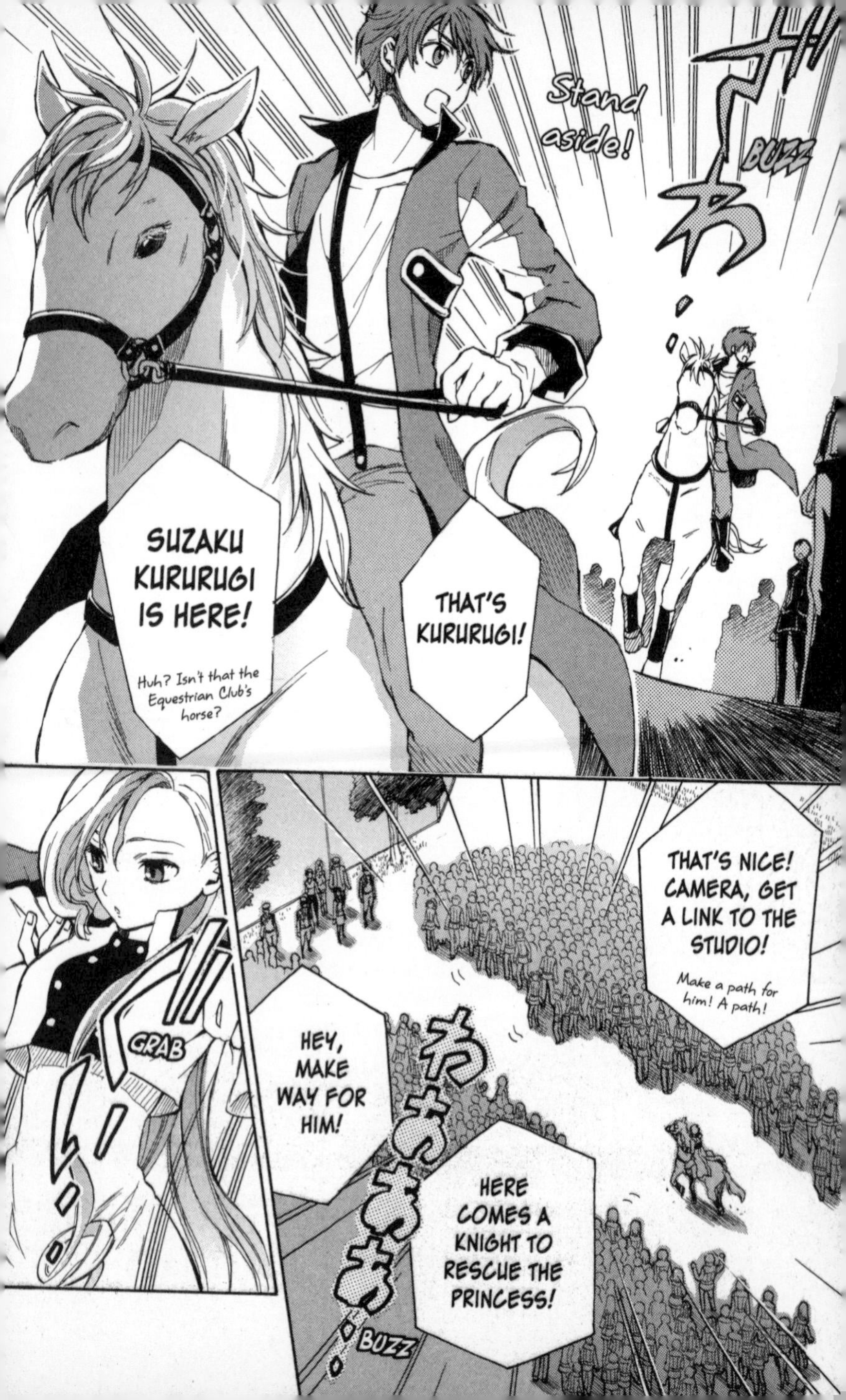
Stand aside!
BUZZ
THAT'S KURURUGI!
SUZAKU KURURUGI IS HERE!
Huh? Isn't that the Equestrian Club's horse?
THAT'S NICE! CAMERA, GET A LINK TO THE STUDIO!
Make a path for him! A path!
HEY, MAKE WAY FOR HIM!
HERE COMES A KNIGHT TO RESCUE THE PRINCESS!
BUZZ
GRAB

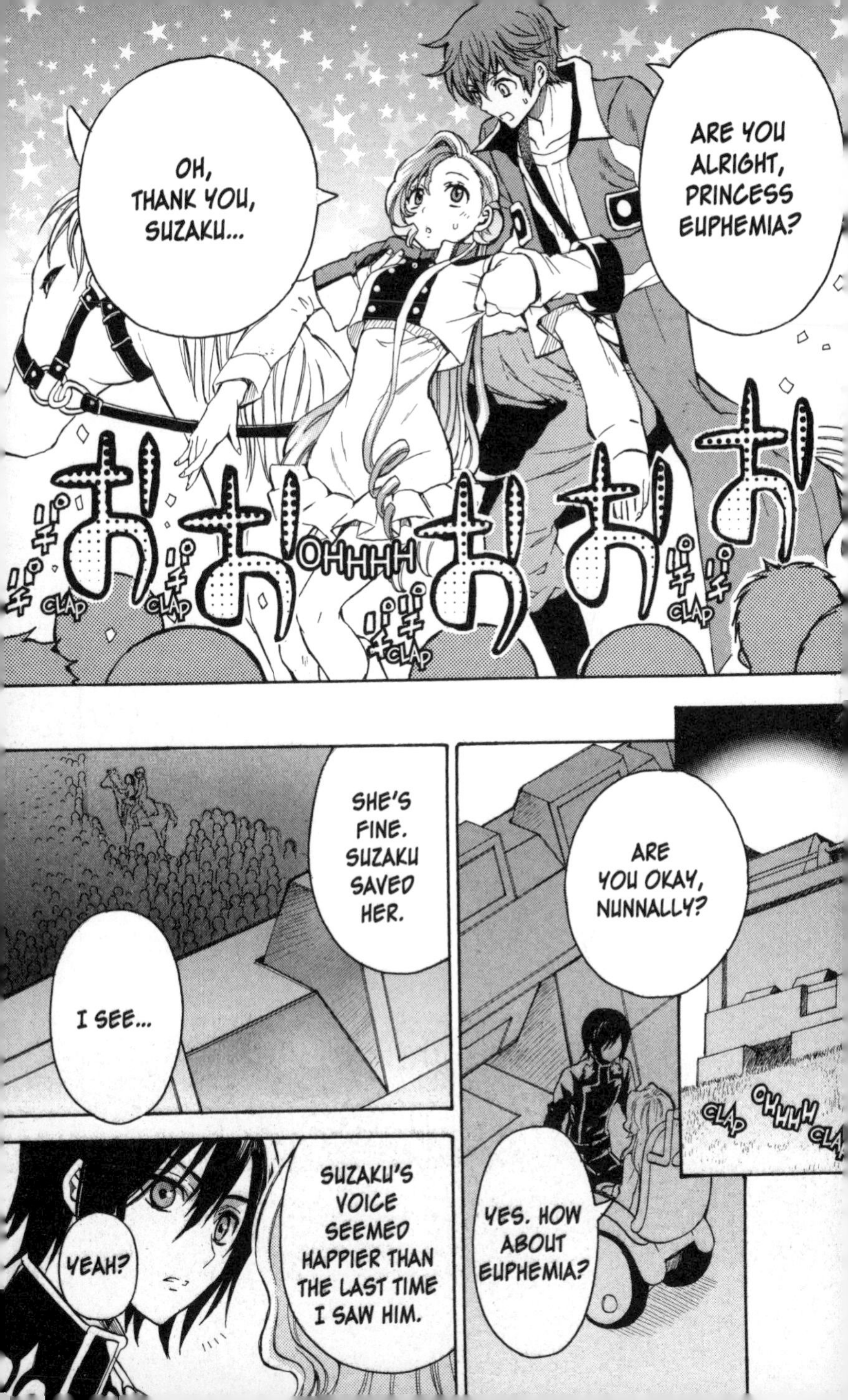
ARE YOU ALRIGHT, PRINCESS EUPHEMIA?
OH, THANK YOU, SUZAKU...
おおおおお
OHHHH
CLAP CLAP CLAP CLAP
ARE YOU OKAY, NUNNALLY?
CLAP OHHHH CLAP
YES. HOW ABOUT EUPHEMIA?
SHE'S FINE. SUZAKU SAVED HER.
I SEE...
SUZAKU'S VOICE SEEMED HAPPIER THAN THE LAST TIME I SAW HIM.
YEAH?

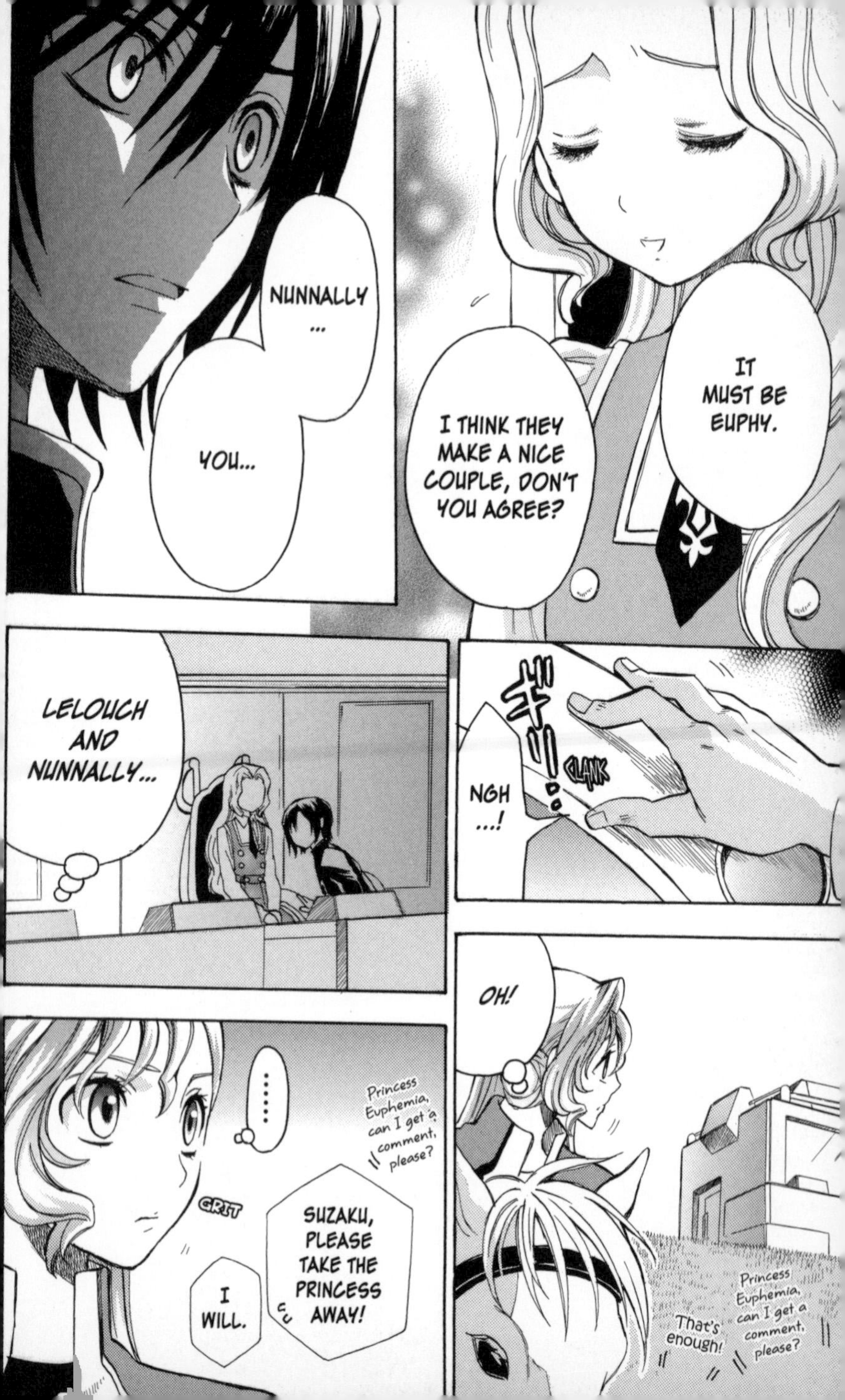
IT MUST BE EUPHY.
I THINK THEY MAKE A NICE COUPLE, DON'T YOU AGREE?
NUNNALLY ...
YOU...
CLANK
NGH ...!
LELOUCH AND NUNNALLY...
OH!
Princess Euphemia, can I get a comment, please?
That's enough!
......
Princess Euphemia, can I get a comment, please?
SUZAKU, PLEASE TAKE THE PRINCESS AWAY!
GRIT
I WILL.

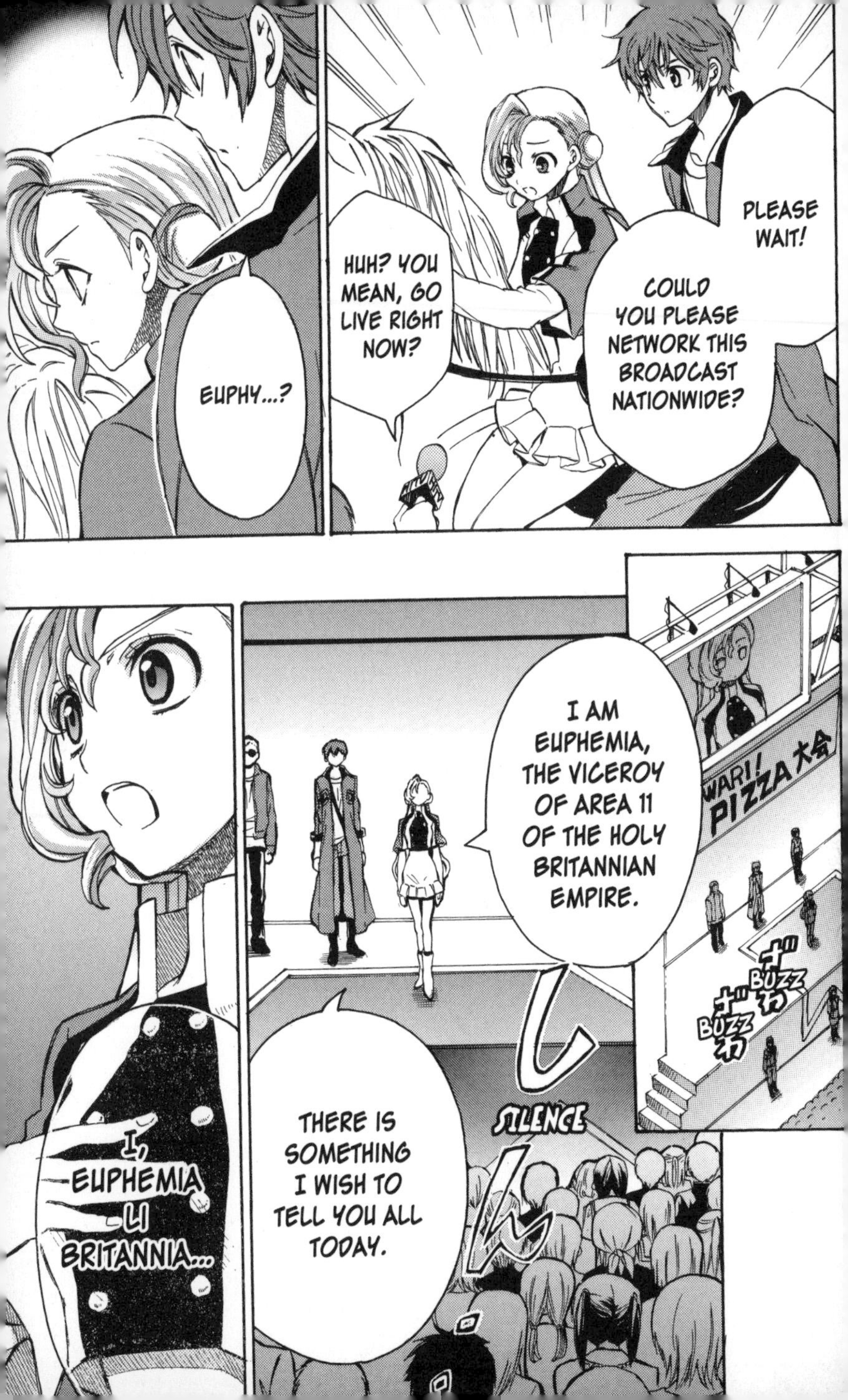
PLEASE WAIT!
COULD YOU PLEASE NETWORK THIS BROADCAST NATIONWIDE?
HUH? YOU MEAN, GO LIVE RIGHT NOW?
EUPHY...?
WARI! PIZZA 大会
BUZZ
BUZZ
I AM EUPHEMIA, THE VICEROY OF AREA 11 OF THE HOLY BRITANNIAN EMPIRE.
SILENCE
THERE IS SOMETHING I WISH TO TELL YOU ALL TODAY.
I, EUPHEMIA LI BRITANNIA...

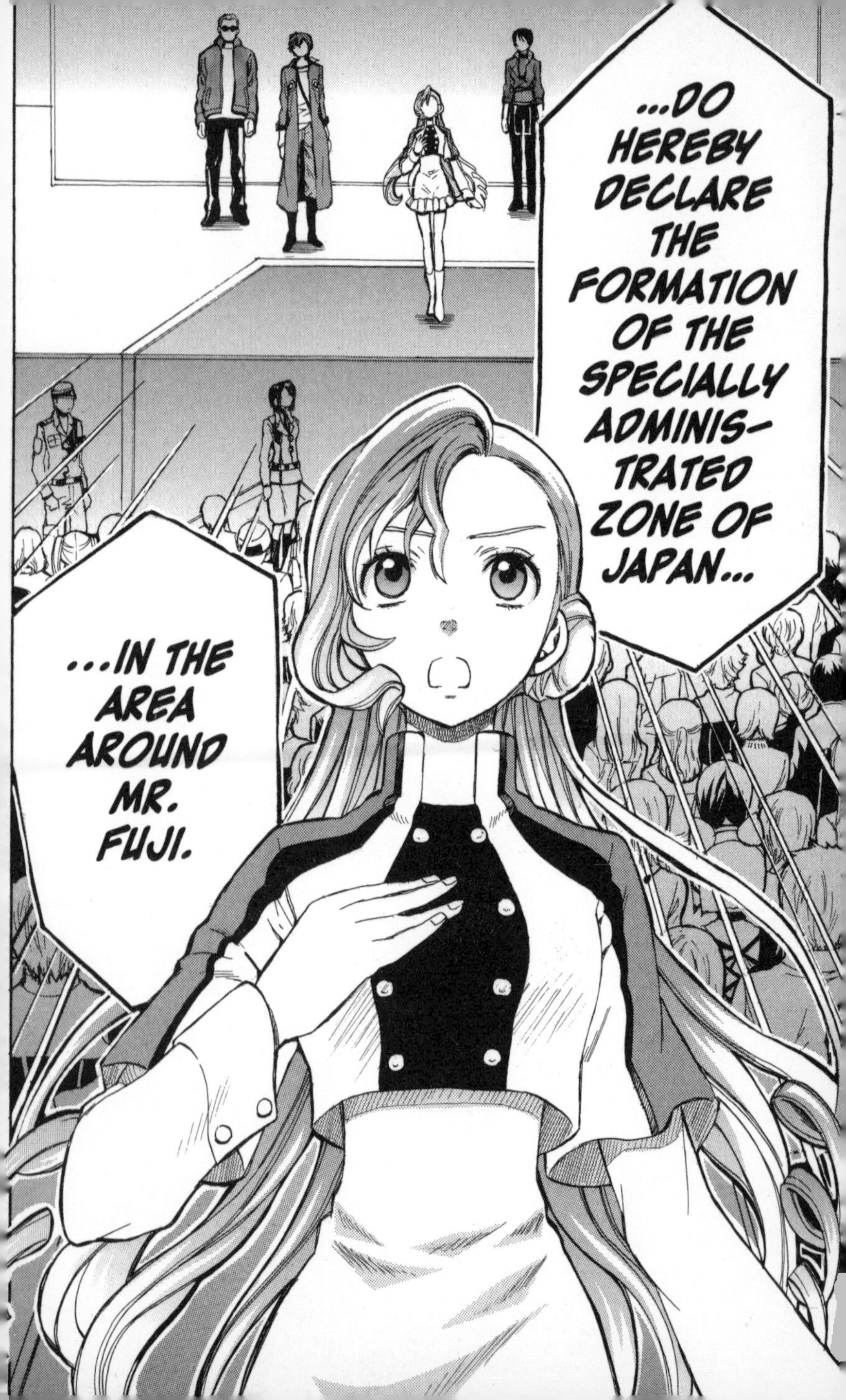
...DO HEREBY DECLARE THE FORMATION OF THE SPECIALLY ADMINIS-TRATED ZONE OF JAPAN...
...IN THE AREA AROUND MR. FUJI.

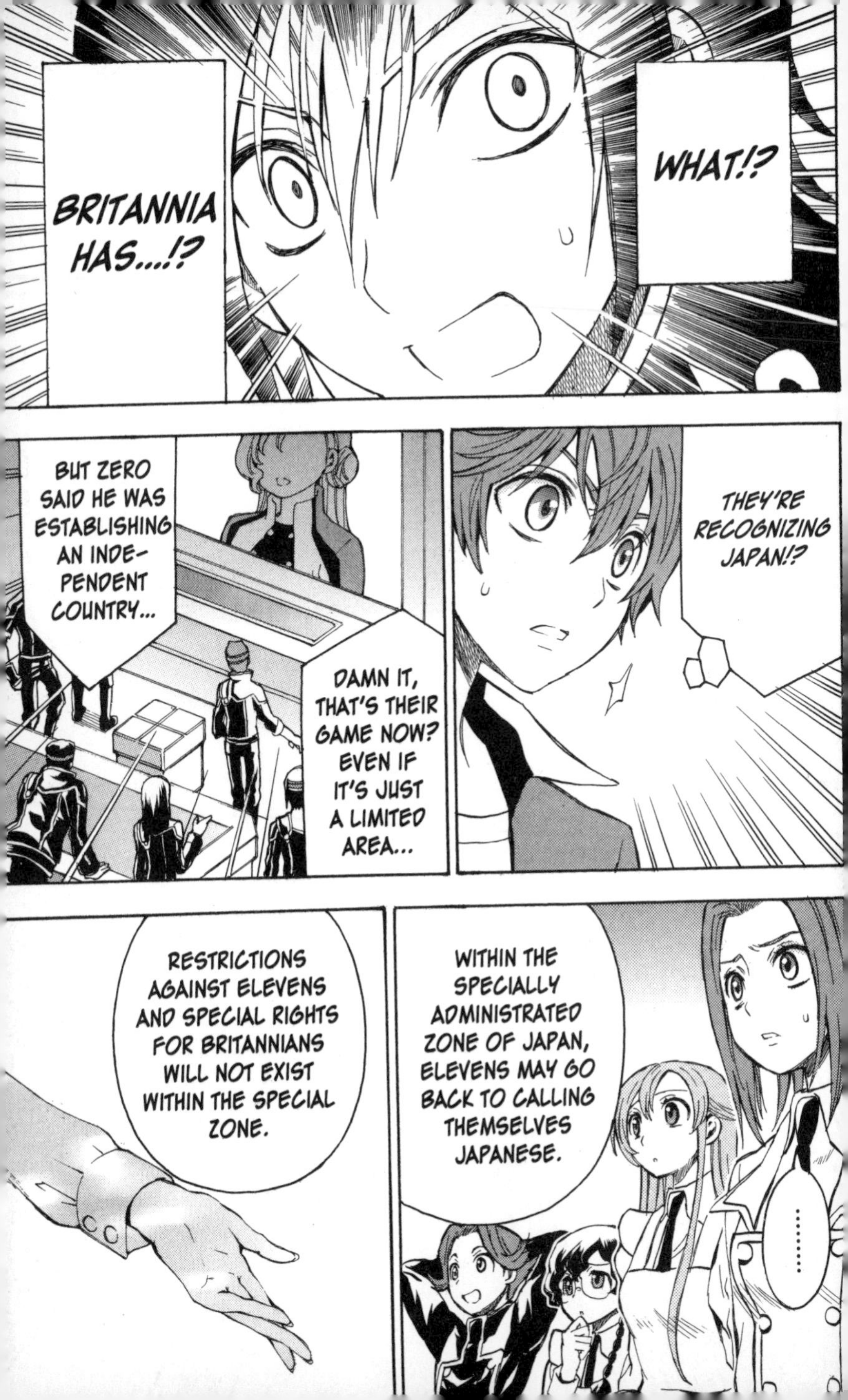
WHAT!?
BRITANNIA HAS...!?
THEY'RE RECOGNIZING JAPAN!?
BUT ZERO SAID HE WAS ESTABLISHING AN INDEPENDENT COUNTRY...
DAMN IT, THAT'S THEIR GAME NOW? EVEN IF IT'S JUST A LIMITED AREA...
WITHIN THE SPECIALLY ADMINISTRATED ZONE OF JAPAN, ELEVENS MAY GO BACK TO CALLING THEMSELVES JAPANESE.
......
RESTRICTIONS AGAINST ELEVENS AND SPECIAL RIGHTS FOR BRITANNIANS WILL NOT EXIST WITHIN THE SPECIAL ZONE.

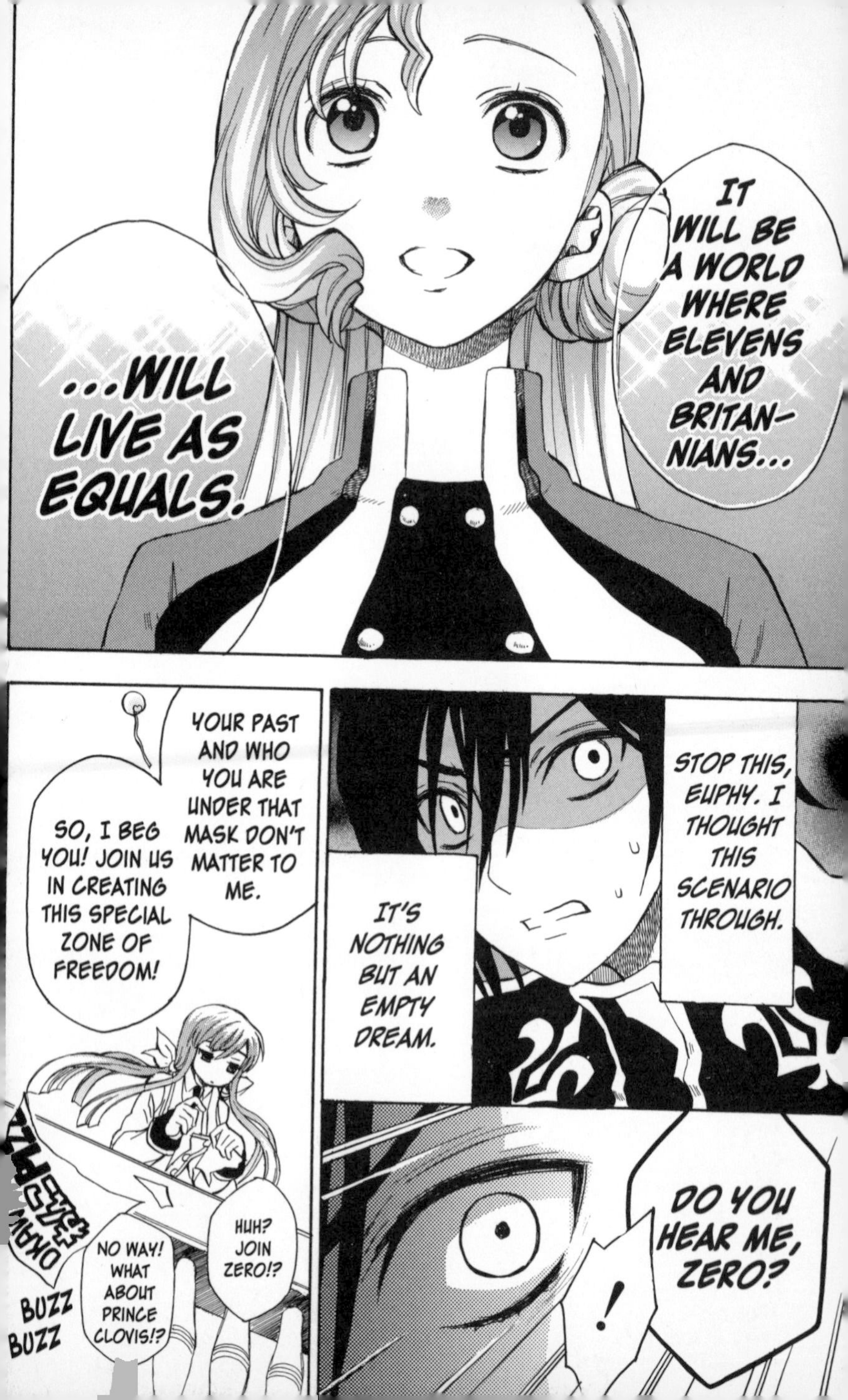
IT WILL BE A WORLD WHERE ELEVENS AND BRITAN-NIANS...
...WILL LIVE AS EQUALS.
STOP THIS, EUPHY. I THOUGHT THIS SCENARIO THROUGH.
IT'S NOTHING BUT AN EMPTY DREAM.
YOUR PAST AND WHO YOU ARE UNDER THAT MASK DON'T MATTER TO ME.
SO, I BEG YOU! JOIN US IN CREATING THIS SPECIAL ZONE OF FREEDOM!
DO YOU HEAR ME, ZERO?
!
HUH? JOIN ZERO!?
NO WAY! WHAT ABOUT PRINCE CLOVIS!?
BUZZ BUZZ

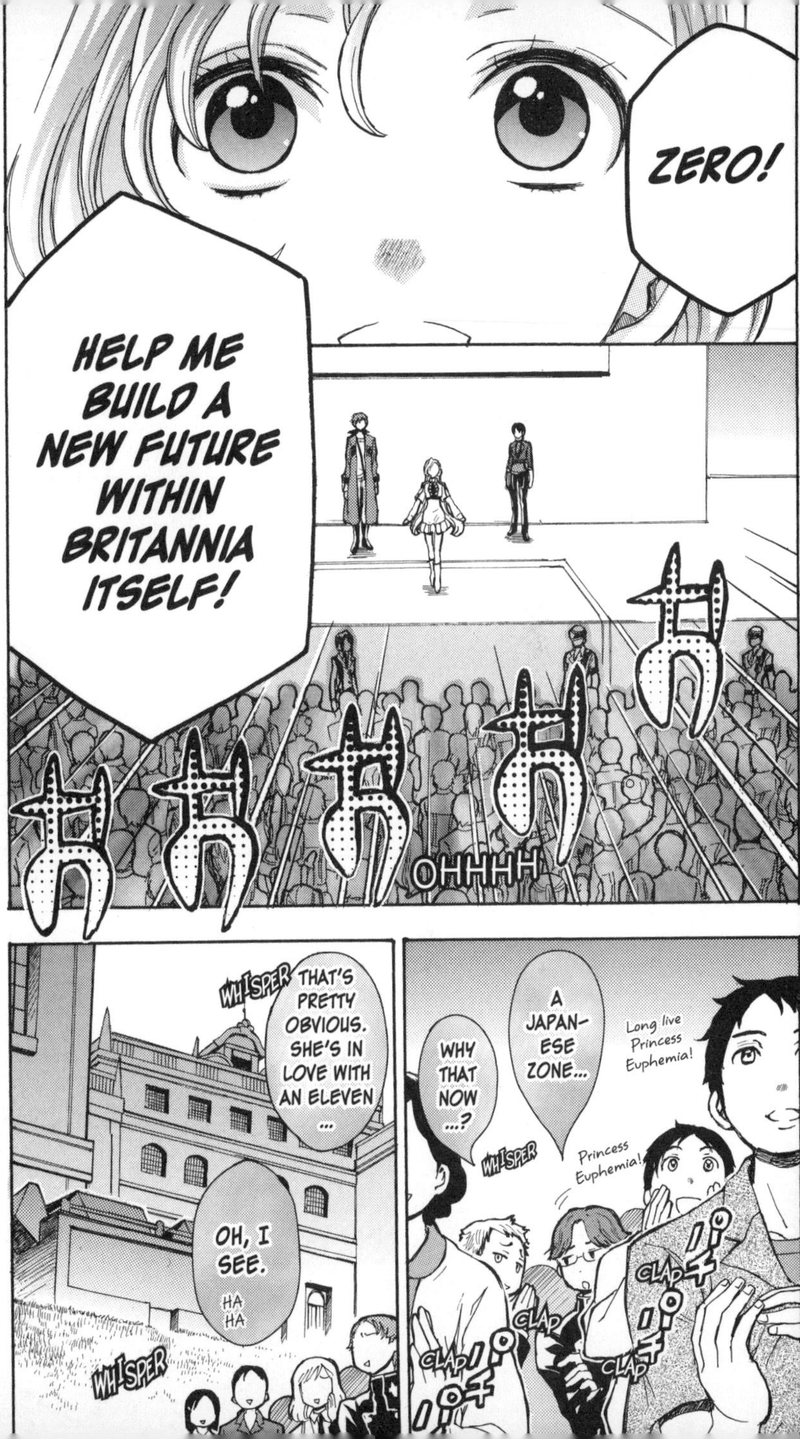
ZERO!
HELP ME BUILD A NEW FUTURE WITHIN BRITANNIA ITSELF!
OHHHH
Long live Princess Euphemia!
A JAPAN-ESE ZONE...
WHY THAT NOW ...?
WHISPER
Princess Euphemia!
CLAP
CLAP
CLAP
CLAP
WHISPER
THAT'S PRETTY OBVIOUS. SHE'S IN LOVE WITH AN ELEVEN ...
OH, I SEE.
HA HA
WHISPER

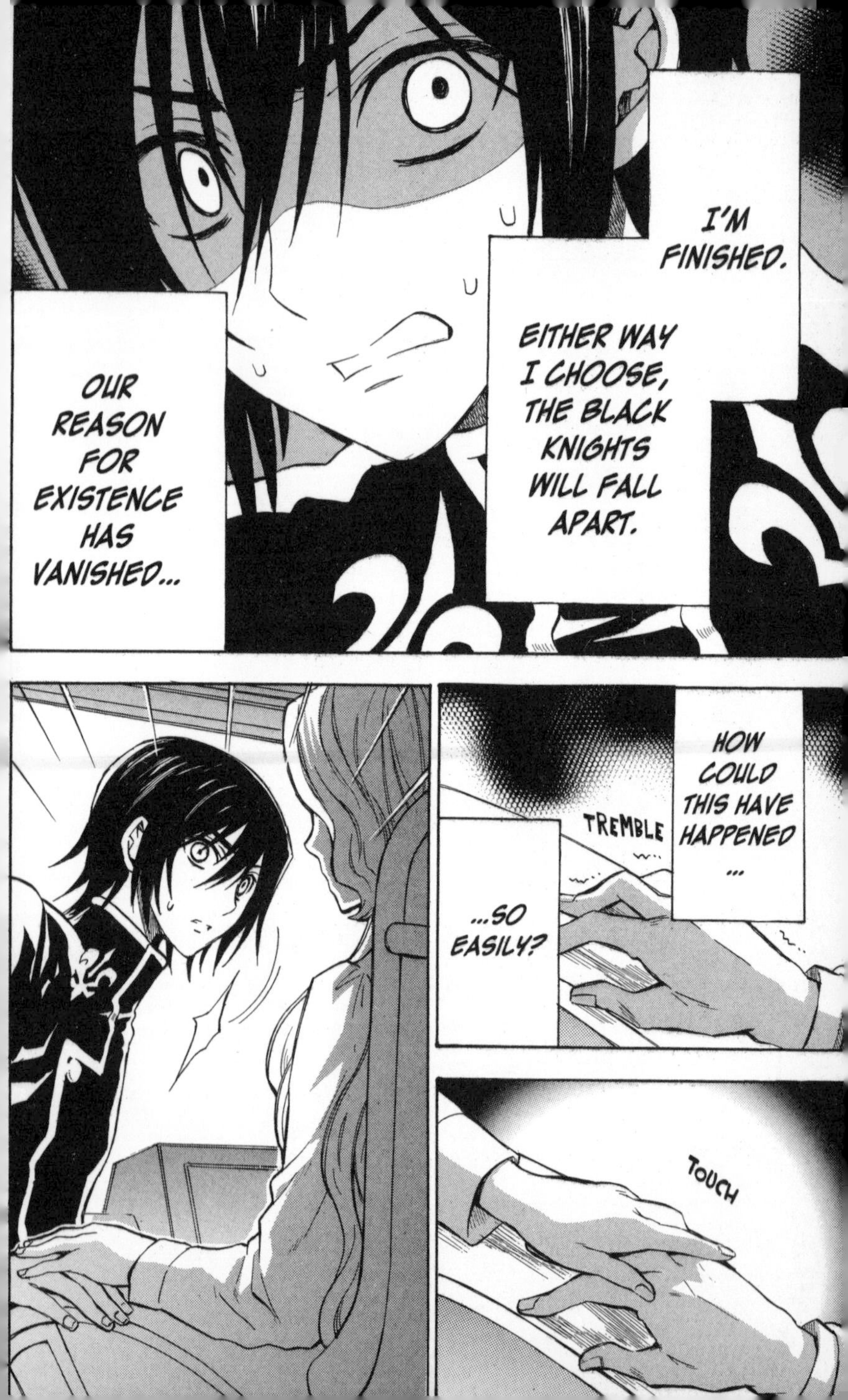
I'M FINISHED.
EITHER WAY I CHOOSE, THE BLACK KNIGHTS WILL FALL APART.
OUR REASON FOR EXISTENCE HAS VANISHED...
HOW COULD THIS HAVE HAPPENED...
TREMBLE
...SO EASILY?
TOUCH

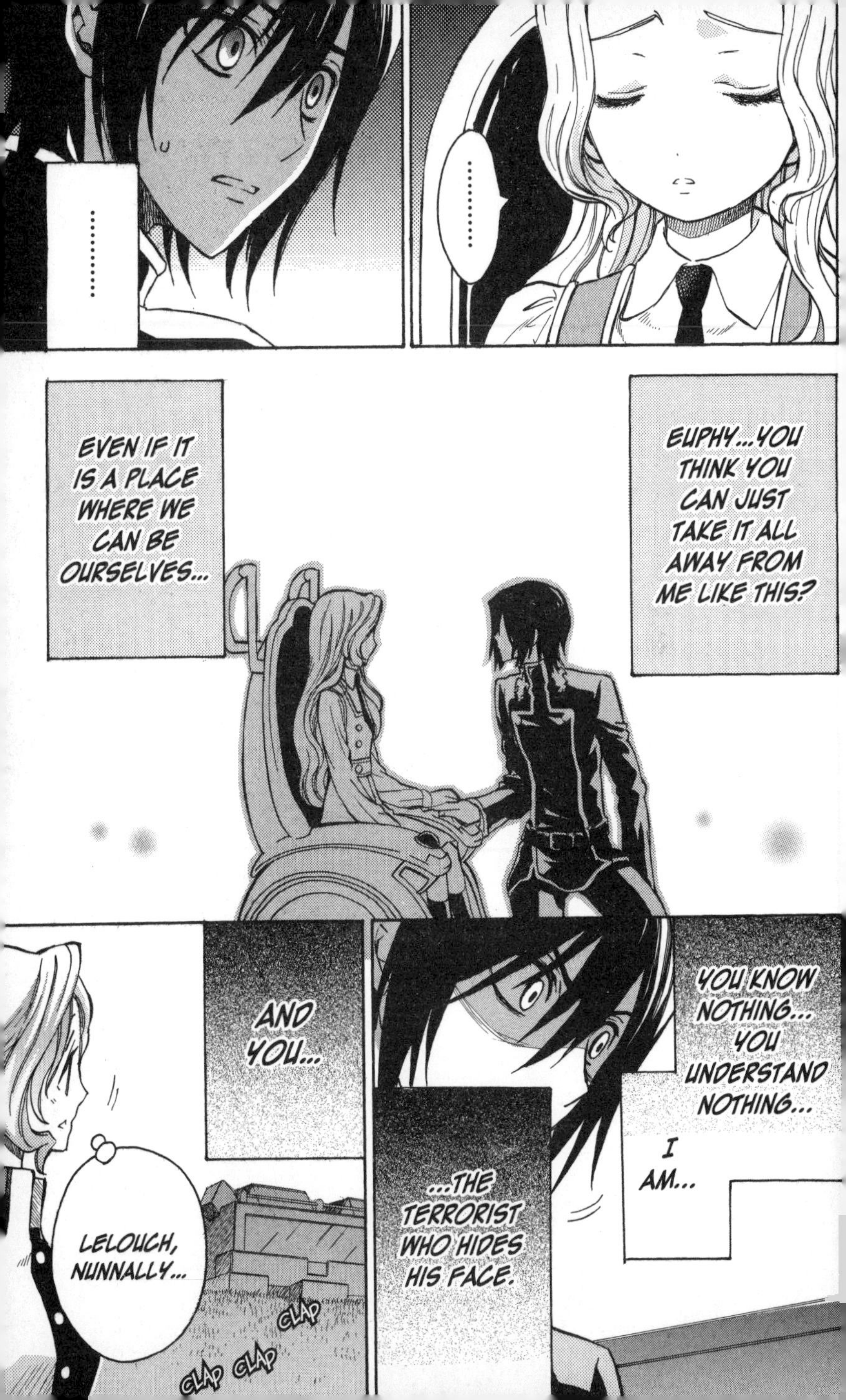
......
......
EUPHY...YOU THINK YOU CAN JUST TAKE IT ALL AWAY FROM ME LIKE THIS?
EVEN IF IT IS A PLACE WHERE WE CAN BE OURSELVES...
YOU KNOW NOTHING... YOU UNDERSTAND NOTHING...
I AM...
...THE TERRORIST WHO HIDES HIS FACE.
AND YOU...
LELOUCH, NUNNALLY...
CLAP
CLAP CLAP

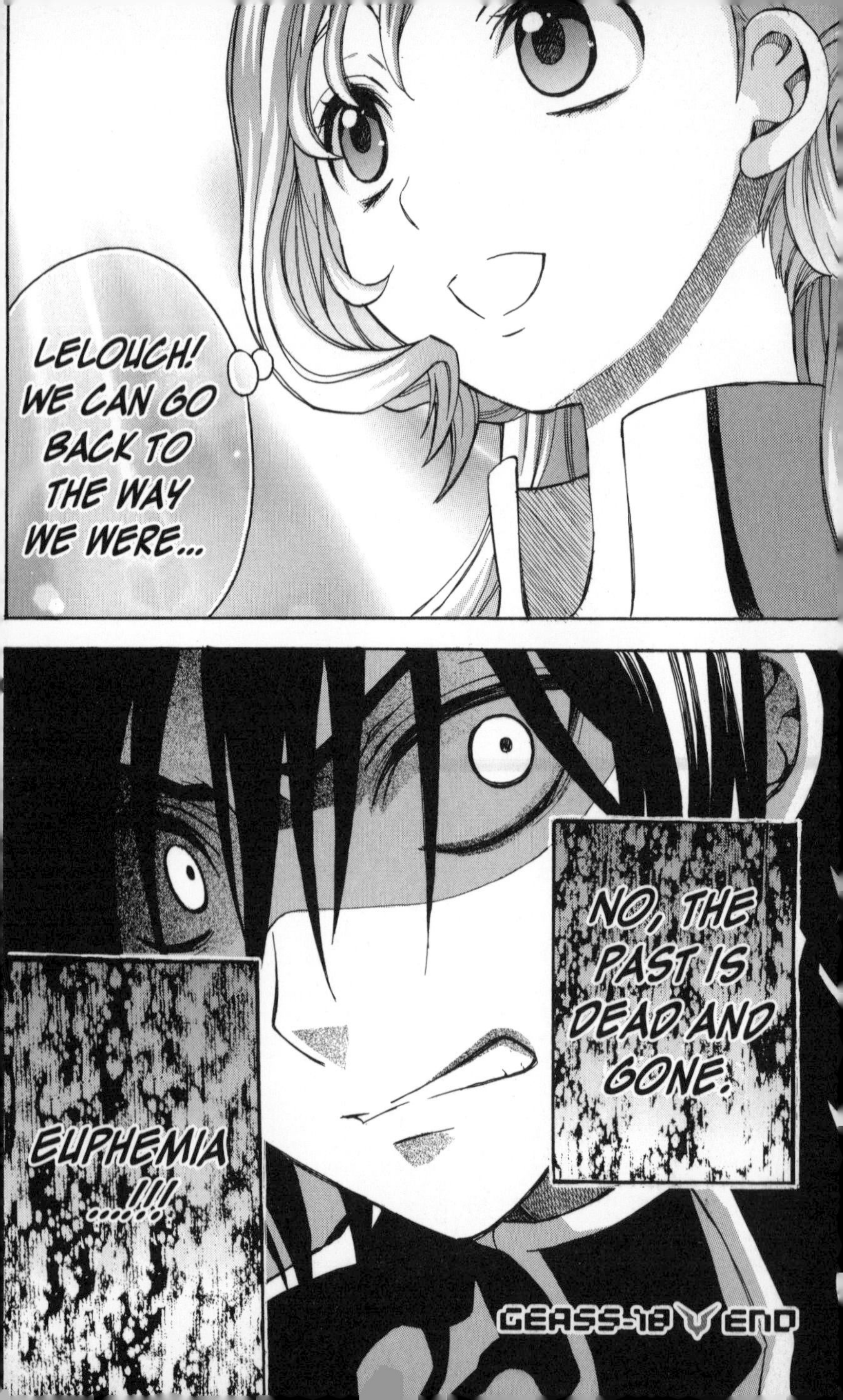
LELOUCH! WE CAN GO BACK TO THE WAY WE WERE...
NO, THE PAST IS DEAD AND GONE.
EUPHEMIA ...!!!
GEASS-18 END

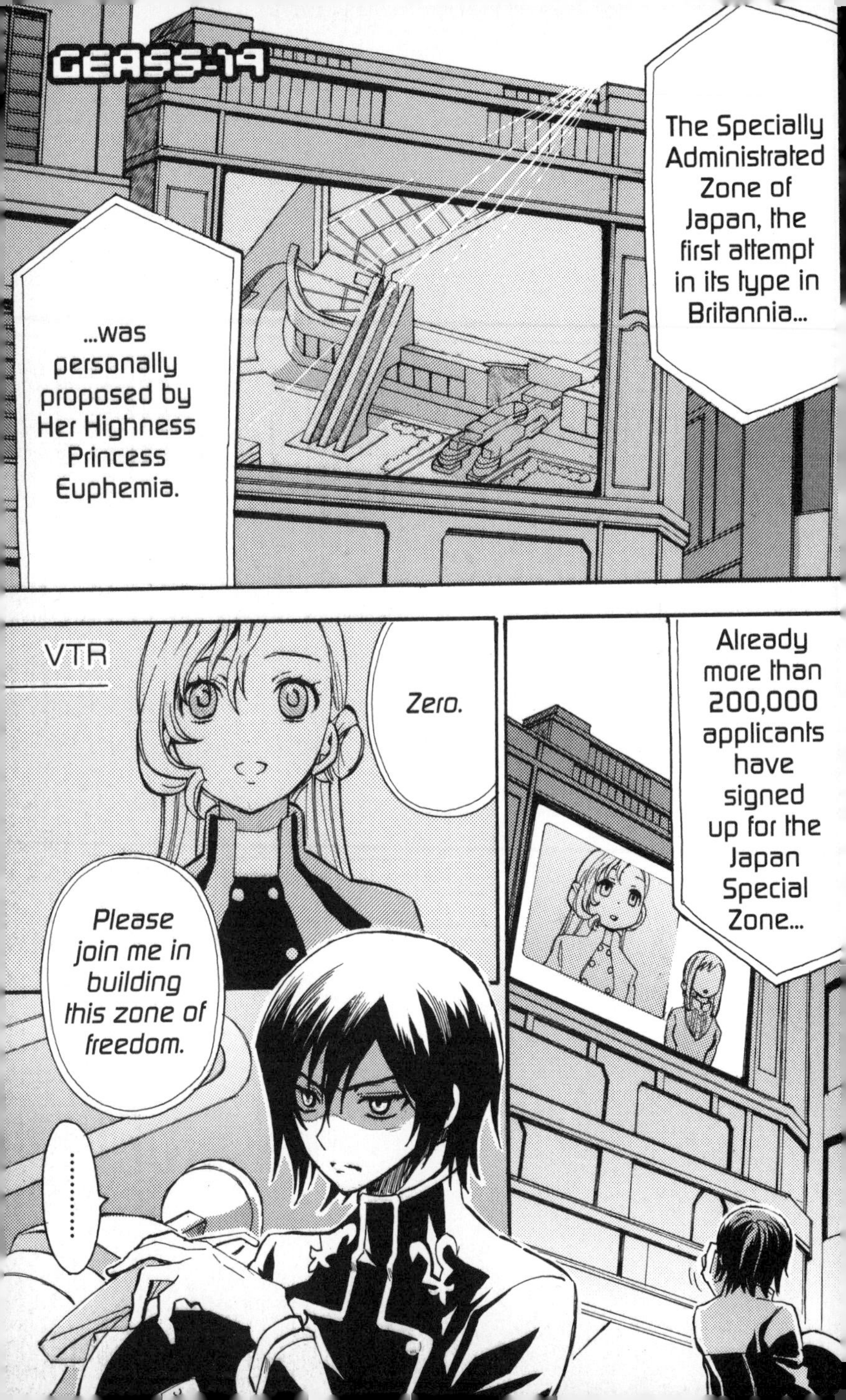
GEASS-19
The Specially Administrated Zone of Japan, the first attempt in its type in Britannia...
...was personally proposed by Her Highness Princess Euphemia.
Already more than 200,000 applicants have signed up for the Japan Special Zone...
Zero.
VTR
Please join me in building this zone of freedom.
....

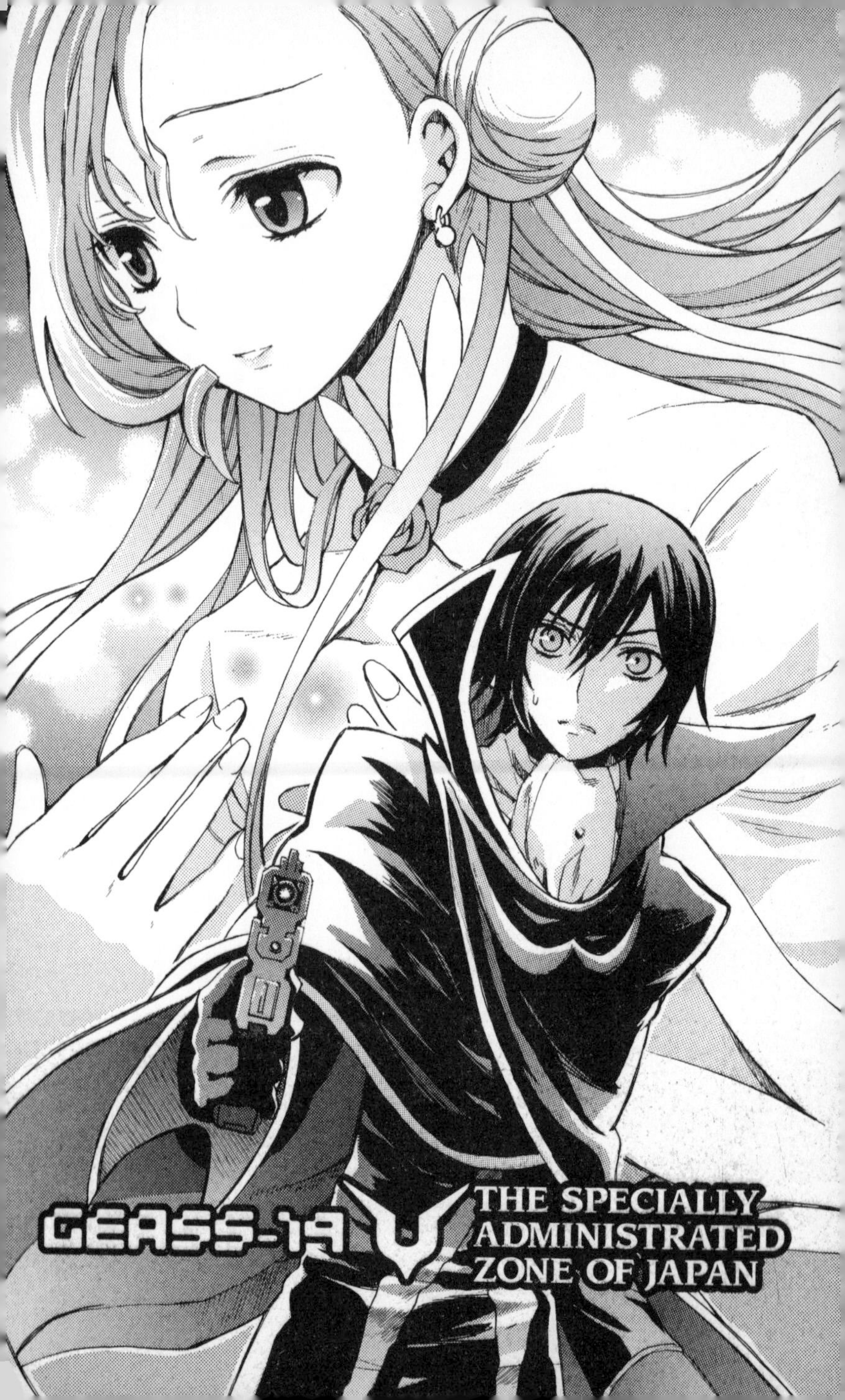
GEASS-19
THE SPECIALLY ADMINISTRATED ZONE OF JAPAN

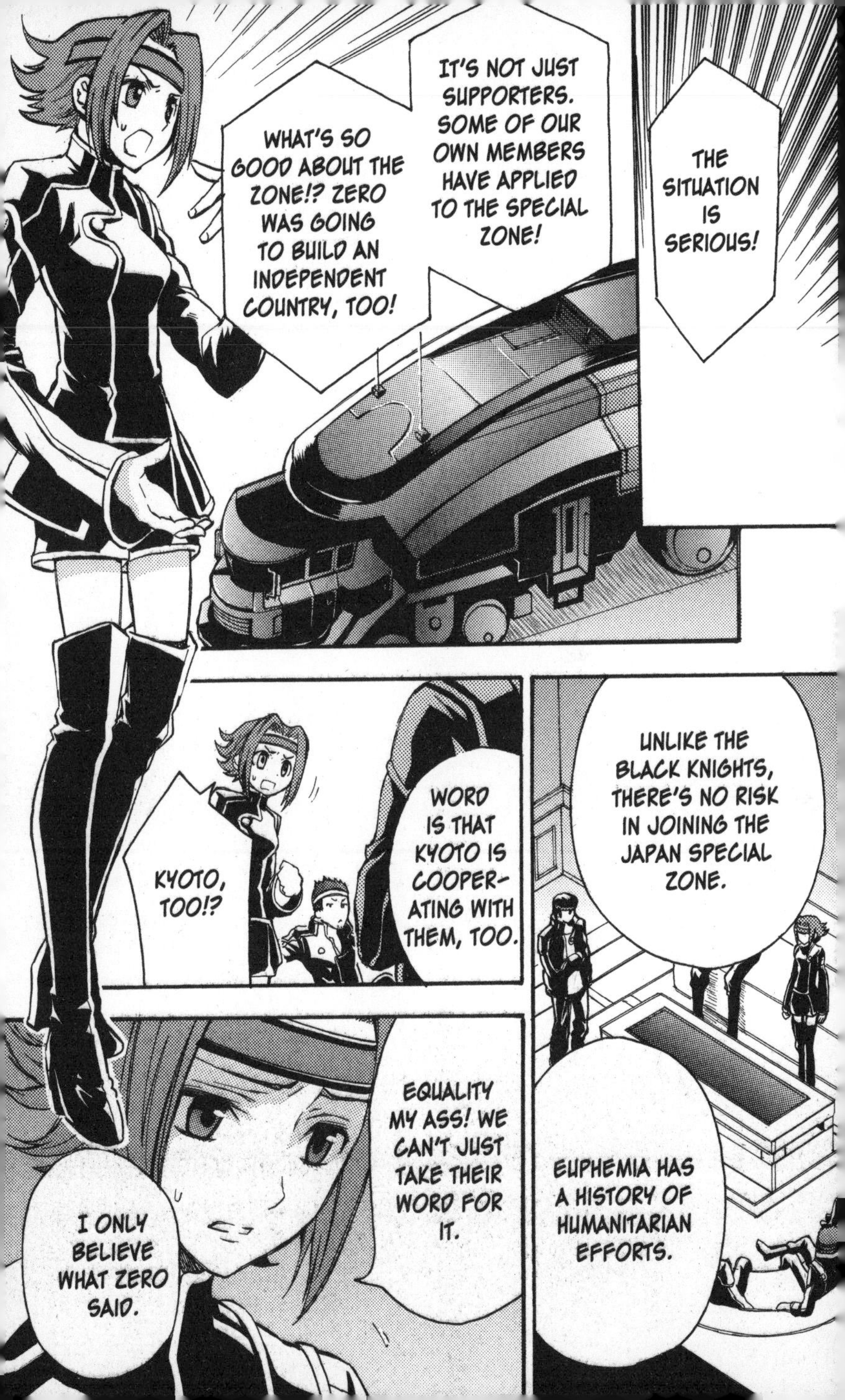
THE SITUATION IS SERIOUS!
IT'S NOT JUST SUPPORTERS. SOME OF OUR OWN MEMBERS HAVE APPLIED TO THE SPECIAL ZONE!
WHAT'S SO GOOD ABOUT THE ZONE!? ZERO WAS GOING TO BUILD AN INDEPENDENT COUNTRY, TOO!
UNLIKE THE BLACK KNIGHTS, THERE'S NO RISK IN JOINING THE JAPAN SPECIAL ZONE.
EUPHEMIA HAS A HISTORY OF HUMANITARIAN EFFORTS.
WORD IS THAT KYOTO IS COOPER-ATING WITH THEM, TOO.
KYOTO, TOO!?
EQUALITY MY ASS! WE CAN'T JUST TAKE THEIR WORD FOR IT.
I ONLY BELIEVE WHAT ZERO SAID.

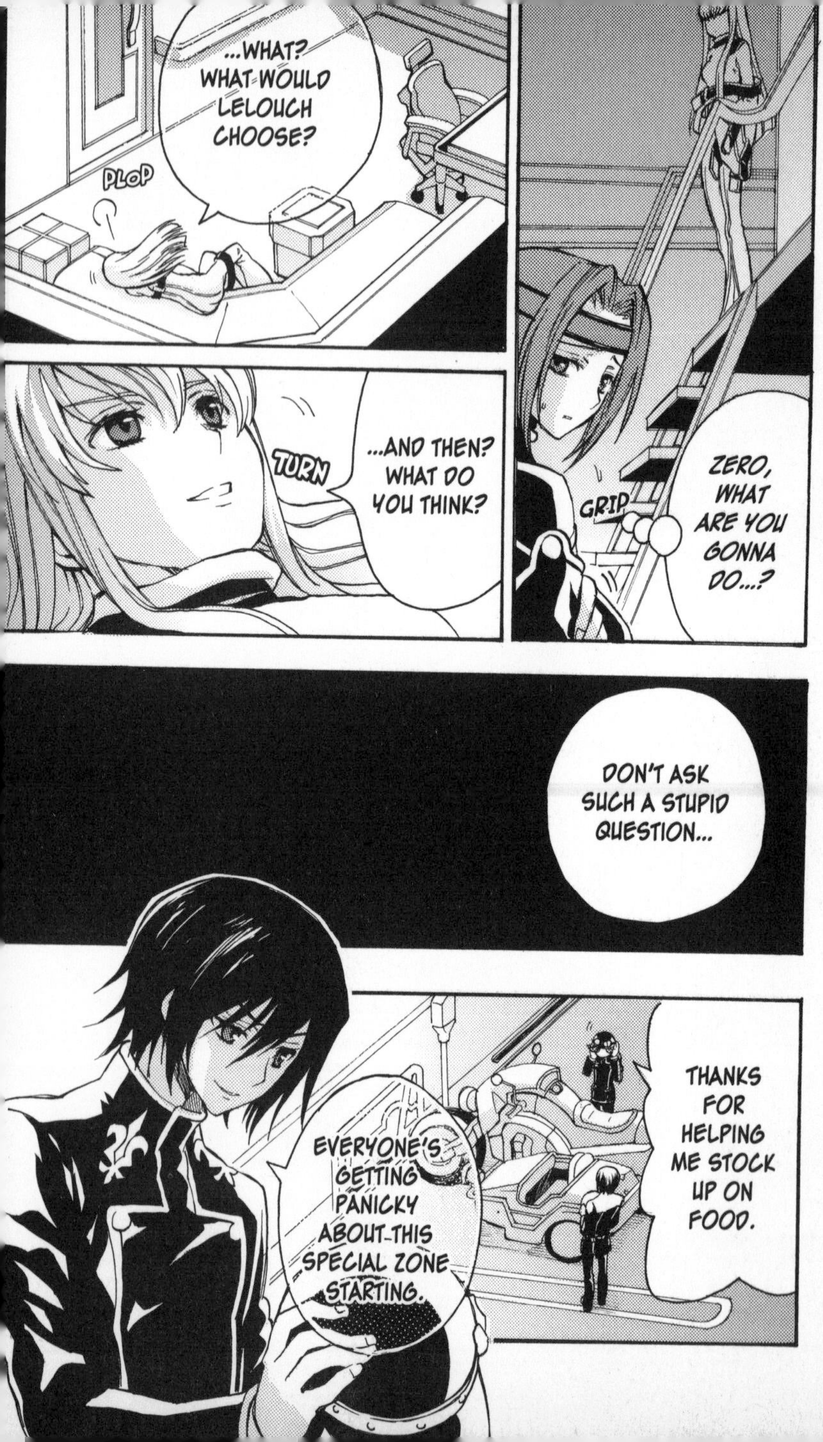
GRIP
ZERO, WHAT ARE YOU GONNA DO...?
PLOP
...WHAT? WHAT WOULD LELOUCH CHOOSE?
TURN
...AND THEN? WHAT DO YOU THINK?
DON'T ASK SUCH A STUPID QUESTION...
THANKS FOR HELPING ME STOCK UP ON FOOD.
EVERYONE'S GETTING PANICKY ABOUT THIS SPECIAL ZONE STARTING.

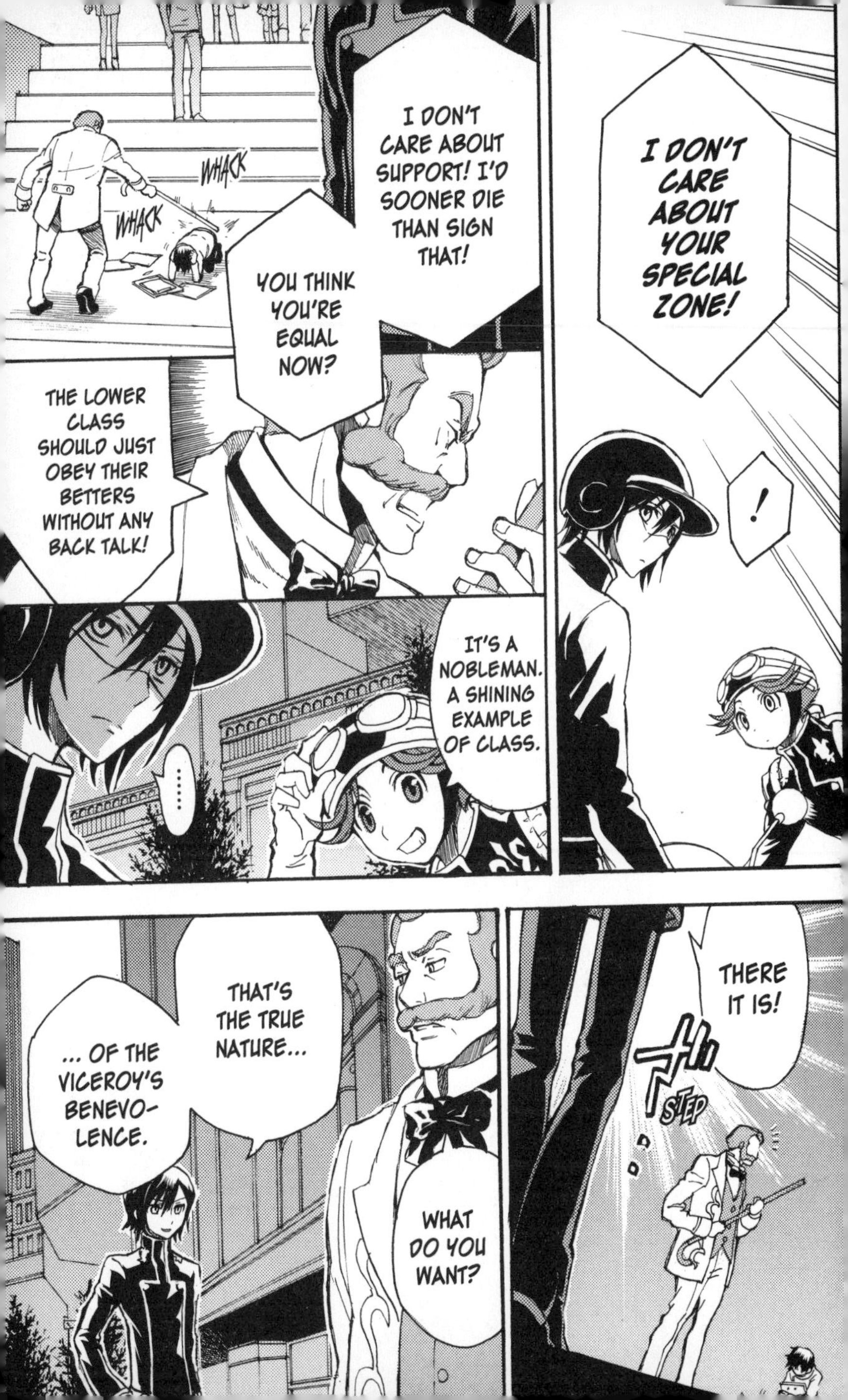
I DON'T CARE ABOUT YOUR SPECIAL ZONE!
!
I DON'T CARE ABOUT SUPPORT! I'D SOONER DIE THAN SIGN THAT!
WHACK
WHACK
YOU THINK YOU'RE EQUAL NOW?
THE LOWER CLASS SHOULD JUST OBEY THEIR BETTERS WITHOUT ANY BACK TALK!
IT'S A NOBLEMAN. A SHINING EXAMPLE OF CLASS.
......
THERE IT IS!
STEP
THAT'S THE TRUE NATURE...
... OF THE VICEROY'S BENEVO-LENCE.
WHAT DO YOU WANT?

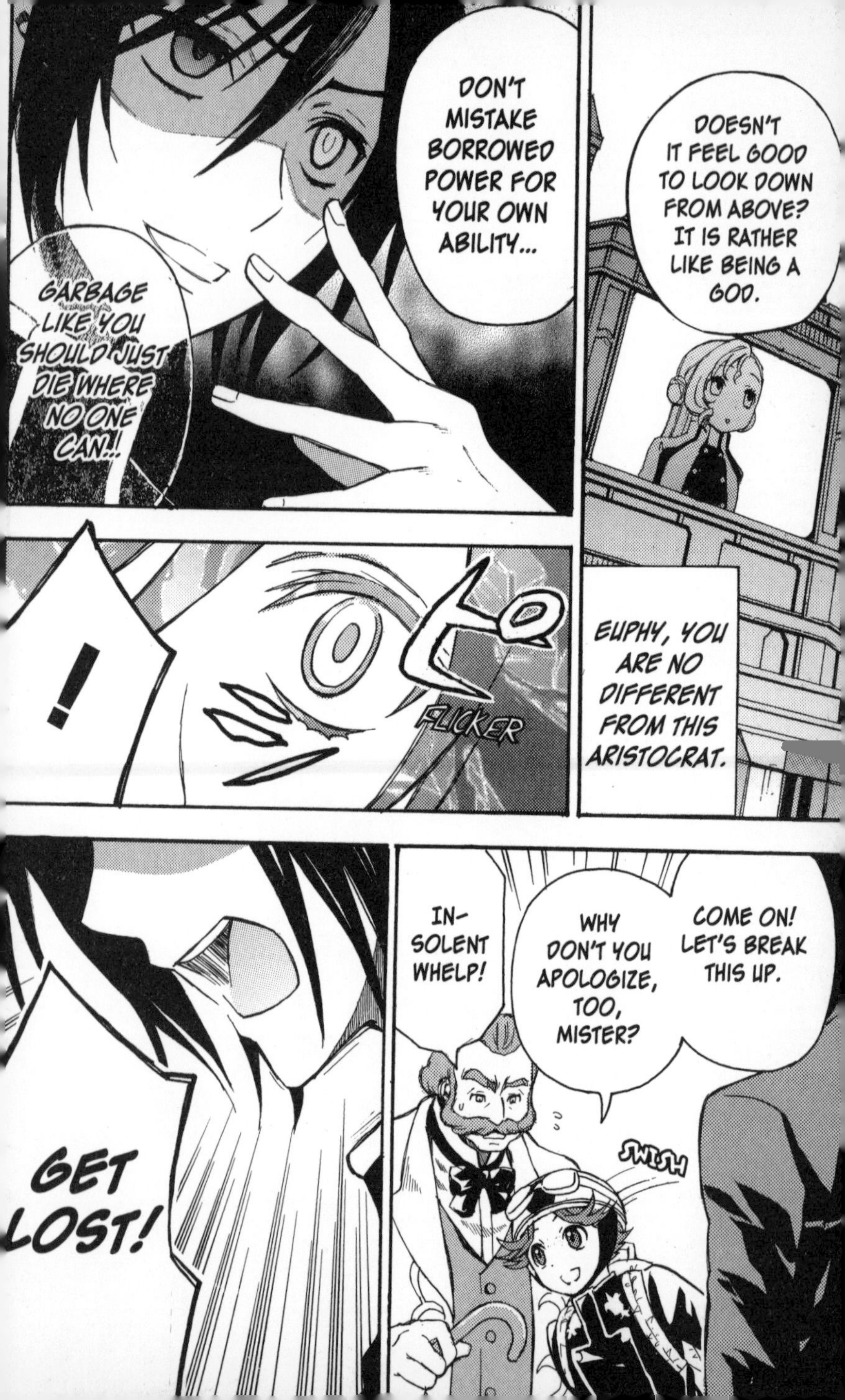
DOESN'T IT FEEL GOOD TO LOOK DOWN FROM ABOVE? IT IS RATHER LIKE BEING A GOD.
EUPHY, YOU ARE NO DIFFERENT FROM THIS ARISTOCRAT.
DON'T MISTAKE BORROWED POWER FOR YOUR OWN ABILITY...
GARBAGE LIKE YOU SHOULD JUST DIE WHERE NO ONE CAN...!!
!
FLICKER
COME ON! LET'S BREAK THIS UP.
WHY DON'T YOU APOLOGIZE, TOO, MISTER?
IN-SOLENT WHELP!
SWISH
GET LOST!

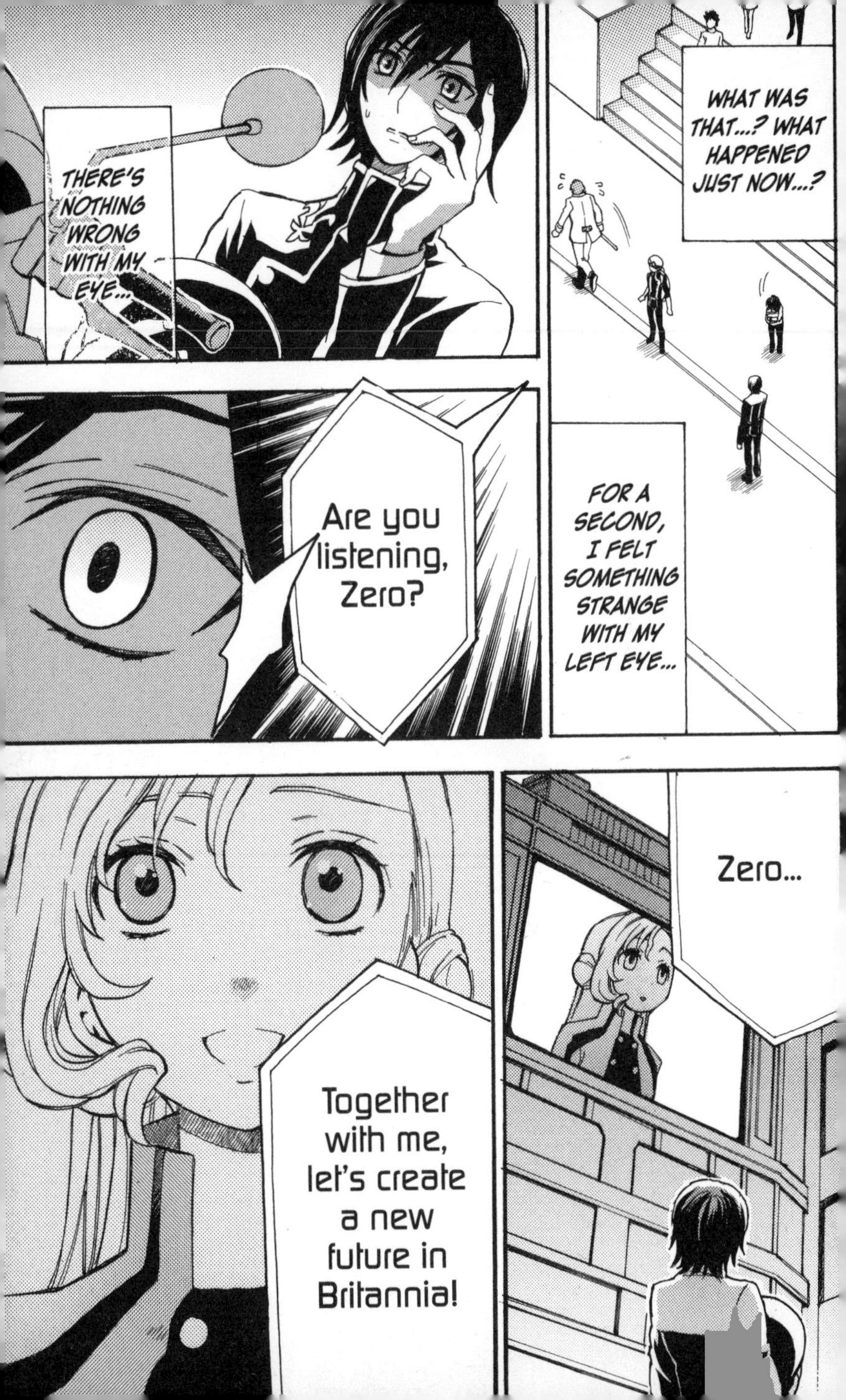
WHAT WAS THAT...? WHAT HAPPENED JUST NOW...?
FOR A SECOND, I FELT SOMETHING STRANGE WITH MY LEFT EYE...
THERE'S NOTHING WRONG WITH MY EYE...
Are you listening, Zero?
Zero...
Together with me, let's create a new future in Britannia!

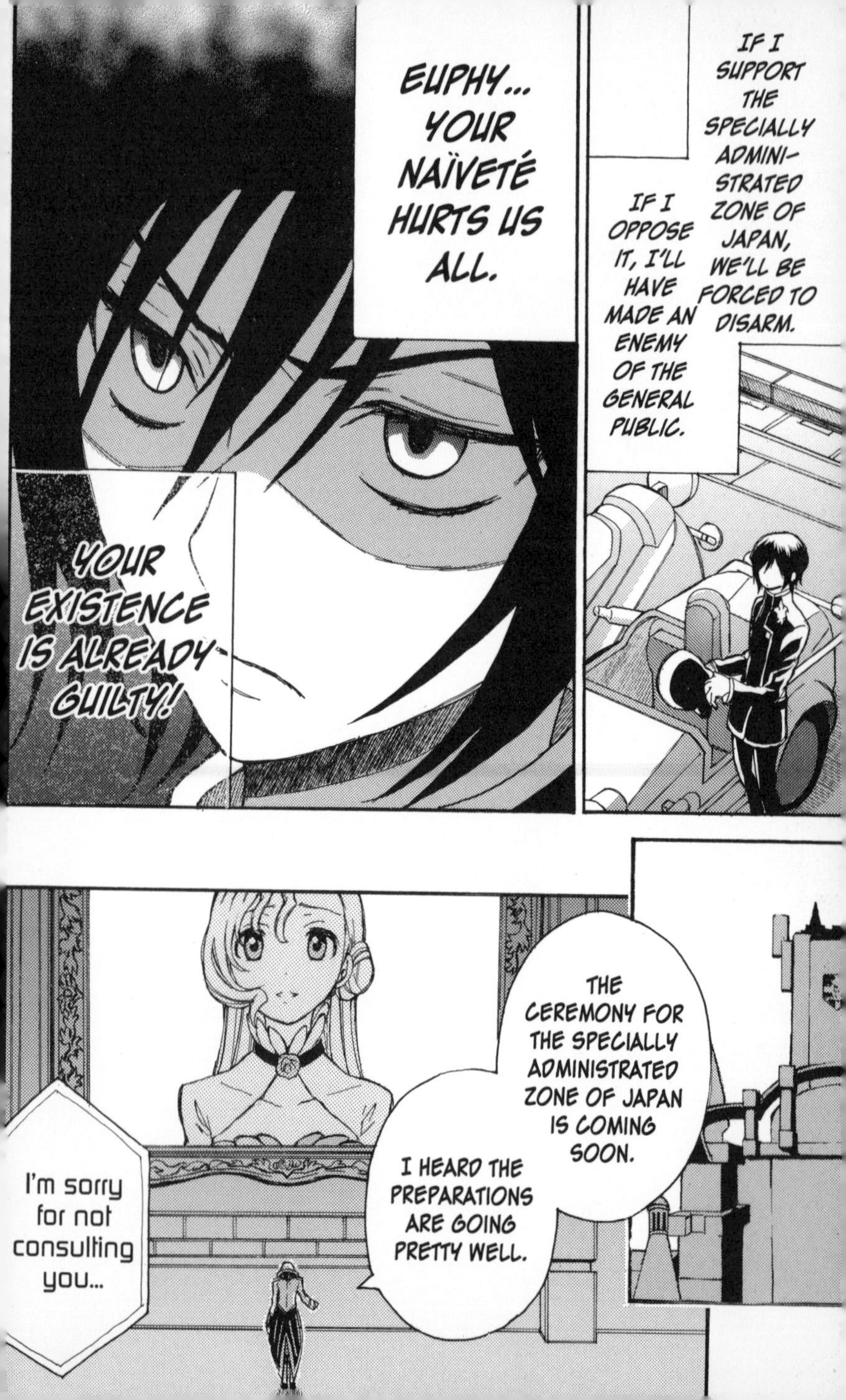
IF I SUPPORT THE SPECIALLY ADMINI-STRATED ZONE OF JAPAN, WE'LL BE FORCED TO DISARM.
IF I OPPOSE IT, I'LL HAVE MADE AN ENEMY OF THE GENERAL PUBLIC.
EUPHY... YOUR NAÏVETÉ HURTS US ALL.
YOUR EXISTENCE IS ALREADY GUILTY!
THE CEREMONY FOR THE SPECIALLY ADMINISTRATED ZONE OF JAPAN IS COMING SOON.
I HEARD THE PREPARATIONS ARE GOING PRETTY WELL.
I'm sorry for not consulting you...

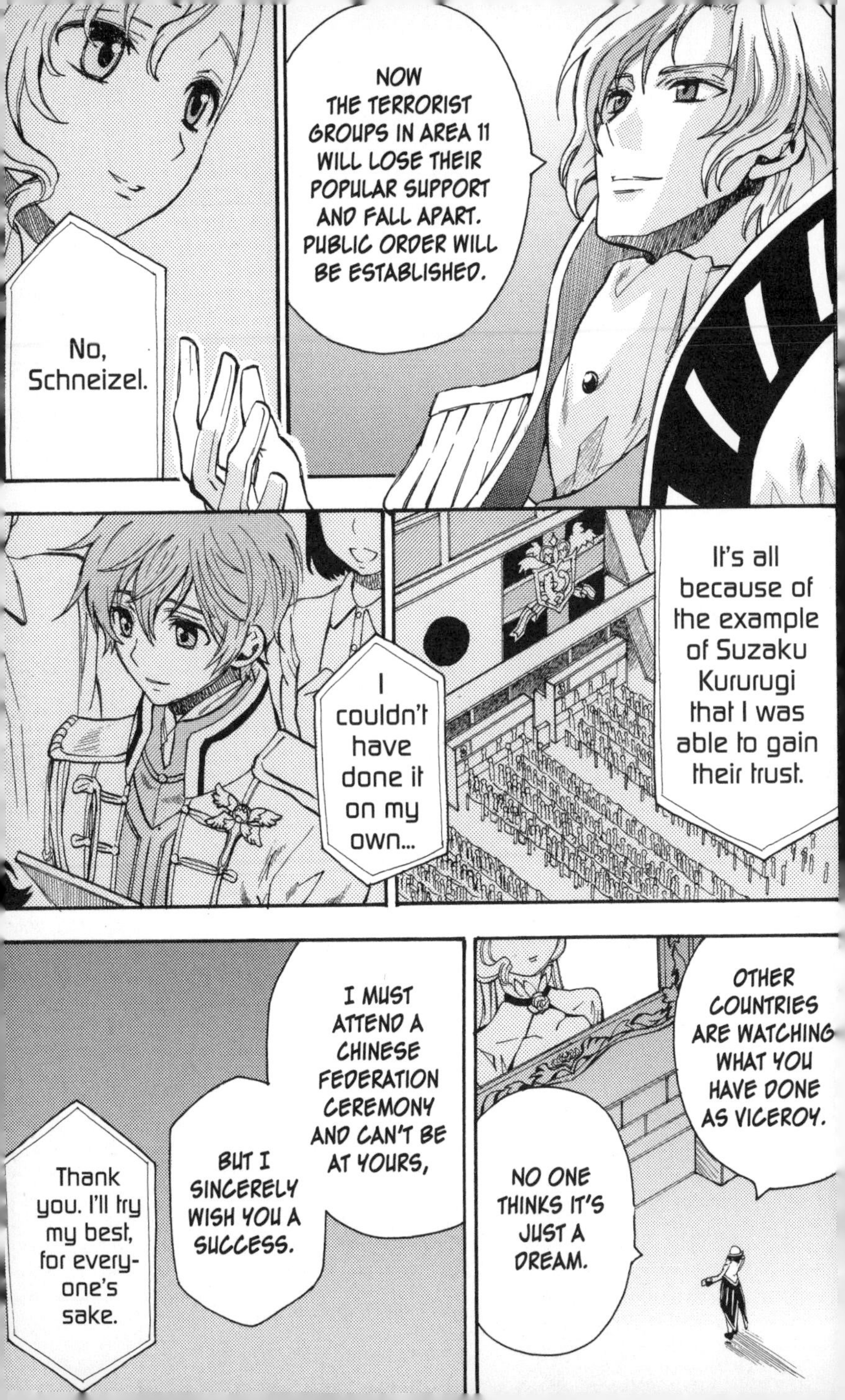
NOW THE TERRORIST GROUPS IN AREA 11 WILL LOSE THEIR POPULAR SUPPORT AND FALL APART. PUBLIC ORDER WILL BE ESTABLISHED.
No, Schneizel.
It's all because of the example of Suzaku Kururugi that I was able to gain their trust.
I couldn't have done it on my own...
OTHER COUNTRIES ARE WATCHING WHAT YOU HAVE DONE AS VICEROY.
NO ONE THINKS IT'S JUST A DREAM.
I MUST ATTEND A CHINESE FEDERATION CEREMONY AND CAN'T BE AT YOURS,
BUT I SINCERELY WISH YOU A SUCCESS.
Thank you. I'll try my best, for every-one's sake.

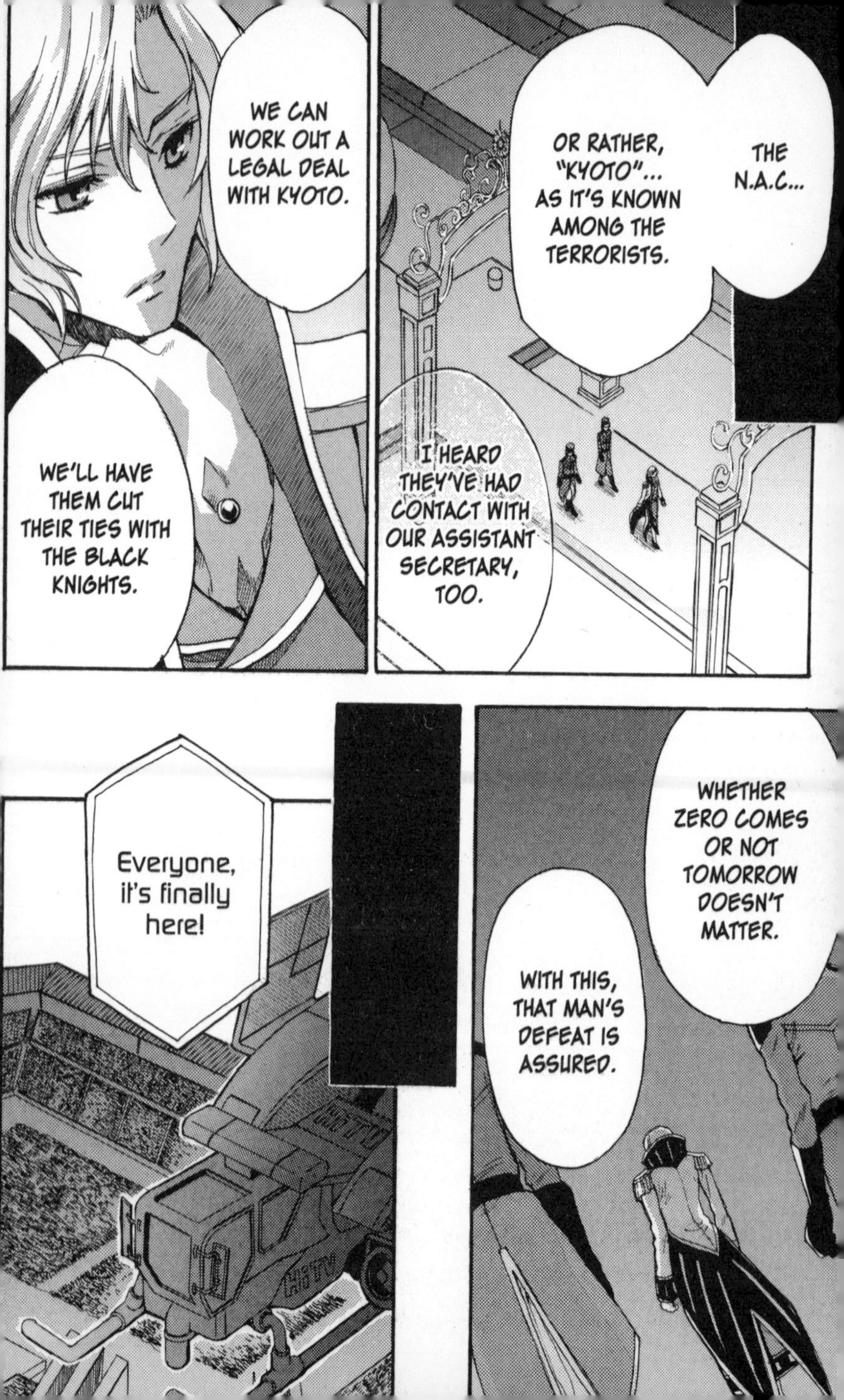
THE N.A.C...
OR RATHER, "KYOTO"... AS IT'S KNOWN AMONG THE TERRORISTS.
I HEARD THEY'VE HAD CONTACT WITH OUR ASSISTANT SECRETARY, TOO.
WE CAN WORK OUT A LEGAL DEAL WITH KYOTO.
WE'LL HAVE THEM CUT THEIR TIES WITH THE BLACK KNIGHTS.
WHETHER ZERO COMES OR NOT TOMORROW DOESN'T MATTER.
WITH THIS, THAT MAN'S DEFEAT IS ASSURED.
Everyone, it's finally here!

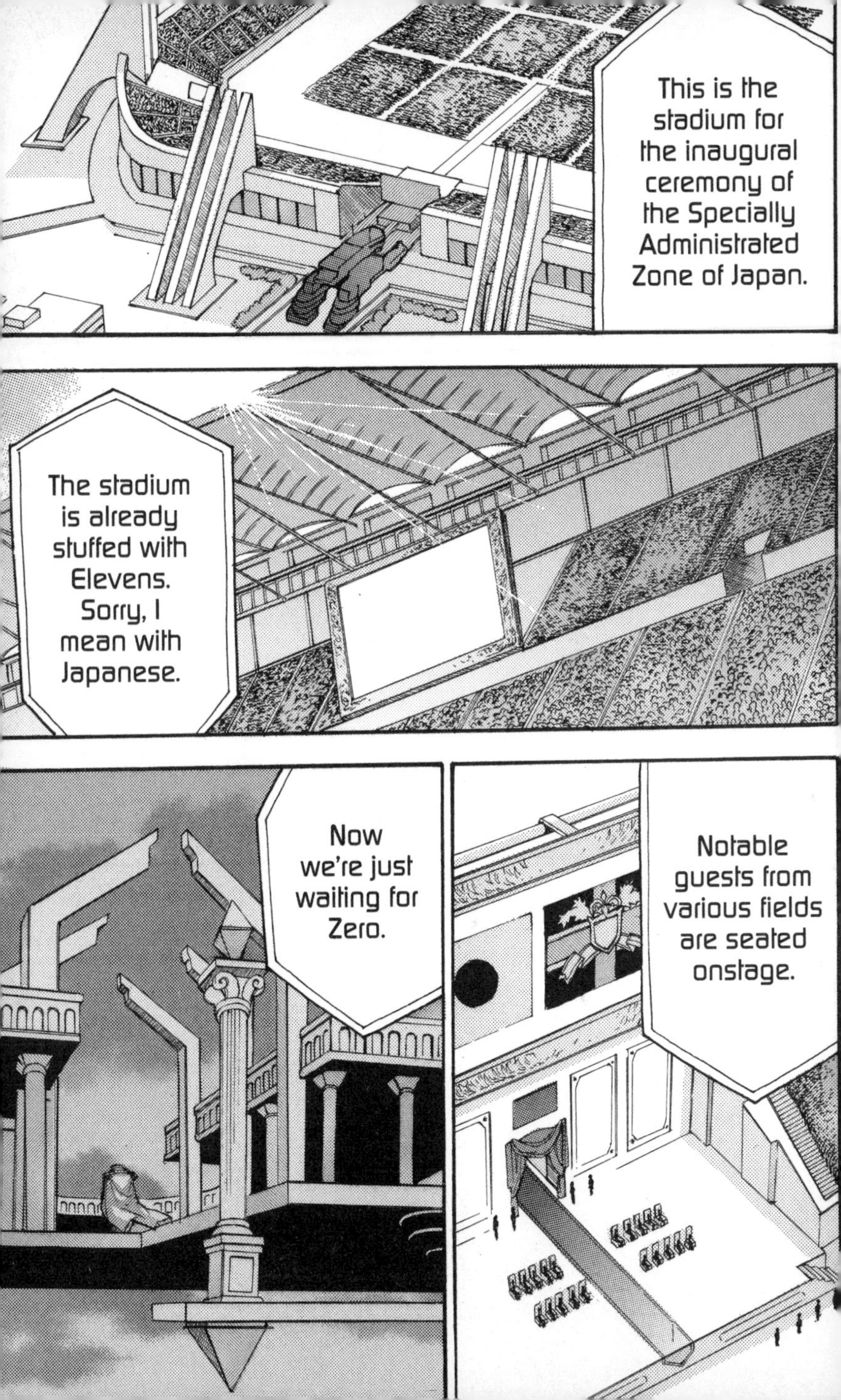
This is the stadium for the inaugural ceremony of the Specially Administrated Zone of Japan.
The stadium is already stuffed with Elevens. Sorry, I mean with Japanese.
Notable guests from various fields are seated onstage.
Now we're just waiting for Zero.

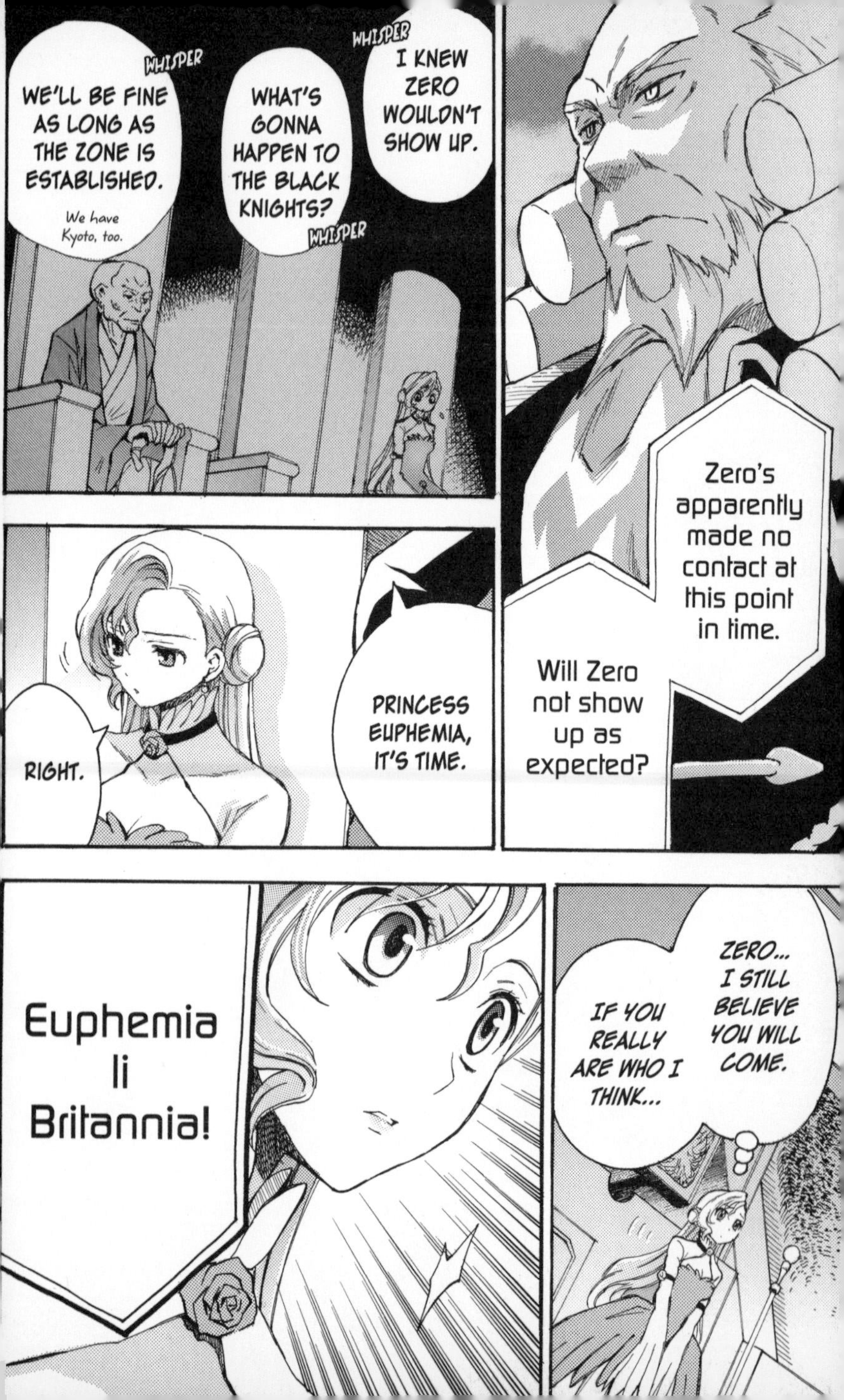
Zero's apparently made no contact at this point in time.
Will Zero not show up as expected?
WHISPER
I KNEW ZERO WOULDN'T SHOW UP.
WHAT'S GONNA HAPPEN TO THE BLACK KNIGHTS?
WHISPER
WHISPER
WE'LL BE FINE AS LONG AS THE ZONE IS ESTABLISHED.
We have Kyoto, too.
PRINCESS EUPHEMIA, IT'S TIME.
RIGHT.
ZERO... I STILL BELIEVE YOU WILL COME.
IF YOU REALLY ARE WHO I THINK...
Euphemia li Britannia!

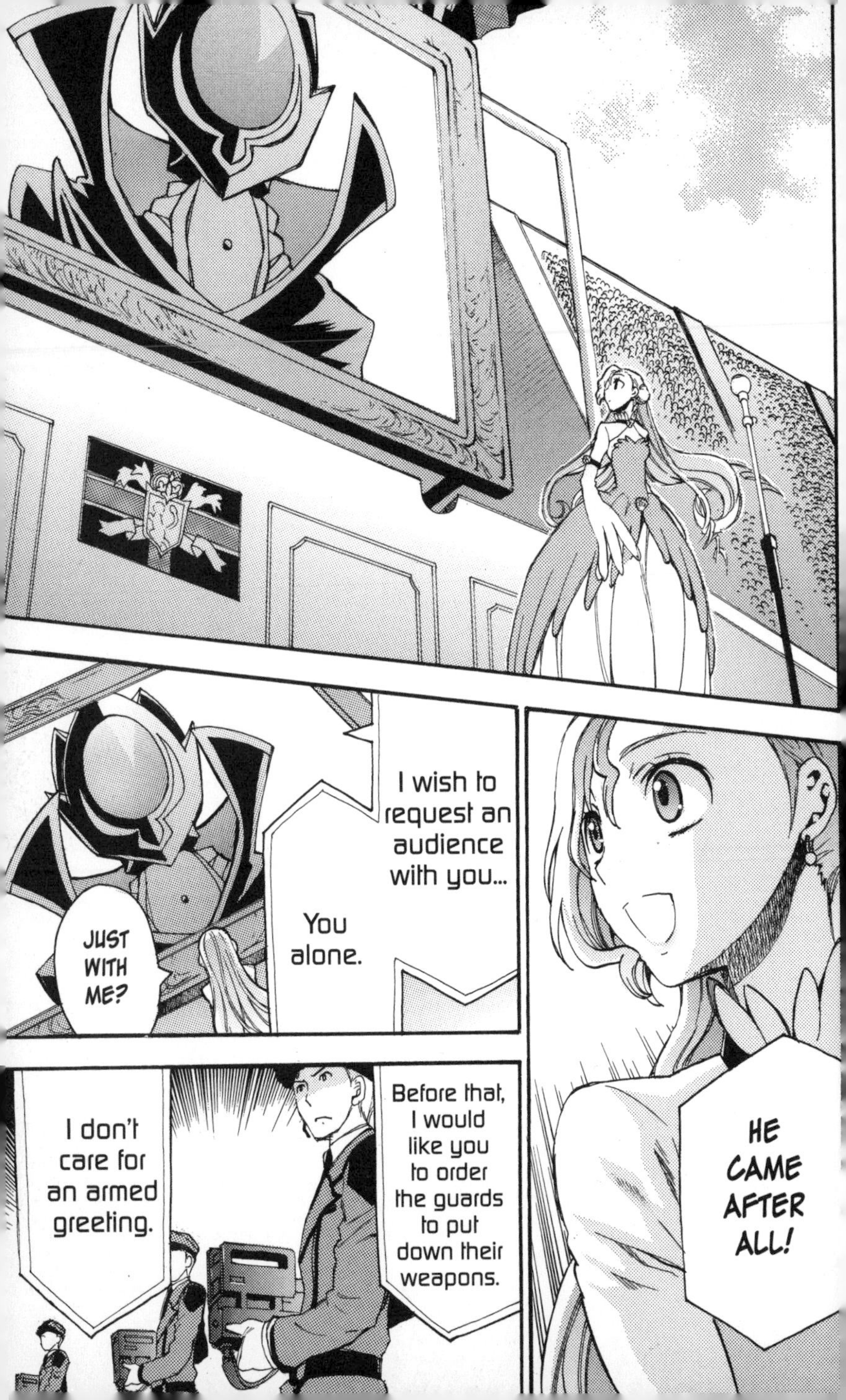
HE CAME AFTER ALL!
I wish to request an audience with you...
You alone.
JUST WITH ME?
Before that, I would like you to order the guards to put down their weapons.
I don't care for an armed greeting.

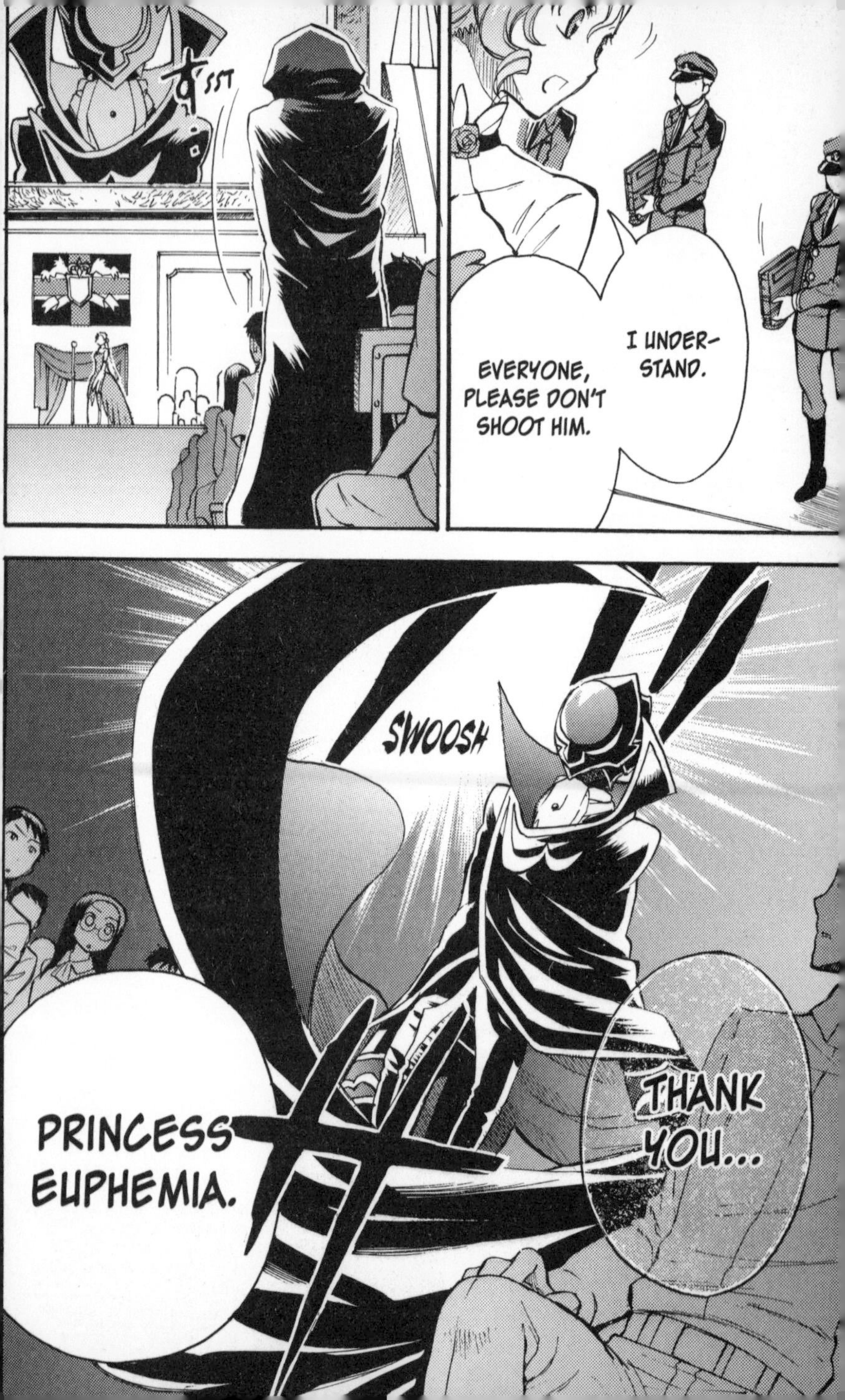
I UNDER-
STAND.
EVERYONE, PLEASE DON'T SHOOT HIM.
SST
SWOOSH
THANK YOU...
PRINCESS EUPHEMIA.

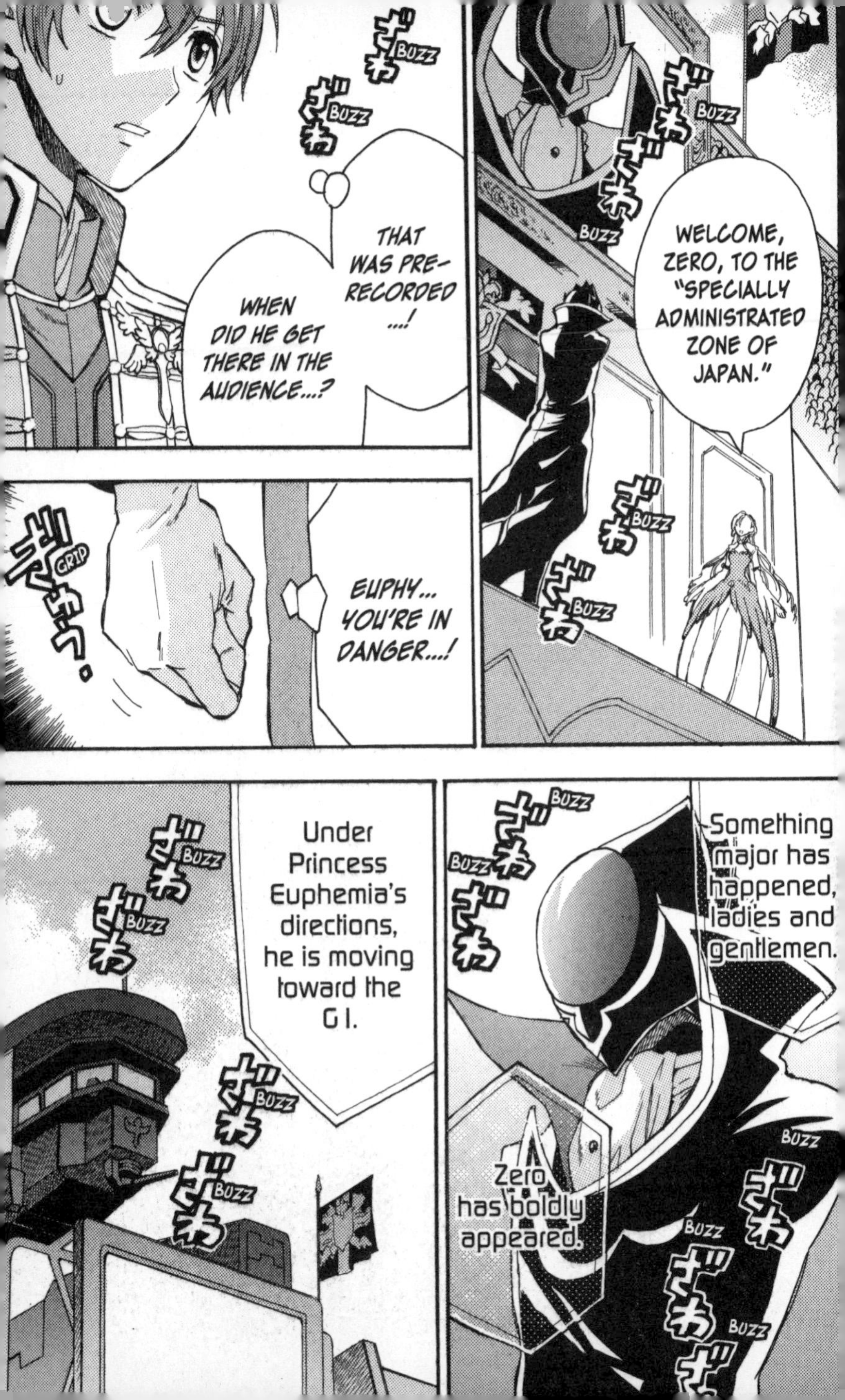

ざわ BUZZ
ざわ BUZZ
WELCOME, ZERO, TO THE "SPECIALLY ADMINISTRATED ZONE OF JAPAN."
ざわ BUZZ
ざわ BUZZ
ざわ BUZZ
ざわ BUZZ
THAT WAS PRE-RECORDED ...!
WHEN DID HE GET THERE IN THE AUDIENCE...?
ぎゅっ。 GRIP
EUPHY... YOU'RE IN DANGER...!
ざわ BUZZ
ざわ BUZZ
Something major has happened, ladies and gentlemen.
Zero has boldly appeared.
ざわ BUZZ
ざわ BUZZ
ざわ BUZZ
ざわ BUZZ
Under Princess Euphemia's directions, he is moving toward the G1.
ざわ BUZZ
ざわ BUZZ
ざわ BUZZ

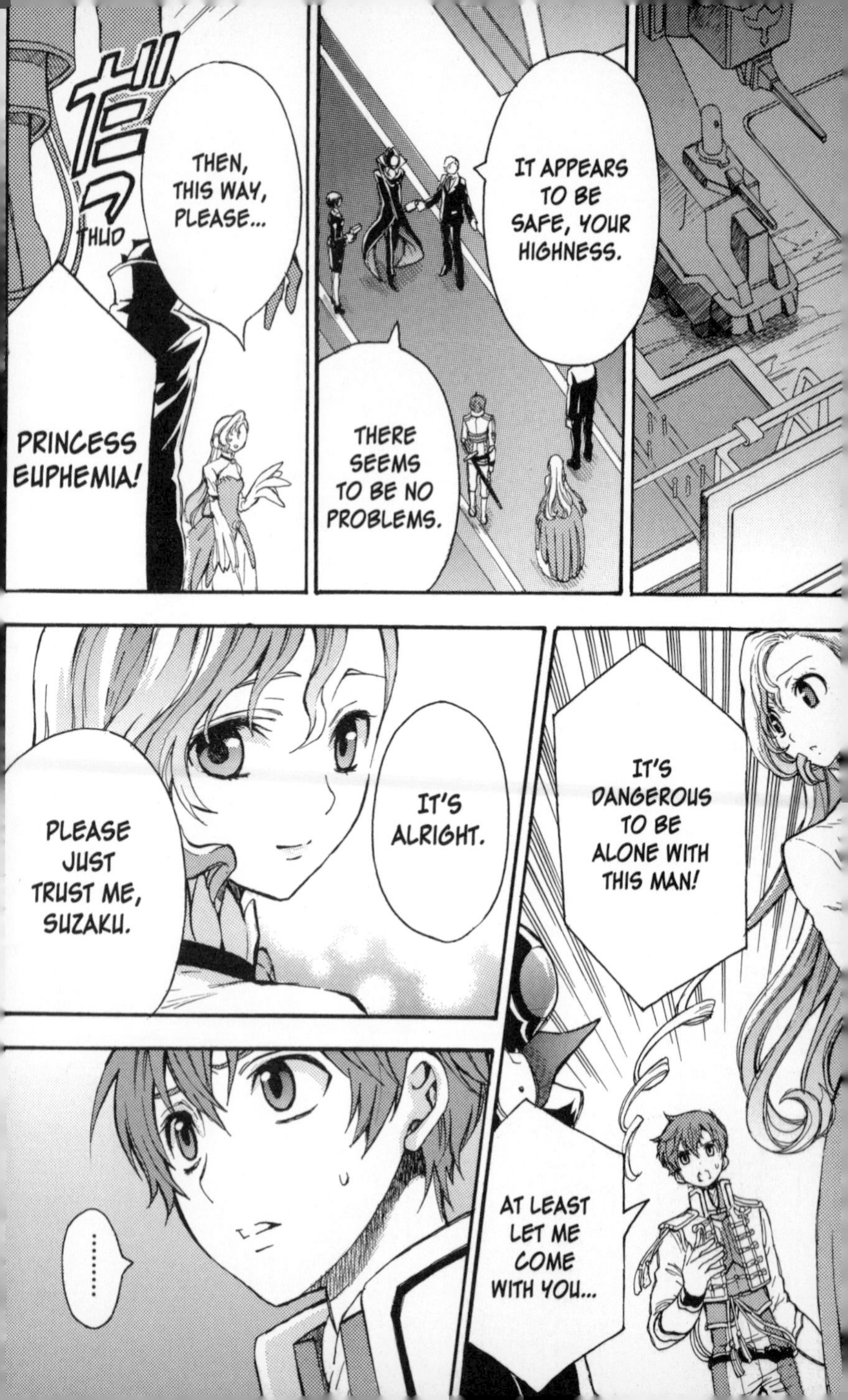
IT APPEARS TO BE SAFE, YOUR HIGHNESS.
THERE SEEMS TO BE NO PROBLEMS.
THEN, THIS WAY, PLEASE...
ガッ
THUD
PRINCESS EUPHEMIA!
IT'S DANGEROUS TO BE ALONE WITH THIS MAN!
AT LEAST LET ME COME WITH YOU...
IT'S ALRIGHT.
PLEASE JUST TRUST ME, SUZAKU.
......

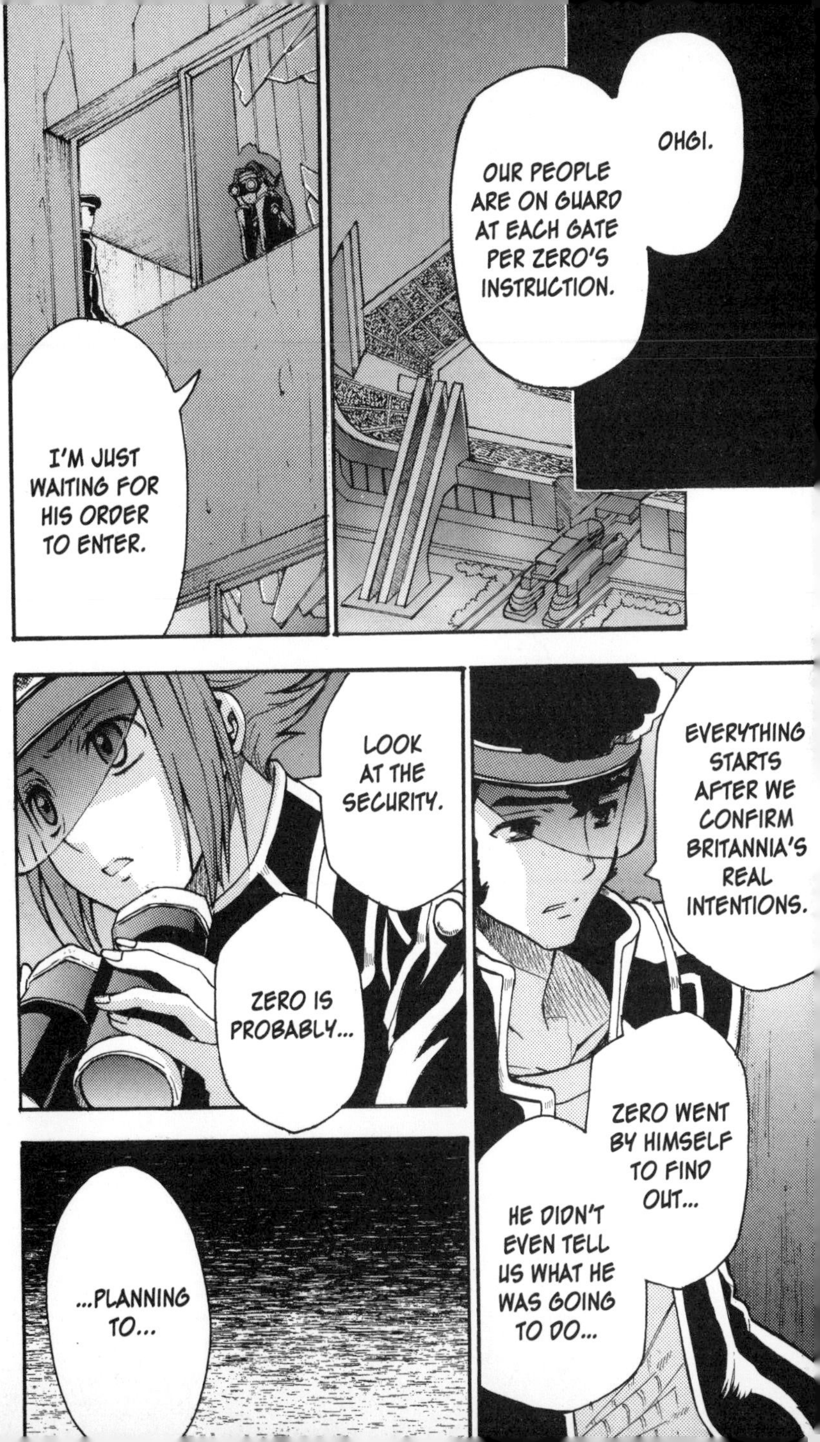

OHGI.
OUR PEOPLE ARE ON GUARD AT EACH GATE PER ZERO'S INSTRUCTION.
I'M JUST WAITING FOR HIS ORDER TO ENTER.
EVERYTHING STARTS AFTER WE CONFIRM BRITANNIA'S REAL INTENTIONS.
ZERO WENT BY HIMSELF TO FIND OUT...
HE DIDN'T EVEN TELL US WHAT HE WAS GOING TO DO...
LOOK AT THE SECURITY.
ZERO IS PROBABLY...
...PLANNING TO...

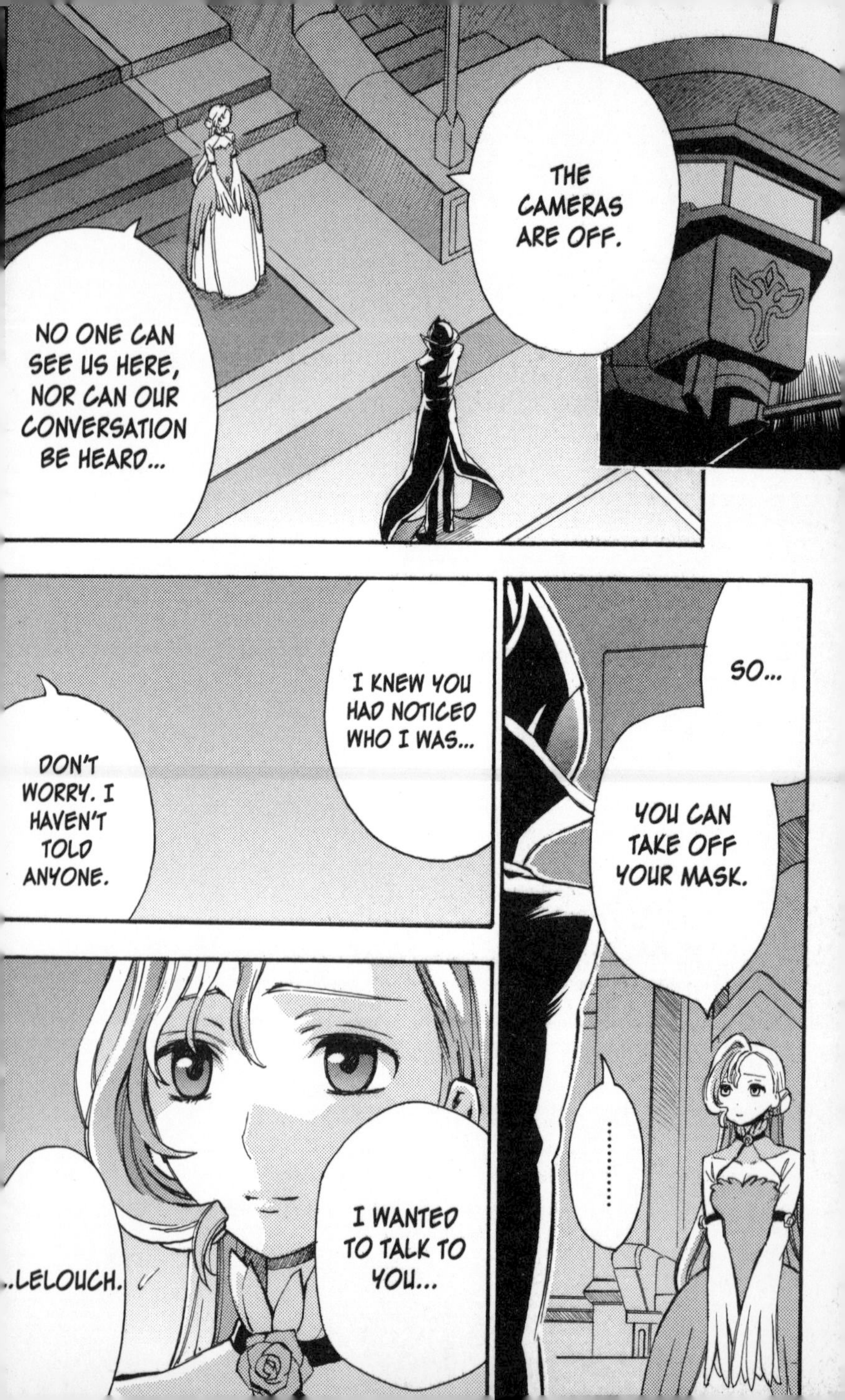
THE CAMERAS ARE OFF.
NO ONE CAN SEE US HERE, NOR CAN OUR CONVERSATION BE HEARD...
SO...
YOU CAN TAKE OFF YOUR MASK.
....
I KNEW YOU HAD NOTICED WHO I WAS...
DON'T WORRY. I HAVEN'T TOLD ANYONE.
I WANTED TO TALK TO YOU...
..LELOUCH.

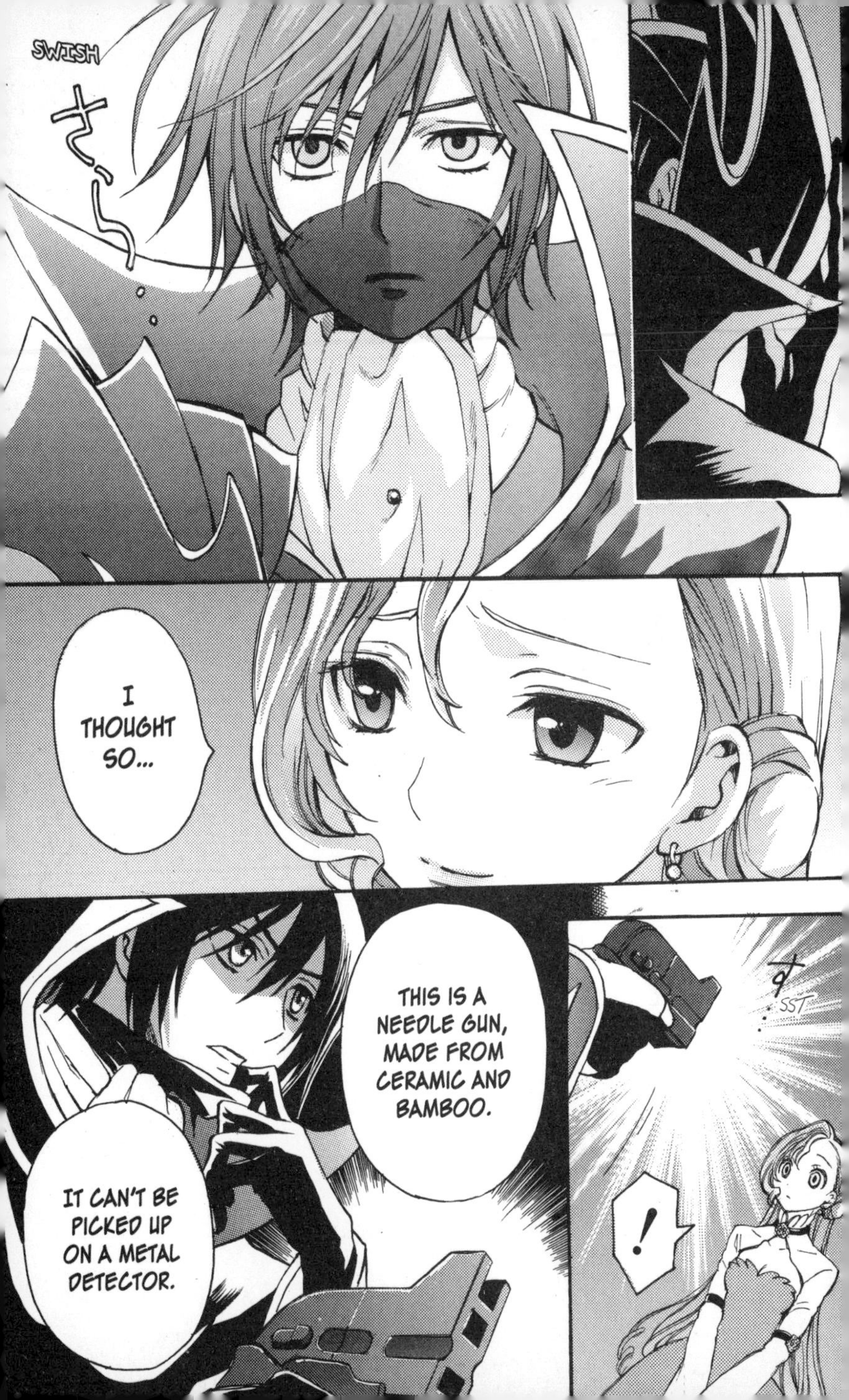
SWISH
I THOUGHT SO...
SST
!
THIS IS A NEEDLE GUN, MADE FROM CERAMIC AND BAMBOO.
IT CAN'T BE PICKED UP ON A METAL DETECTOR.

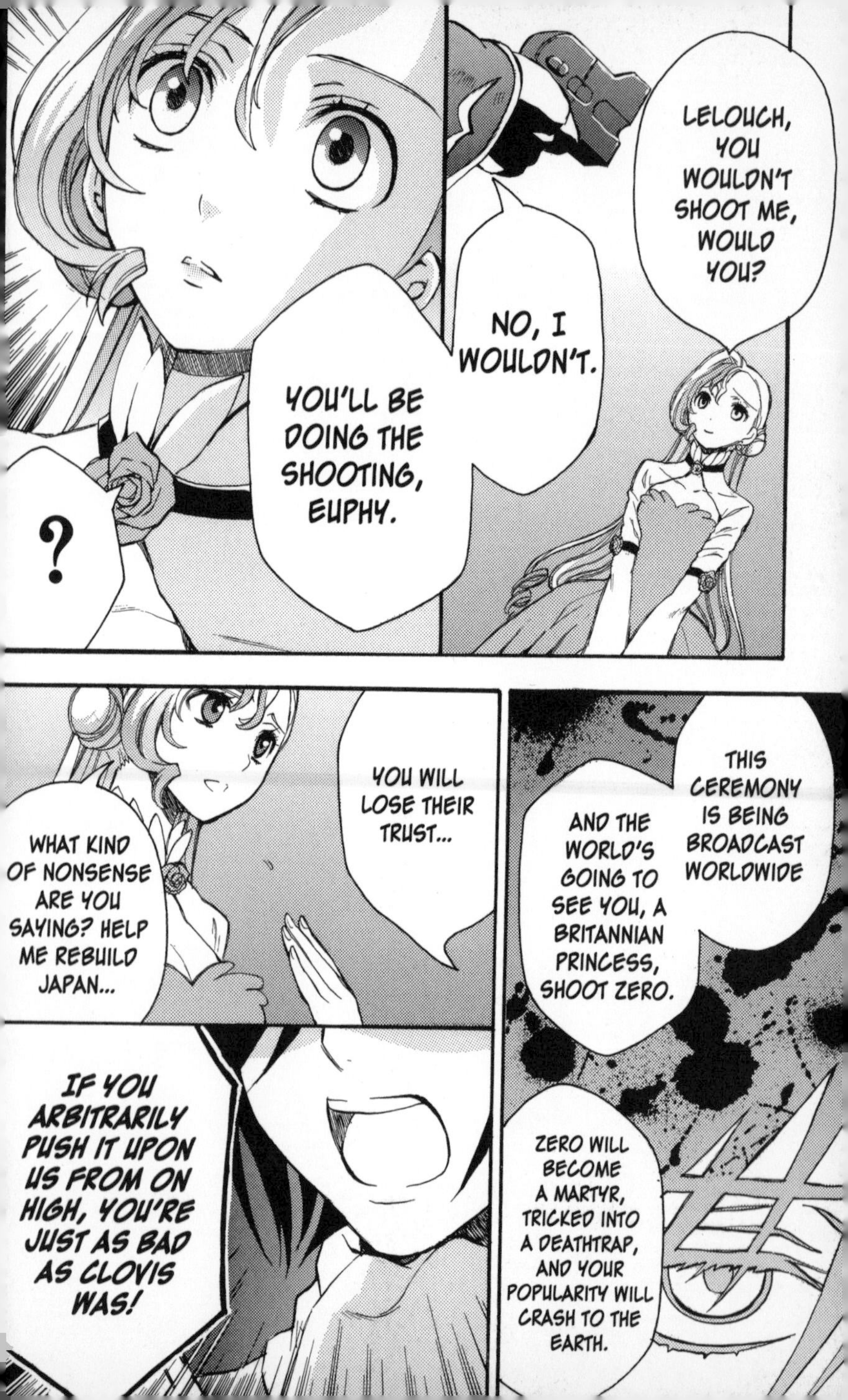
LELOUCH, YOU WOULDN'T SHOOT ME, WOULD YOU?
NO, I WOULDN'T.
YOU'LL BE DOING THE SHOOTING, EUPHY.
?
THIS CEREMONY IS BEING BROADCAST WORLDWIDE
AND THE WORLD'S GOING TO SEE YOU, A BRITANNIAN PRINCESS, SHOOT ZERO.
ZERO WILL BECOME A MARTYR, TRICKED INTO A DEATHTRAP, AND YOUR POPULARITY WILL CRASH TO THE EARTH.
YOU WILL LOSE THEIR TRUST...
WHAT KIND OF NONSENSE ARE YOU SAYING? HELP ME REBUILD JAPAN...
IF YOU ARBITRARILY PUSH IT UPON US FROM ON HIGH, YOU'RE JUST AS BAD AS CLOVIS WAS!

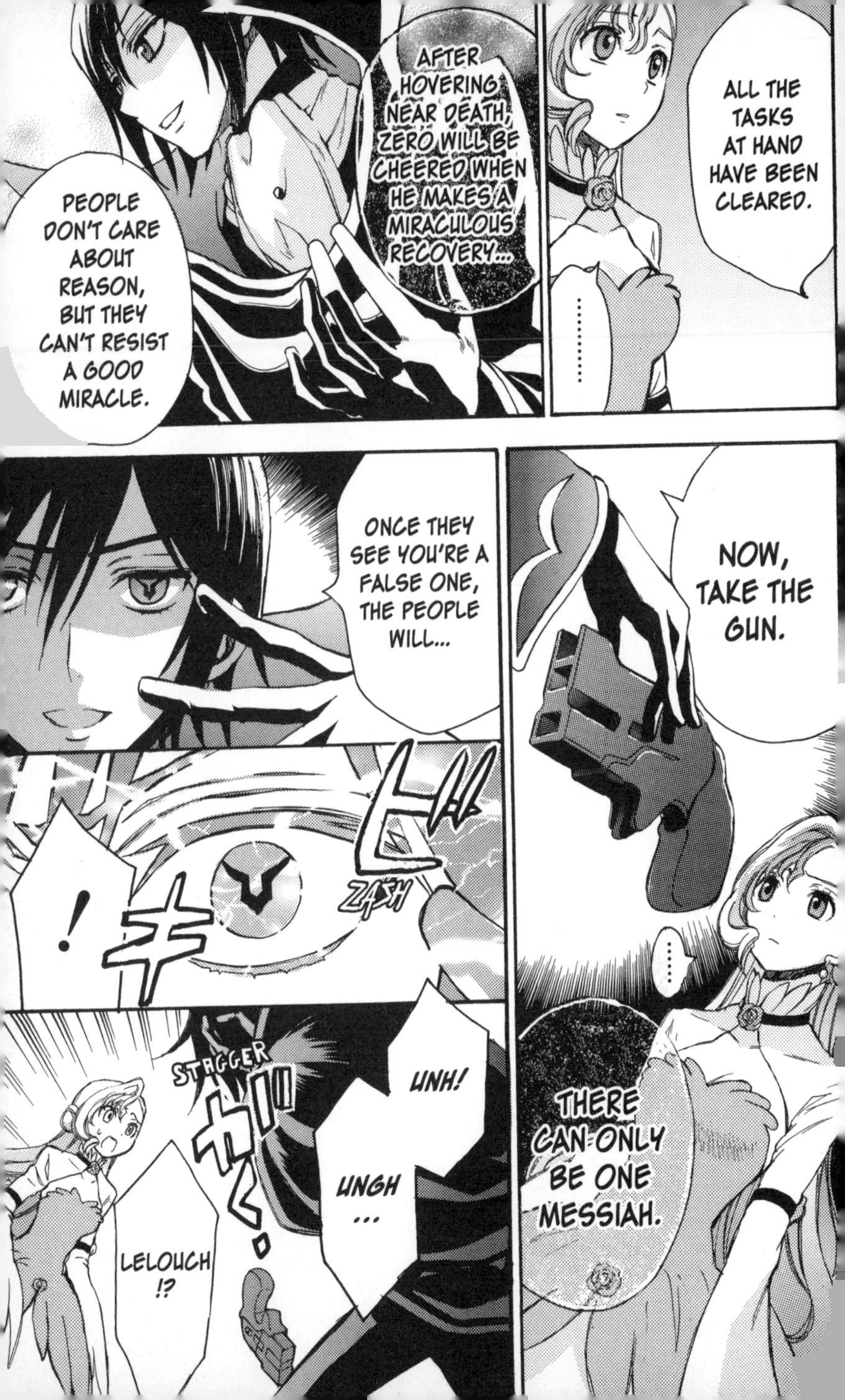

ALL THE TASKS AT HAND HAVE BEEN CLEARED.
......
AFTER HOVERING NEAR DEATH, ZERO WILL BE CHEERED WHEN HE MAKES A MIRACULOUS RECOVERY...
PEOPLE DON'T CARE ABOUT REASON, BUT THEY CAN'T RESIST A GOOD MIRACLE.
NOW, TAKE THE GUN.
......
THERE CAN ONLY BE ONE MESSIAH.
ONCE THEY SEE YOU'RE A FALSE ONE, THE PEOPLE WILL...
ZASH
!
UNH!
UNGH ...
STAGGER
LELOUCH !?

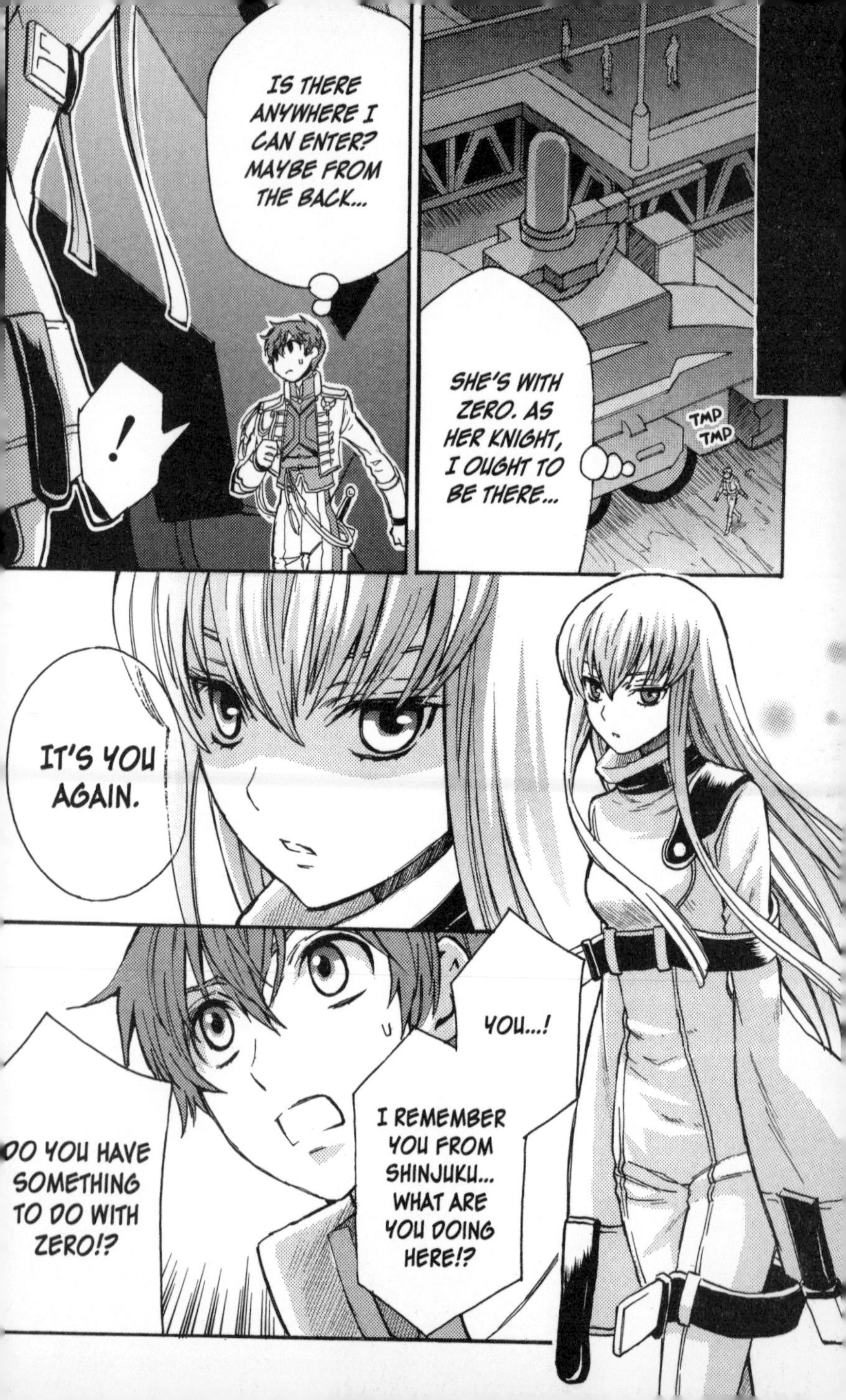
SHE'S WITH ZERO. AS HER KNIGHT, I OUGHT TO BE THERE...
TMP TMP
IS THERE ANYWHERE I CAN ENTER? MAYBE FROM THE BACK...
!
IT'S YOU AGAIN.
YOU...!
I REMEMBER YOU FROM SHINJUKU... WHAT ARE YOU DOING HERE!?
DO YOU HAVE SOMETHING TO DO WITH ZERO!?

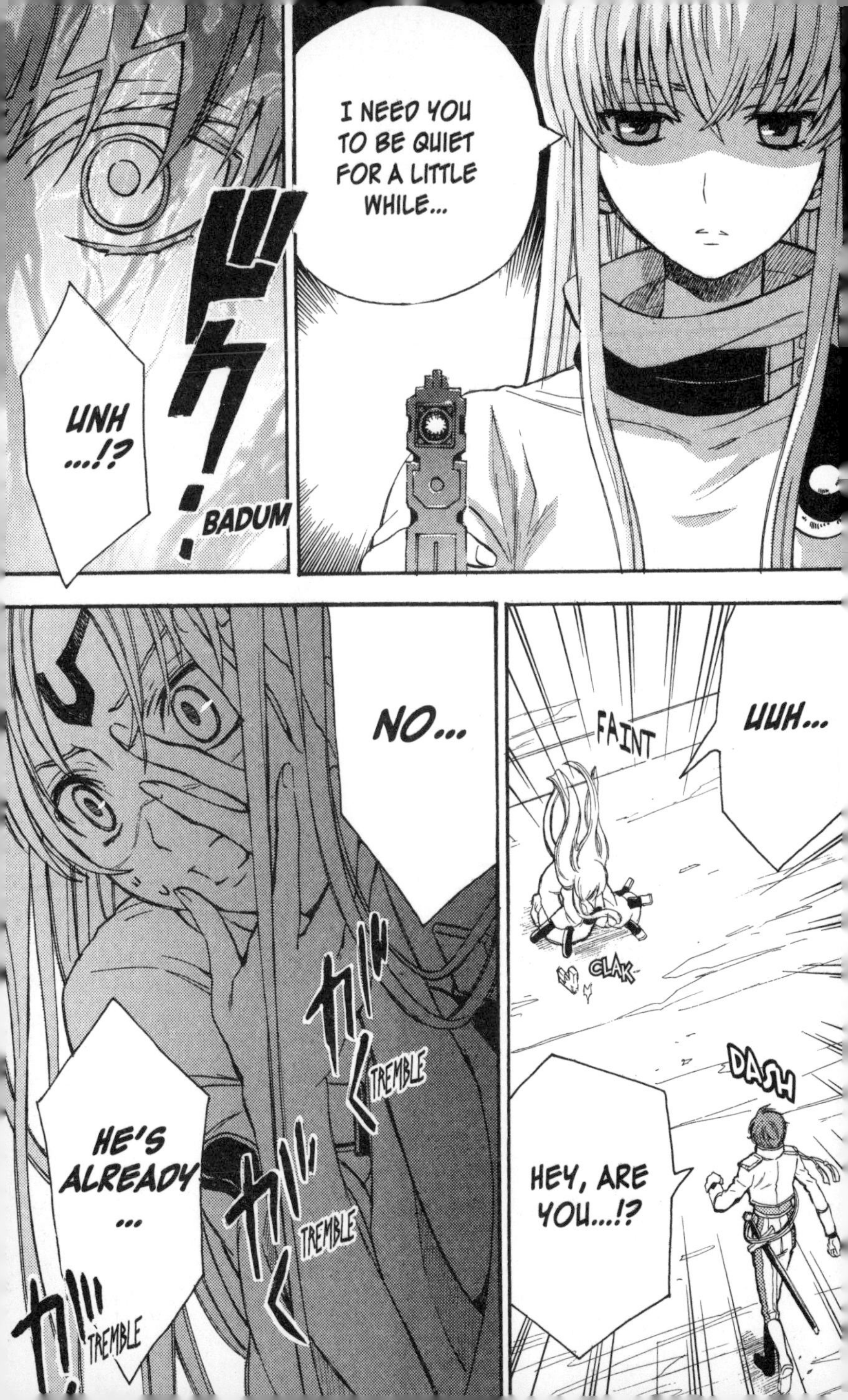
I NEED YOU TO BE QUIET FOR A LITTLE WHILE...
BADUM
UNH ...!?
UUH...
FAINT
CLAK
DASH
HEY, ARE YOU...!?
NO...
TREMBLE
TREMBLE
HE'S ALREADY ...
TREMBLE

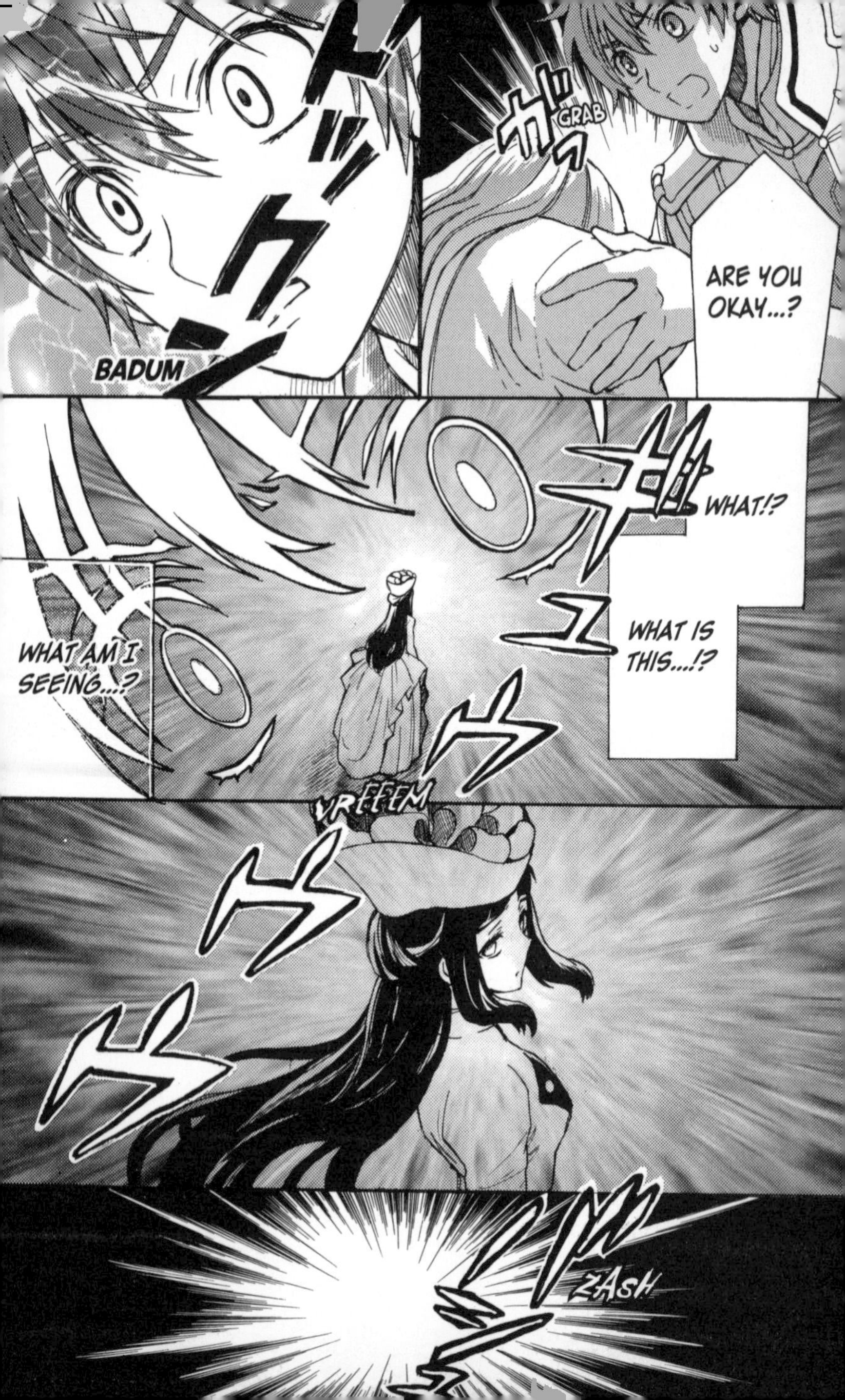
GRAB
ARE YOU OKAY...?
BADUM
WHAT!?
WHAT IS THIS...!?
WHAT AM I SEEING...?
VREEEM
ZASH

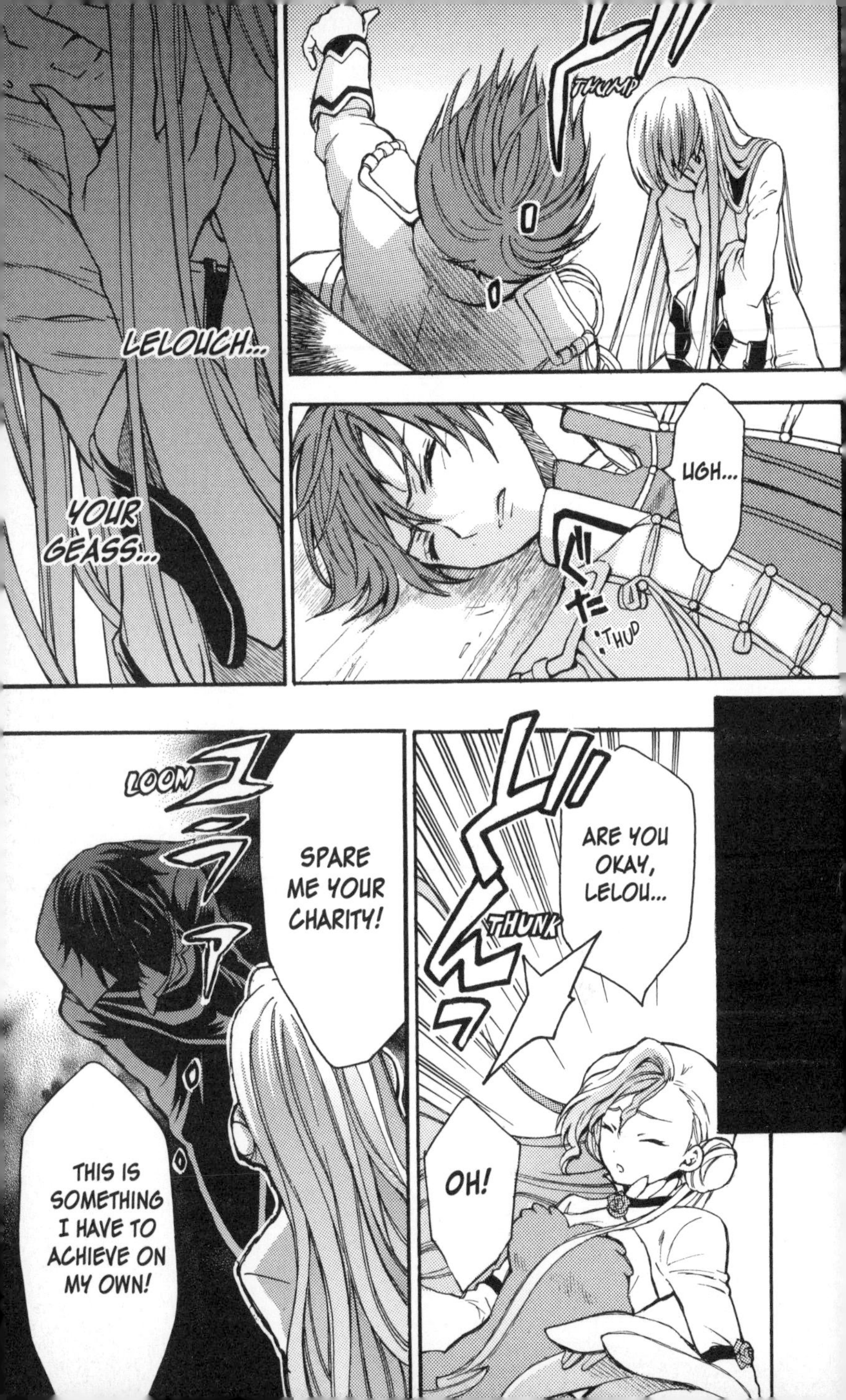
THUMP
UGH...
THUD
LELOUCH...
YOUR GEASS...
ARE YOU OKAY, LELOU...
THUNK
OH!
LOOM
SPARE ME YOUR CHARITY!
THIS IS SOMETHING I HAVE TO ACHIEVE ON MY OWN!

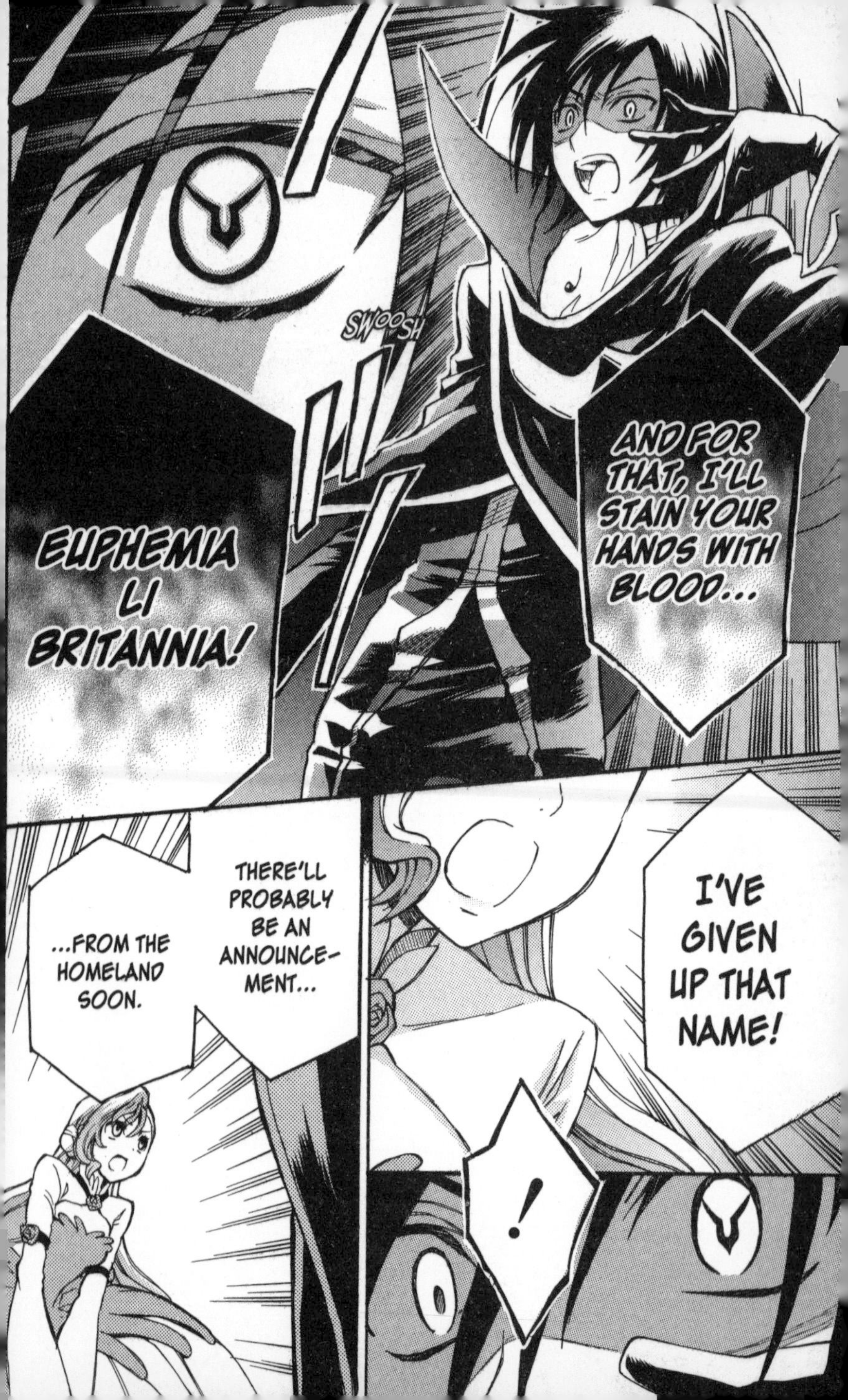
SWOOSH
AND FOR THAT, I'LL STAIN YOUR HANDS WITH BLOOD...
EUPHEMIA LI BRITANNIA!
I'VE GIVEN UP THAT NAME!
!
THERE'LL PROBABLY BE AN ANNOUNCEMENT...
...FROM THE HOMELAND SOON.

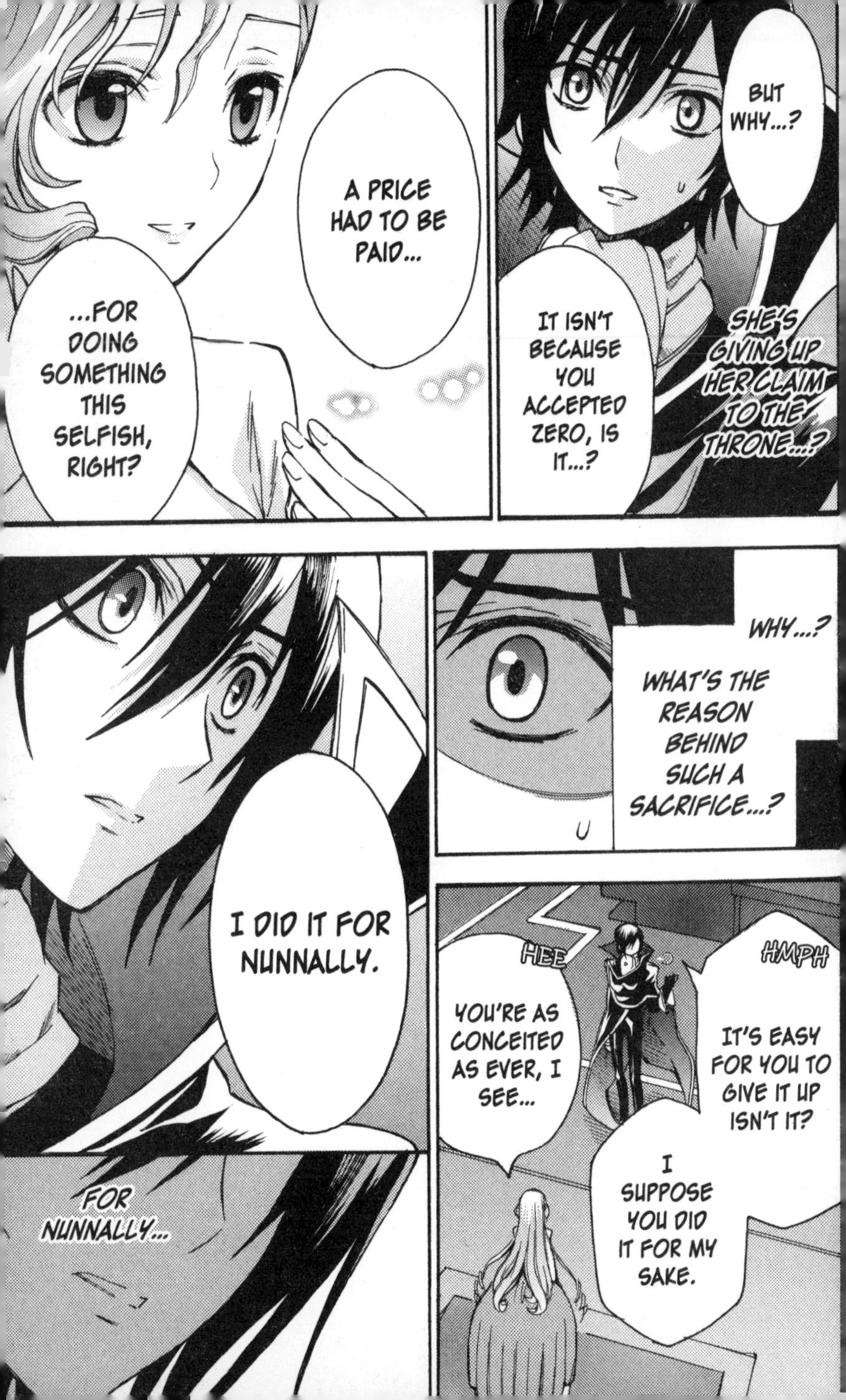
BUT WHY...?
IT ISN'T BECAUSE YOU ACCEPTED ZERO, IS IT...?
SHE'S GIVING UP HER CLAIM TO THE THRONE...?
A PRICE HAD TO BE PAID...
...FOR DOING SOMETHING THIS SELFISH, RIGHT?
WHY...?
WHAT'S THE REASON BEHIND SUCH A SACRIFICE...?
HMPH
IT'S EASY FOR YOU TO GIVE IT UP ISN'T IT?
HEE
YOU'RE AS CONCEITED AS EVER, I SEE...
I SUPPOSE YOU DID IT FOR MY SAKE.
I DID IT FOR NUNNALLY.
FOR NUNNALLY...

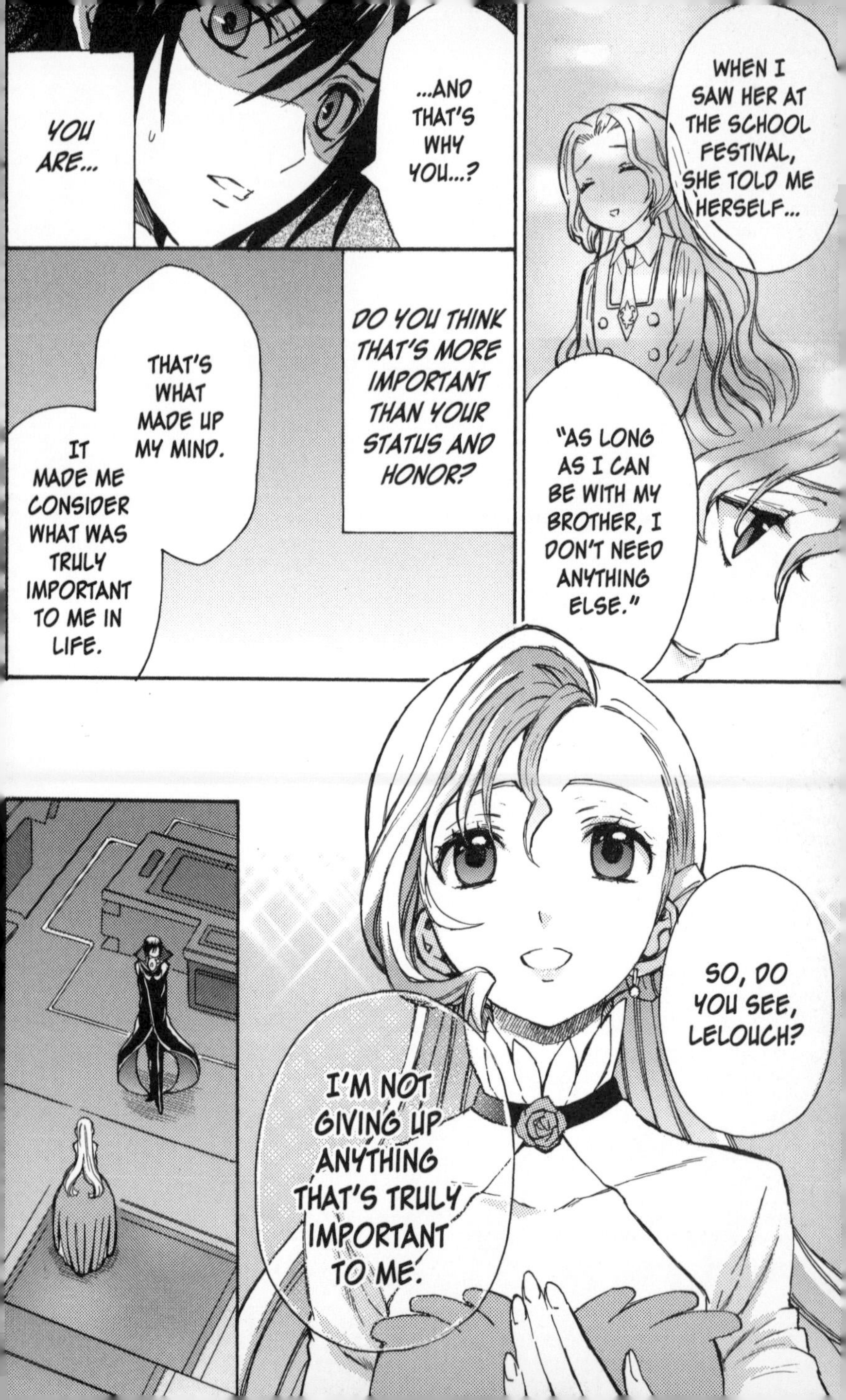
WHEN I SAW HER AT THE SCHOOL FESTIVAL, SHE TOLD ME HERSELF...
"AS LONG AS I CAN BE WITH MY BROTHER, I DON'T NEED ANYTHING ELSE."
...AND THAT'S WHY YOU...?
YOU ARE...
DO YOU THINK THAT'S MORE IMPORTANT THAN YOUR STATUS AND HONOR?
THAT'S WHAT MADE UP MY MIND.
IT MADE ME CONSIDER WHAT WAS TRULY IMPORTANT TO ME IN LIFE.
SO, DO YOU SEE, LELOUCH?
I'M NOT GIVING UP ANYTHING THAT'S TRULY IMPORTANT TO ME.

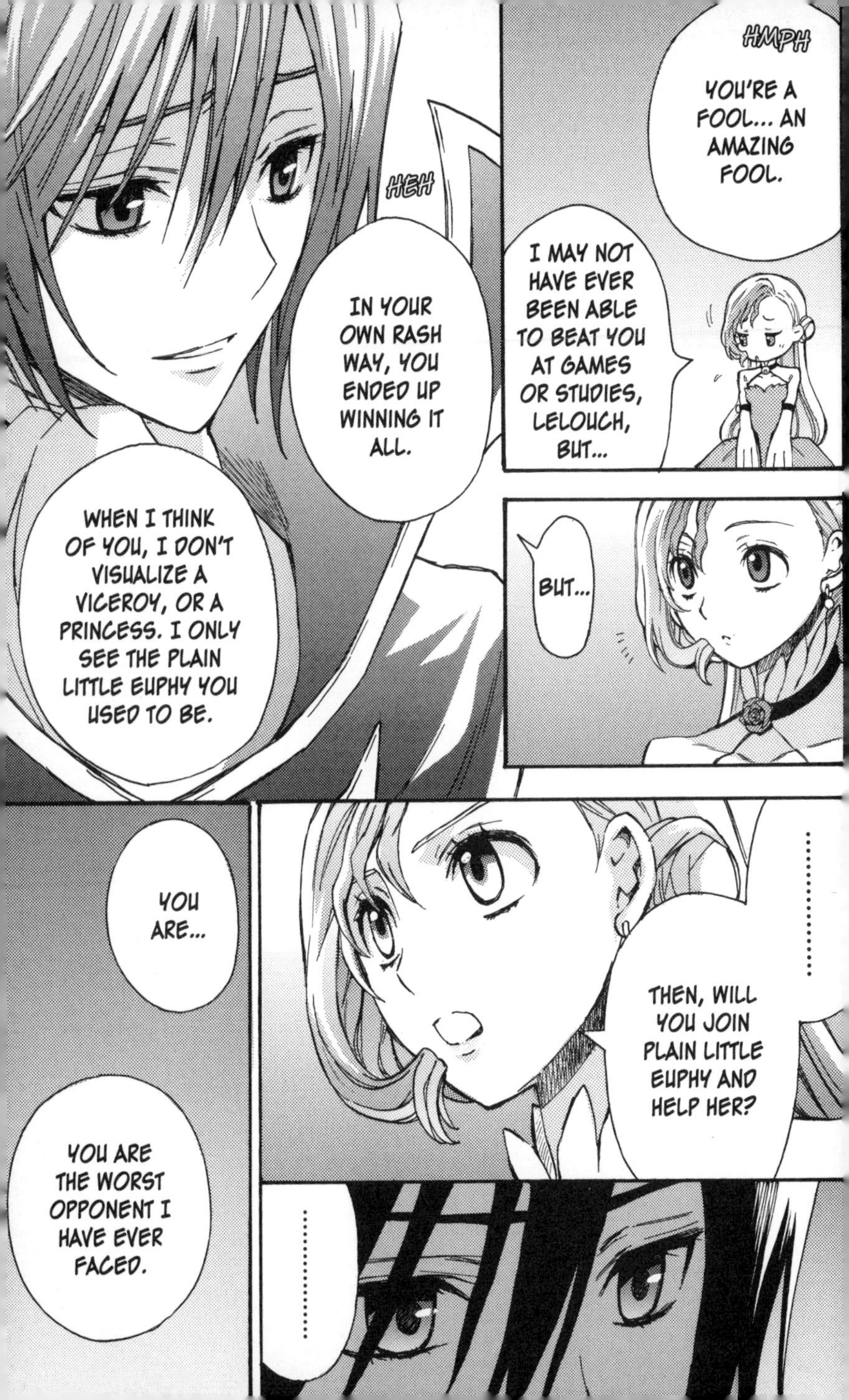
HMPH
YOU'RE A FOOL... AN AMAZING FOOL.
I MAY NOT HAVE EVER BEEN ABLE TO BEAT YOU AT GAMES OR STUDIES, LELOUCH, BUT...
BUT...
HEH
IN YOUR OWN RASH WAY, YOU ENDED UP WINNING IT ALL.
WHEN I THINK OF YOU, I DON'T VISUALIZE A VICEROY, OR A PRINCESS. I ONLY SEE THE PLAIN LITTLE EUPHY YOU USED TO BE.
......
THEN, WILL YOU JOIN PLAIN LITTLE EUPHY AND HELP HER?
......
YOU ARE...
YOU ARE THE WORST OPPONENT I HAVE EVER FACED.

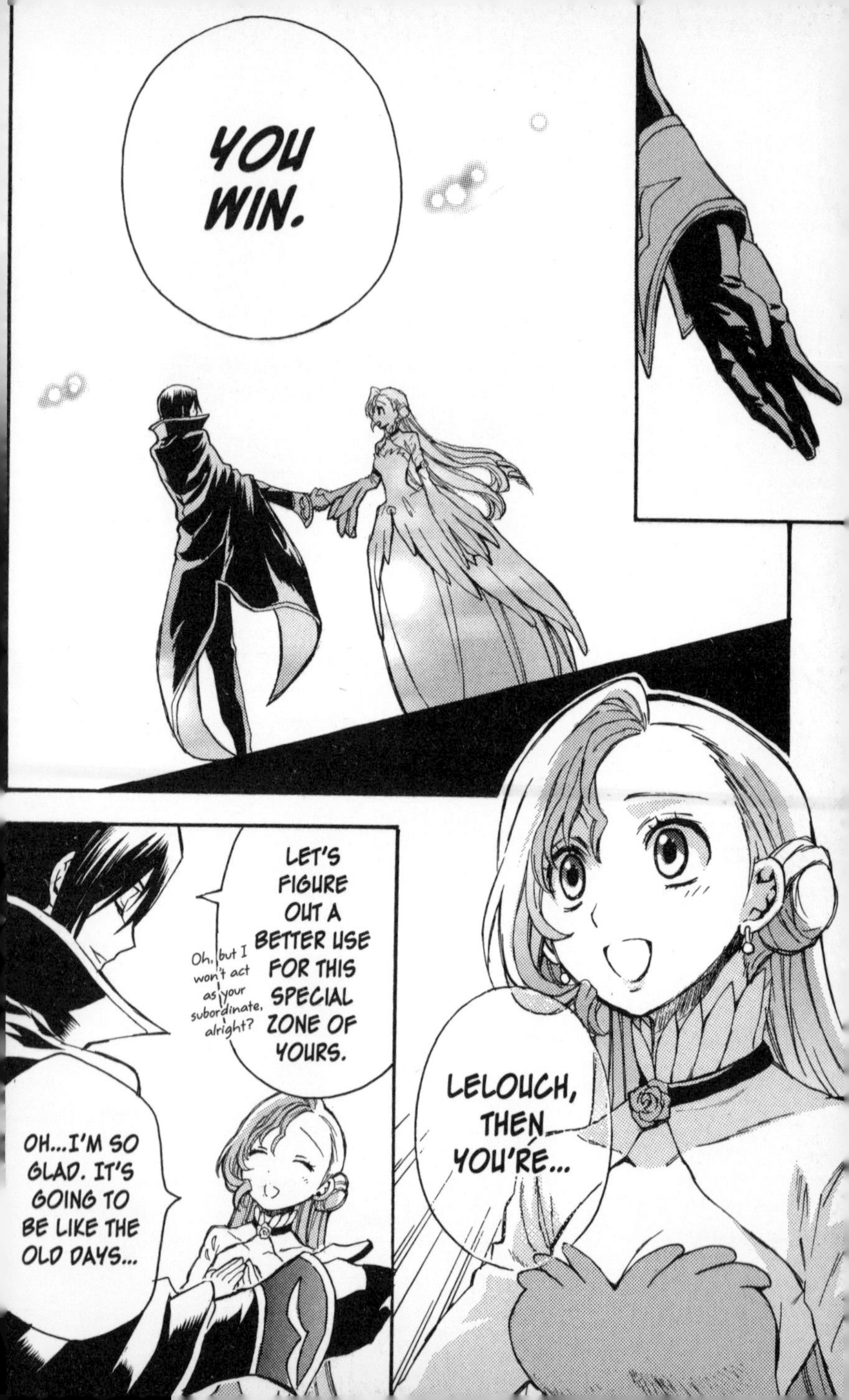
YOU WIN.
LELOUCH, THEN YOU'RE...
LET'S FIGURE OUT A BETTER USE FOR THIS SPECIAL ZONE OF YOURS.
Oh, but I won't act as your subordinate, alright?
OH...I'M SO GLAD. IT'S GOING TO BE LIKE THE OLD DAYS...

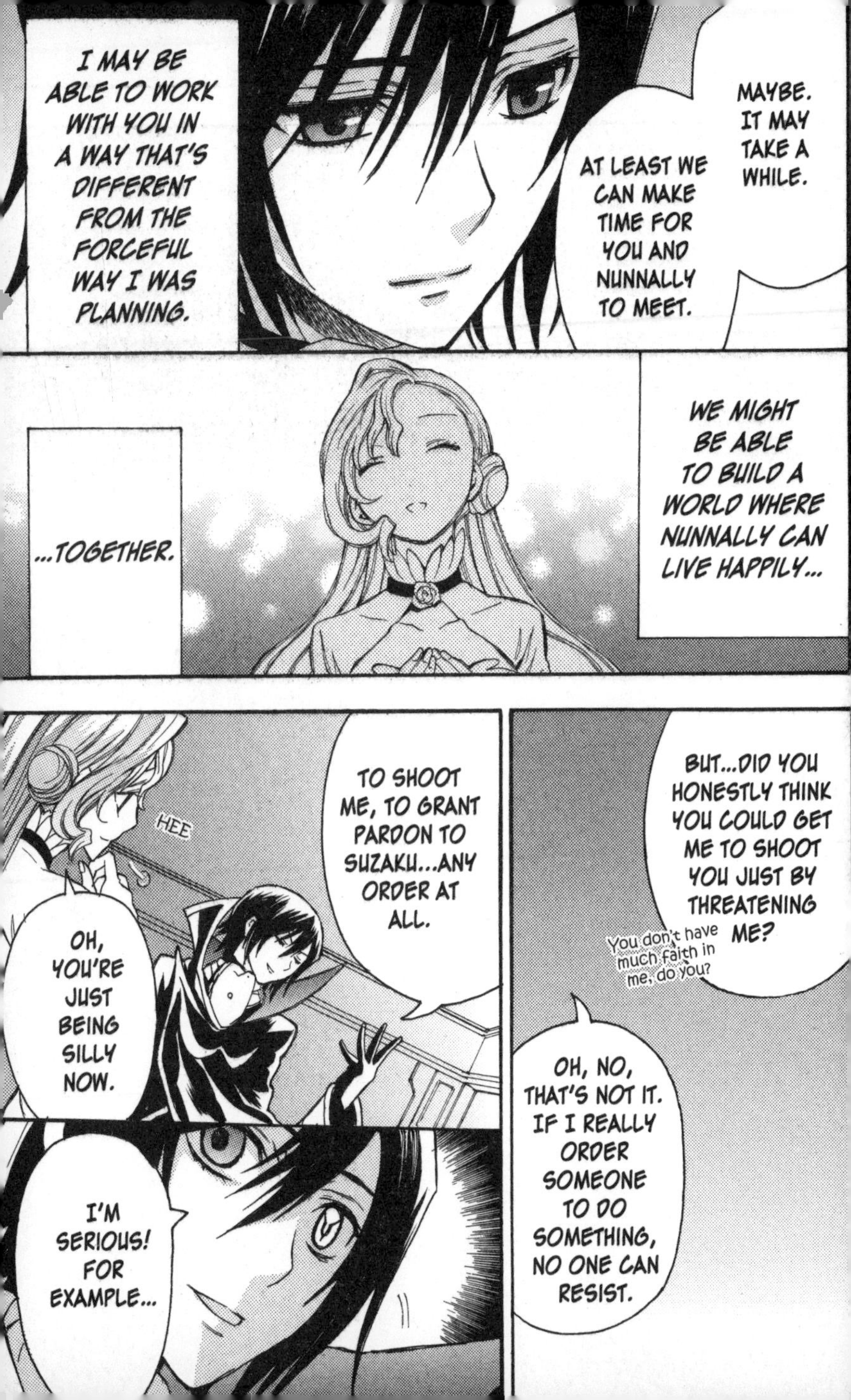
MAYBE. IT MAY TAKE A WHILE.
AT LEAST WE CAN MAKE TIME FOR YOU AND NUNNALLY TO MEET.
I MAY BE ABLE TO WORK WITH YOU IN A WAY THAT'S DIFFERENT FROM THE FORCEFUL WAY I WAS PLANNING.
WE MIGHT BE ABLE TO BUILD A WORLD WHERE NUNNALLY CAN LIVE HAPPILY...
...TOGETHER.
BUT...DID YOU HONESTLY THINK YOU COULD GET ME TO SHOOT YOU JUST BY THREATENING ME?
You don't have much faith in me, do you?
OH, NO, THAT'S NOT IT. IF I REALLY ORDER SOMEONE TO DO SOMETHING, NO ONE CAN RESIST.
TO SHOOT ME, TO GRANT PARDON TO SUZAKU...ANY ORDER AT ALL.
HEE
OH, YOU'RE JUST BEING SILLY NOW.
I'M SERIOUS! FOR EXAMPLE...

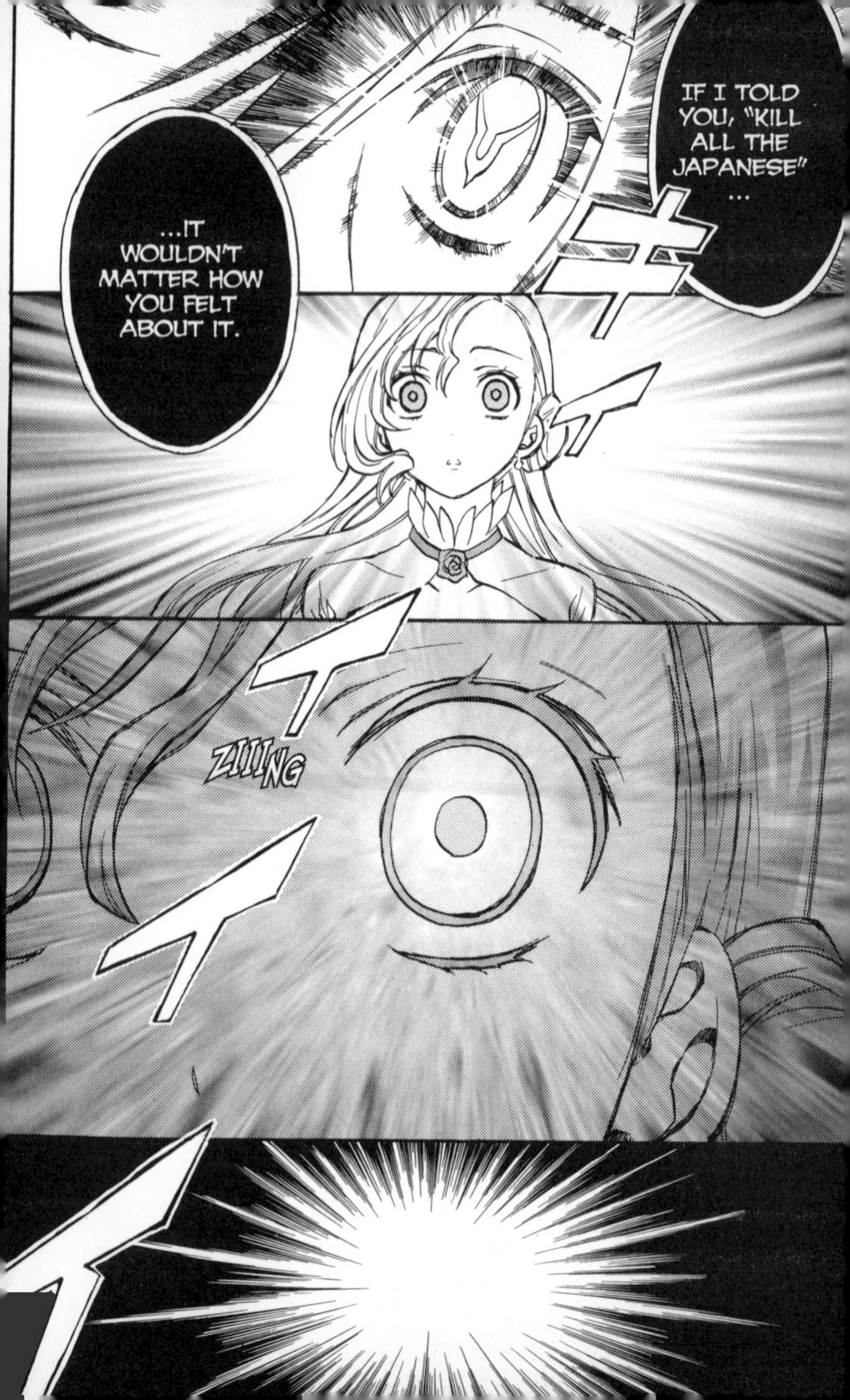
IF I TOLD YOU, "KILL ALL THE JAPANESE" ...
...IT WOULDN'T MATTER HOW YOU FELT ABOUT IT.
ZIIING

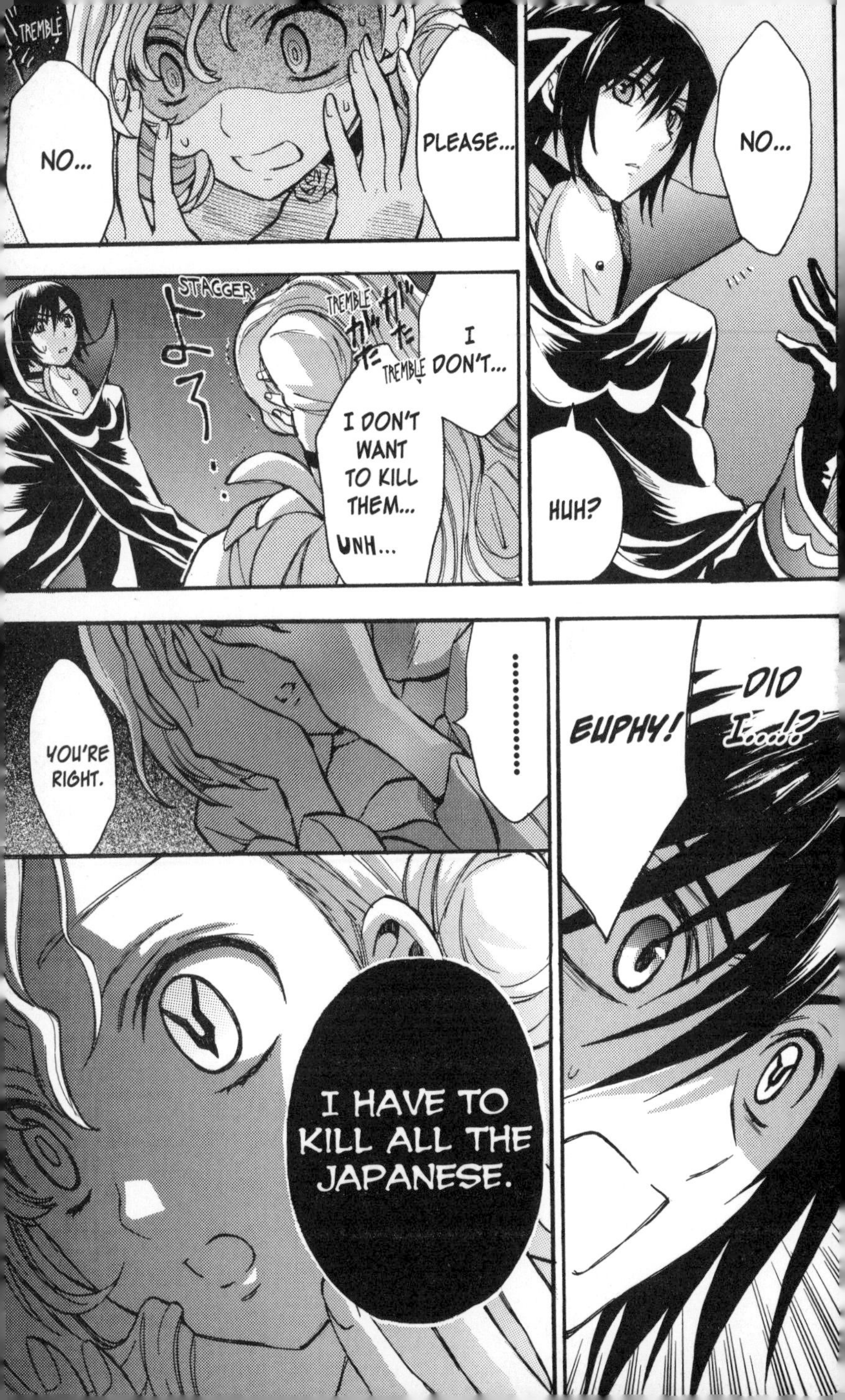
NO...
HUH?
TREMBLE
PLEASE...
NO...
TREMBLE
I DON'T...
TREMBLE
I DON'T WANT TO KILL THEM...
UNH...
STAGGER
DID I...!?
EUPHY!
....
YOU'RE RIGHT.
I HAVE TO KILL ALL THE JAPANESE.

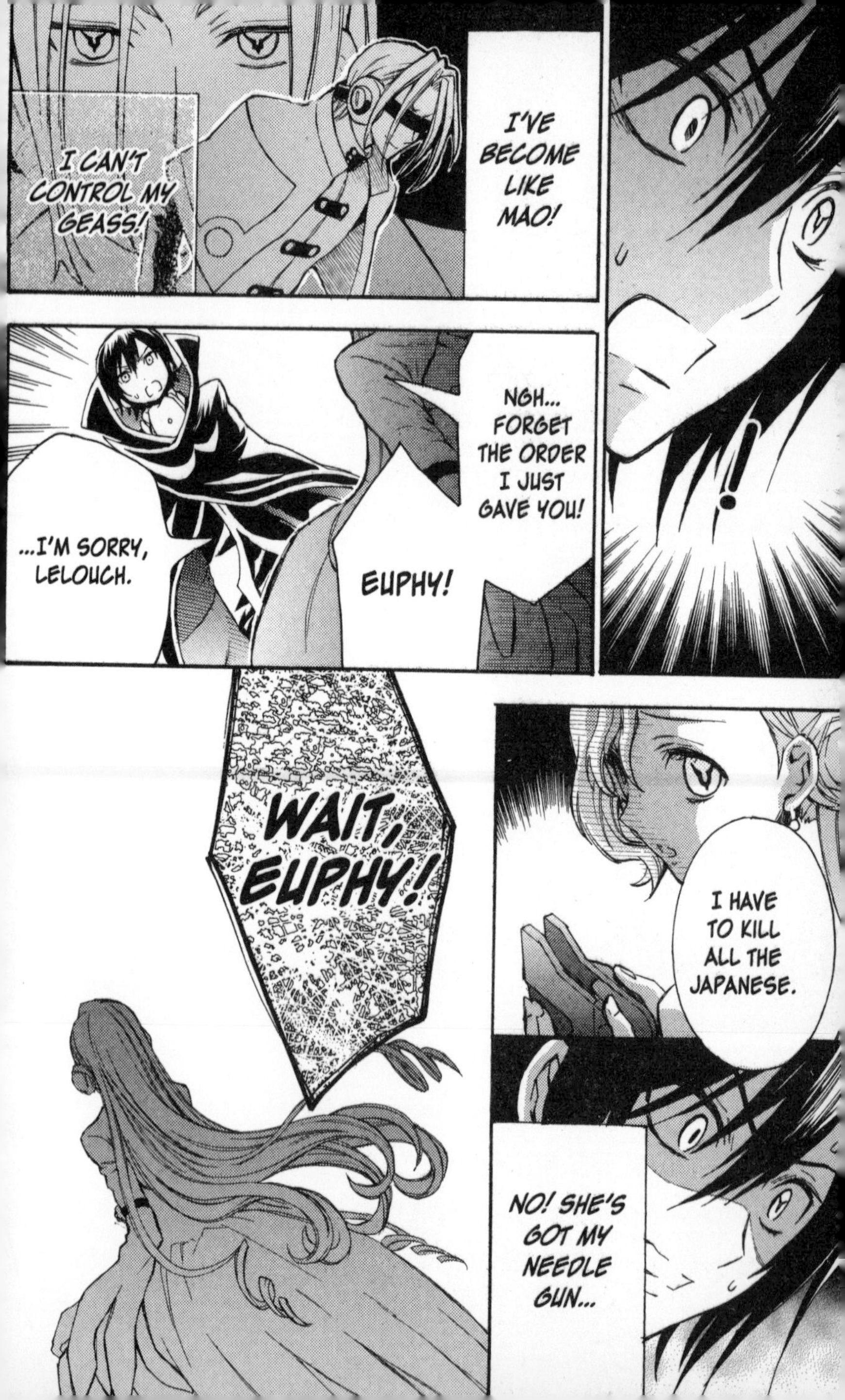
!
I'VE BECOME LIKE MAO!
I CAN'T CONTROL MY GEASS!
NGH... FORGET THE ORDER I JUST GAVE YOU!
EUPHY!
...I'M SORRY, LELOUCH.
I HAVE TO KILL ALL THE JAPANESE.
NO! SHE'S GOT MY NEEDLE GUN...
WAIT, EUPHY!

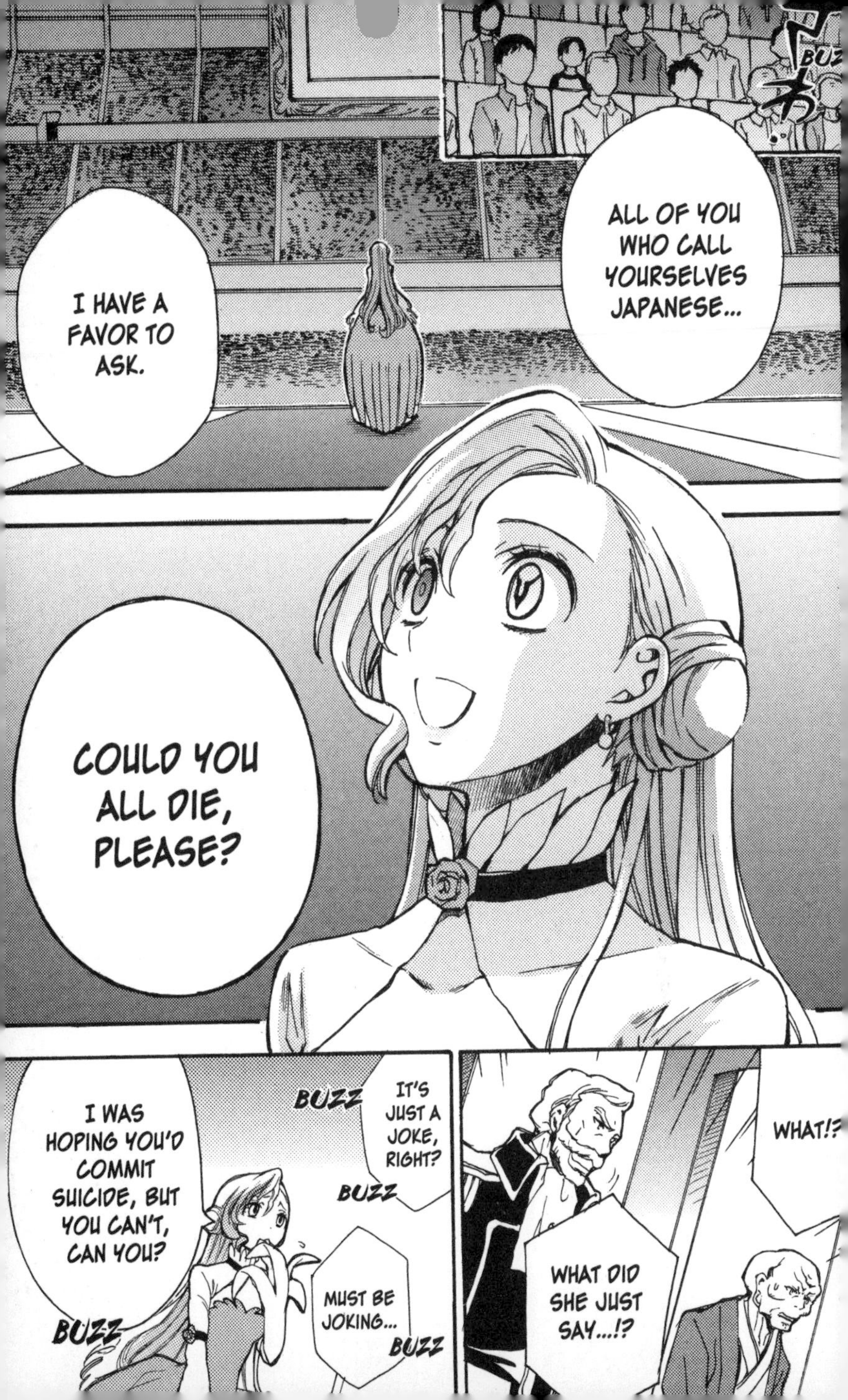
BUZ
ALL OF YOU WHO CALL YOURSELVES JAPANESE...
I HAVE A FAVOR TO ASK.
COULD YOU ALL DIE, PLEASE?
WHAT!?
WHAT DID SHE JUST SAY...!?
IT'S JUST A JOKE, RIGHT?
BUZZ
BUZZ
I WAS HOPING YOU'D COMMIT SUICIDE, BUT YOU CAN'T, CAN YOU?
MUST BE JOKING...
BUZZ
BUZZ

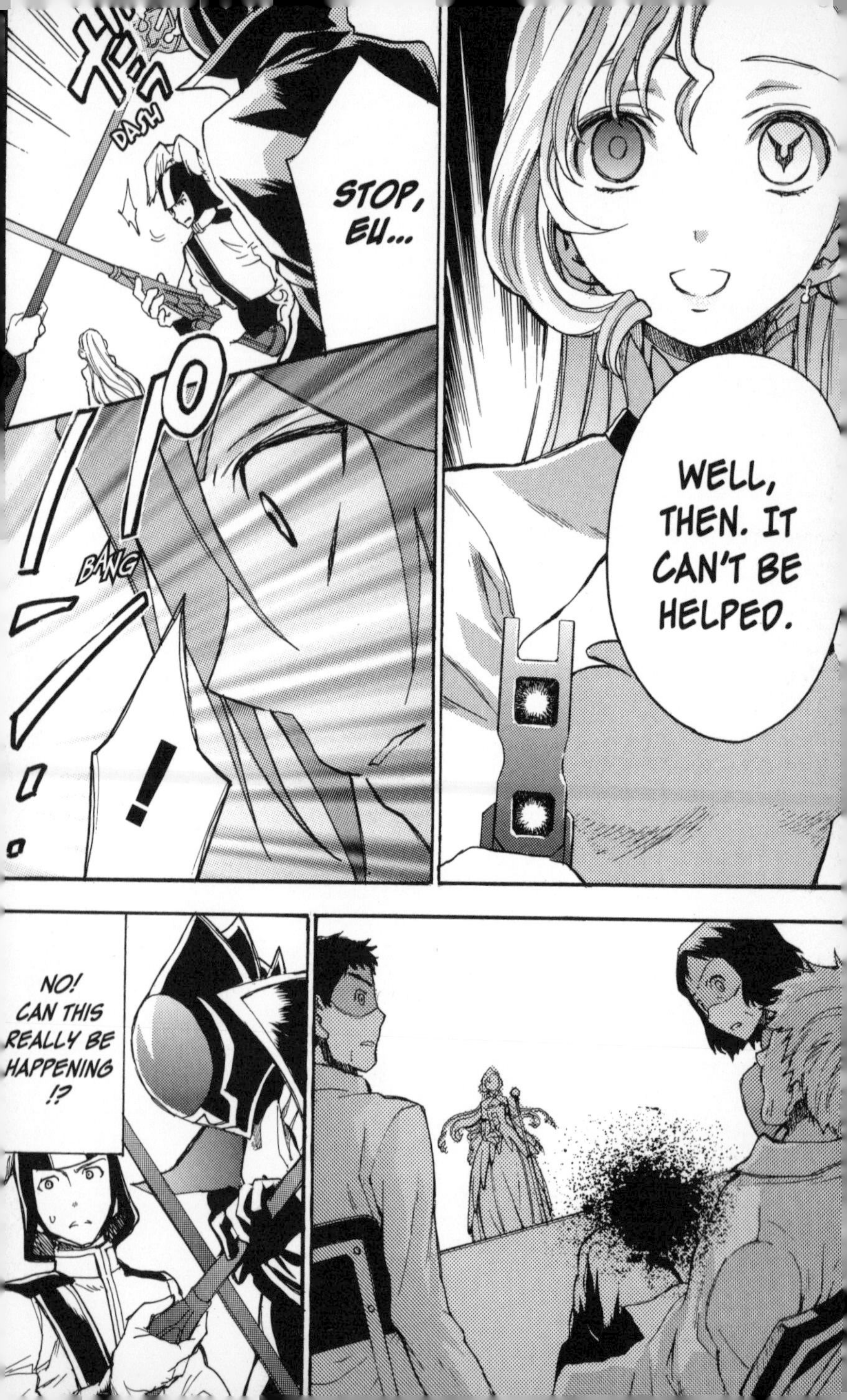
WELL, THEN. IT CAN'T BE HELPED.
DASH
STOP, EU...
BANG
!
NO! CAN THIS REALLY BE HAPPENING!?

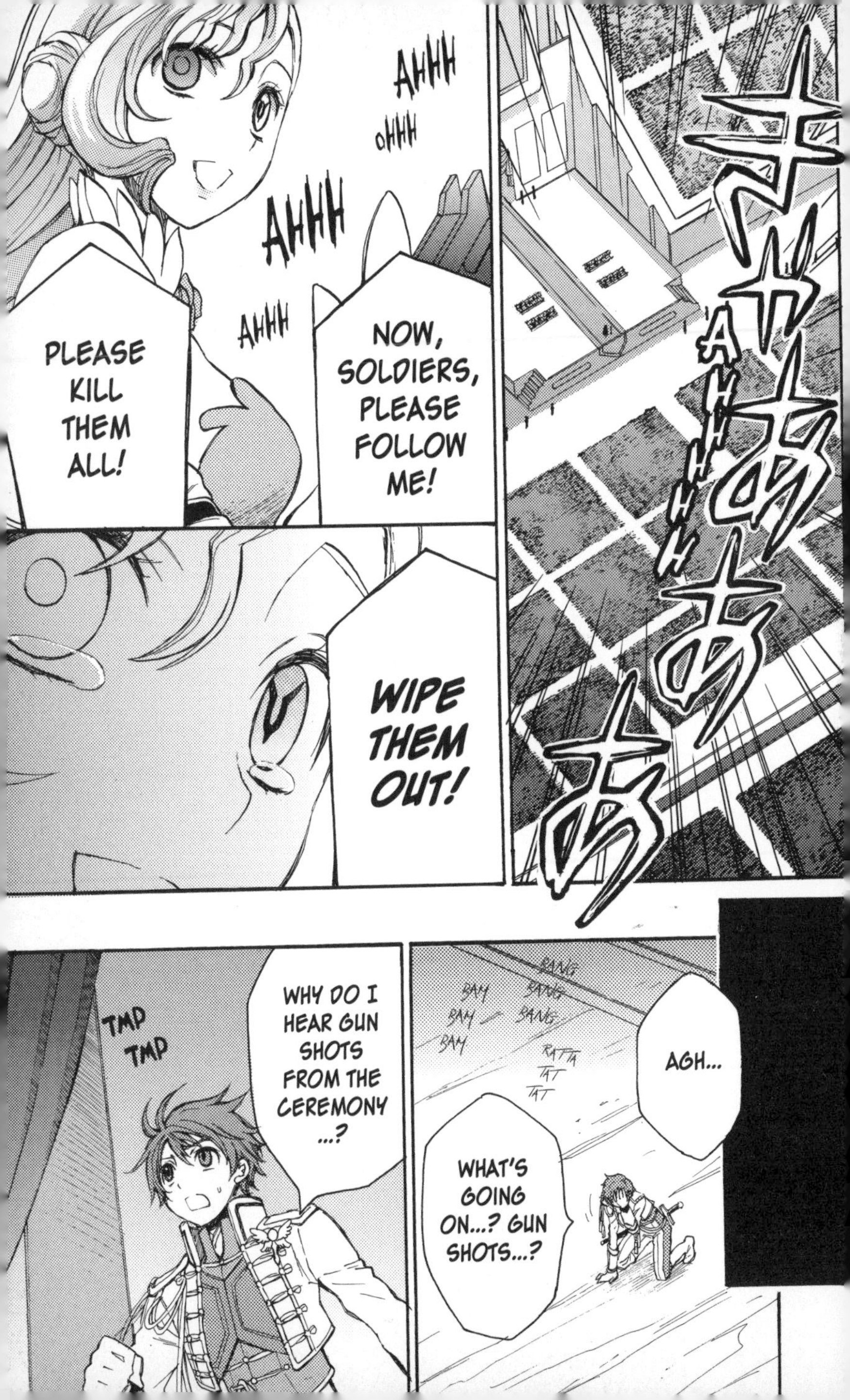

きゃあああ
AHHHHHHH
NOW, SOLDIERS, PLEASE FOLLOW ME!
AHHH
OHHH
AHHH
AHHH
PLEASE KILL THEM ALL!
WIPE THEM OUT!
AGH...
BANG BANG BANG
BAM BAM BAM
RATTA TAT TAT
WHAT'S GOING ON...? GUN SHOTS...?
WHY DO I HEAR GUN SHOTS FROM THE CEREMONY ...?
TMP TMP

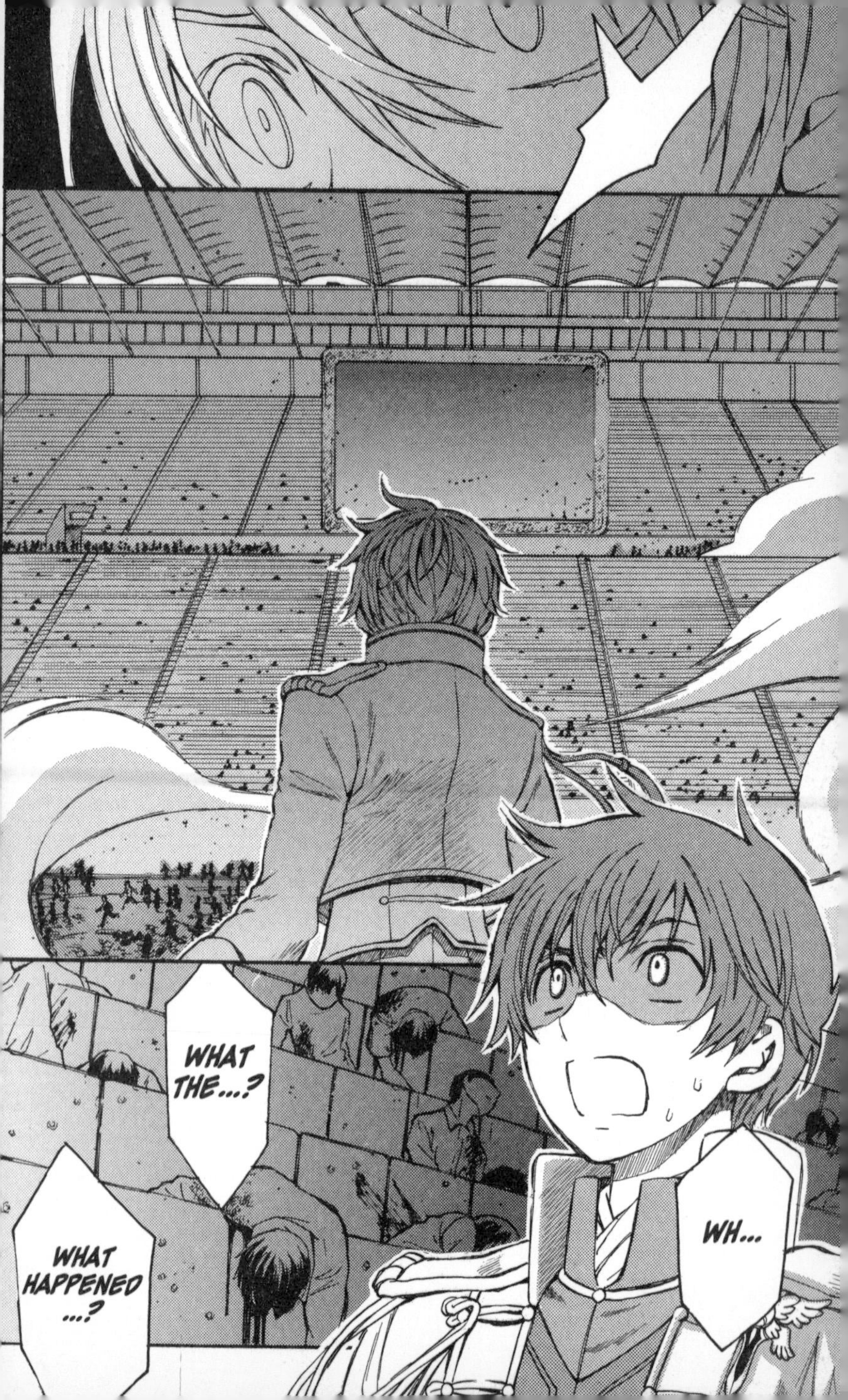
WH...
WHAT THE...?
WHAT HAPPENED ...?

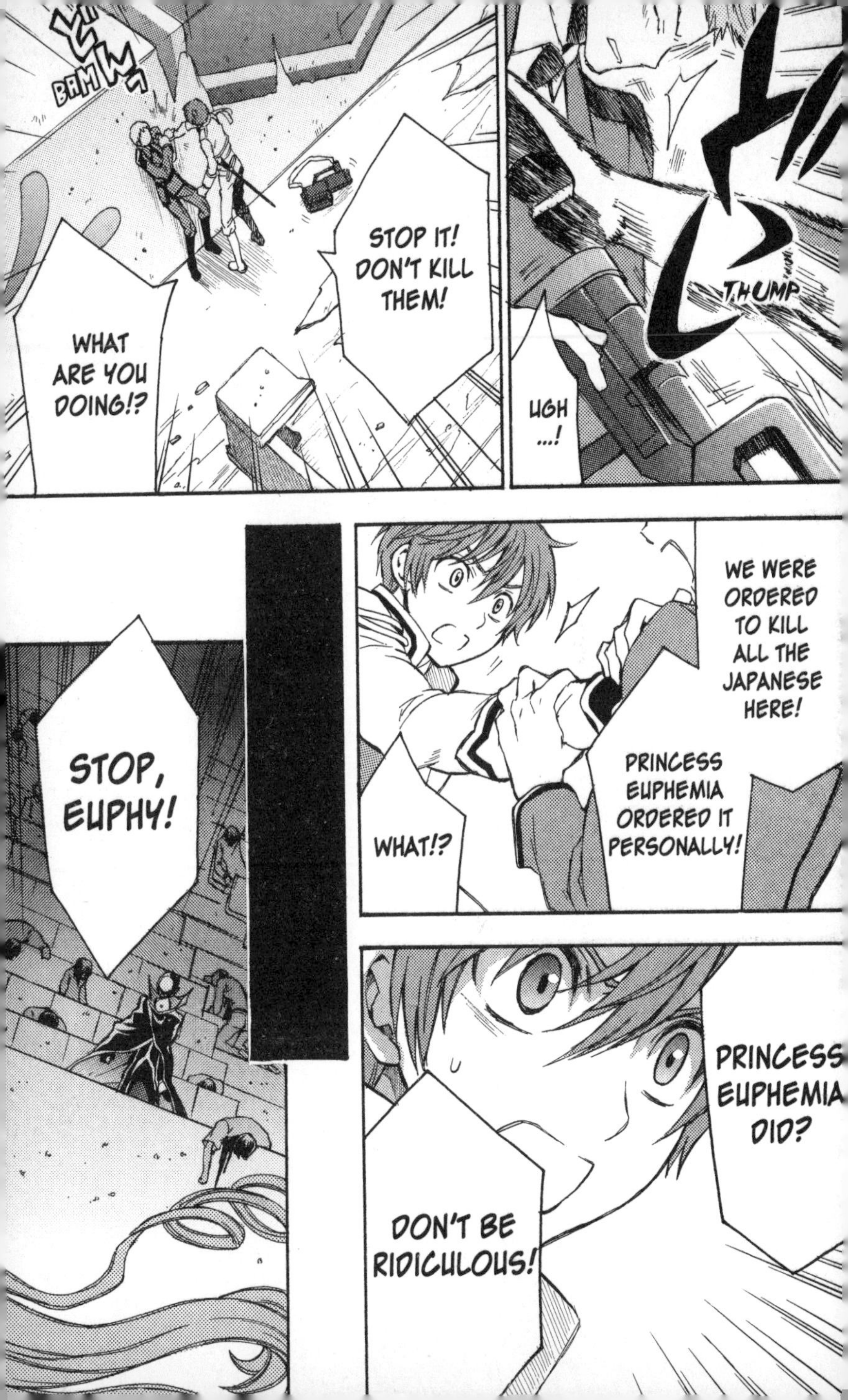
THUMP
UGH ...!
BAM
STOP IT! DON'T KILL THEM!
WHAT ARE YOU DOING!?
WE WERE ORDERED TO KILL ALL THE JAPANESE HERE!
PRINCESS EUPHEMIA ORDERED IT PERSONALLY!
WHAT!?
PRINCESS EUPHEMIA DID?
DON'T BE RIDICULOUS!
STOP, EUPHY!

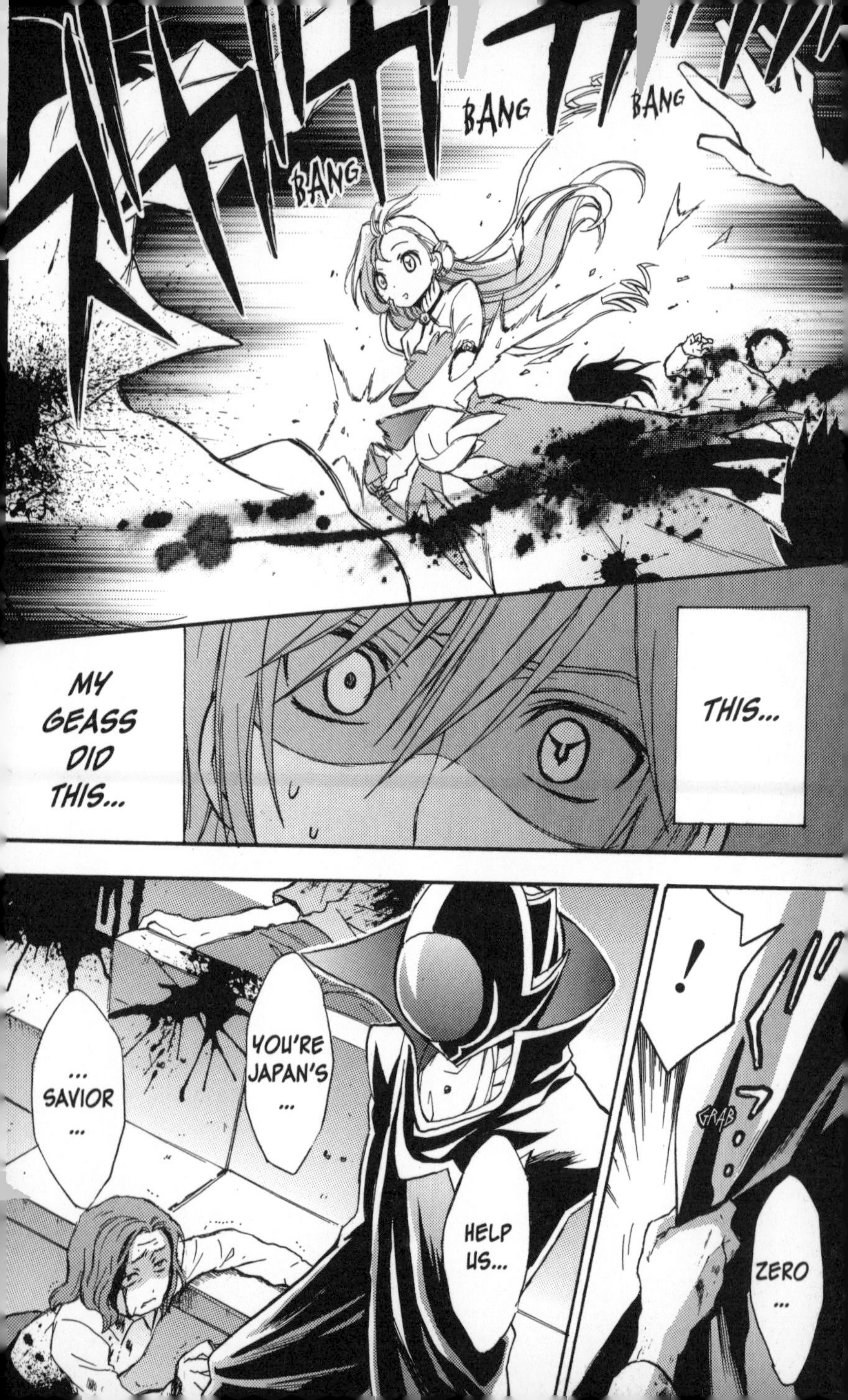
BANG
BANG
BANG
THIS...
MY GEASS DID THIS...
!
ZERO ...
GRAB
HELP US...
YOU'RE JAPAN'S ...
... SAVIOR ...

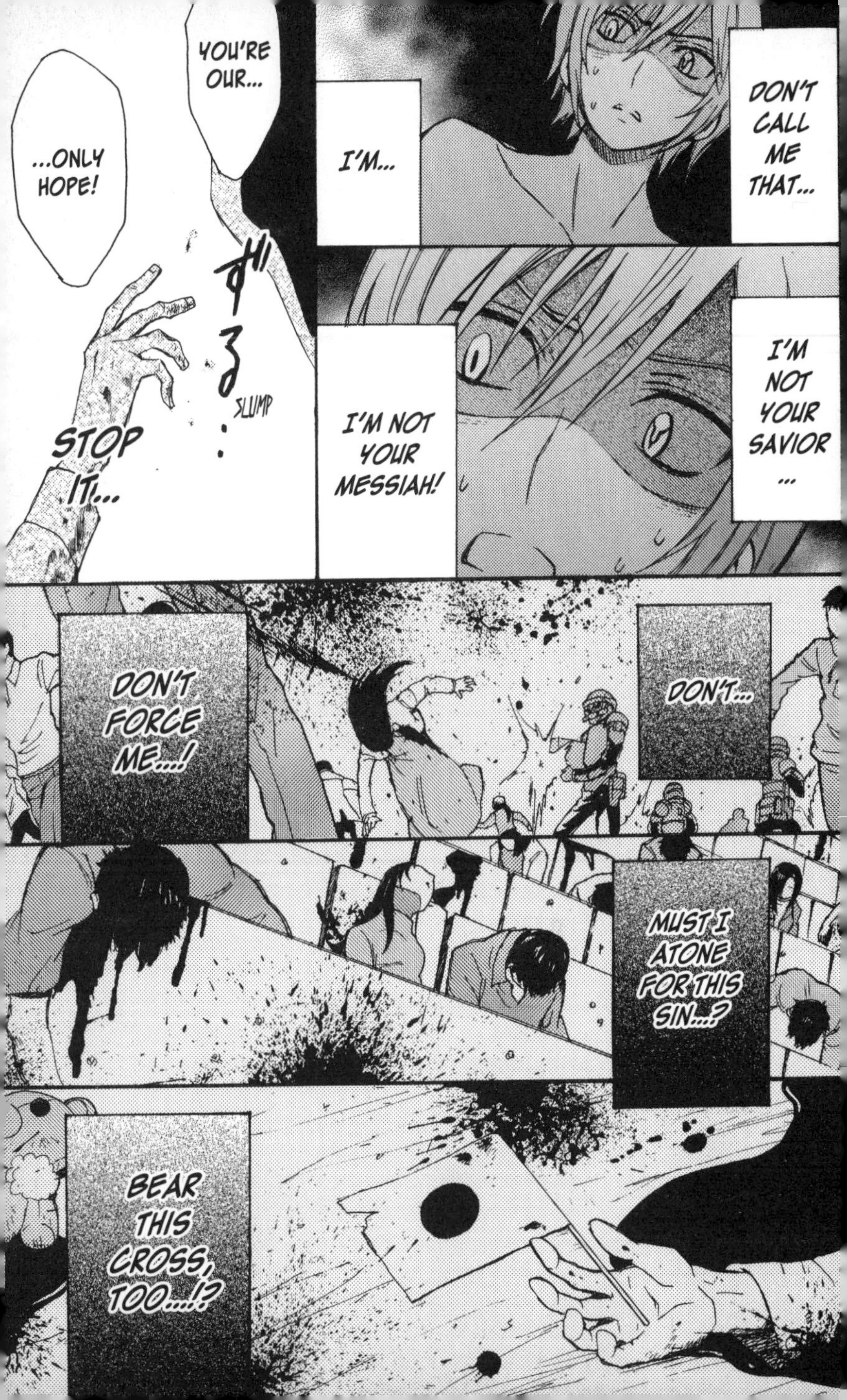
DON'T CALL ME THAT...
I'M...
I'M NOT YOUR SAVIOR...
I'M NOT YOUR MESSIAH!
YOU'RE OUR...
...ONLY HOPE!
ずる
SLUMP
STOP IT...
DON'T...
DON'T FORCE ME...!
MUST I ATONE FOR THIS SIN...?
BEAR THIS CROSS, TOO...!?

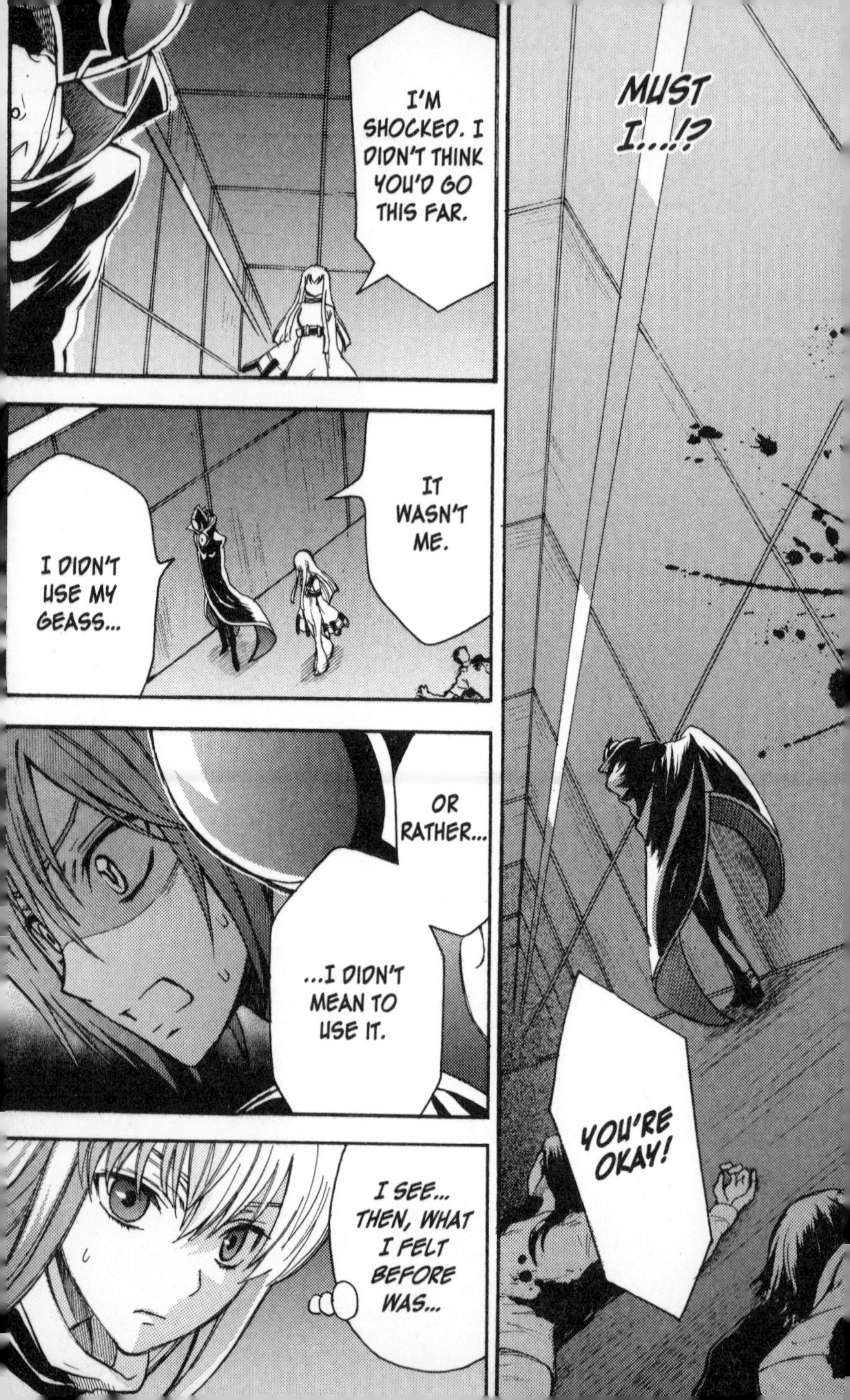
MUST I...!?
YOU'RE OKAY!
I'M SHOCKED. I DIDN'T THINK YOU'D GO THIS FAR.
IT WASN'T ME.
I DIDN'T USE MY GEASS...
OR RATHER...
...I DIDN'T MEAN TO USE IT.
I SEE... THEN, WHAT I FELT BEFORE WAS...

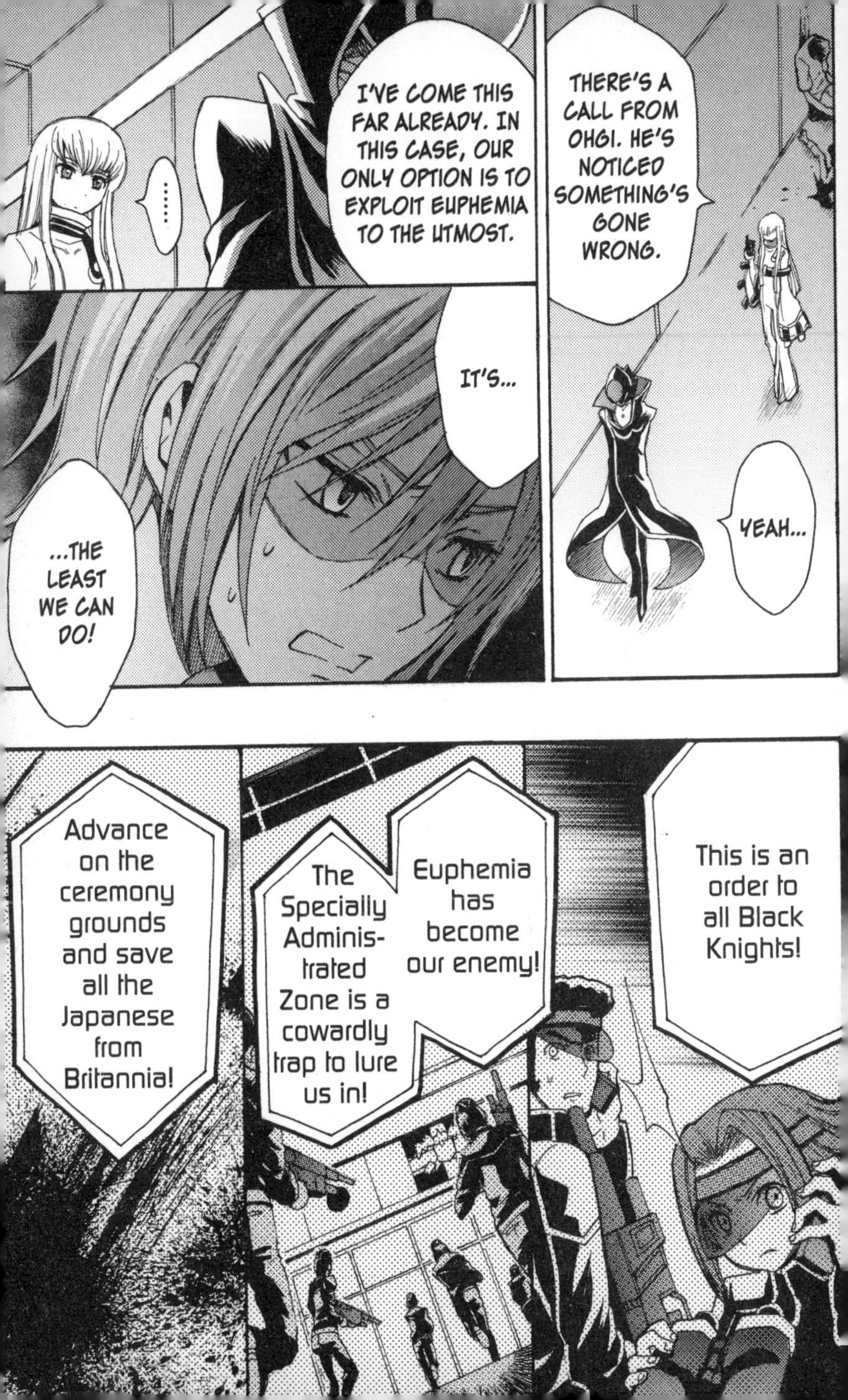
THERE'S A CALL FROM OHGI. HE'S NOTICED SOMETHING'S GONE WRONG.
YEAH...
I'VE COME THIS FAR ALREADY. IN THIS CASE, OUR ONLY OPTION IS TO EXPLOIT EUPHEMIA TO THE UTMOST.
......
IT'S...
...THE LEAST WE CAN DO!
This is an order to all Black Knights!
Euphemia has become our enemy!
The Specially Adminis-trated Zone is a cowardly trap to lure us in!
Advance on the ceremony grounds and save all the Japanese from Britannia!

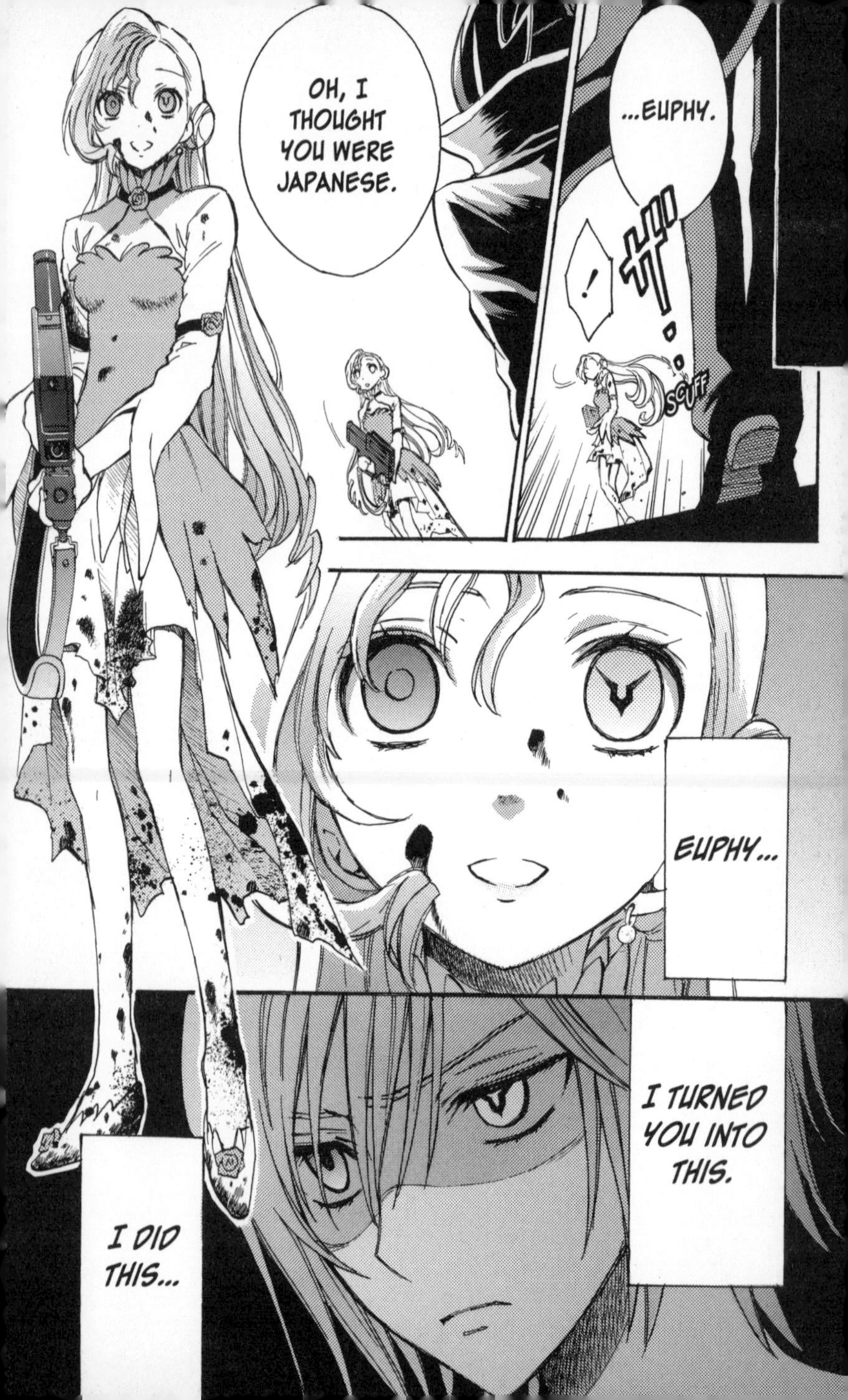
...EUPHY.
!
SCUFF
OH, I THOUGHT YOU WERE JAPANESE.
EUPHY...
I TURNED YOU INTO THIS.
I DID THIS...

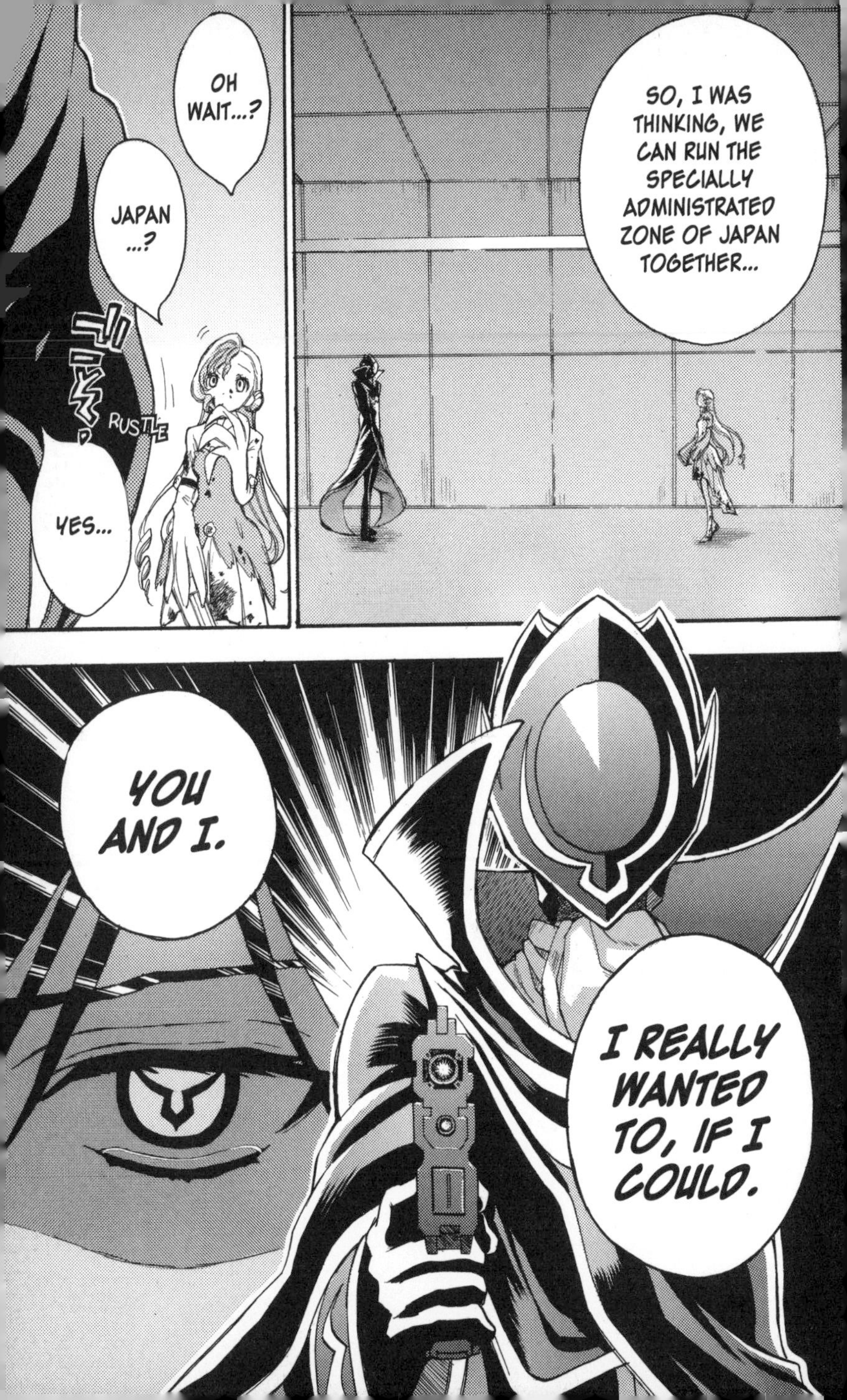
SO, I WAS THINKING, WE CAN RUN THE SPECIALLY ADMINISTRATED ZONE OF JAPAN TOGETHER...
OH WAIT...?
JAPAN ...?
RUSTLE
YES...
YOU AND I.
I REALLY WANTED TO, IF I COULD.

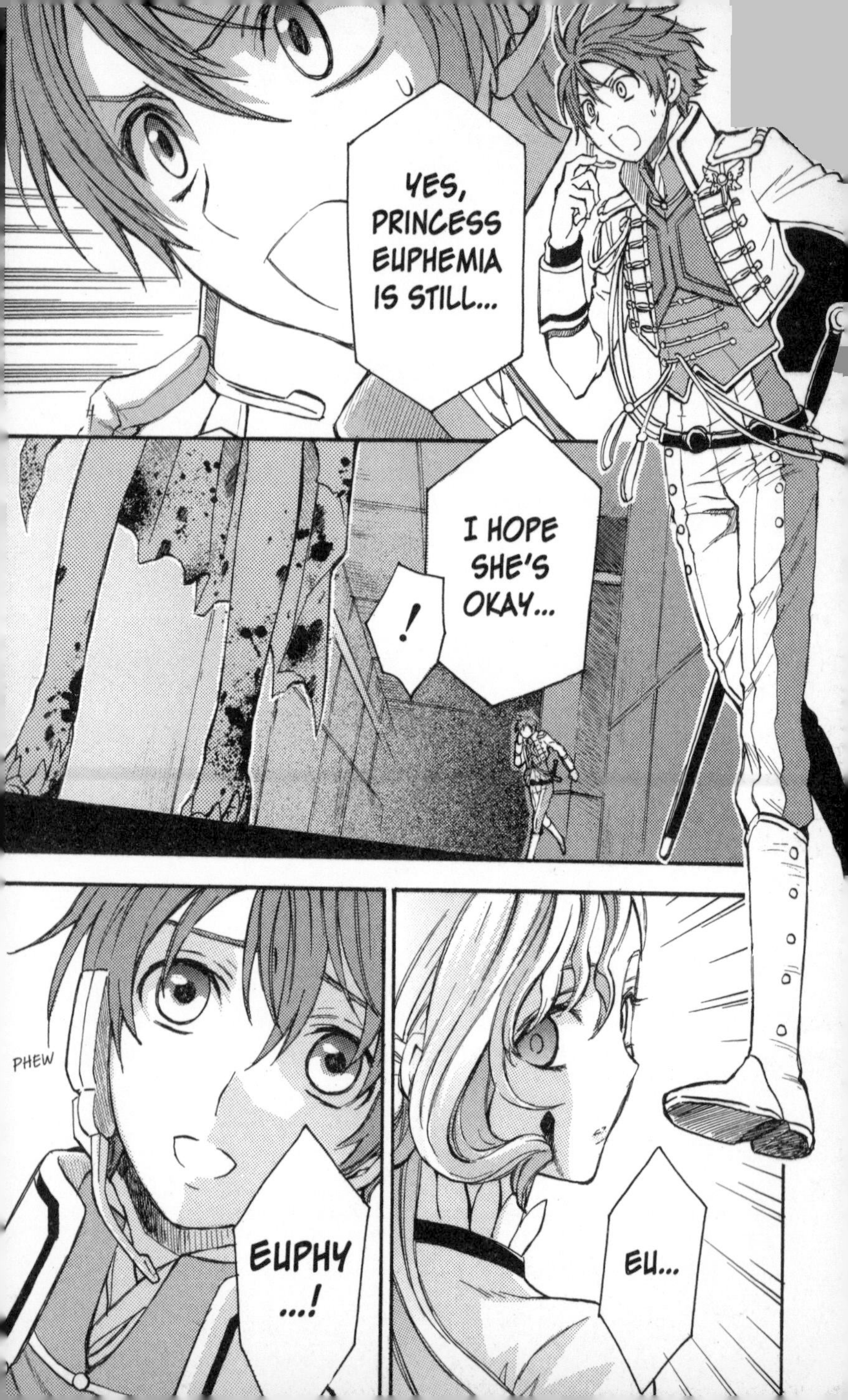
YES, PRINCESS EUPHEMIA IS STILL...
I HOPE SHE'S OKAY...
!
EU...
PHEW
EUPHY ...!

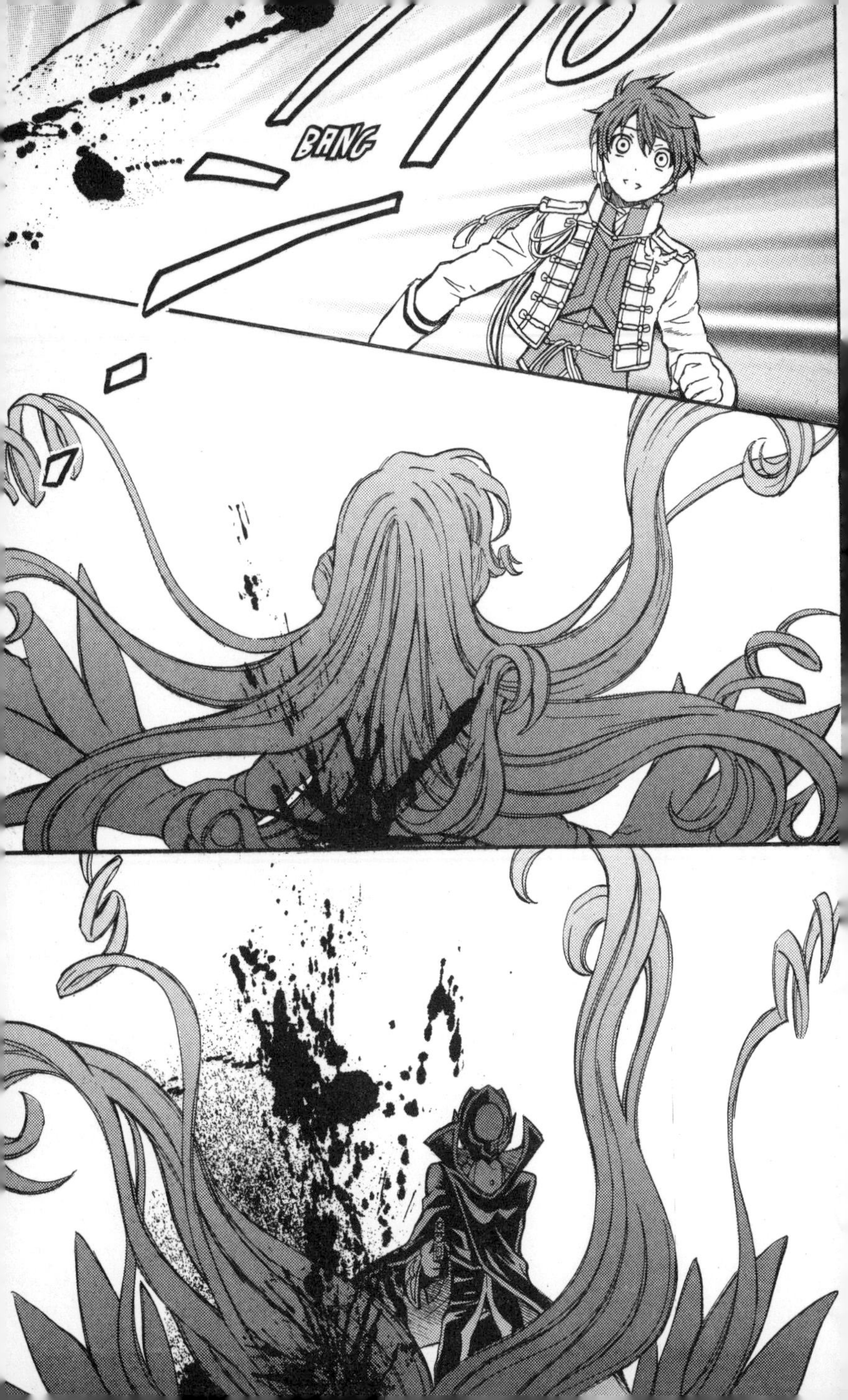
BANG

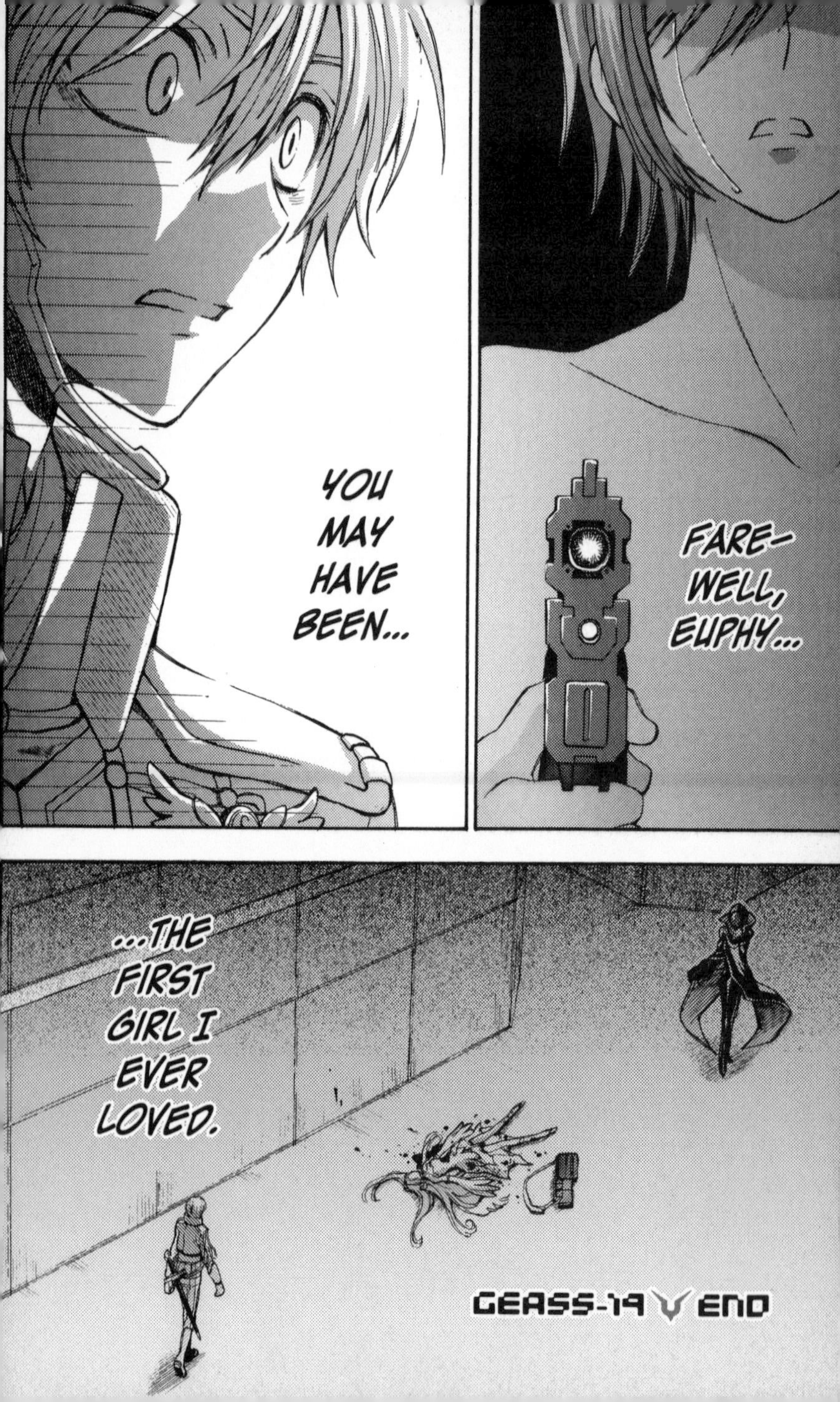
FARE-WELL, EUPHY...
YOU MAY HAVE BEEN...
...THE FIRST GIRL I EVER LOVED.
GEASS-19 END

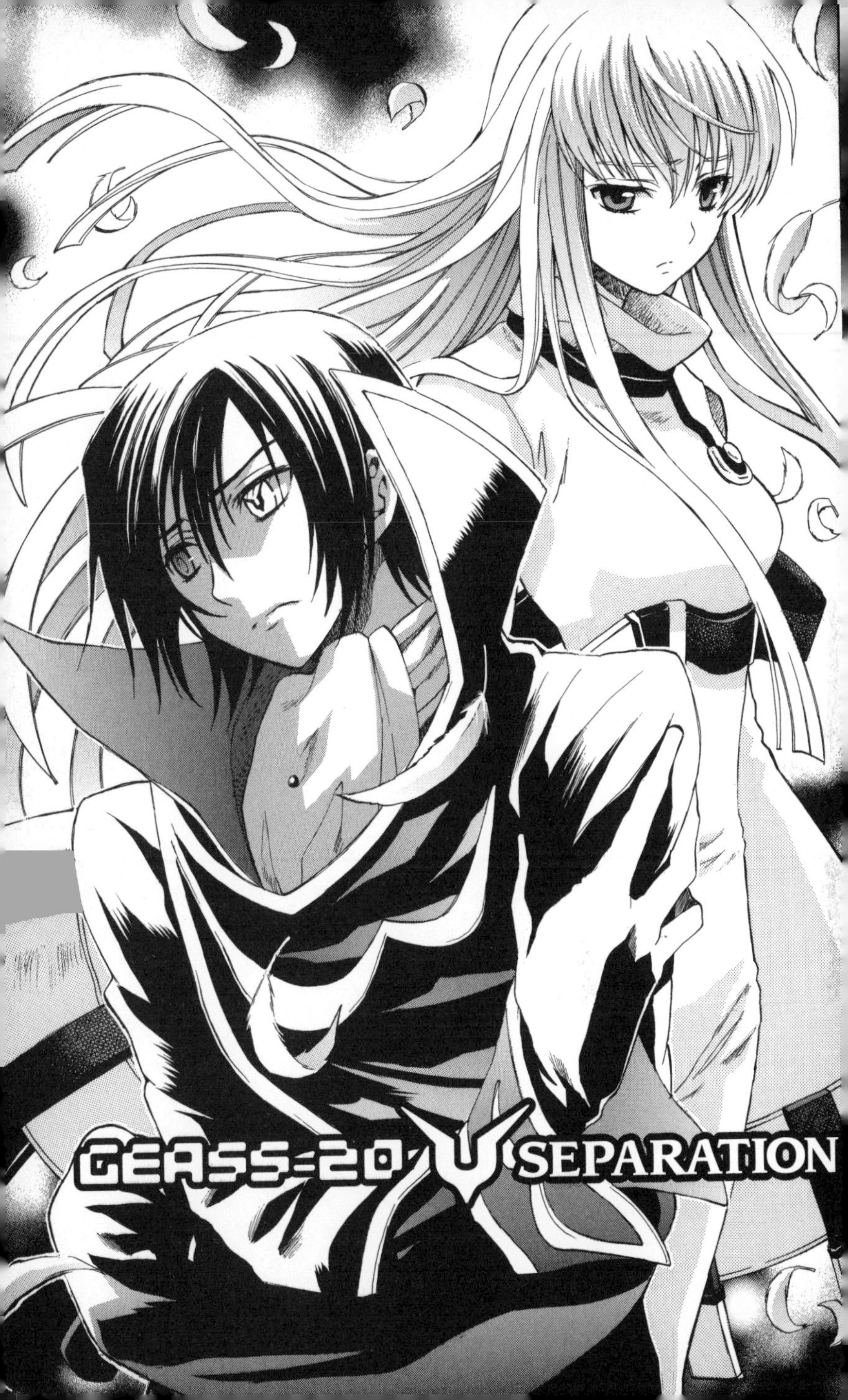
GEASS-20 SEPARATION

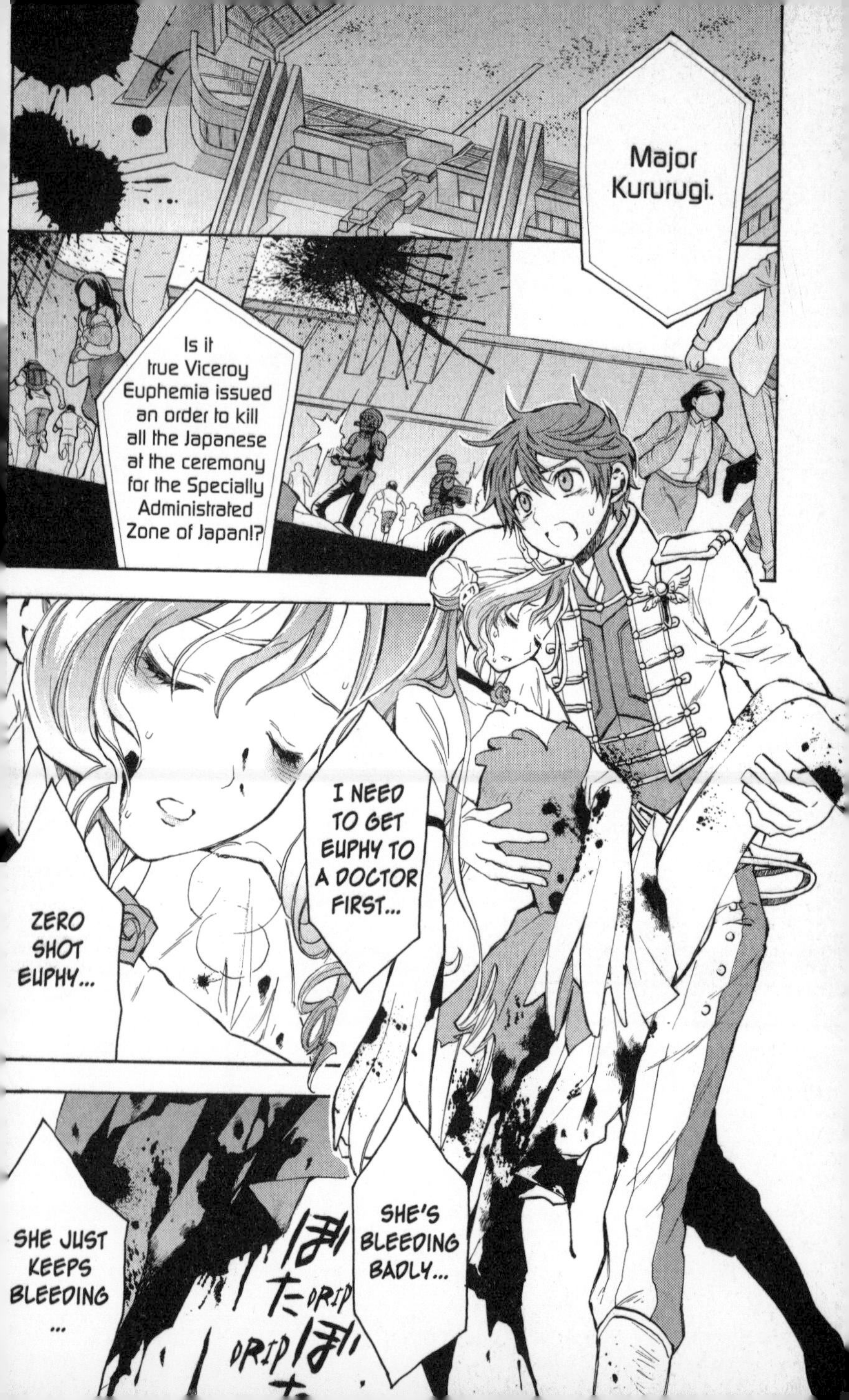
Major Kururugi.
...
Is it true Viceroy Euphemia issued an order to kill all the Japanese at the ceremony for the Specially Administrated Zone of Japan!?
I NEED TO GET EUPHY TO A DOCTOR FIRST...
ZERO SHOT EUPHY...
SHE'S BLEEDING BADLY...
ぽた DRIP
DRIP
SHE JUST KEEPS BLEEDING ...

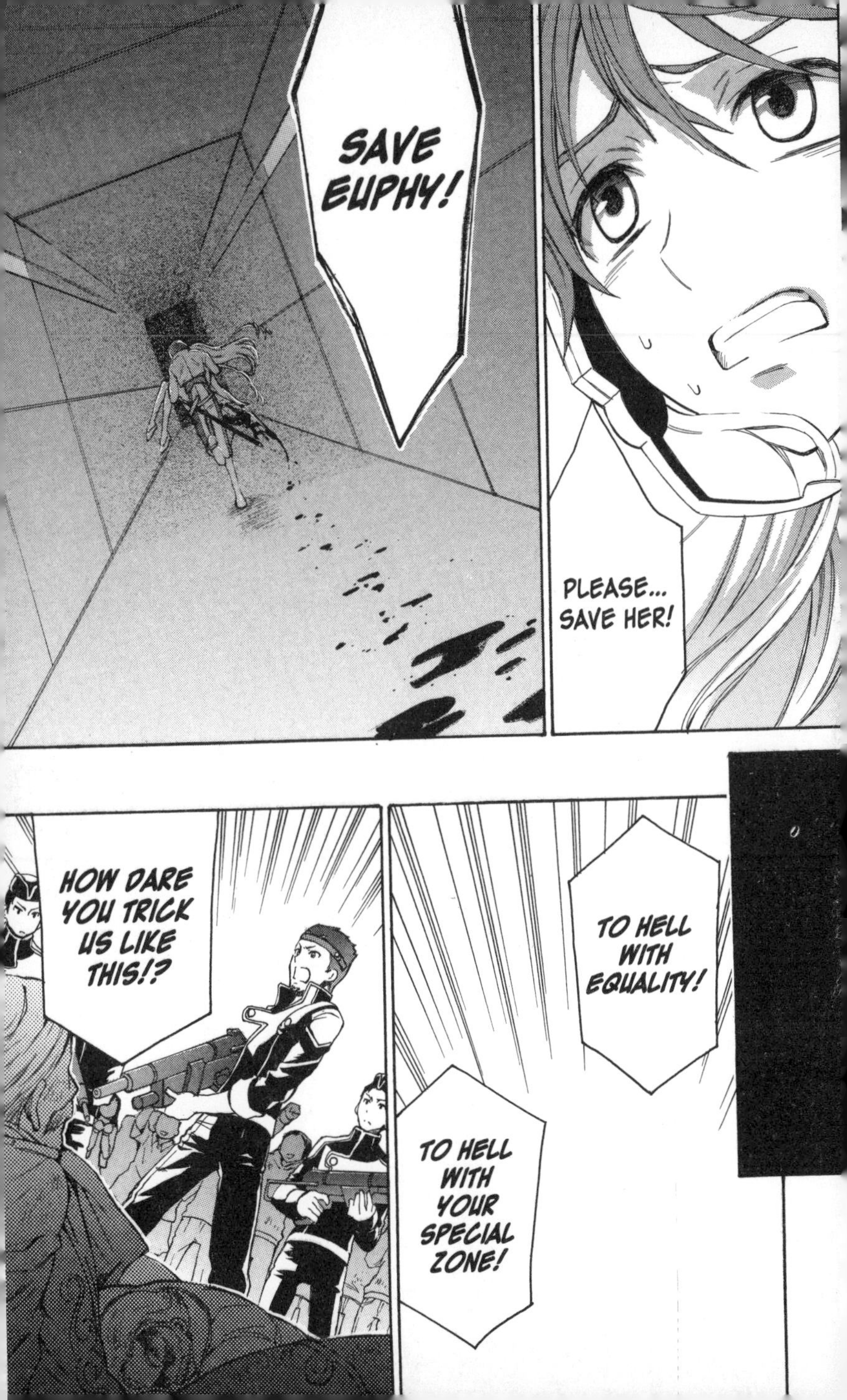
PLEASE... SAVE HER!
SAVE EUPHY!
TO HELL WITH EQUALITY!
TO HELL WITH YOUR SPECIAL ZONE!
HOW DARE YOU TRICK US LIKE THIS!?

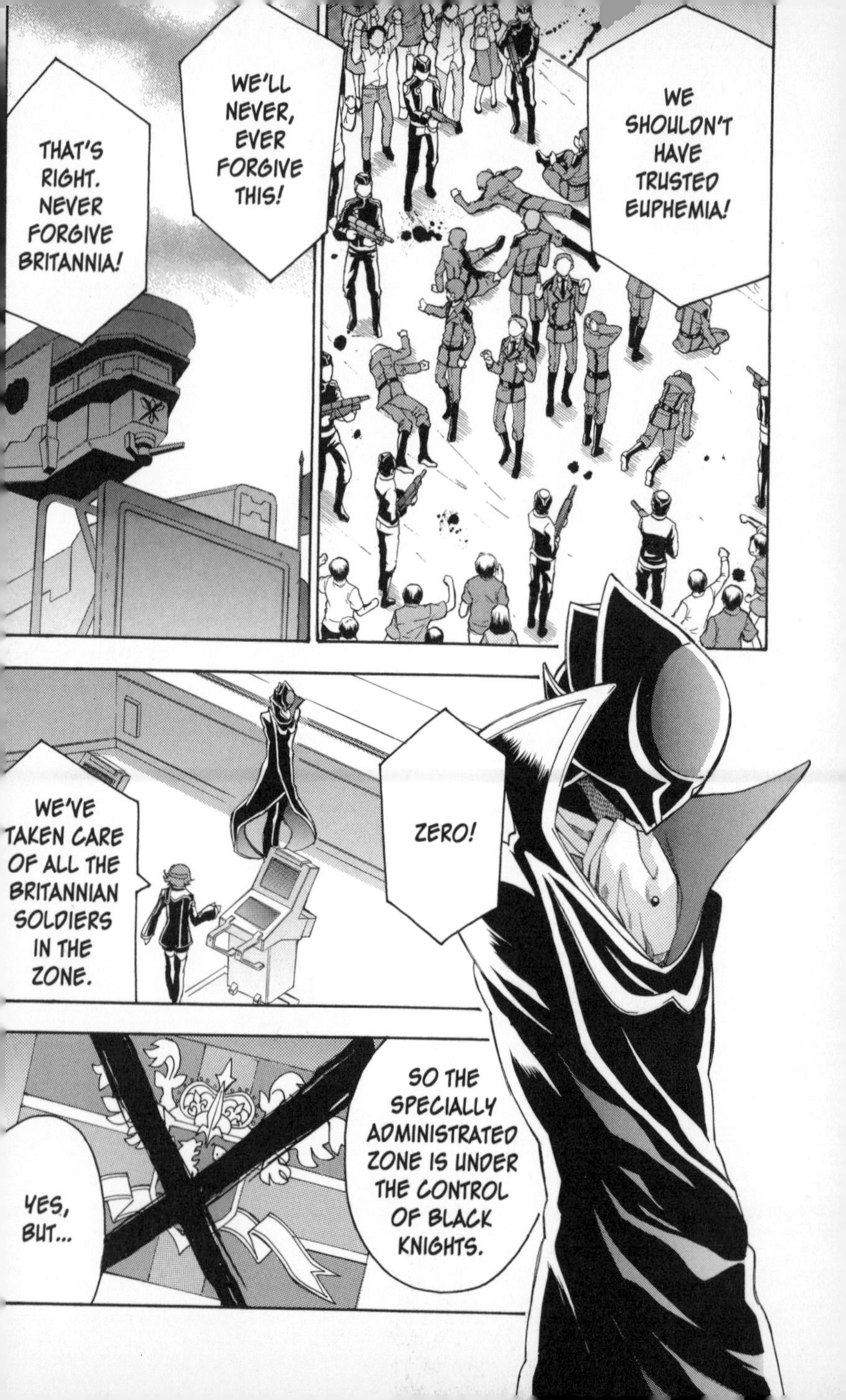
WE SHOULDN'T HAVE TRUSTED EUPHEMIA!
WE'LL NEVER, EVER FORGIVE THIS!
THAT'S RIGHT. NEVER FORGIVE BRITANNIA!
ZERO!
WE'VE TAKEN CARE OF ALL THE BRITANNIAN SOLDIERS IN THE ZONE.
SO THE SPECIALLY ADMINISTRATED ZONE IS UNDER THE CONTROL OF BLACK KNIGHTS.
YES, BUT...

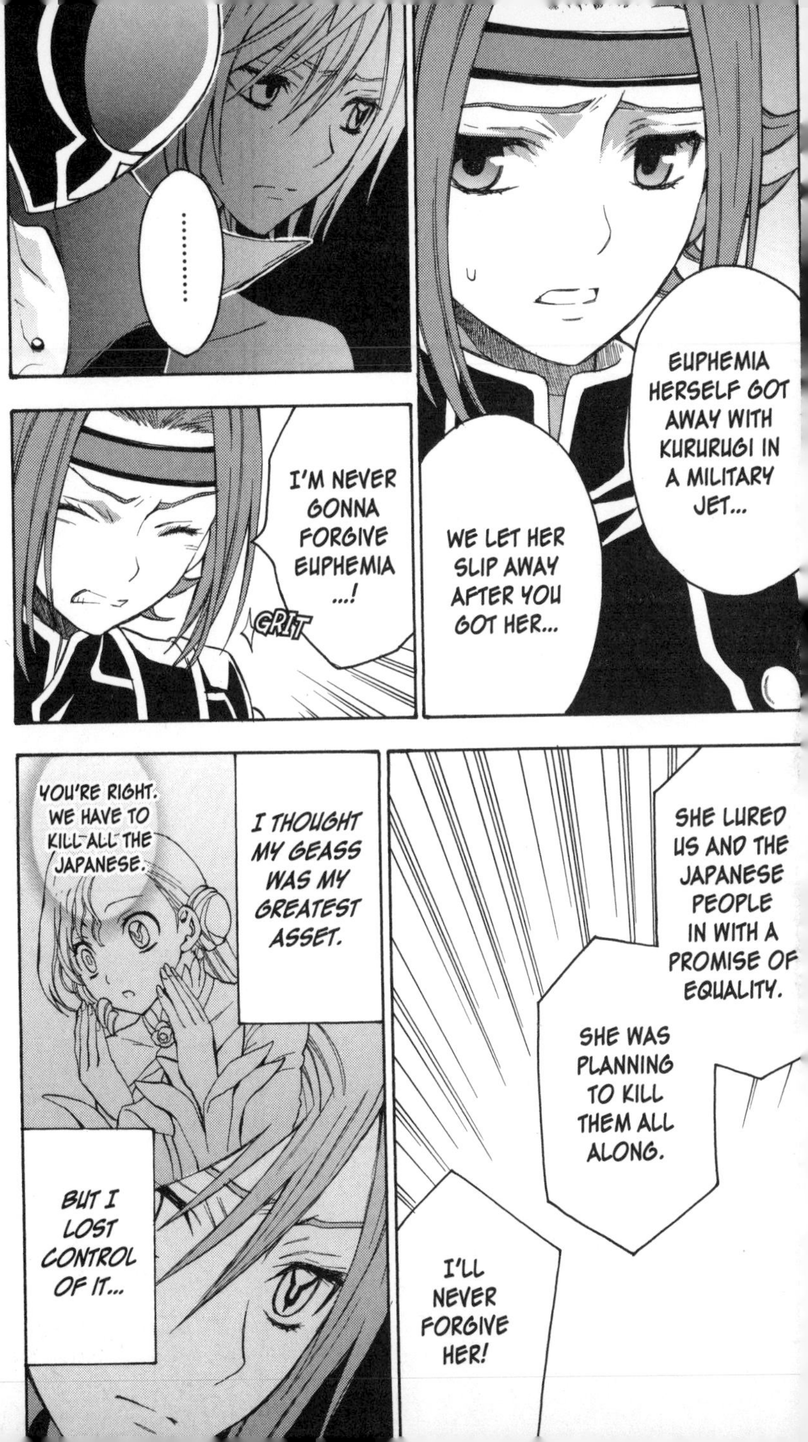
EUPHEMIA HERSELF GOT AWAY WITH KURURUGI IN A MILITARY JET...
WE LET HER SLIP AWAY AFTER YOU GOT HER...
......
I'M NEVER GONNA FORGIVE EUPHEMIA ...!
GRIT
SHE LURED US AND THE JAPANESE PEOPLE IN WITH A PROMISE OF EQUALITY.
SHE WAS PLANNING TO KILL THEM ALL ALONG.
I'LL NEVER FORGIVE HER!
I THOUGHT MY GEASS WAS MY GREATEST ASSET.
YOU'RE RIGHT. WE HAVE TO KILL ALL THE JAPANESE.
BUT I LOST CONTROL OF IT...

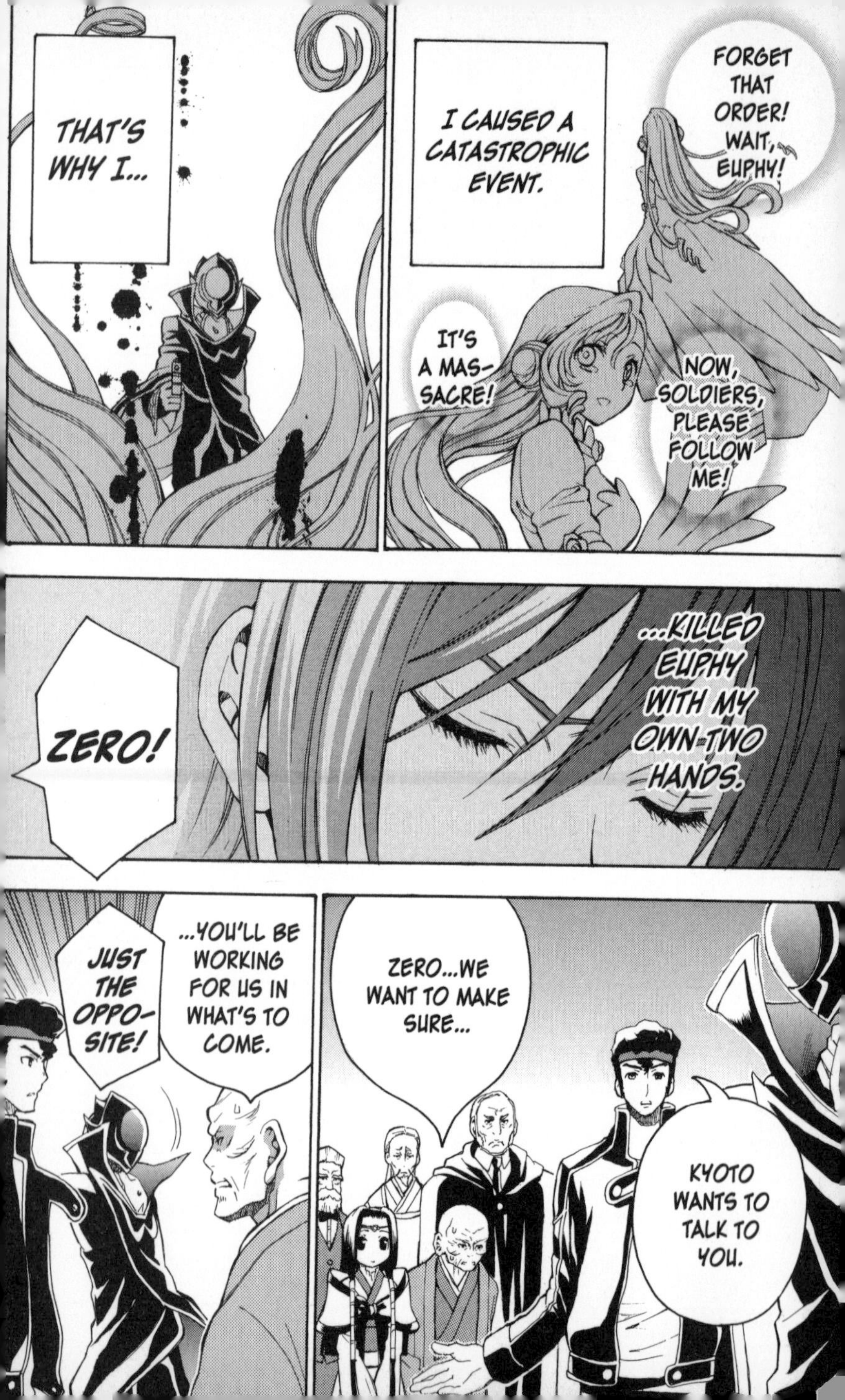
FORGET THAT ORDER! WAIT, EUPHY!
I CAUSED A CATASTROPHIC EVENT.
NOW, SOLDIERS, PLEASE FOLLOW ME!
IT'S A MAS-SACRE!
THAT'S WHY I...
...KILLED EUPHY WITH MY OWN TWO HANDS.
ZERO!
KYOTO WANTS TO TALK TO YOU.
ZERO...WE WANT TO MAKE SURE...
...YOU'LL BE WORKING FOR US IN WHAT'S TO COME.
JUST THE OPPO-SITE!

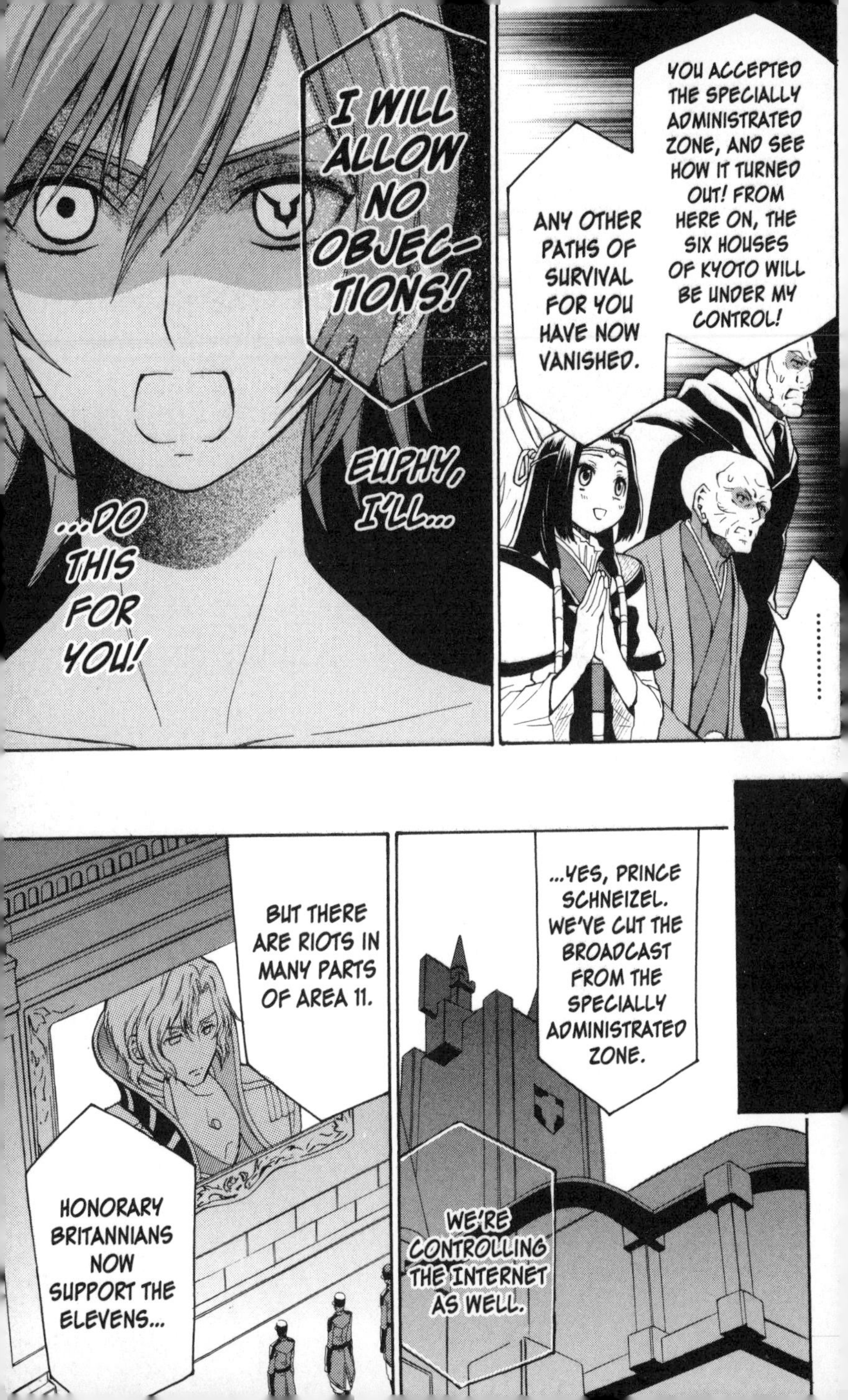
YOU ACCEPTED THE SPECIALLY ADMINISTRATED ZONE, AND SEE HOW IT TURNED OUT! FROM HERE ON, THE SIX HOUSES OF KYOTO WILL BE UNDER MY CONTROL!
ANY OTHER PATHS OF SURVIVAL FOR YOU HAVE NOW VANISHED.
I WILL ALLOW NO OBJEC-TIONS!
EUPHY, I'LL...
...DO THIS FOR YOU!
...YES, PRINCE SCHNEIZEL. WE'VE CUT THE BROADCAST FROM THE SPECIALLY ADMINISTRATED ZONE.
WE'RE CONTROLLING THE INTERNET AS WELL.
BUT THERE ARE RIOTS IN MANY PARTS OF AREA 11.
HONORARY BRITANNIANS NOW SUPPORT THE ELEVENS...

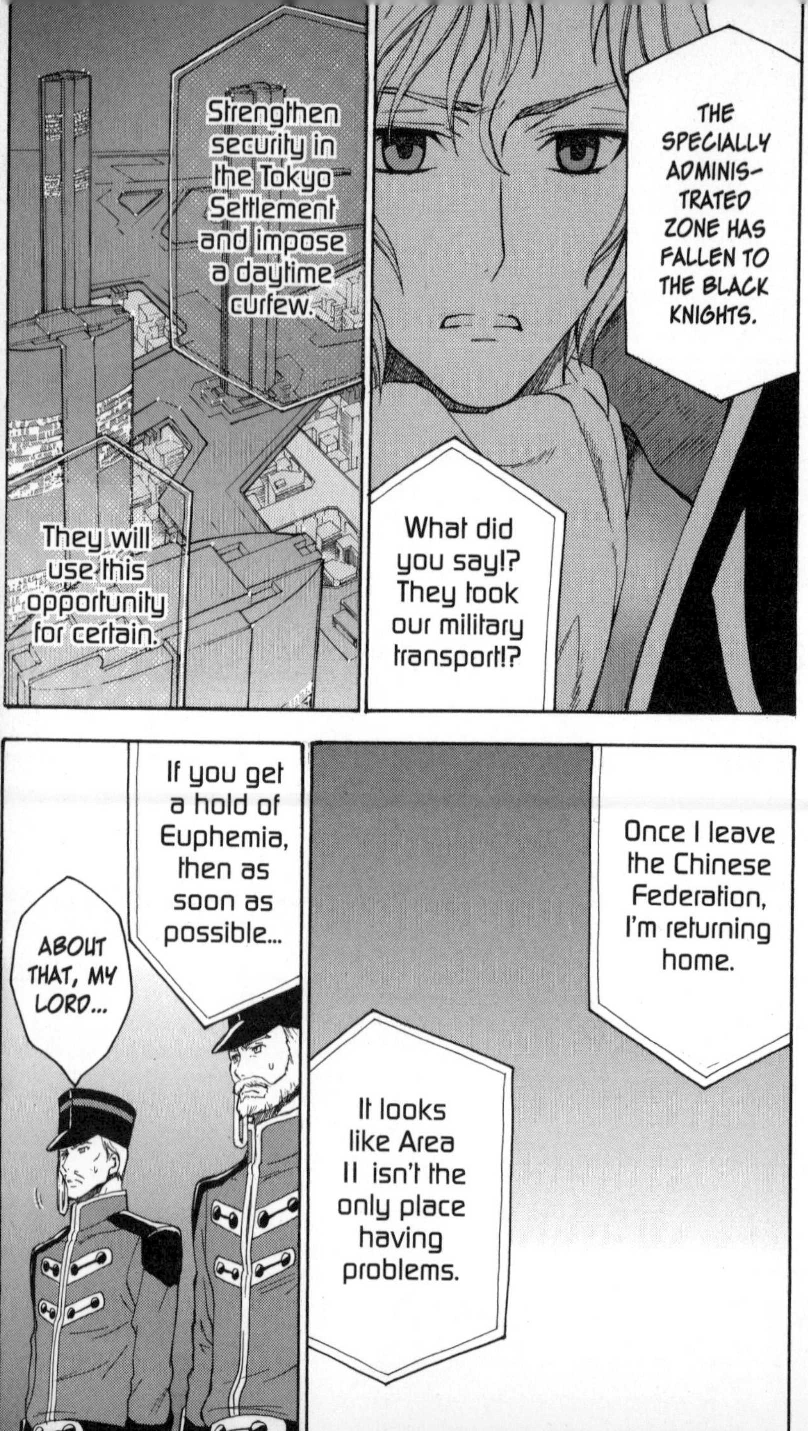
THE SPECIALLY ADMINIS-TRATED ZONE HAS FALLEN TO THE BLACK KNIGHTS.
What did you say!? They took our military transport!?
Strengthen security in the Tokyo Settlement and impose a daytime curfew.
They will use this opportunity for certain.
Once I leave the Chinese Federation, I'm returning home.
It looks like Area 11 isn't the only place having problems.
If you get a hold of Euphemia, then as soon as possible...
ABOUT THAT, MY LORD...

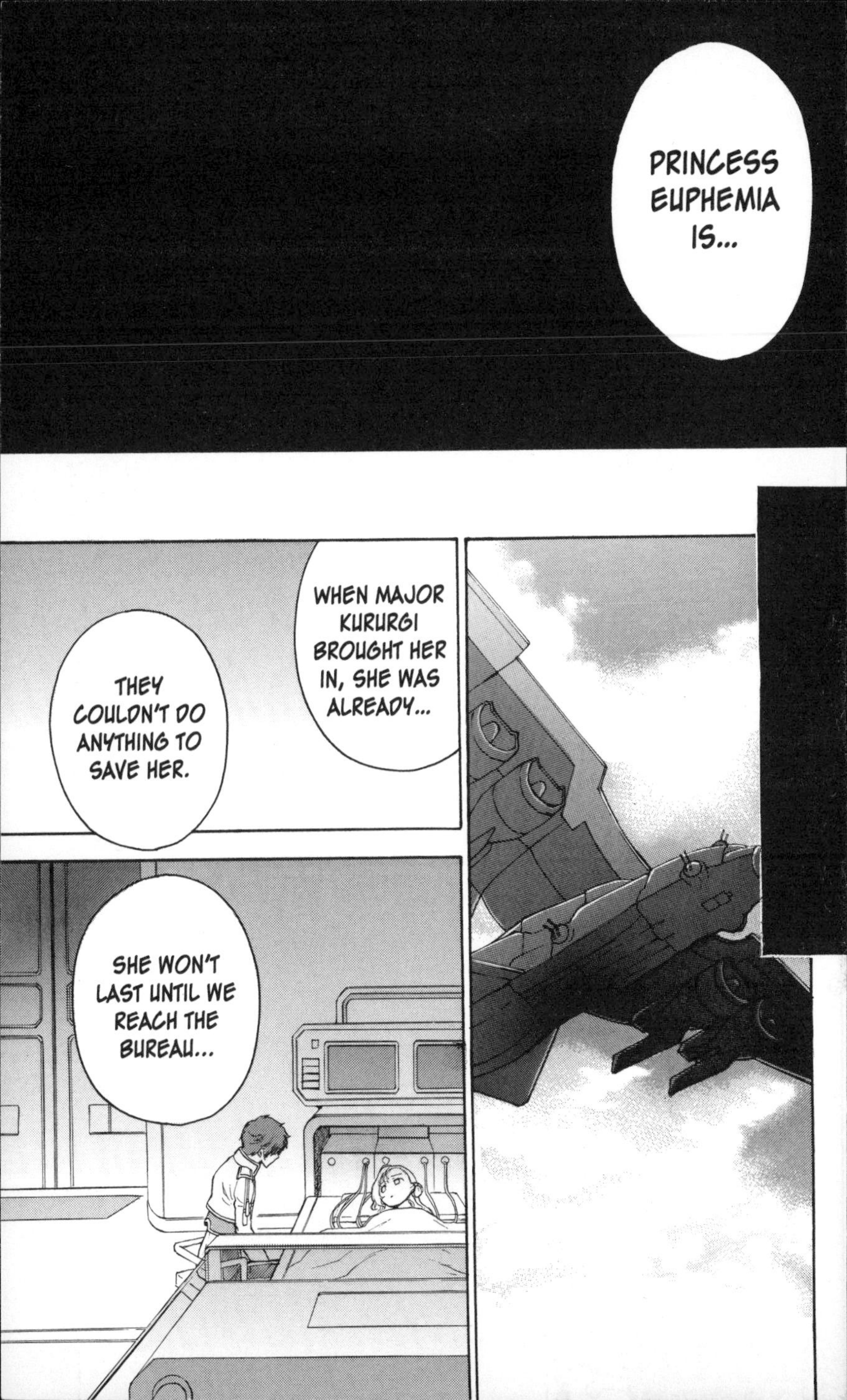
PRINCESS EUPHEMIA IS...
WHEN MAJOR KURURGI BROUGHT HER IN, SHE WAS ALREADY...
THEY COULDN'T DO ANYTHING TO SAVE HER.
SHE WON'T LAST UNTIL WE REACH THE BUREAU...

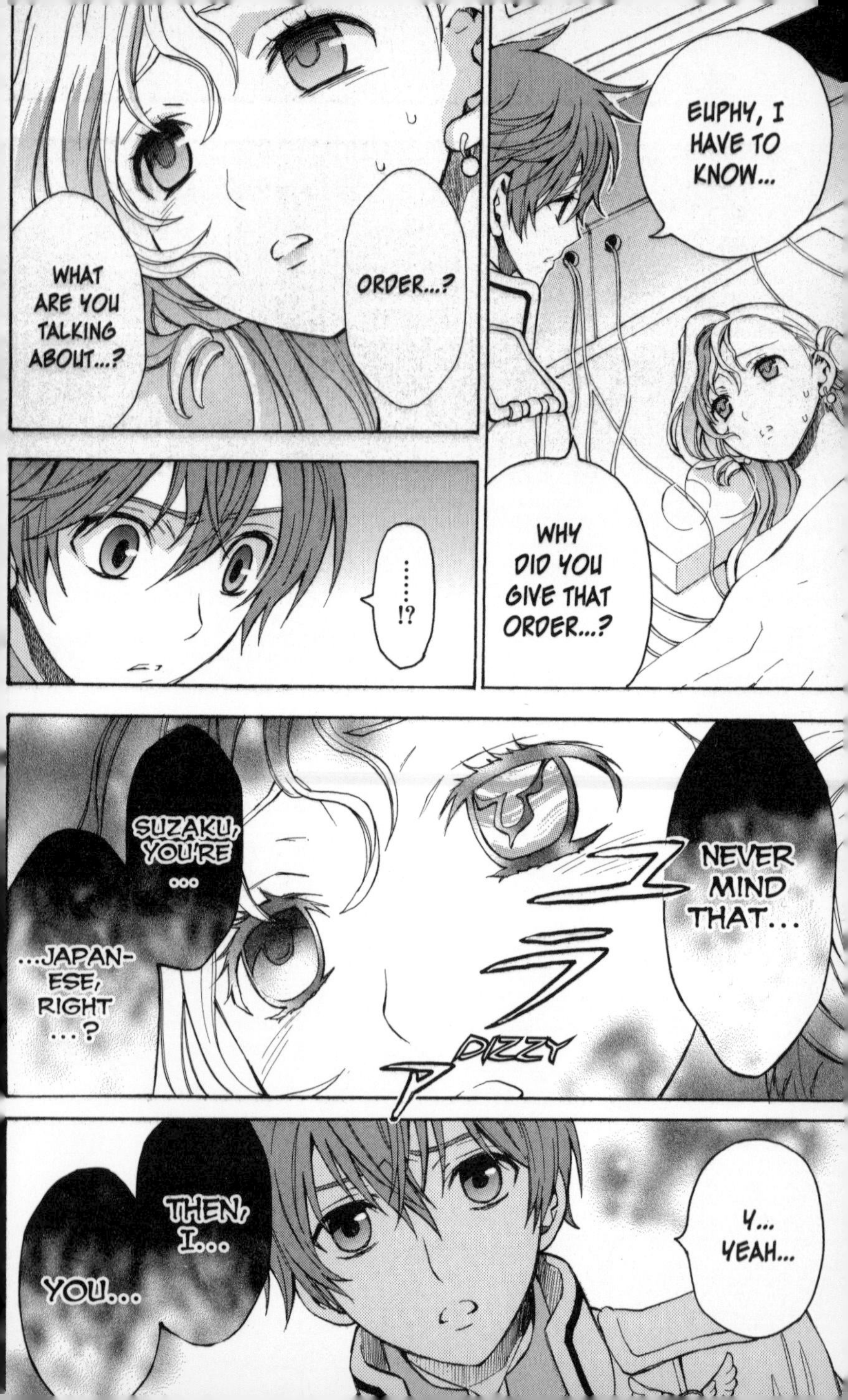
EUPHY, I HAVE TO KNOW...
WHY DID YOU GIVE THAT ORDER...?
ORDER...?
WHAT ARE YOU TALKING ABOUT...?
......!?
NEVER MIND THAT...
DIZZY
SUZAKU, YOU'RE ...
...JAPAN-ESE, RIGHT ...?
Y... YEAH...
THEN, I...
YOU...

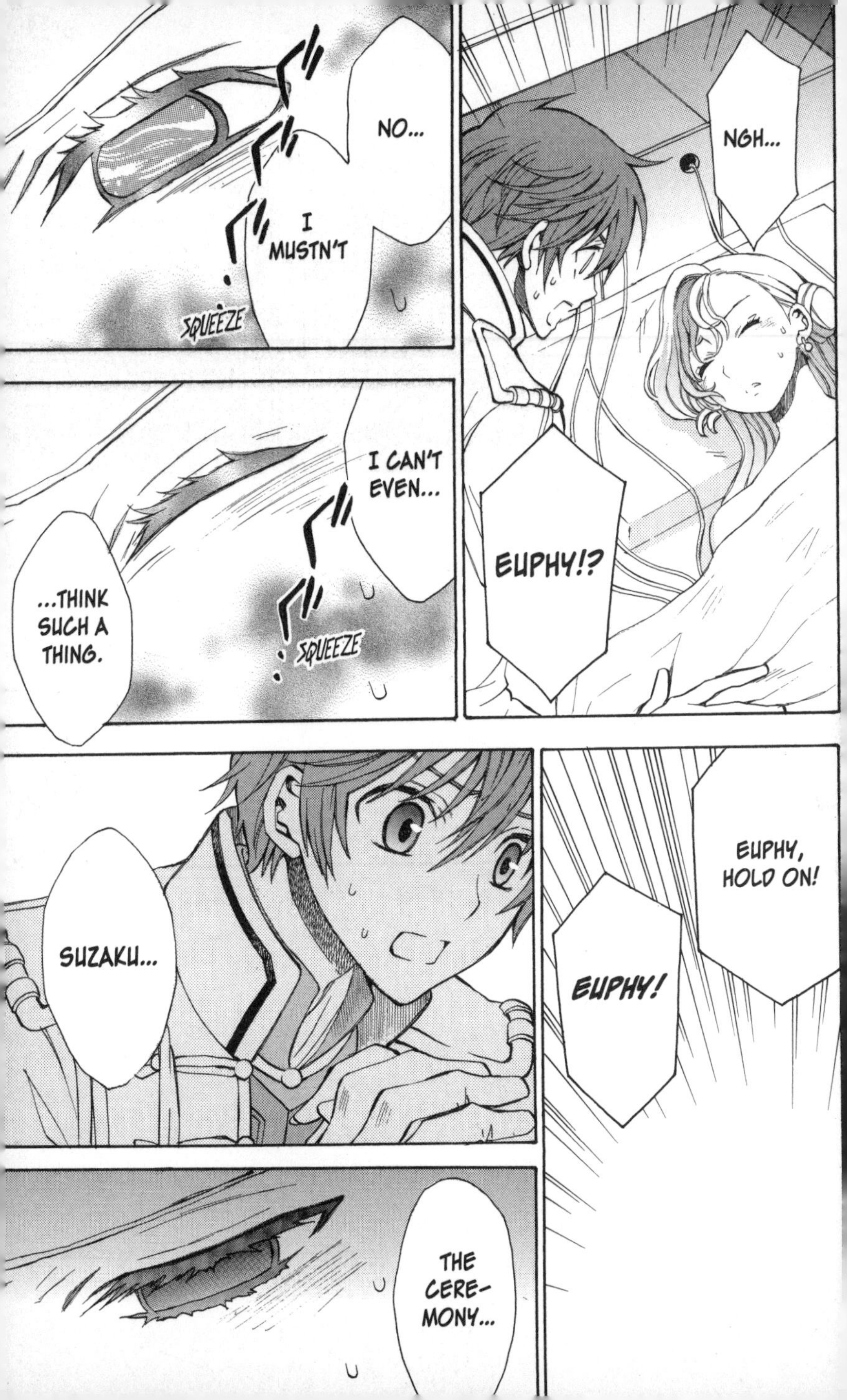
NGH...
EUPHY!?
NO...
I MUSTN'T
SQUEEZE
I CAN'T EVEN...
...THINK SUCH A THING.
SQUEEZE
EUPHY, HOLD ON!
EUPHY!
SUZAKU...
THE CERE-MONY...

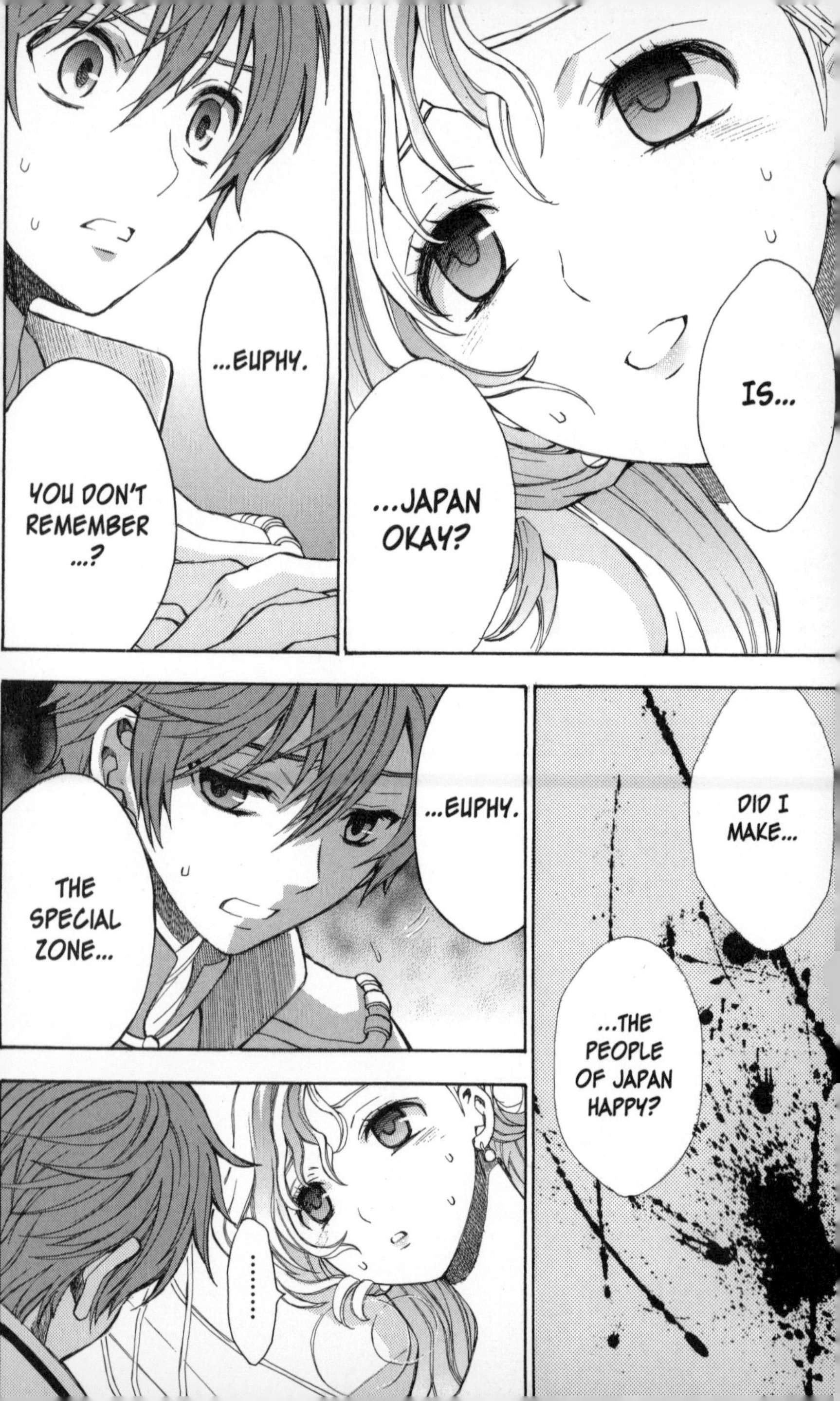
IS...
...JAPAN OKAY?
...EUPHY.
YOU DON'T REMEMBER ...?
DID I MAKE...
...THE PEOPLE OF JAPAN HAPPY?
...EUPHY.
THE SPECIAL ZONE...
......

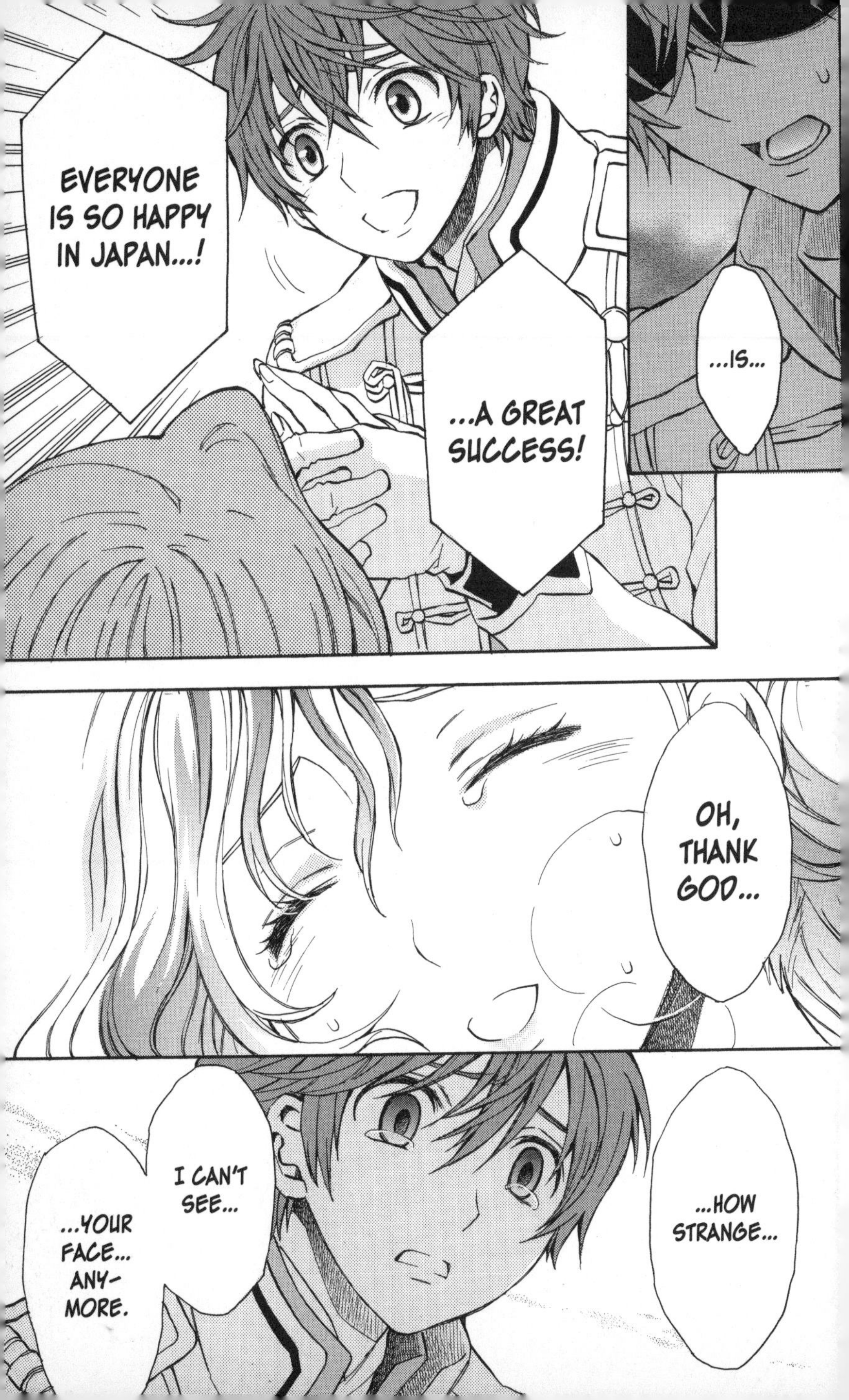
...IS...
EVERYONE IS SO HAPPY IN JAPAN...!
...A GREAT SUCCESS!
OH, THANK GOD...
...HOW STRANGE...
I CAN'T SEE...
...YOUR FACE... ANY-MORE.

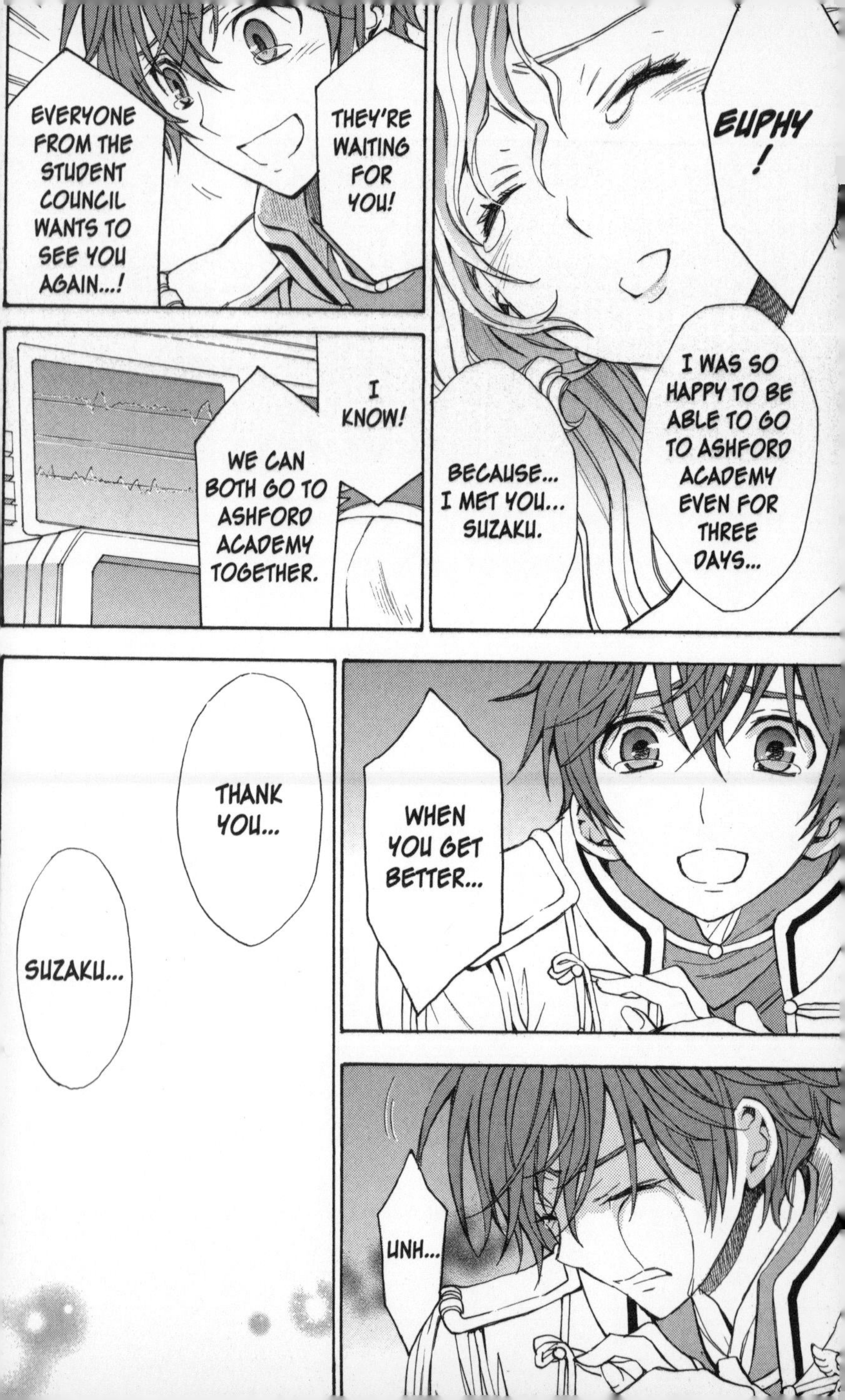
EUPHY!
I WAS SO HAPPY TO BE ABLE TO GO TO ASHFORD ACADEMY EVEN FOR THREE DAYS...
BECAUSE... I MET YOU... SUZAKU.
THEY'RE WAITING FOR YOU!
EVERYONE FROM THE STUDENT COUNCIL WANTS TO SEE YOU AGAIN...!
I KNOW!
WE CAN BOTH GO TO ASHFORD ACADEMY TOGETHER.
WHEN YOU GET BETTER...
UNH...
THANK YOU...
SUZAKU...

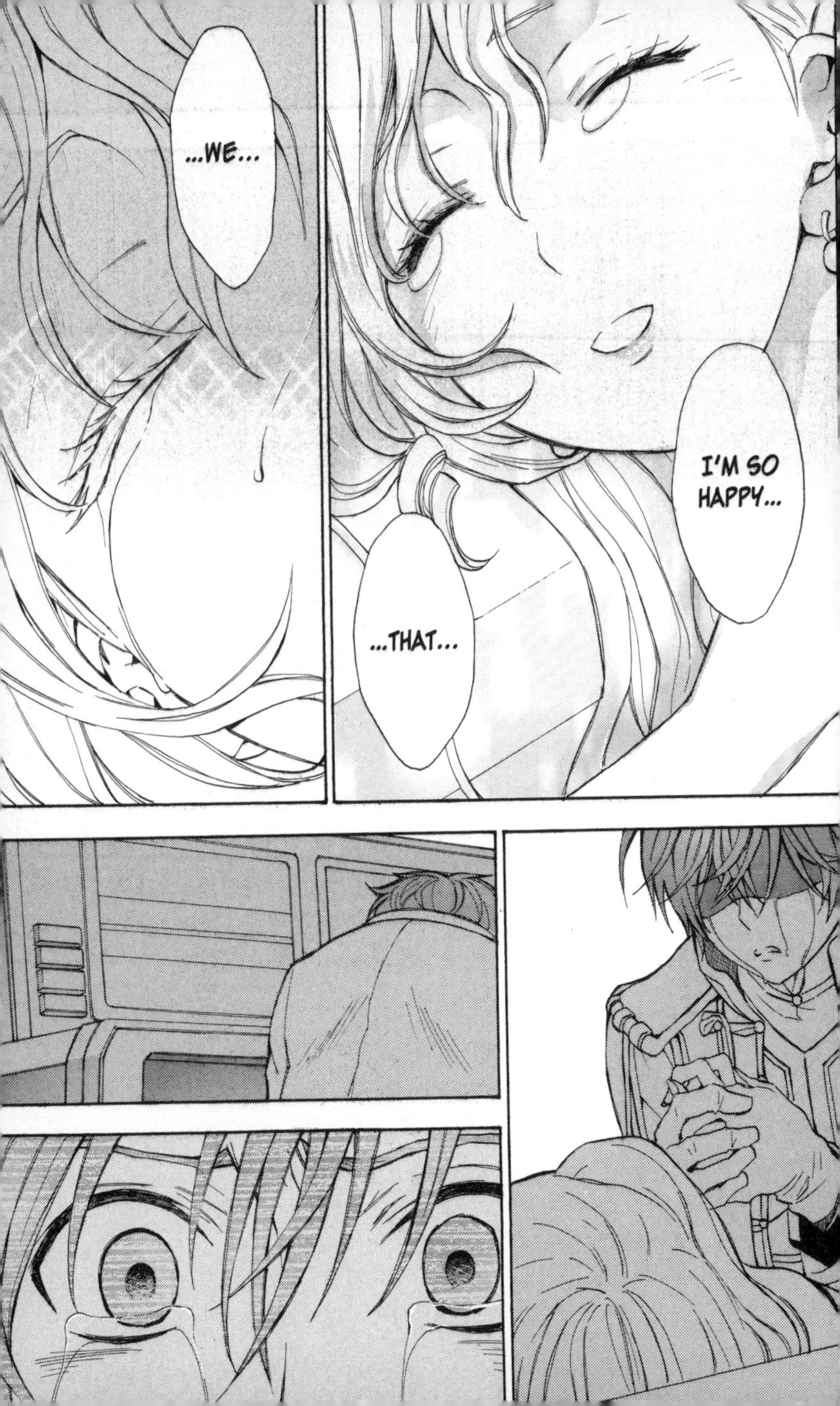
I'M SO HAPPY...
...THAT...
...WE...

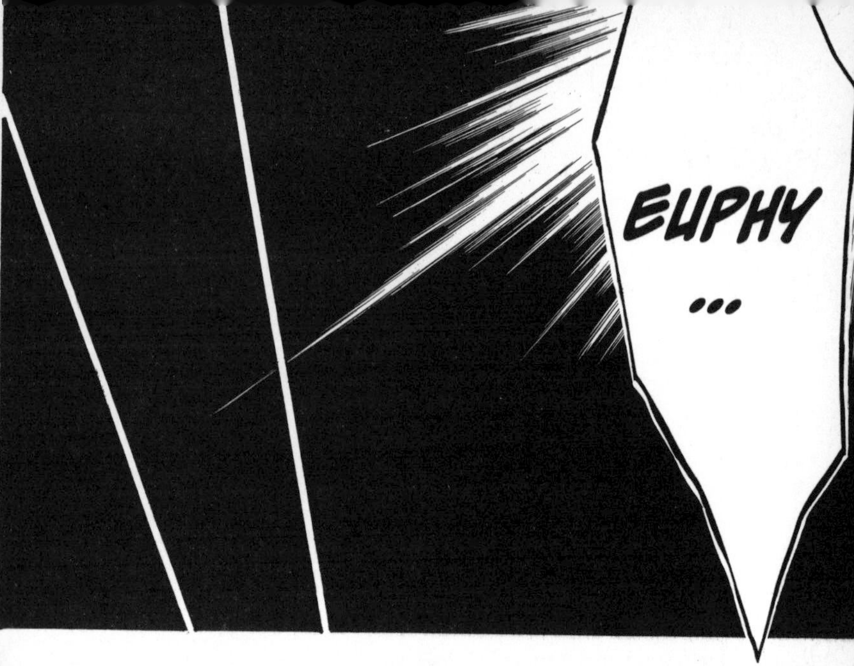
EUPHY
...

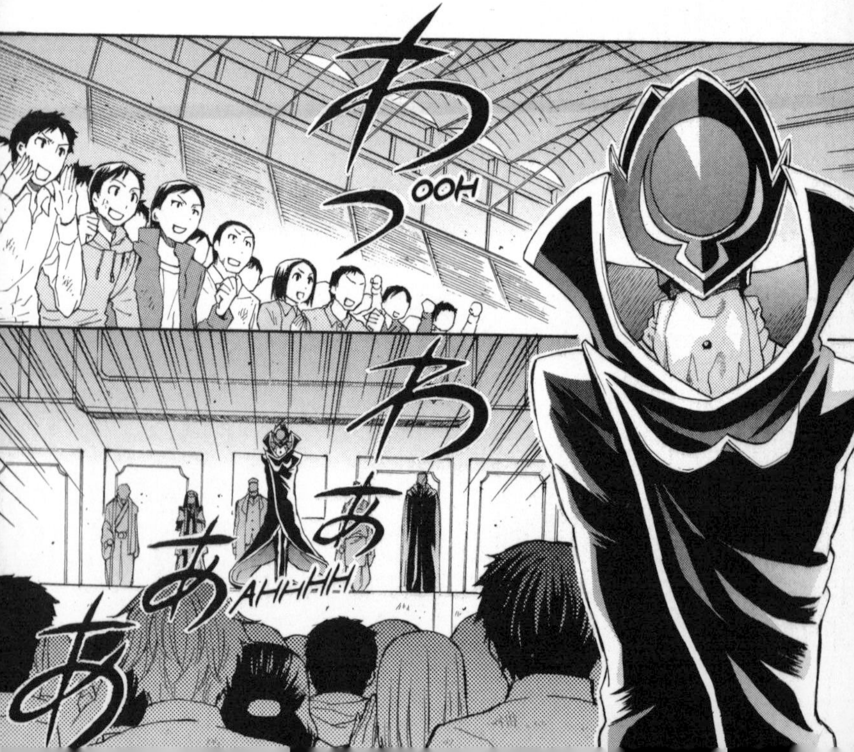
わっ
OOH
ああああ
AHHHH

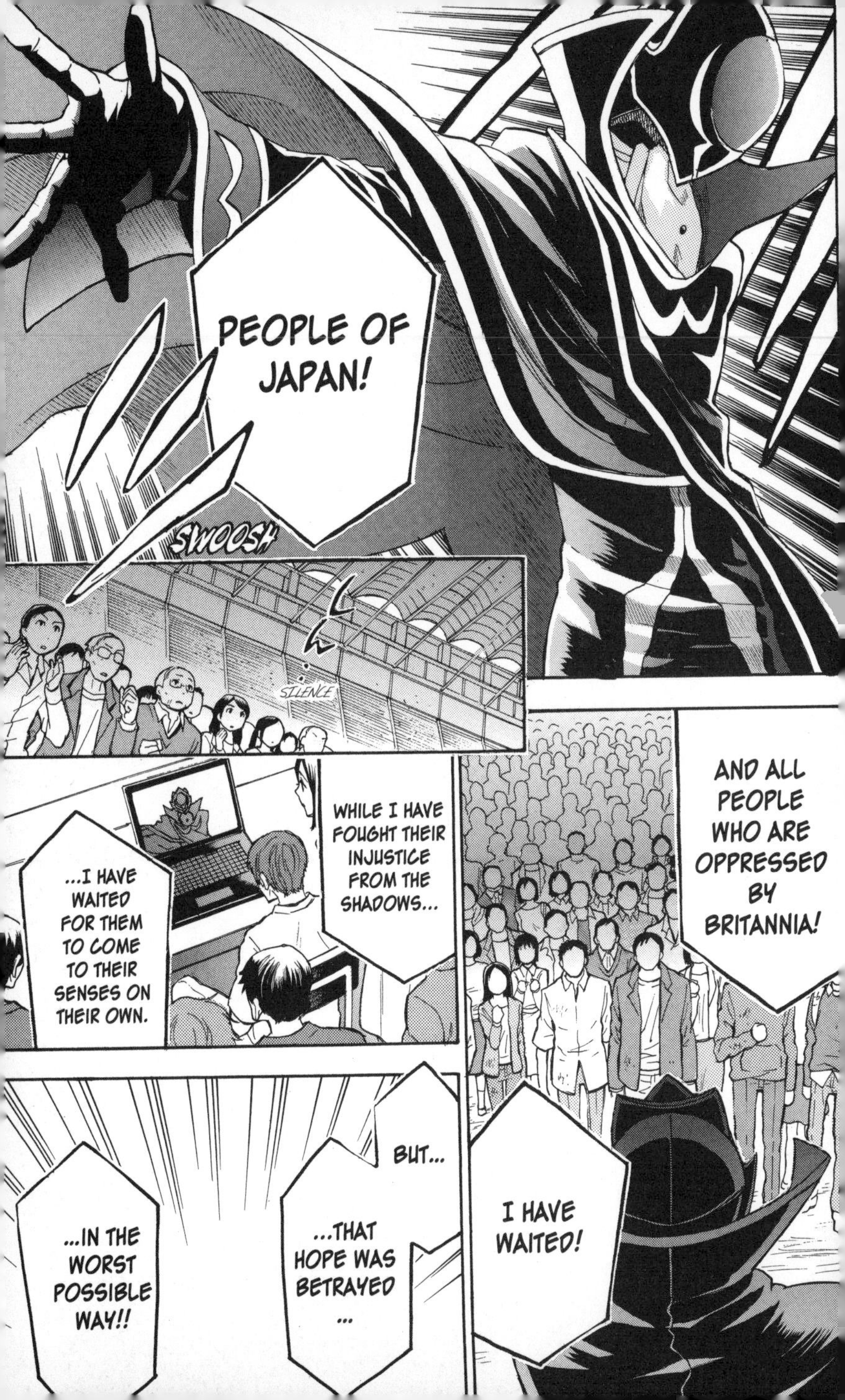
PEOPLE OF JAPAN!
SWOOSH
SILENCE
AND ALL PEOPLE WHO ARE OPPRESSED BY BRITANNIA!
WHILE I HAVE FOUGHT THEIR INJUSTICE FROM THE SHADOWS...
...I HAVE WAITED FOR THEM TO COME TO THEIR SENSES ON THEIR OWN.
I HAVE WAITED!
BUT...
...THAT HOPE WAS BETRAYED ...
...IN THE WORST POSSIBLE WAY!!

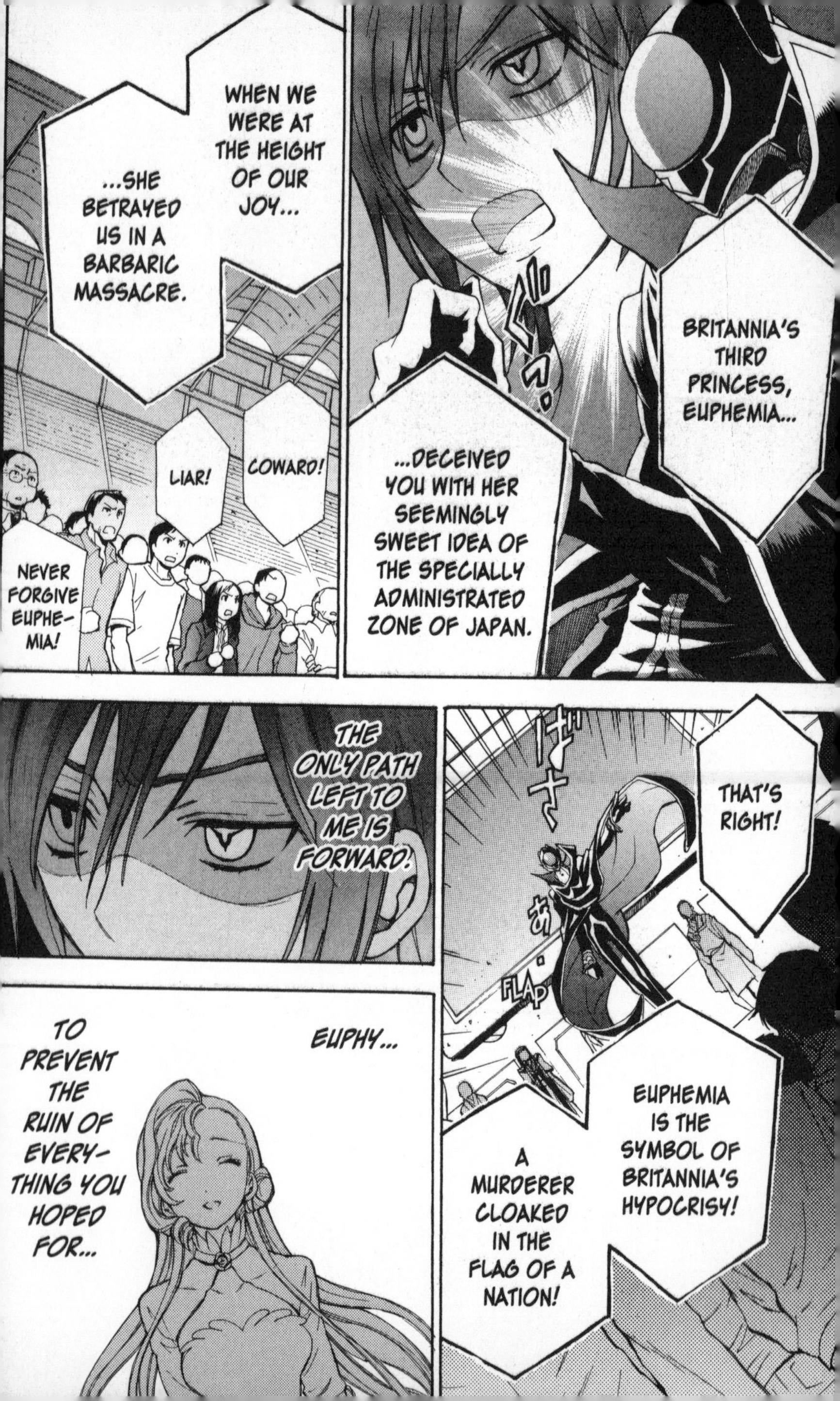
BRITANNIA'S THIRD PRINCESS, EUPHEMIA...
...DECEIVED YOU WITH HER SEEMINGLY SWEET IDEA OF THE SPECIALLY ADMINISTRATED ZONE OF JAPAN.
WHEN WE WERE AT THE HEIGHT OF OUR JOY...
...SHE BETRAYED US IN A BARBARIC MASSACRE.
COWARD!
LIAR!
NEVER FORGIVE EUPHEMIA!
THAT'S RIGHT!
FLAP
EUPHEMIA IS THE SYMBOL OF BRITANNIA'S HYPOCRISY!
A MURDERER CLOAKED IN THE FLAG OF A NATION!
THE ONLY PATH LEFT TO ME IS FORWARD.
EUPHY...
TO PREVENT THE RUIN OF EVERYTHING YOU HOPED FOR...

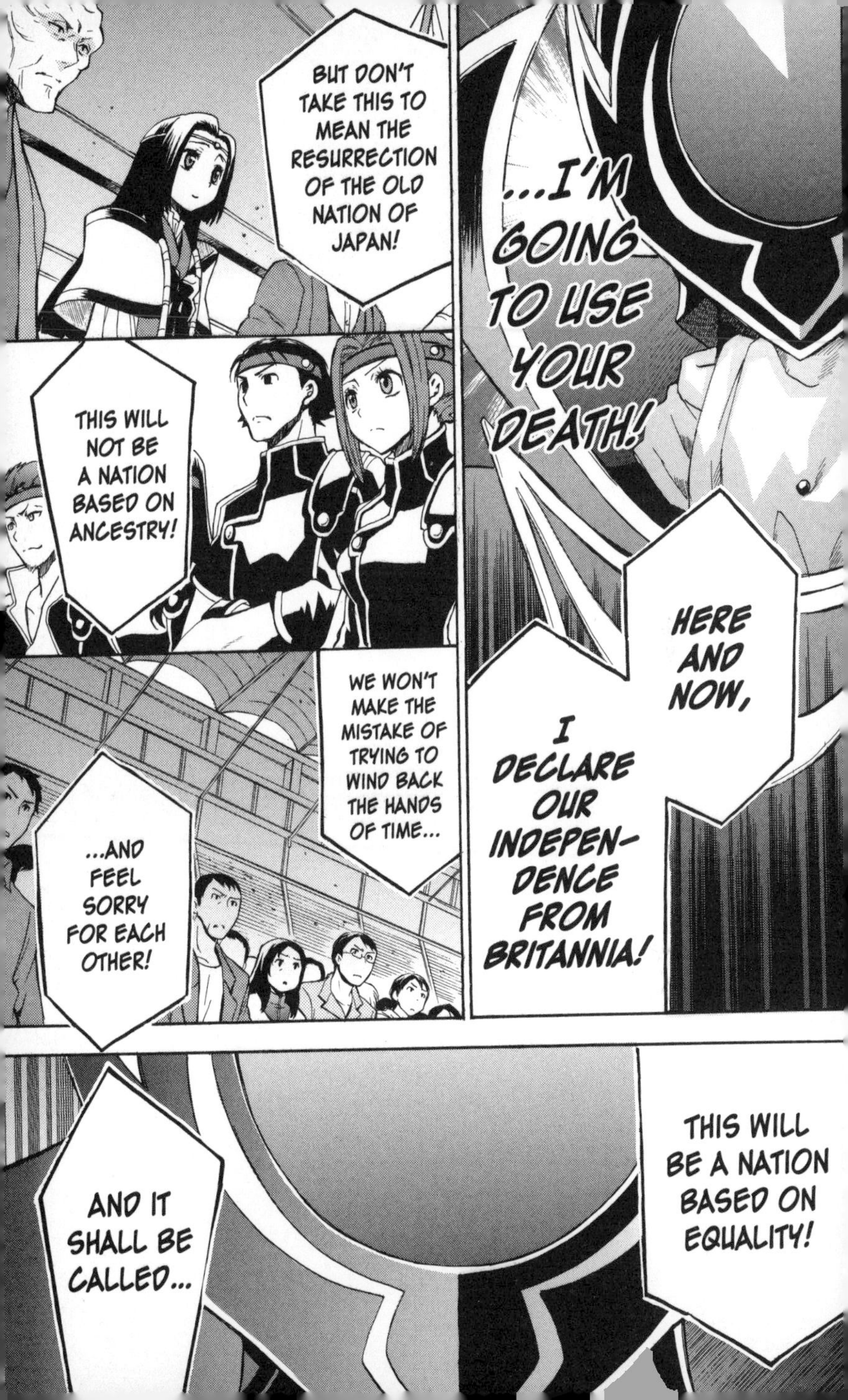
...I'M GOING TO USE YOUR DEATH!
HERE AND NOW,
I DECLARE OUR INDEPENDENCE FROM BRITANNIA!
BUT DON'T TAKE THIS TO MEAN THE RESURRECTION OF THE OLD NATION OF JAPAN!
THIS WILL NOT BE A NATION BASED ON ANCESTRY!
WE WON'T MAKE THE MISTAKE OF TRYING TO WIND BACK THE HANDS OF TIME...
...AND FEEL SORRY FOR EACH OTHER!
THIS WILL BE A NATION BASED ON EQUALITY!
AND IT SHALL BE CALLED...

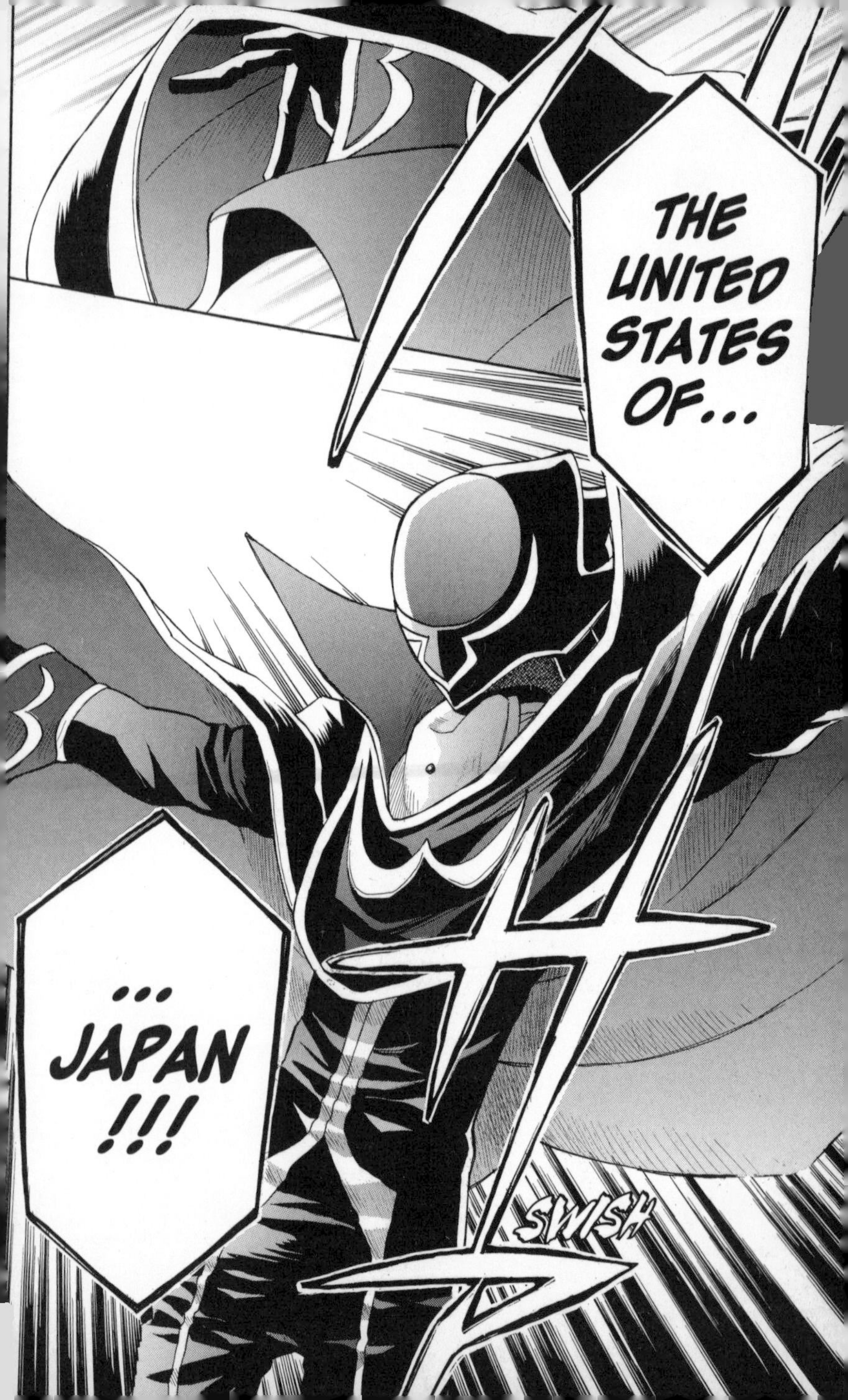
THE UNITED STATES OF...
...JAPAN!!!
SWISH

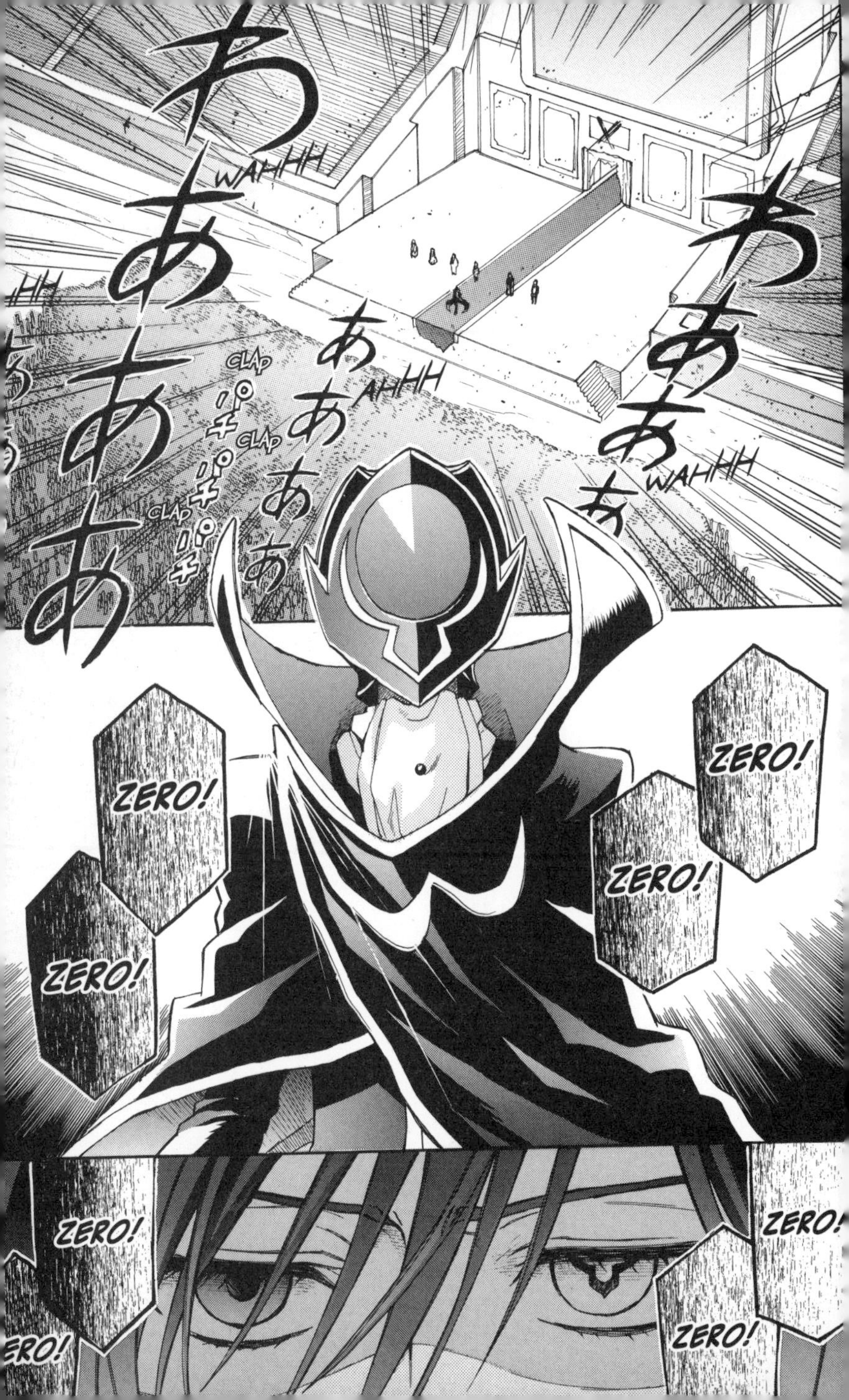

WAHHH
AHHH
CLAP
CLAP
CLAP
WAHHH
ZERO!
ZERO!
ZERO!
ZERO!
ZERO!
ZERO!
ZERO!

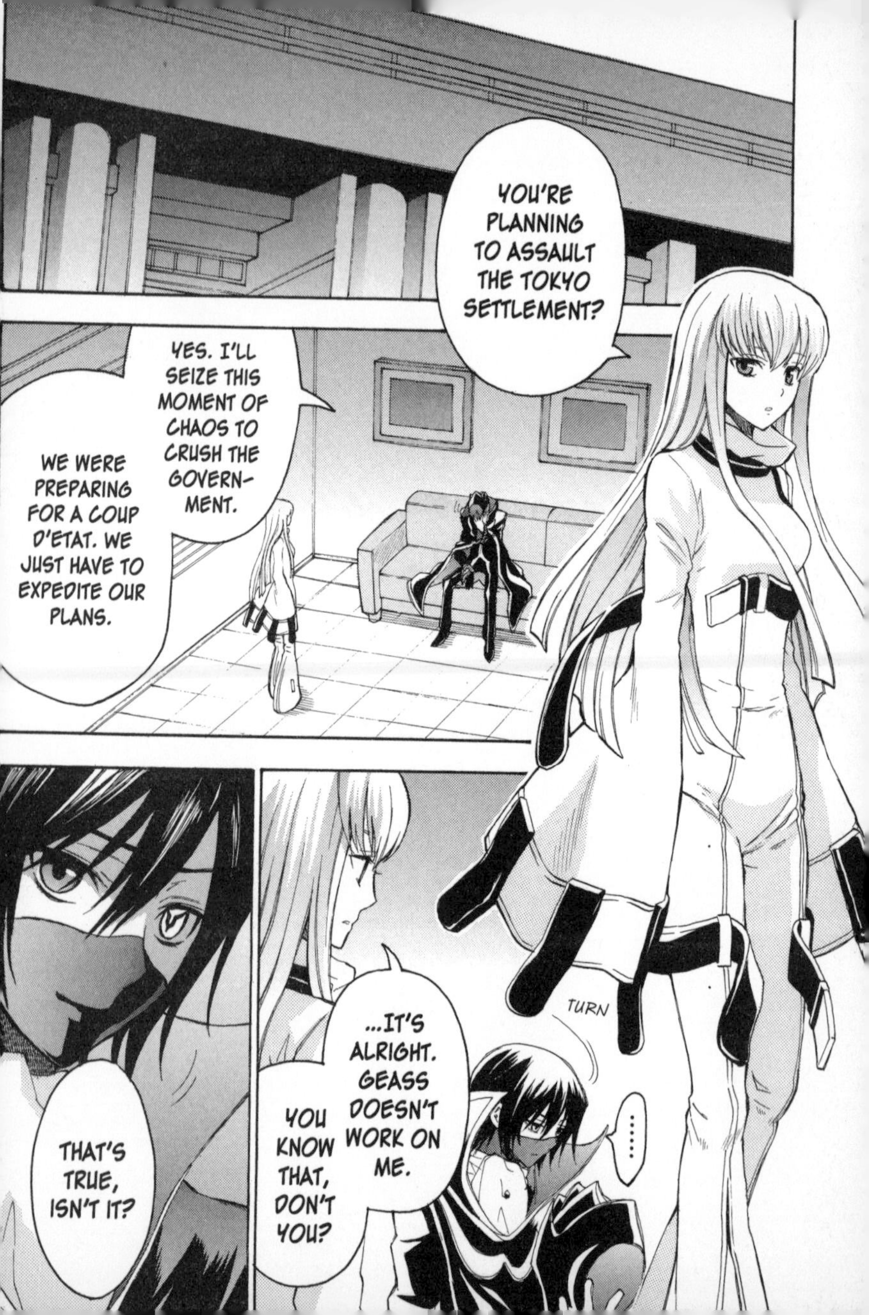

YOU'RE PLANNING TO ASSAULT THE TOKYO SETTLEMENT?
YES. I'LL SEIZE THIS MOMENT OF CHAOS TO CRUSH THE GOVERN-MENT.
WE WERE PREPARING FOR A COUP D'ETAT. WE JUST HAVE TO EXPEDITE OUR PLANS.
TURN
......
...IT'S ALRIGHT. GEASS DOESN'T WORK ON ME.
YOU KNOW THAT, DON'T YOU?
THAT'S TRUE, ISN'T IT?

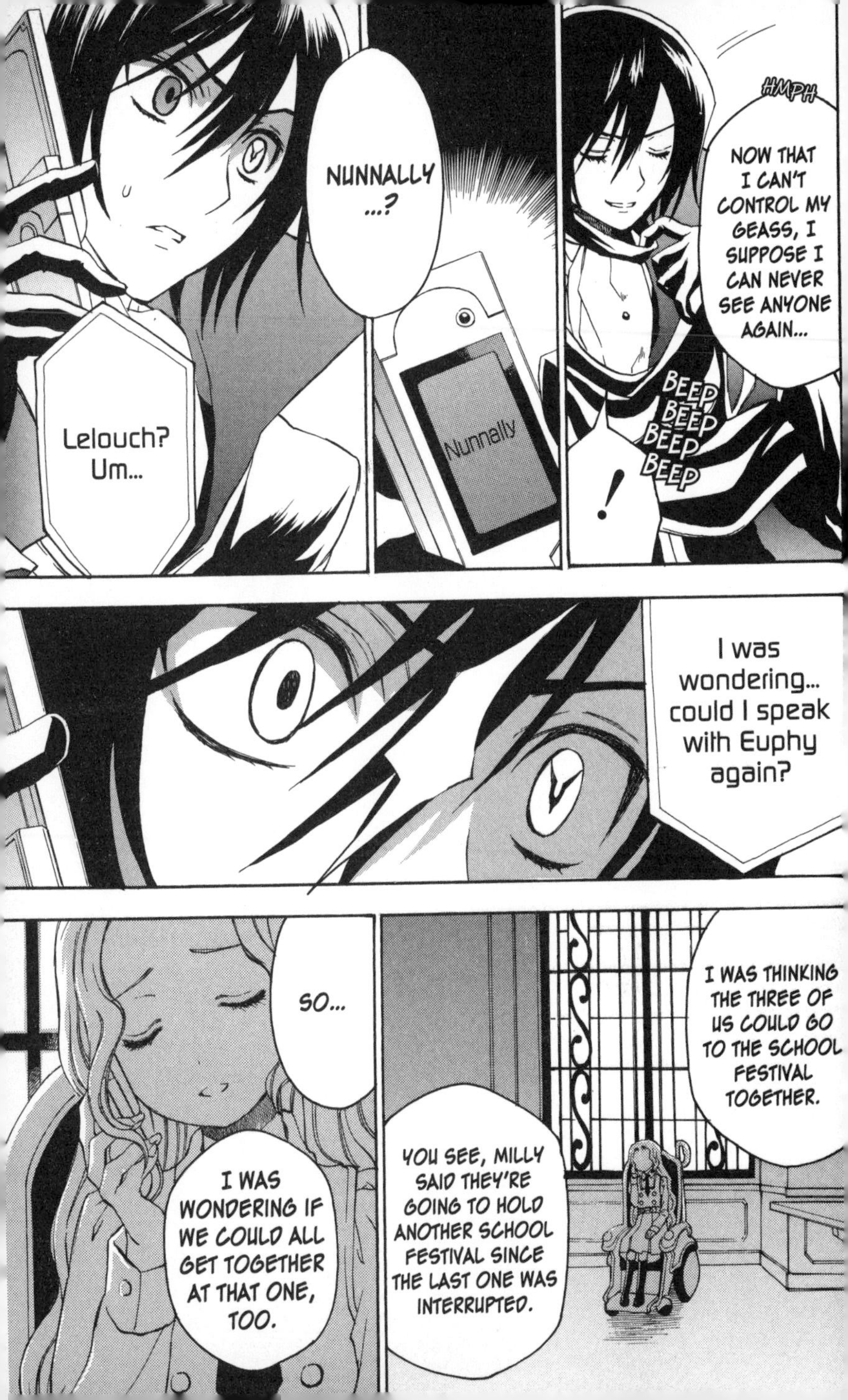
HMPH
NOW THAT I CAN'T CONTROL MY GEASS, I SUPPOSE I CAN NEVER SEE ANYONE AGAIN...
BEEP BEEP BEEP BEEP
!
Nunnally
NUNNALLY ...?
Lelouch? Um...
I was wondering... could I speak with Euphy again?
I WAS THINKING THE THREE OF US COULD GO TO THE SCHOOL FESTIVAL TOGETHER.
YOU SEE, MILLY SAID THEY'RE GOING TO HOLD ANOTHER SCHOOL FESTIVAL SINCE THE LAST ONE WAS INTERRUPTED.
SO...
I WAS WONDERING IF WE COULD ALL GET TOGETHER AT THAT ONE, TOO.

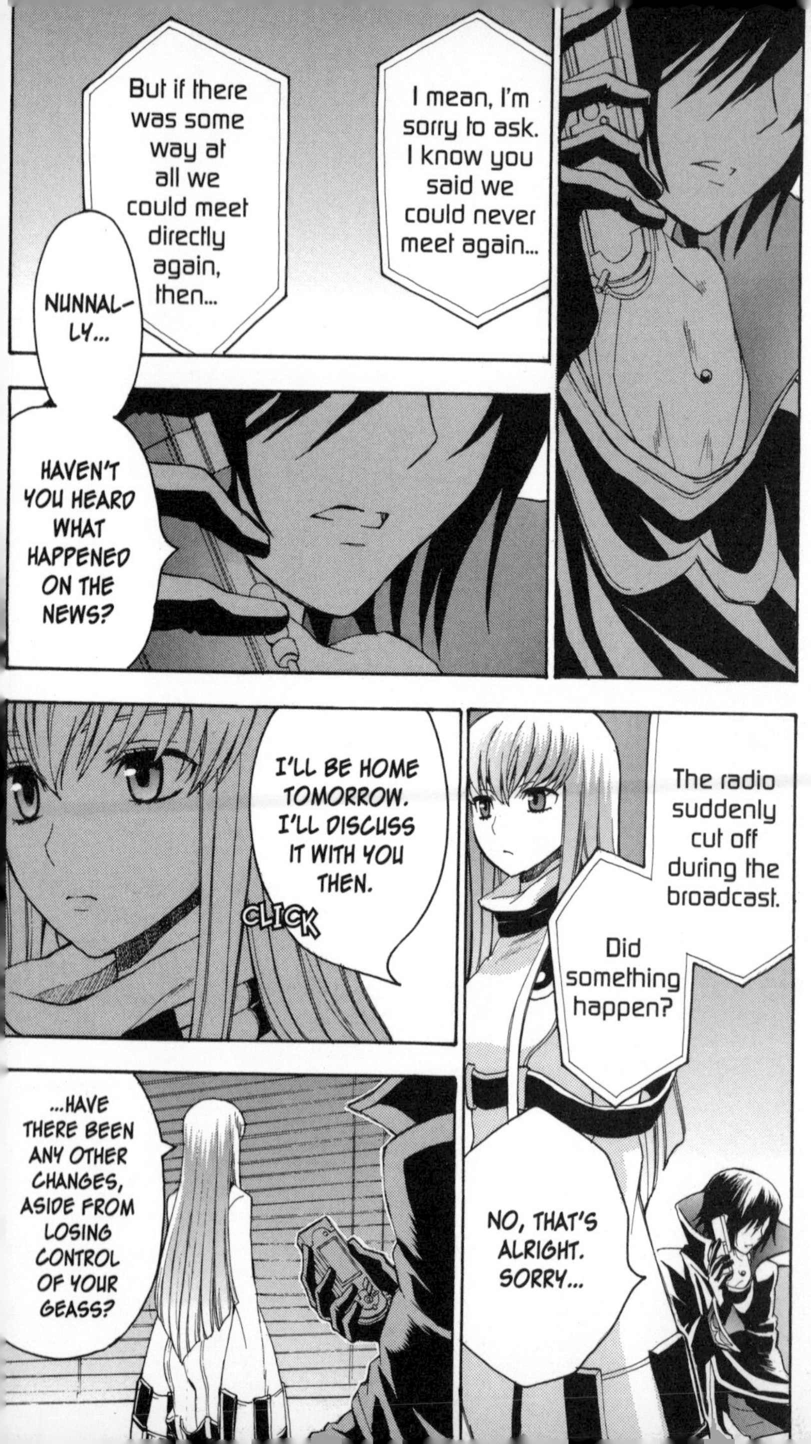

I mean, I'm sorry to ask. I know you said we could never meet again...
But if there was some way at all we could meet directly again, then...
NUNNALLY...
HAVEN'T YOU HEARD WHAT HAPPENED ON THE NEWS?
The radio suddenly cut off during the broadcast.
Did something happen?
NO, THAT'S ALRIGHT. SORRY...
I'LL BE HOME TOMORROW. I'LL DISCUSS IT WITH YOU THEN.
CLICK
...HAVE THERE BEEN ANY OTHER CHANGES, ASIDE FROM LOSING CONTROL OF YOUR GEASS?

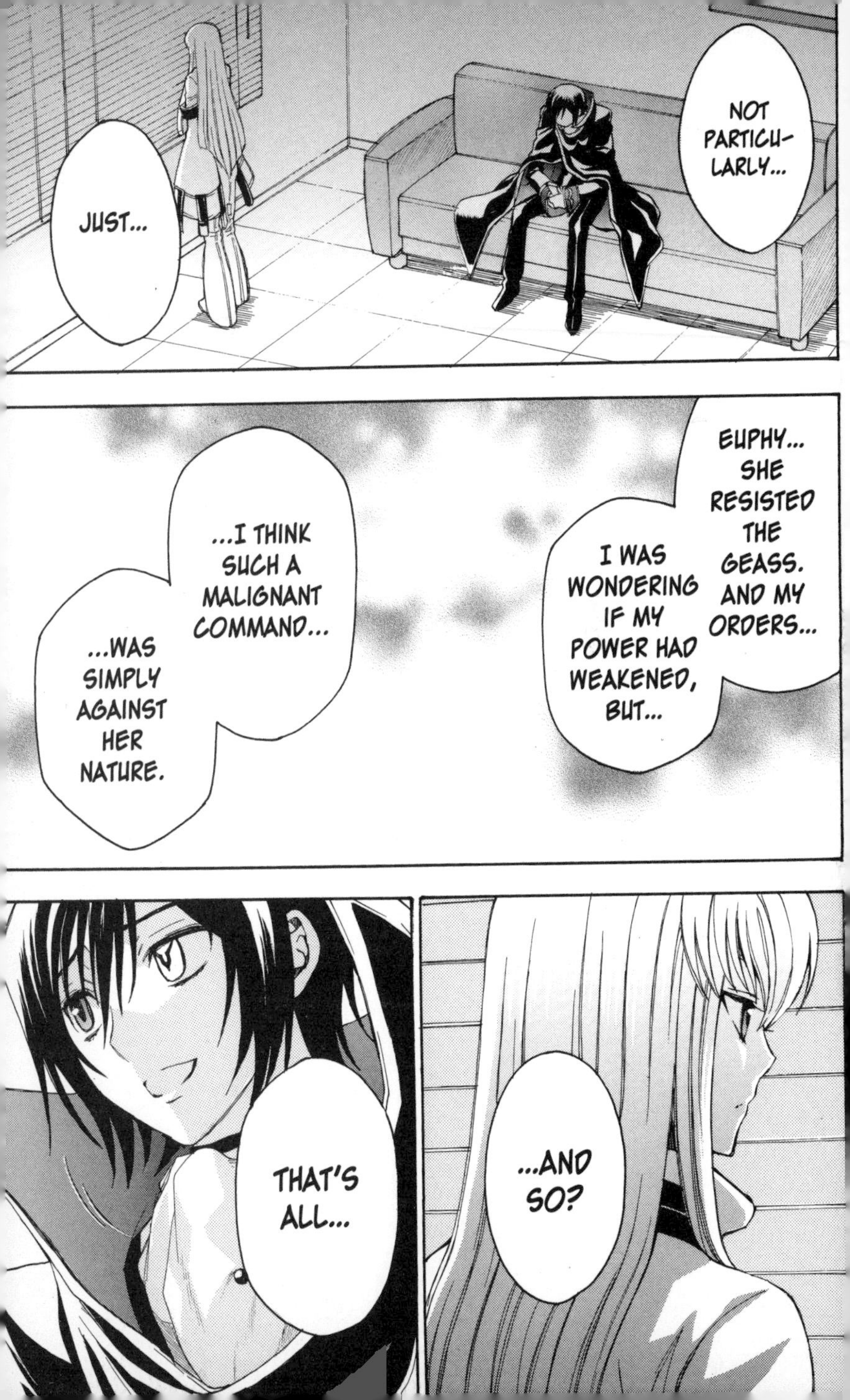
NOT PARTICU-LARLY...
JUST...
EUPHY... SHE RESISTED THE GEASS. AND MY ORDERS...
I WAS WONDERING IF MY POWER HAD WEAKENED, BUT...
...I THINK SUCH A MALIGNANT COMMAND...
...WAS SIMPLY AGAINST HER NATURE.
...AND SO?
THAT'S ALL...

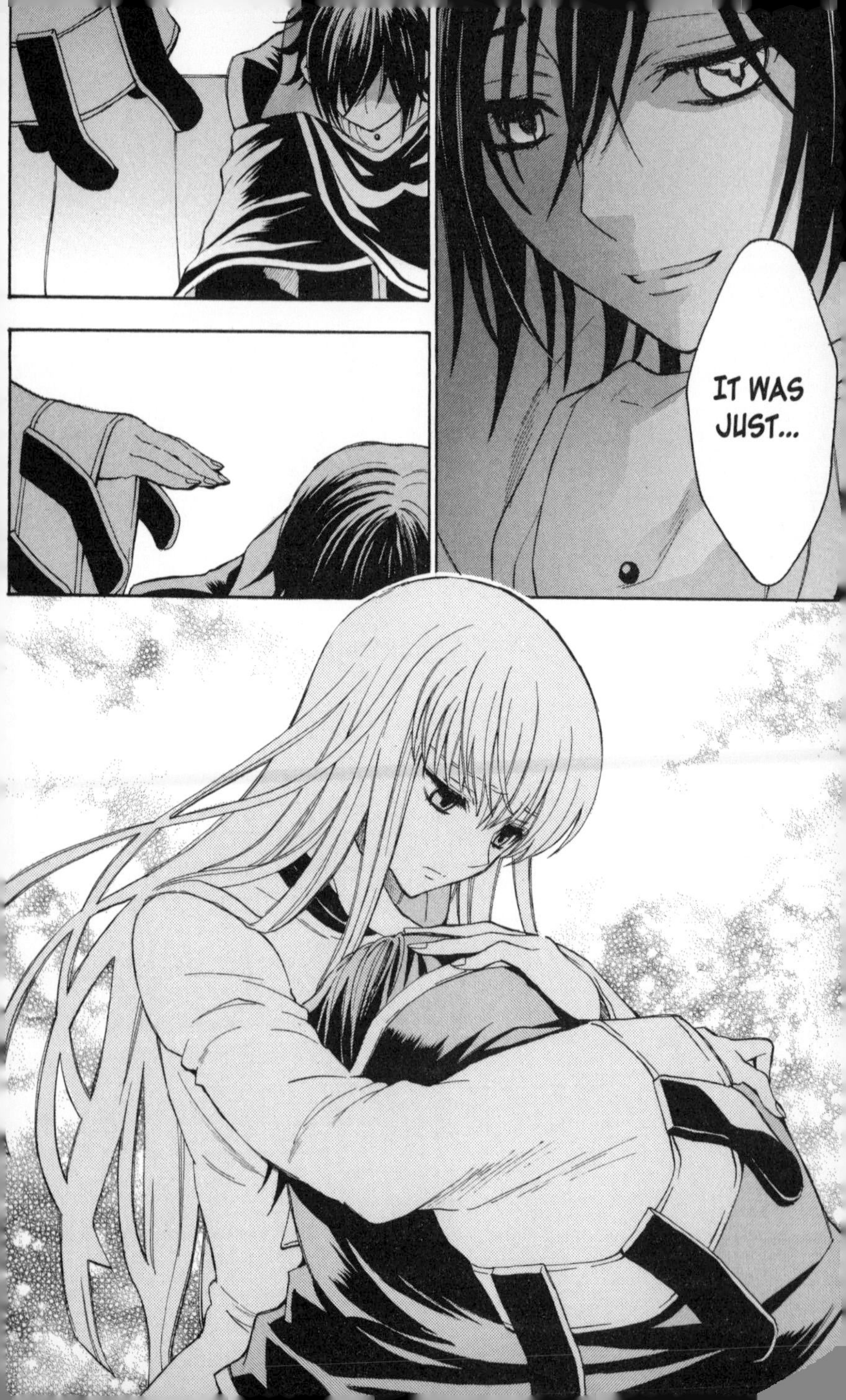
IT WAS JUST...

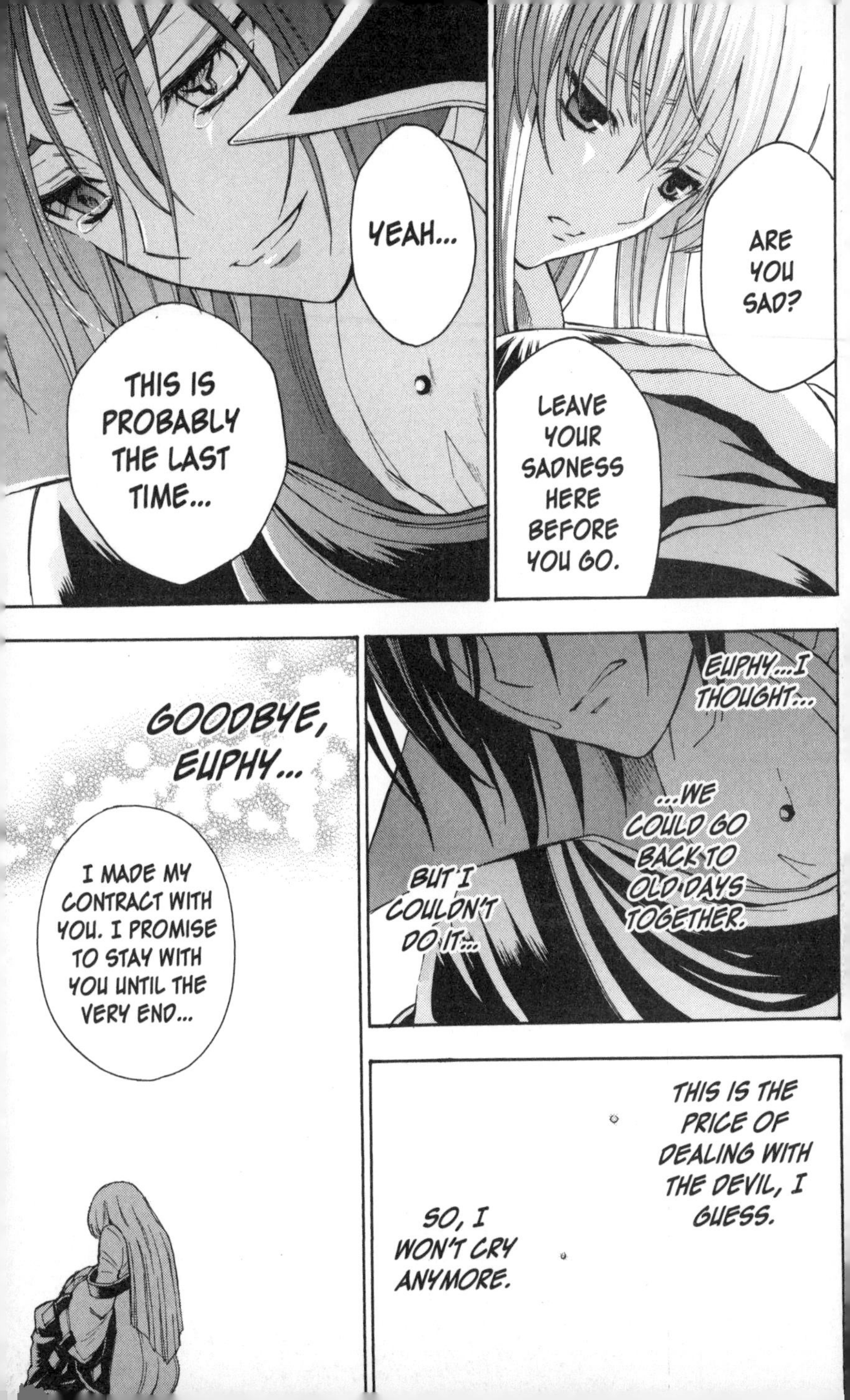
ARE YOU SAD?
LEAVE YOUR SADNESS HERE BEFORE YOU GO.
YEAH...
THIS IS PROBABLY THE LAST TIME...
EUPHY...I THOUGHT...
...WE COULD GO BACK TO OLD DAYS TOGETHER.
BUT I COULDN'T DO IT...
THIS IS THE PRICE OF DEALING WITH THE DEVIL, I GUESS.
SO, I WON'T CRY ANYMORE.
GOODBYE, EUPHY...
I MADE MY CONTRACT WITH YOU. I PROMISE TO STAY WITH YOU UNTIL THE VERY END...

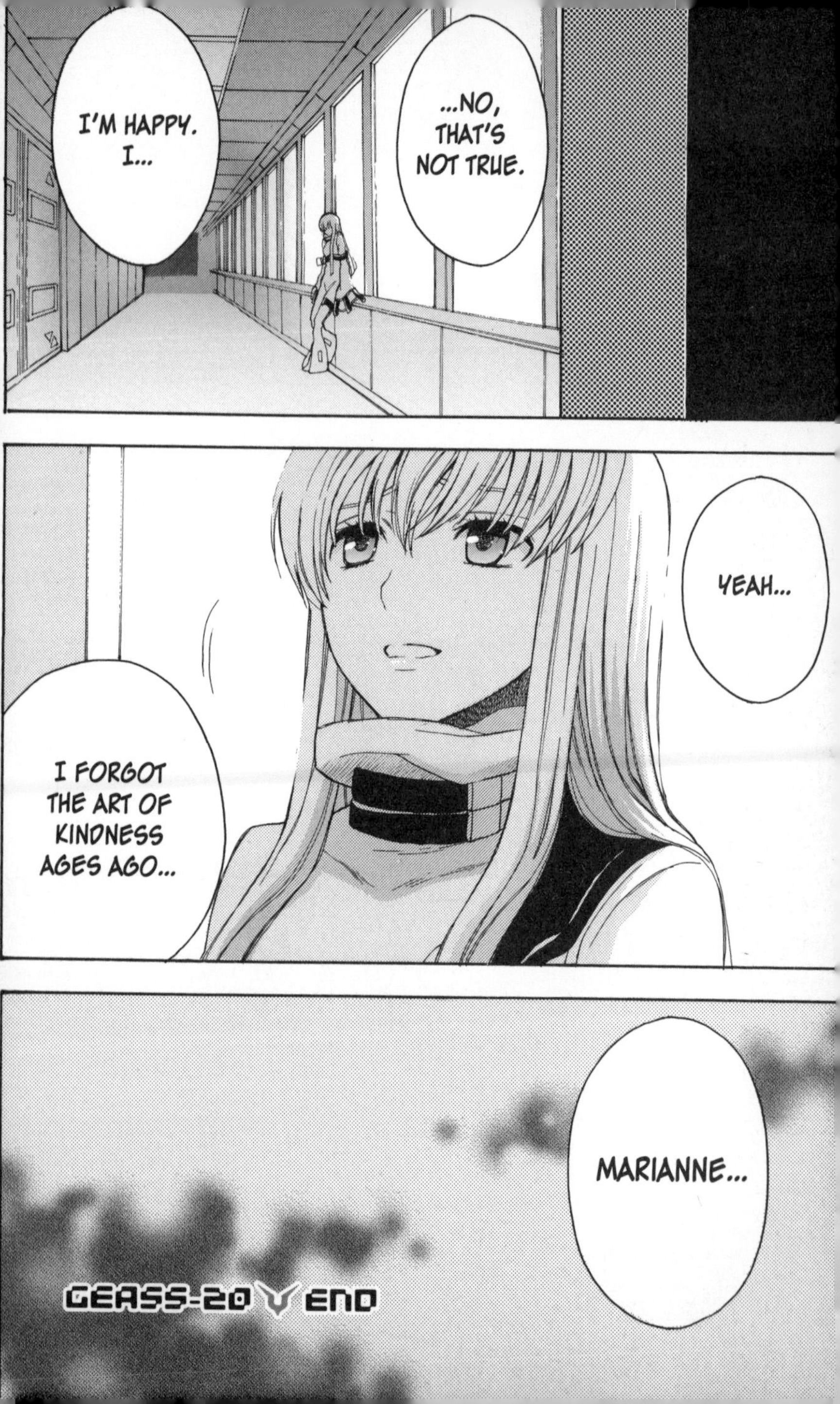
...NO, THAT'S NOT TRUE.
I'M HAPPY. I...
YEAH...
I FORGOT THE ART OF KINDNESS AGES AGO...
MARIANNE...
GEASS-20 END

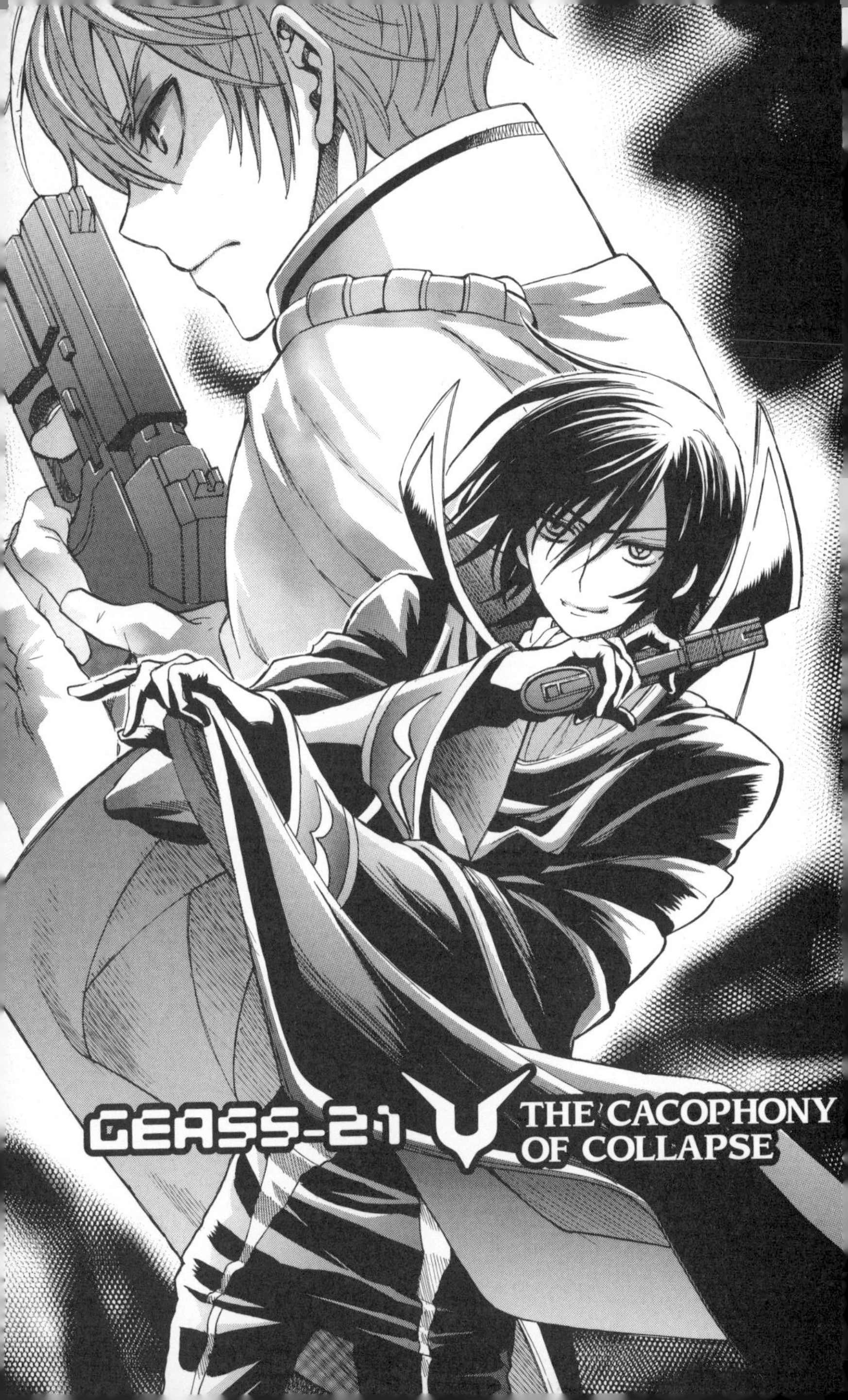
GEASS-21
THE CACOPHONY OF COLLAPSE

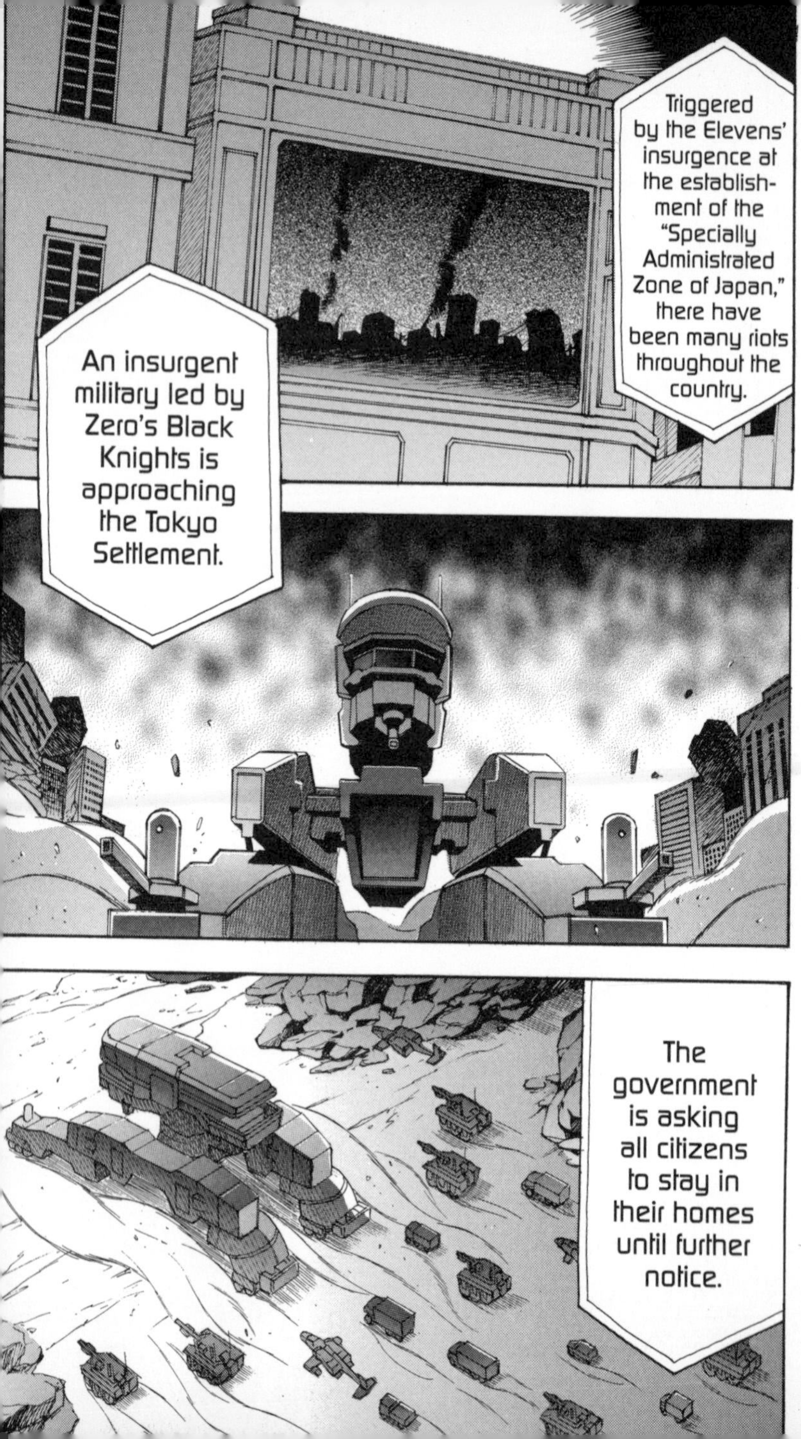
Triggered by the Elevens' insurgence at the establishment of the "Specially Administrated Zone of Japan," there have been many riots throughout the country.
An insurgent military led by Zero's Black Knights is approaching the Tokyo Settlement.
The government is asking all citizens to stay in their homes until further notice.

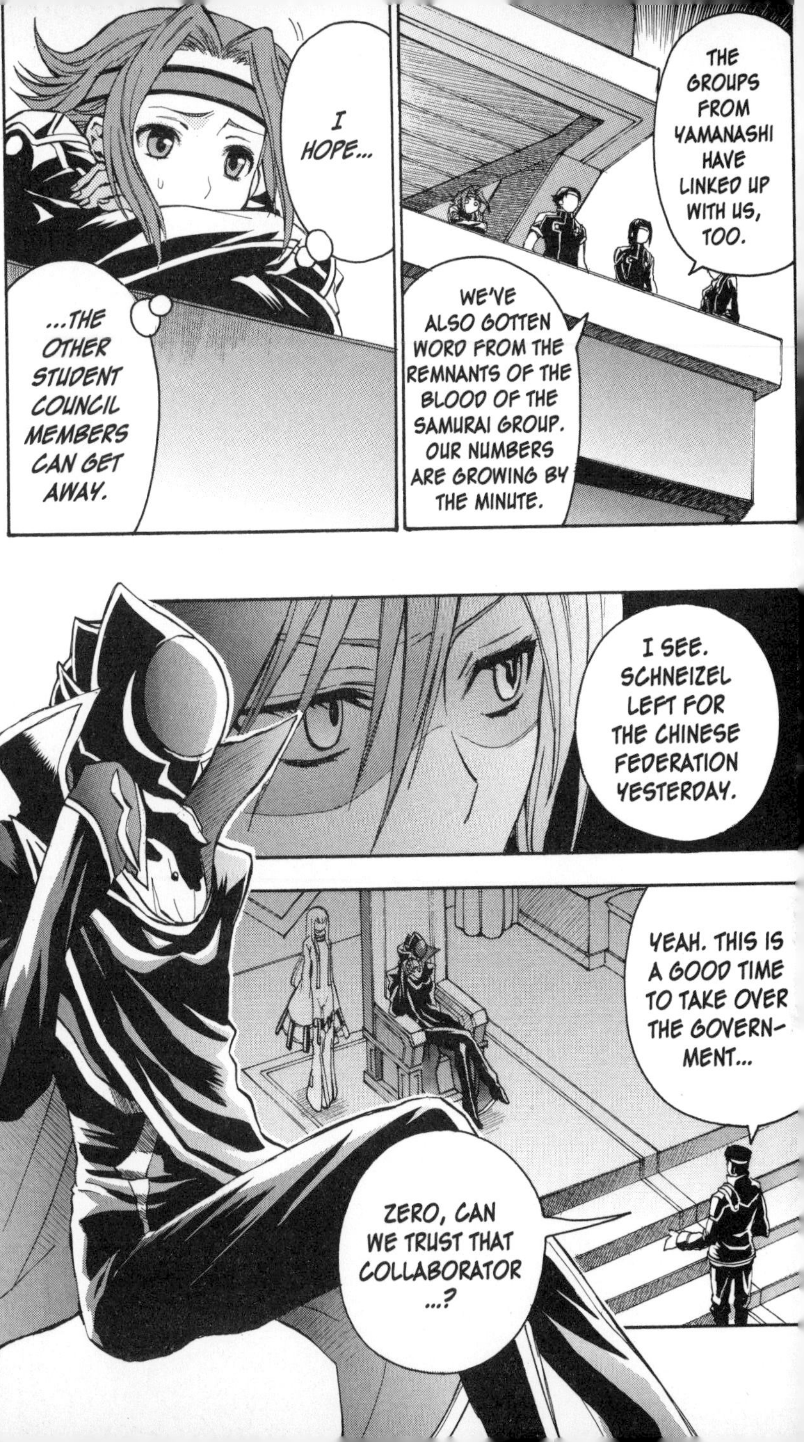
THE GROUPS FROM YAMANASHI HAVE LINKED UP WITH US, TOO.
WE'VE ALSO GOTTEN WORD FROM THE REMNANTS OF THE BLOOD OF THE SAMURAI GROUP. OUR NUMBERS ARE GROWING BY THE MINUTE.
I HOPE...
...THE OTHER STUDENT COUNCIL MEMBERS CAN GET AWAY.
I SEE. SCHNEIZEL LEFT FOR THE CHINESE FEDERATION YESTERDAY.
YEAH. THIS IS A GOOD TIME TO TAKE OVER THE GOVERN-MENT...
ZERO, CAN WE TRUST THAT COLLABORATOR ...?

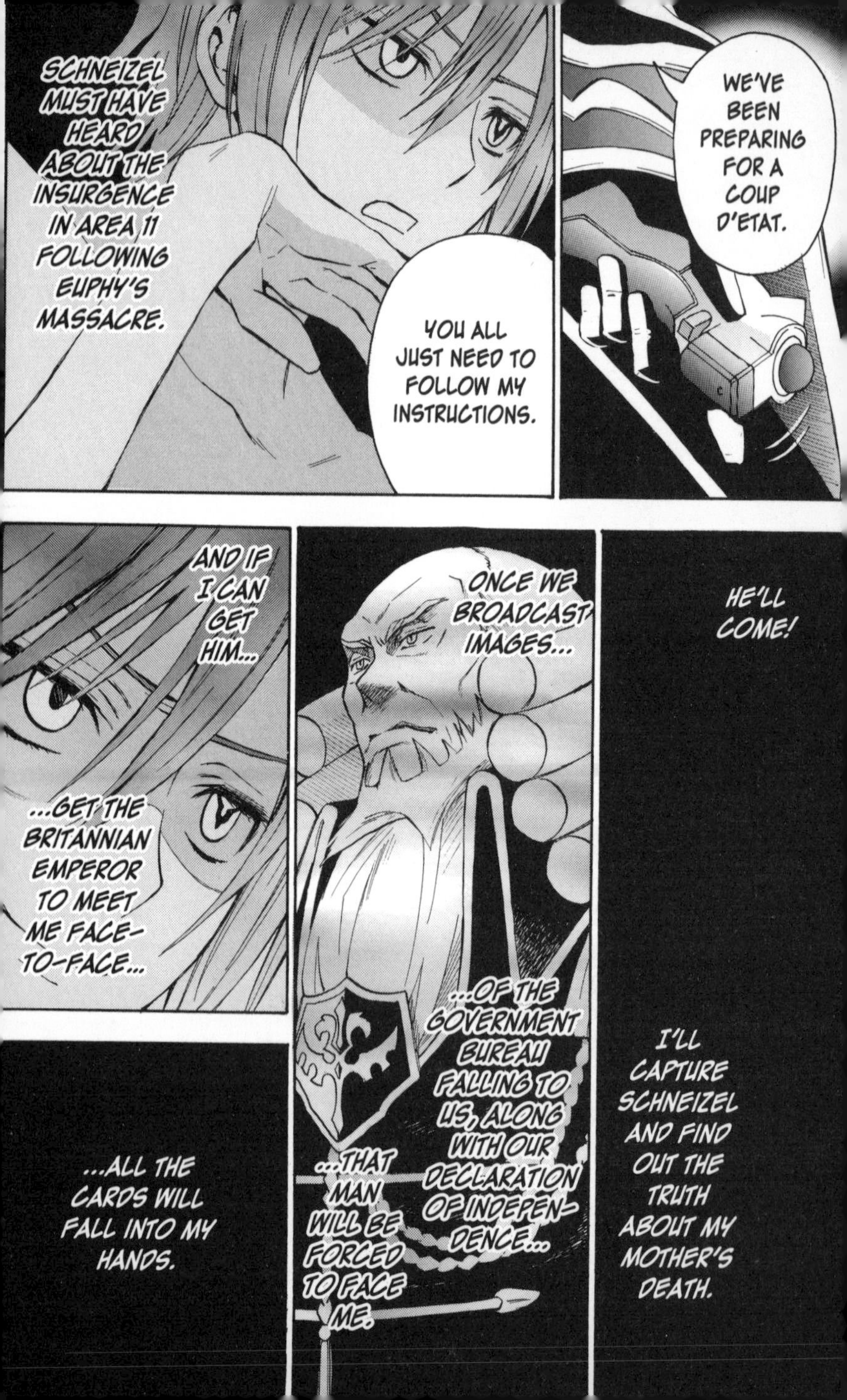
WE'VE BEEN PREPARING FOR A COUP D'ETAT.
YOU ALL JUST NEED TO FOLLOW MY INSTRUCTIONS.
SCHNEIZEL MUST HAVE HEARD ABOUT THE INSURGENCE IN AREA 11 FOLLOWING EUPHY'S MASSACRE.
HE'LL COME!
I'LL CAPTURE SCHNEIZEL AND FIND OUT THE TRUTH ABOUT MY MOTHER'S DEATH.
ONCE WE BROADCAST IMAGES...
...OF THE GOVERNMENT BUREAU FALLING TO US, ALONG WITH OUR DECLARATION OF INDEPEN-DENCE...
...THAT MAN WILL BE FORCED TO FACE ME.
AND IF I CAN GET HIM...
...GET THE BRITANNIAN EMPEROR TO MEET ME FACE-TO-FACE...
...ALL THE CARDS WILL FALL INTO MY HANDS.

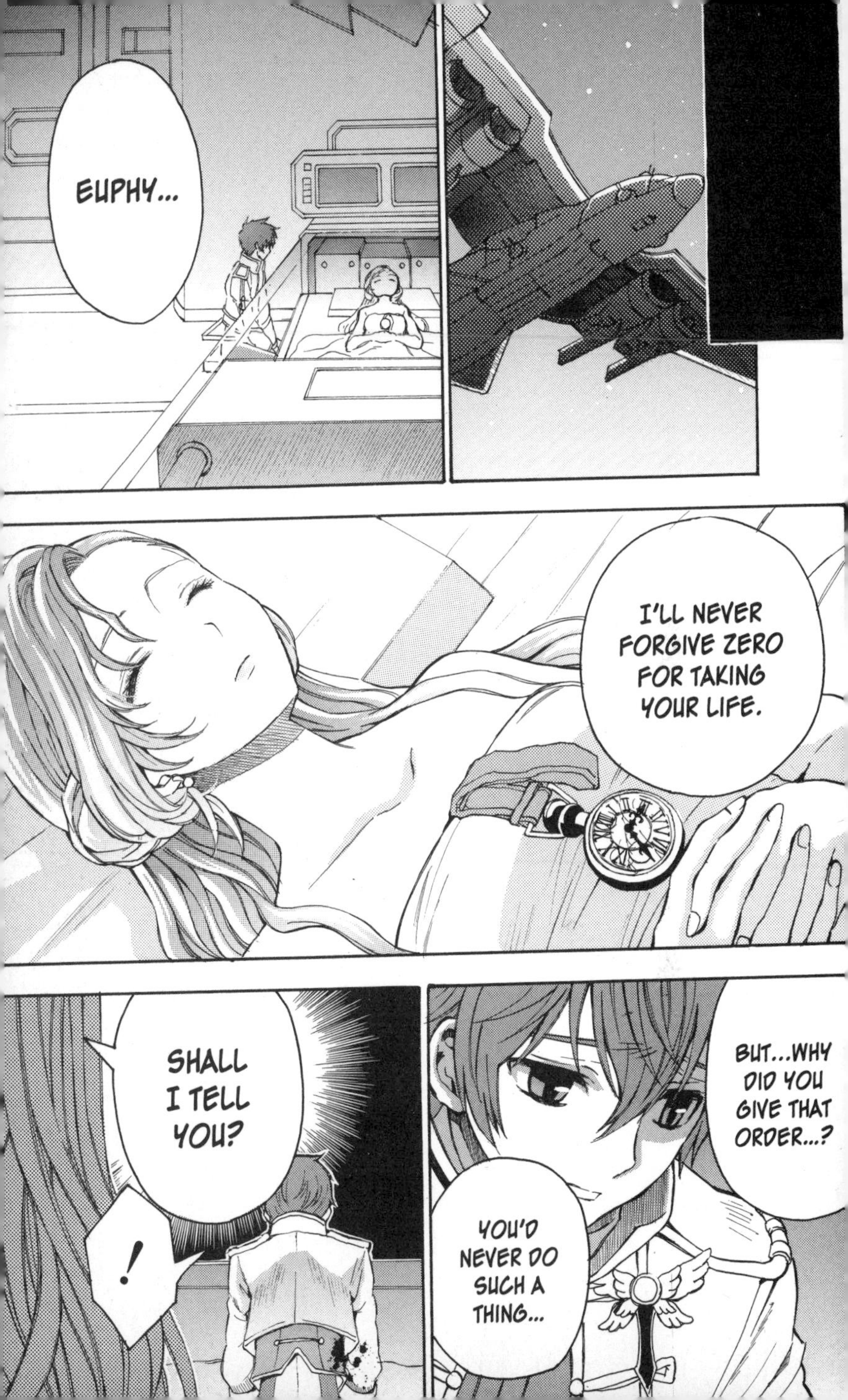
EUPHY...
I'LL NEVER FORGIVE ZERO FOR TAKING YOUR LIFE.
BUT...WHY DID YOU GIVE THAT ORDER...?
YOU'D NEVER DO SUCH A THING...
SHALL I TELL YOU?
!

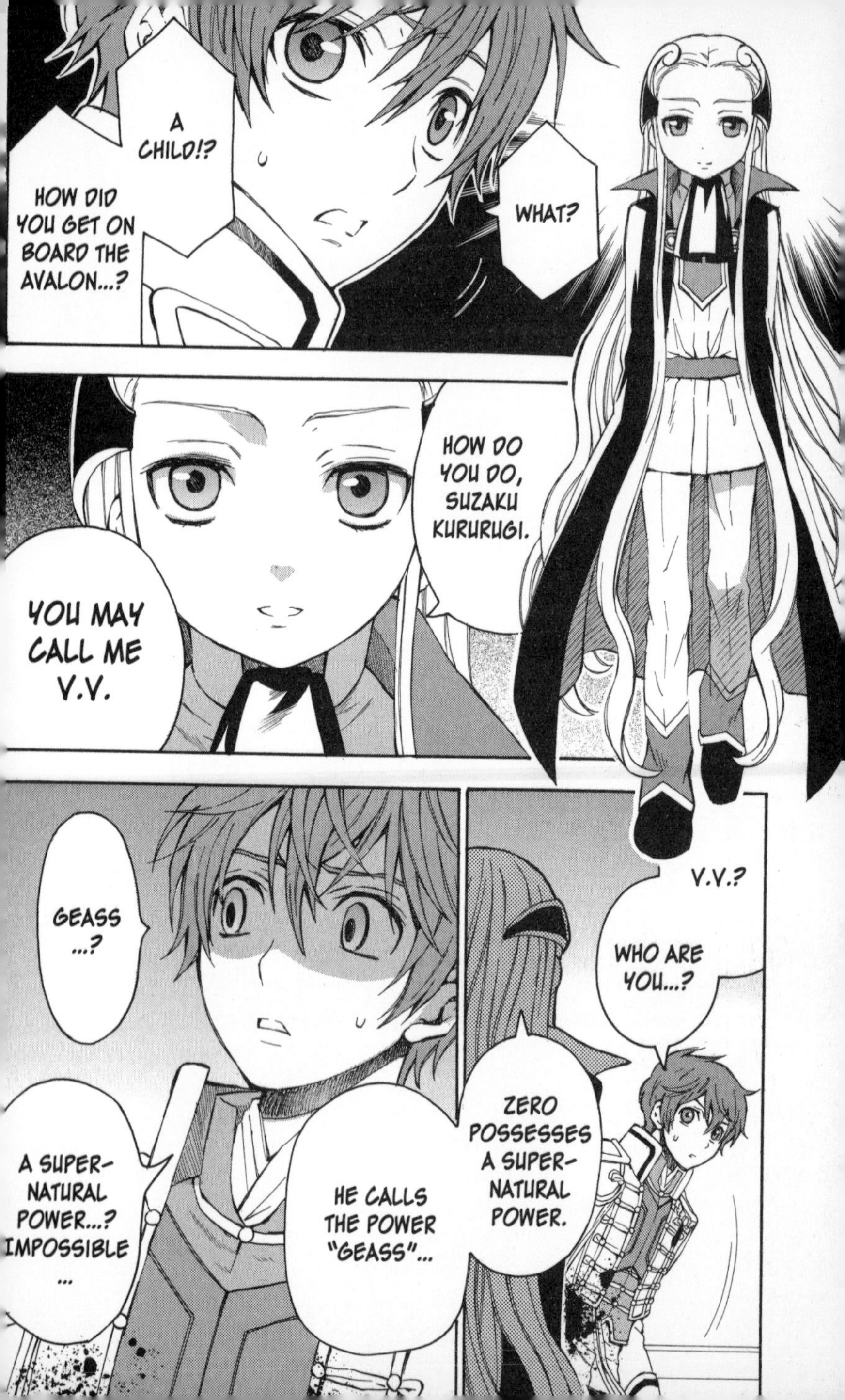
WHAT?
A CHILD!?
HOW DID YOU GET ON BOARD THE AVALON...?
HOW DO YOU DO, SUZAKU KURURUGI.
YOU MAY CALL ME V.V.
V.V.?
WHO ARE YOU...?
ZERO POSSESSES A SUPER-NATURAL POWER.
HE CALLS THE POWER "GEASS"...
GEASS ...?
A SUPER-NATURAL POWER...? IMPOSSIBLE ...

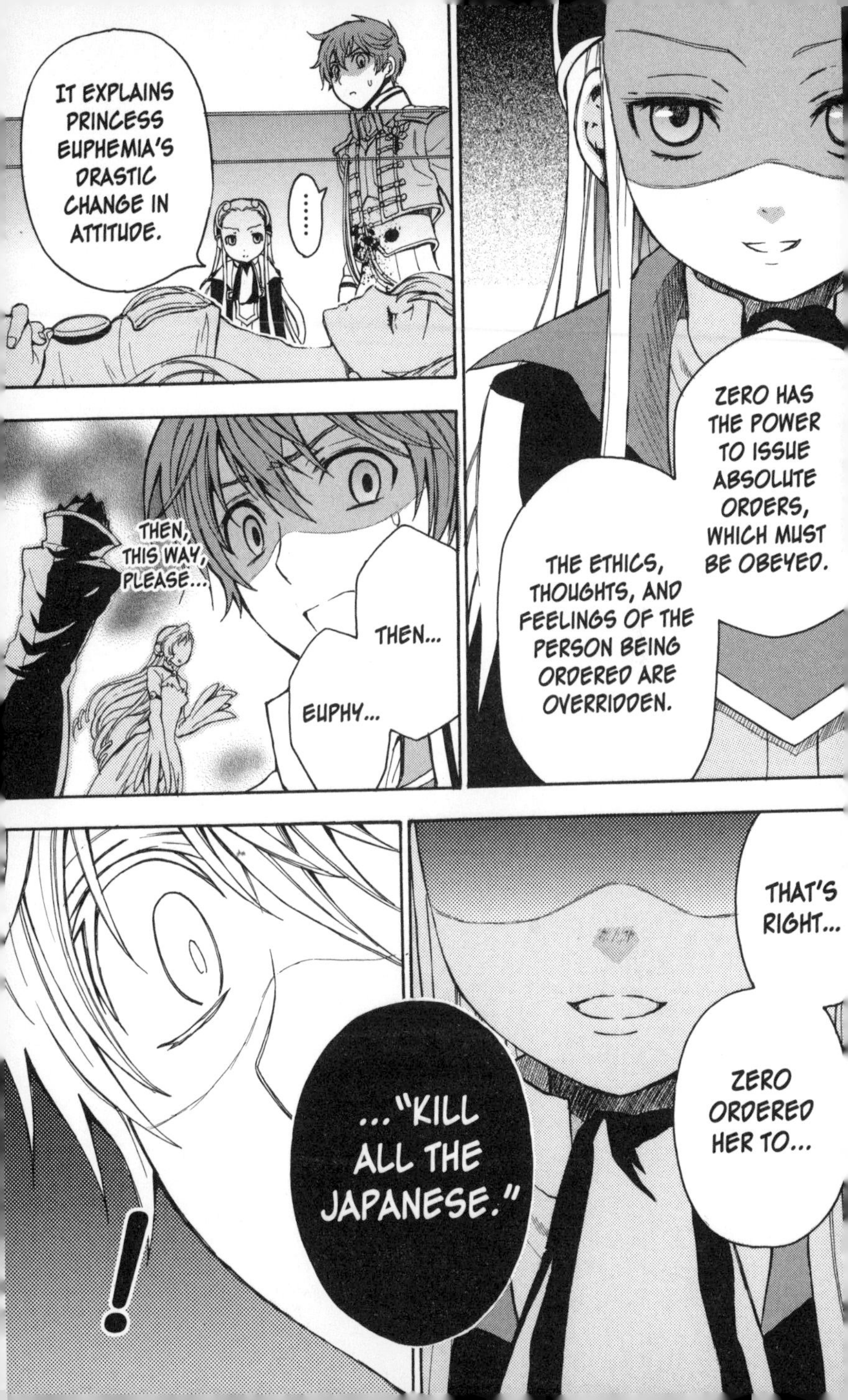
ZERO HAS THE POWER TO ISSUE ABSOLUTE ORDERS, WHICH MUST BE OBEYED.
THE ETHICS, THOUGHTS, AND FEELINGS OF THE PERSON BEING ORDERED ARE OVERRIDDEN.
IT EXPLAINS PRINCESS EUPHEMIA'S DRASTIC CHANGE IN ATTITUDE.
......
THEN...
EUPHY...
THEN, THIS WAY, PLEASE...
THAT'S RIGHT...
ZERO ORDERED HER TO...
..."KILL ALL THE JAPANESE."
!

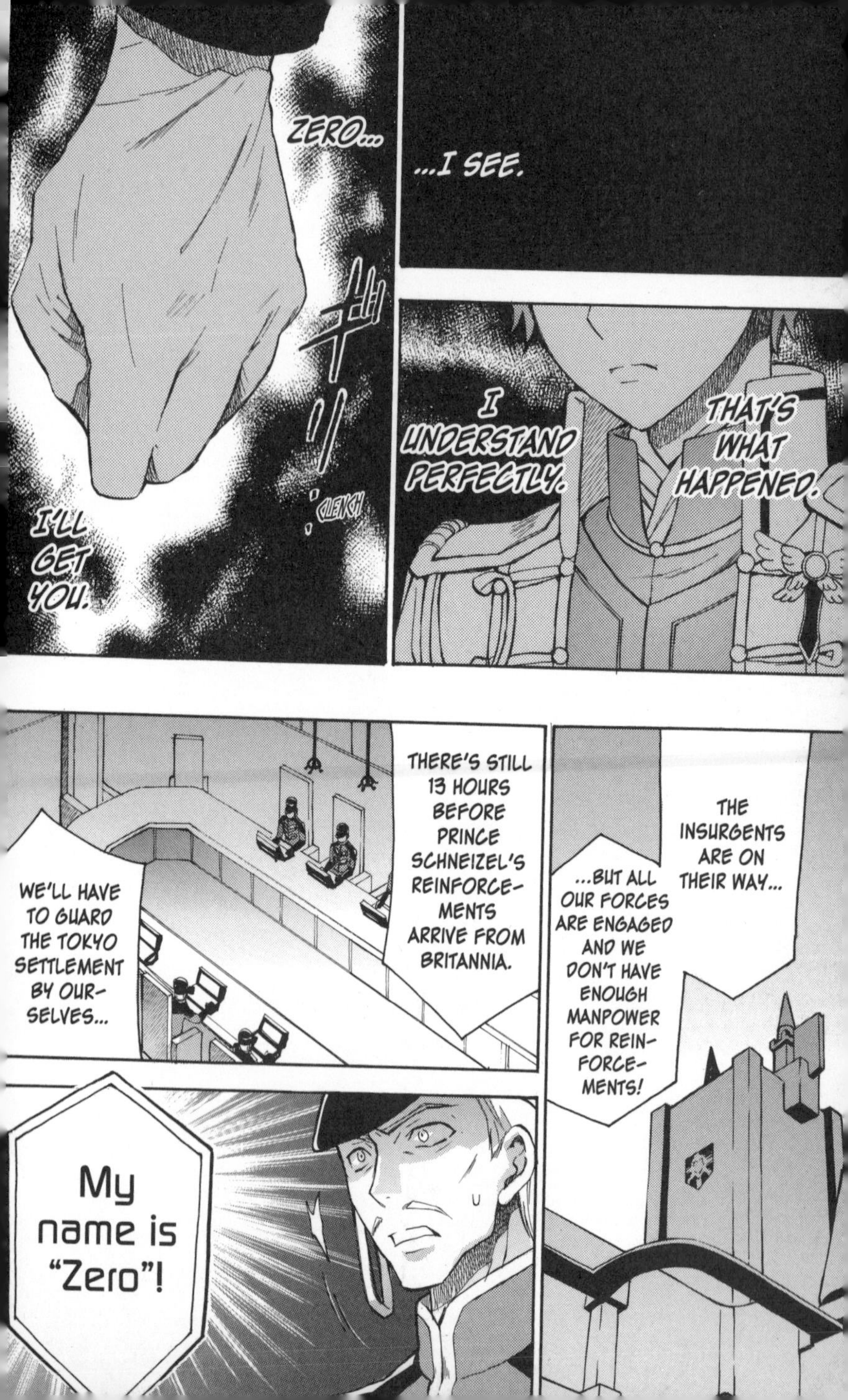
...I SEE.
THAT'S WHAT HAPPENED.
I UNDERSTAND PERFECTLY.
ZERO...
CLENCH
I'LL GET YOU.
THE INSURGENTS ARE ON THEIR WAY...
...BUT ALL OUR FORCES ARE ENGAGED AND WE DON'T HAVE ENOUGH MANPOWER FOR REIN-FORCE-MENTS!
THERE'S STILL 13 HOURS BEFORE PRINCE SCHNEIZEL'S REINFORCE-MENTS ARRIVE FROM BRITANNIA.
WE'LL HAVE TO GUARD THE TOKYO SETTLEMENT BY OUR-SELVES...
My name is "Zero"!

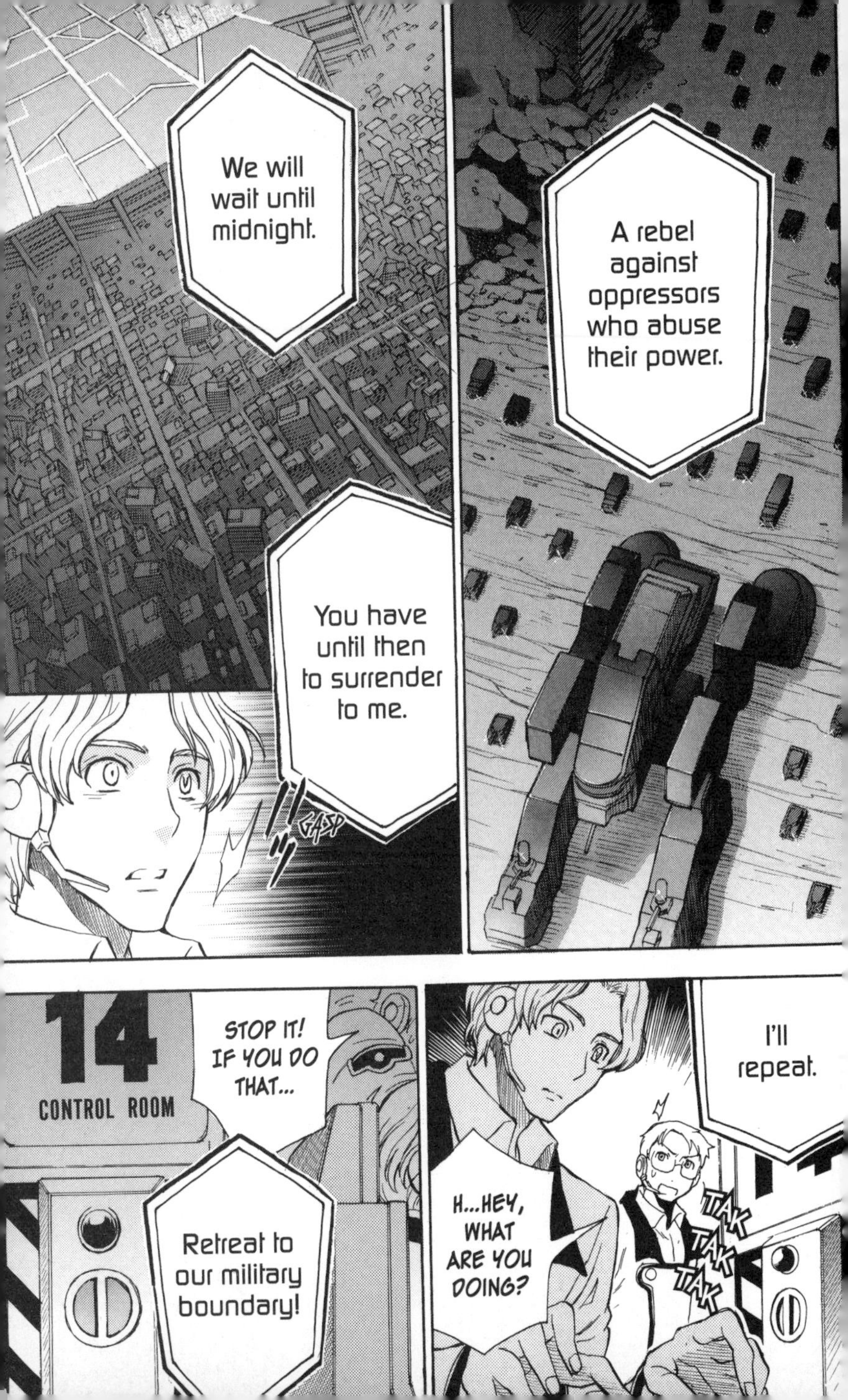
A rebel against oppressors who abuse their power.
We will wait until midnight.
You have until then to surrender to me.
GASP
I'll repeat.
H...HEY, WHAT ARE YOU DOING?
TAK TAK TAK
14
CONTROL ROOM
STOP IT! IF YOU DO THAT...
Retreat to our military boundary!

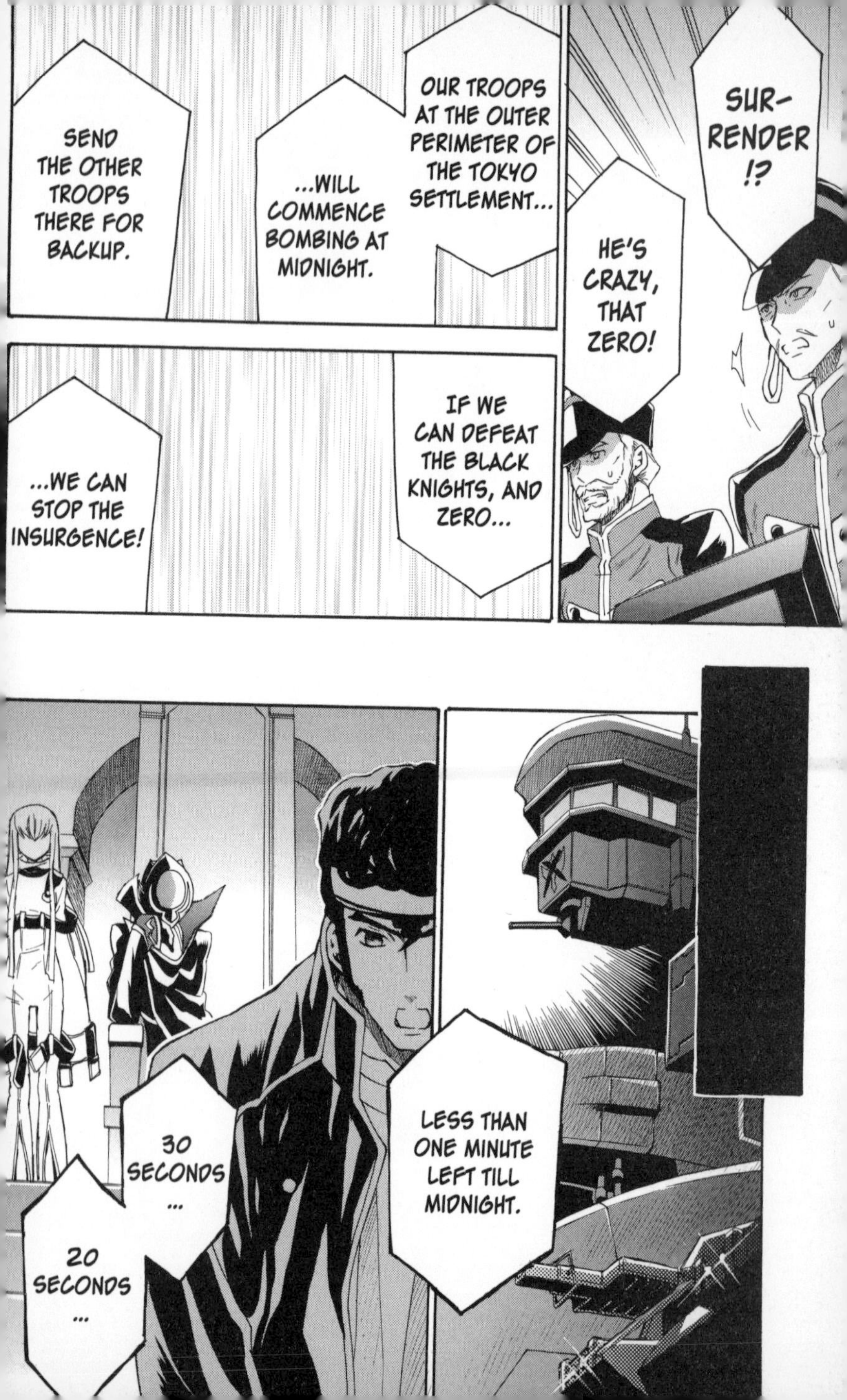
SUR-RENDER!?
HE'S CRAZY, THAT ZERO!
OUR TROOPS AT THE OUTER PERIMETER OF THE TOKYO SETTLEMENT...
...WILL COMMENCE BOMBING AT MIDNIGHT.
SEND THE OTHER TROOPS THERE FOR BACKUP.
IF WE CAN DEFEAT THE BLACK KNIGHTS, AND ZERO...
...WE CAN STOP THE INSURGENCE!
LESS THAN ONE MINUTE LEFT TILL MIDNIGHT.
30 SECONDS ...
20 SECONDS ...

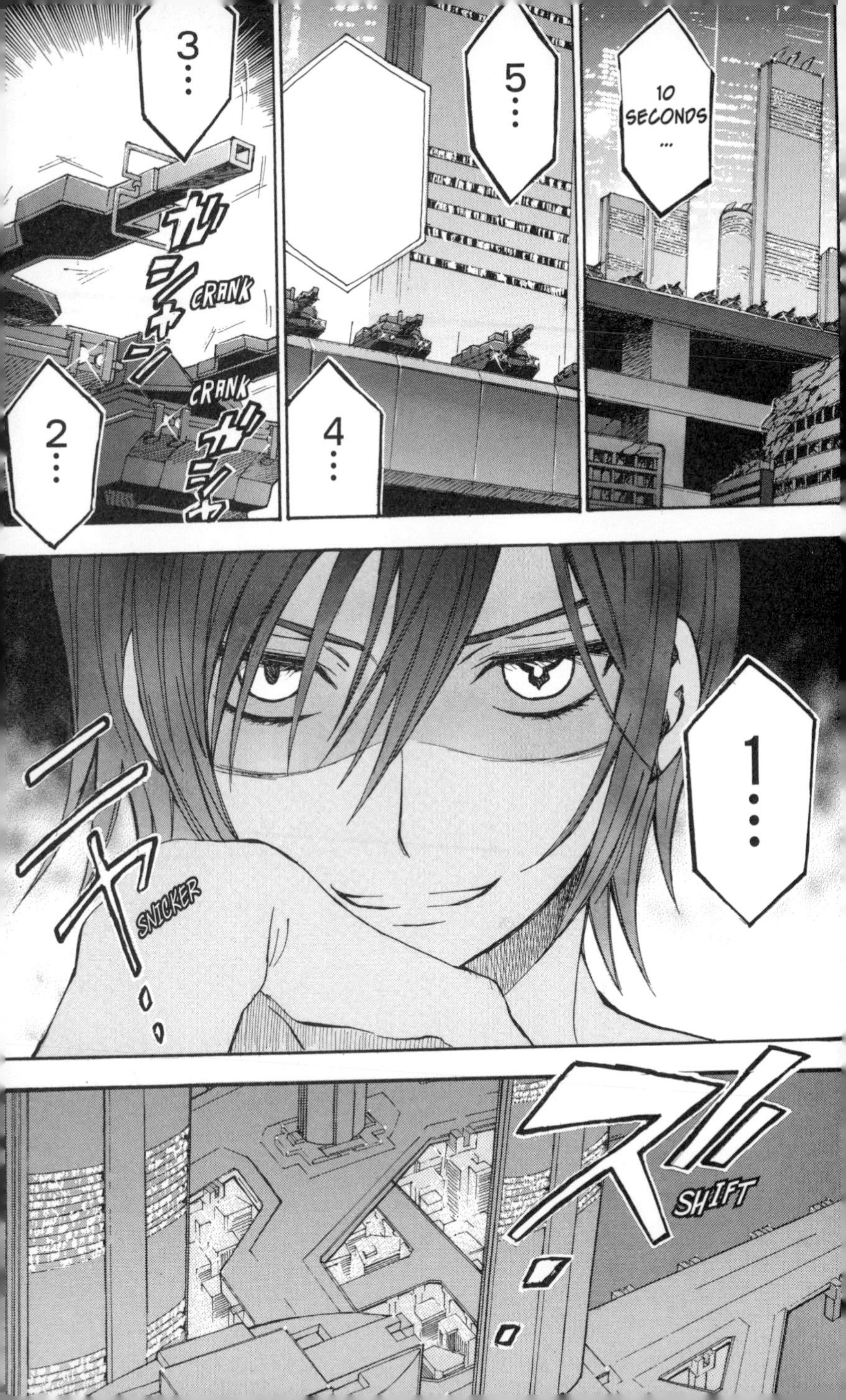
10 SECONDS ...
5...
4...
3...
CRANK
CRANK
2...
1...
SNICKER
SHIFT

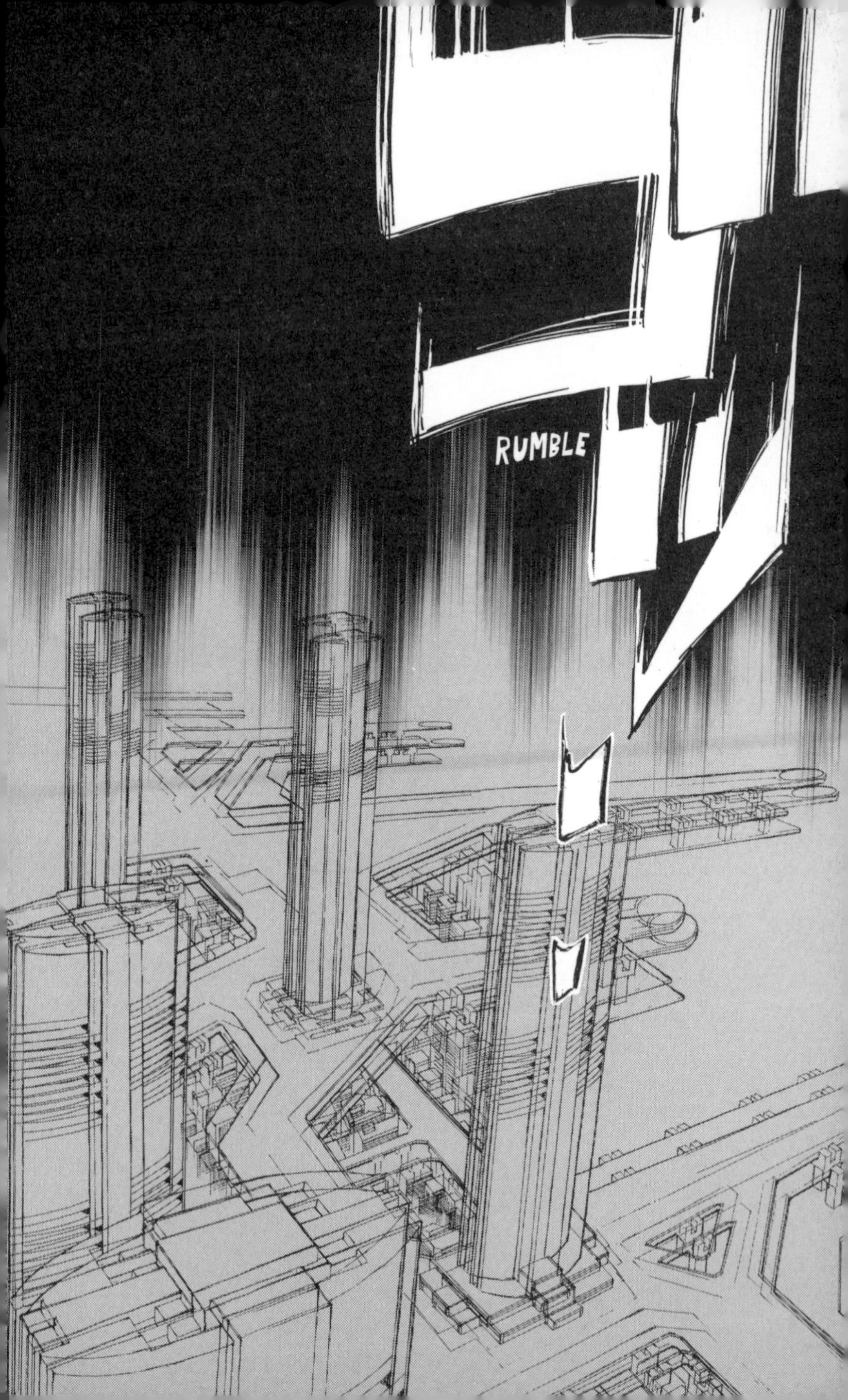
ゴゴゴ
RUMBLE

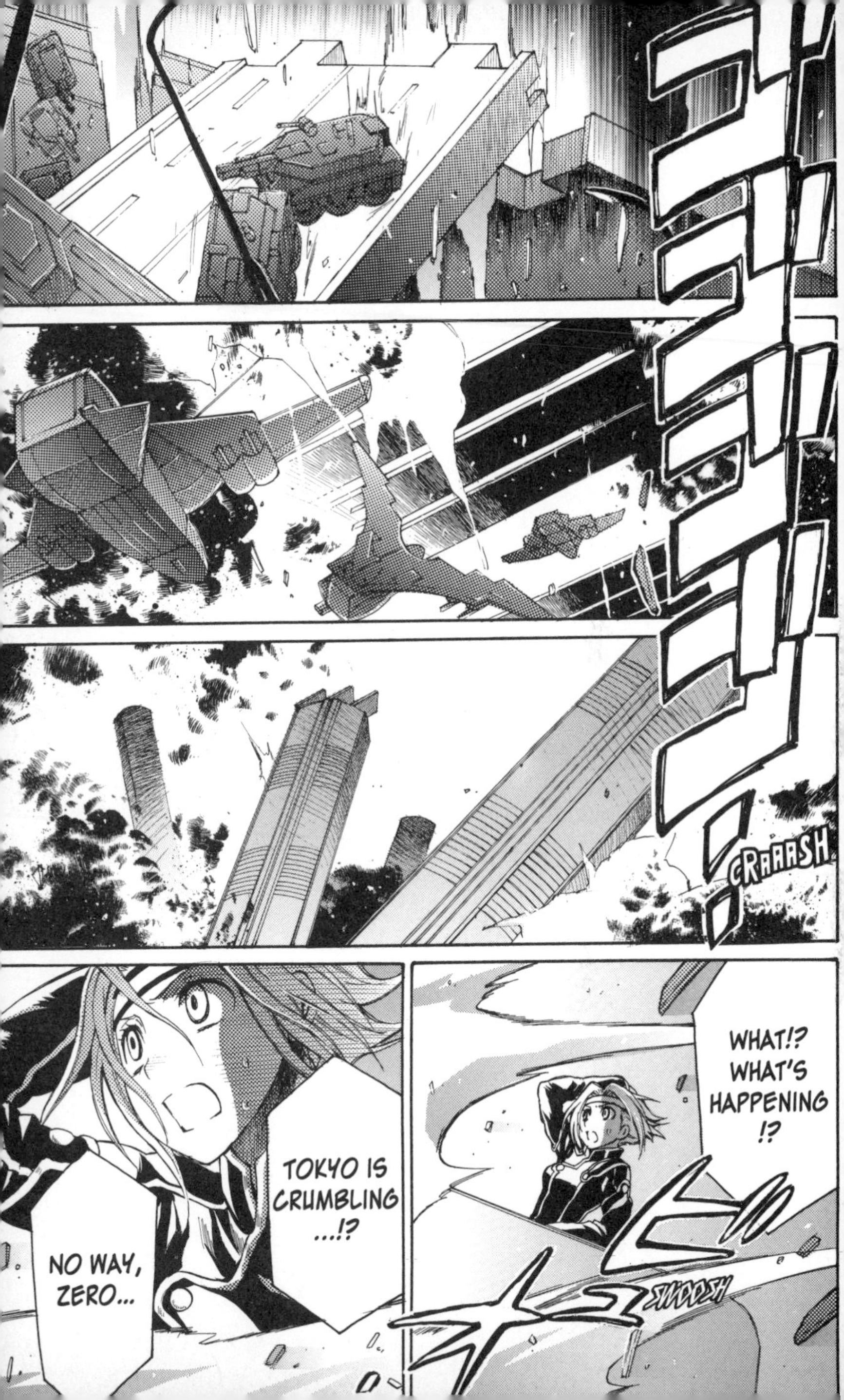
CRAAASH
WHAT!? WHAT'S HAPPENING !?
SWOOSH
TOKYO IS CRUMBLING ...!?
NO WAY, ZERO...

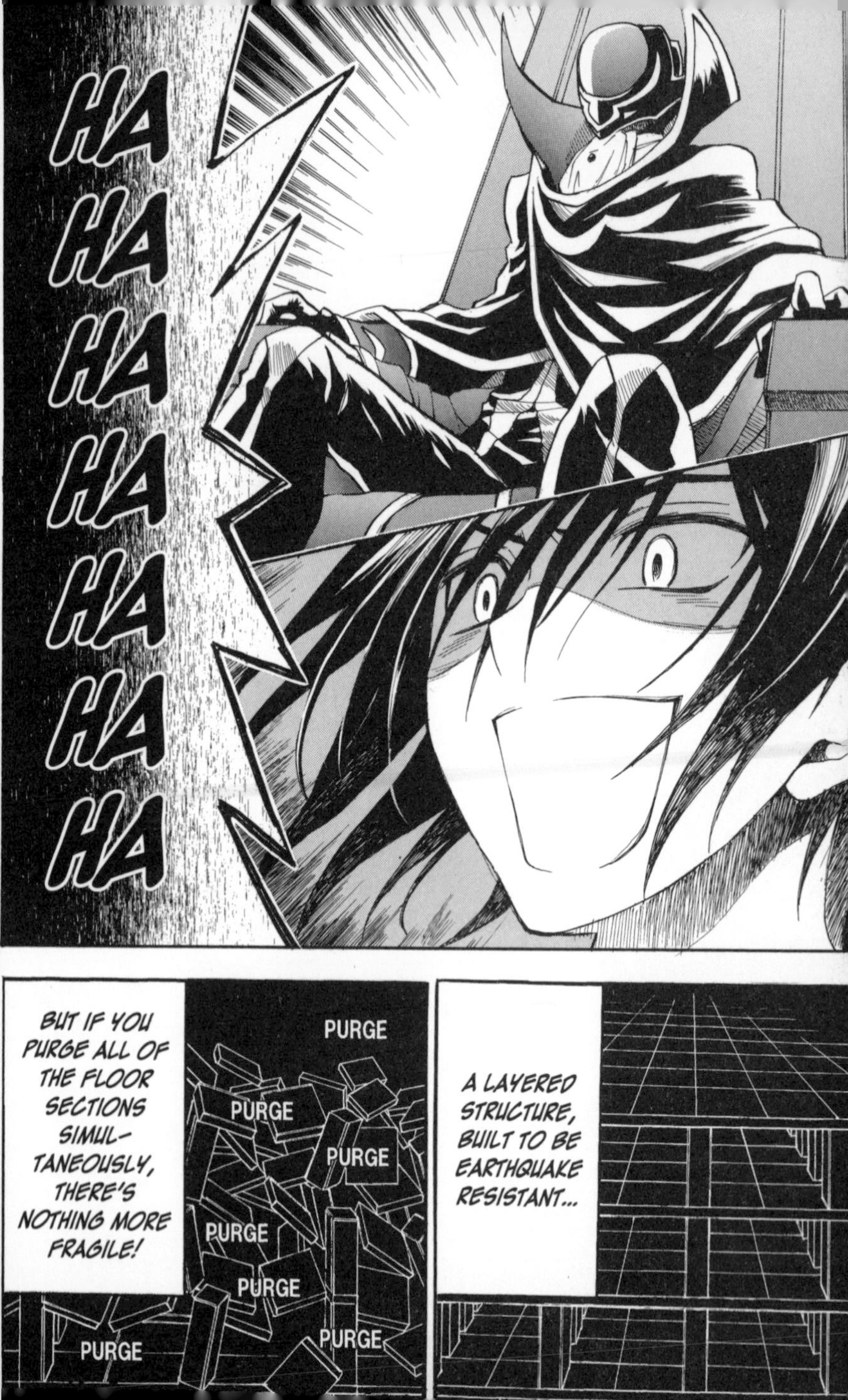
HA HA HA HA HA HA HA
A LAYERED STRUCTURE, BUILT TO BE EARTHQUAKE RESISTANT...
BUT IF YOU PURGE ALL OF THE FLOOR SECTIONS SIMUL-TANEOUSLY, THERE'S NOTHING MORE FRAGILE!
PURGE
PURGE
PURGE
PURGE
PURGE
PURGE
PURGE

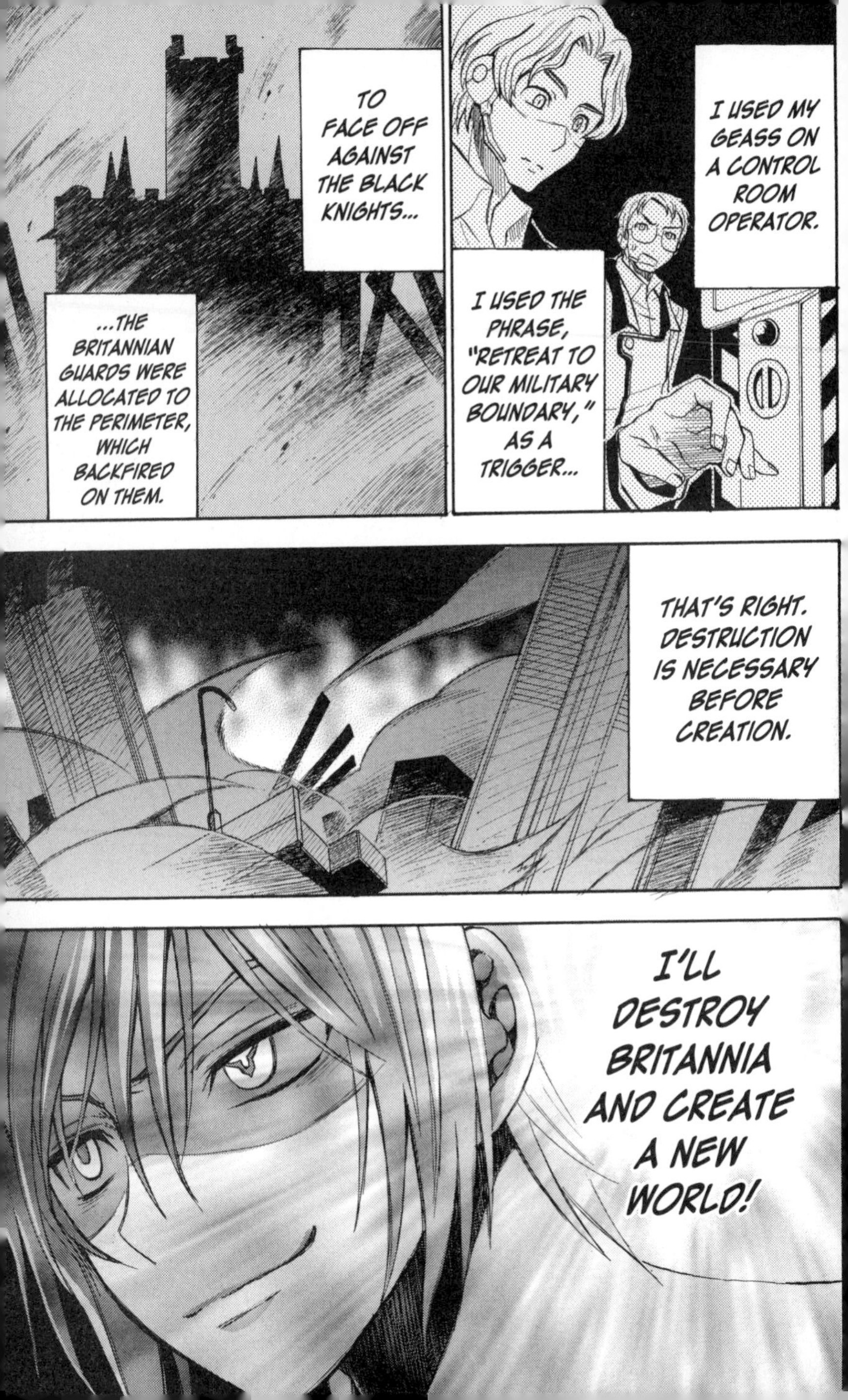
I USED MY GEASS ON A CONTROL ROOM OPERATOR.
I USED THE PHRASE, "RETREAT TO OUR MILITARY BOUNDARY," AS A TRIGGER...
TO FACE OFF AGAINST THE BLACK KNIGHTS...
...THE BRITANNIAN GUARDS WERE ALLOCATED TO THE PERIMETER, WHICH BACKFIRED ON THEM.
THAT'S RIGHT. DESTRUCTION IS NECESSARY BEFORE CREATION.
I'LL DESTROY BRITANNIA AND CREATE A NEW WORLD!

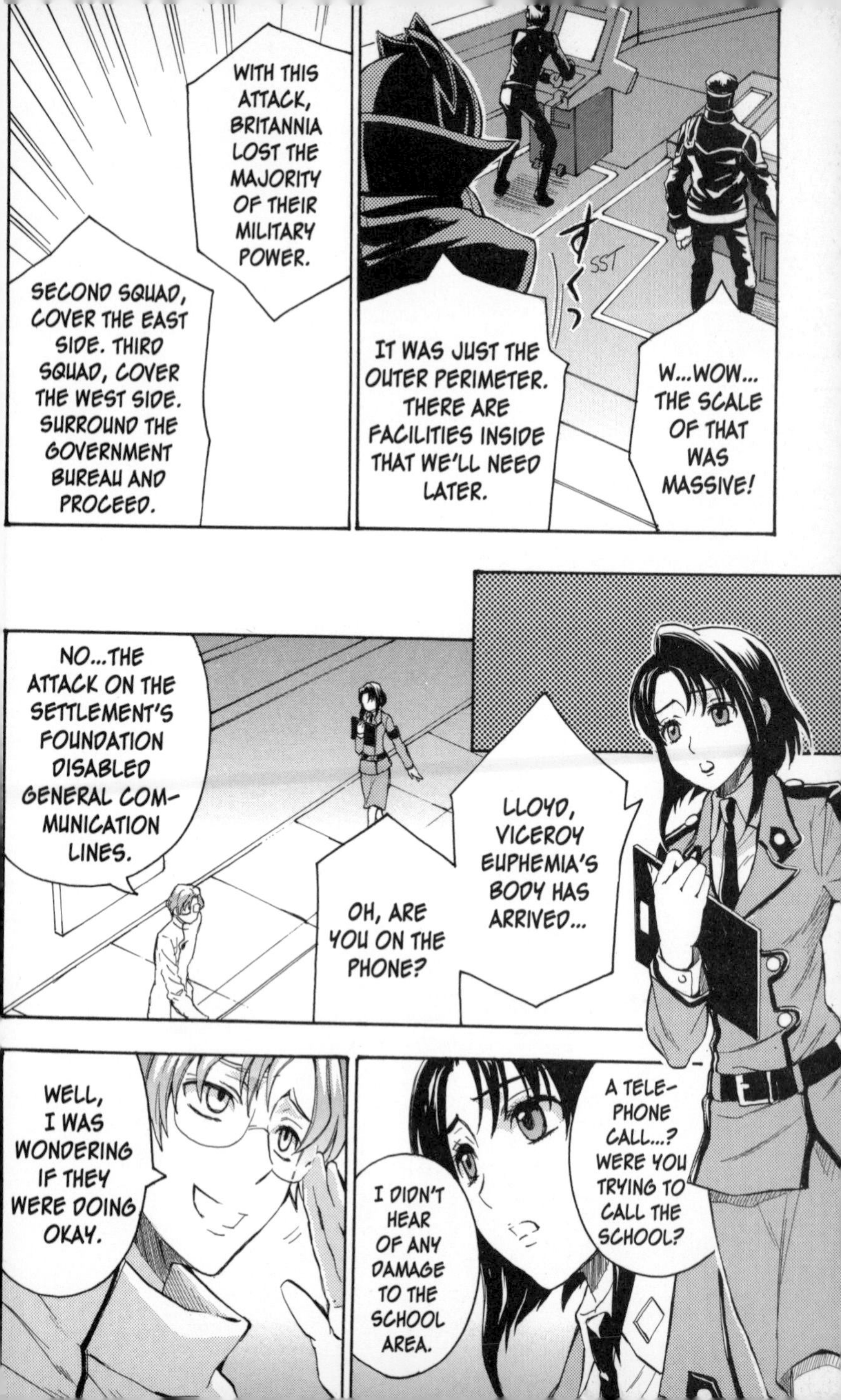
W...WOW... THE SCALE OF THAT WAS MASSIVE!
SST
IT WAS JUST THE OUTER PERIMETER. THERE ARE FACILITIES INSIDE THAT WE'LL NEED LATER.
WITH THIS ATTACK, BRITANNIA LOST THE MAJORITY OF THEIR MILITARY POWER.
SECOND SQUAD, COVER THE EAST SIDE. THIRD SQUAD, COVER THE WEST SIDE. SURROUND THE GOVERNMENT BUREAU AND PROCEED.
LLOYD, VICEROY EUPHEMIA'S BODY HAS ARRIVED...
OH, ARE YOU ON THE PHONE?
NO...THE ATTACK ON THE SETTLEMENT'S FOUNDATION DISABLED GENERAL COM-MUNICATION LINES.
A TELE-PHONE CALL...? WERE YOU TRYING TO CALL THE SCHOOL?
I DIDN'T HEAR OF ANY DAMAGE TO THE SCHOOL AREA.
WELL, I WAS WONDERING IF THEY WERE DOING OKAY.

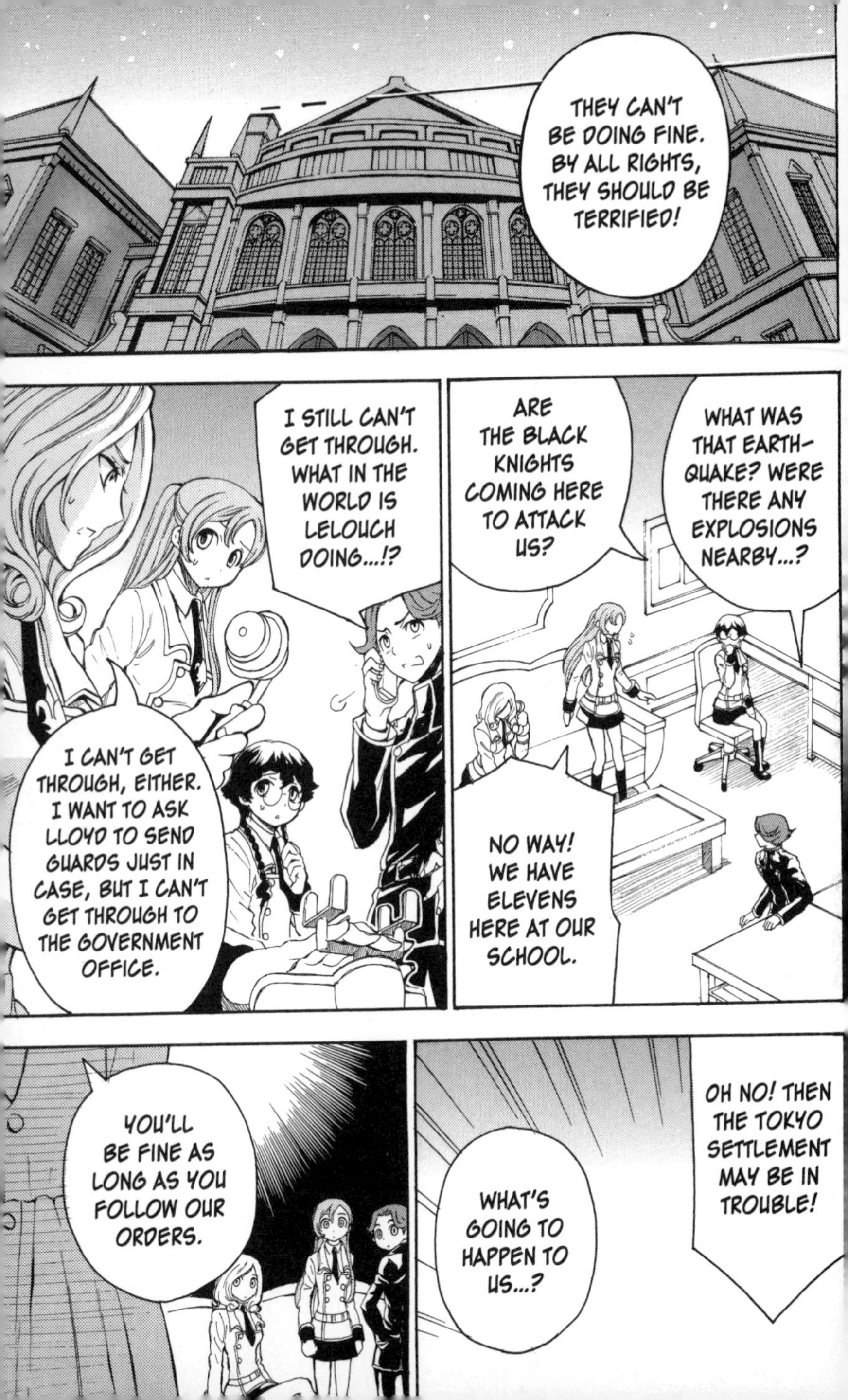
THEY CAN'T BE DOING FINE. BY ALL RIGHTS, THEY SHOULD BE TERRIFIED!
WHAT WAS THAT EARTH-QUAKE? WERE THERE ANY EXPLOSIONS NEARBY...?
ARE THE BLACK KNIGHTS COMING HERE TO ATTACK US?
NO WAY! WE HAVE ELEVENS HERE AT OUR SCHOOL.
I STILL CAN'T GET THROUGH. WHAT IN THE WORLD IS LELOUCH DOING...!?
I CAN'T GET THROUGH, EITHER. I WANT TO ASK LLOYD TO SEND GUARDS JUST IN CASE, BUT I CAN'T GET THROUGH TO THE GOVERNMENT OFFICE.
OH NO! THEN THE TOKYO SETTLEMENT MAY BE IN TROUBLE!
WHAT'S GOING TO HAPPEN TO US...?
YOU'LL BE FINE AS LONG AS YOU FOLLOW OUR ORDERS.

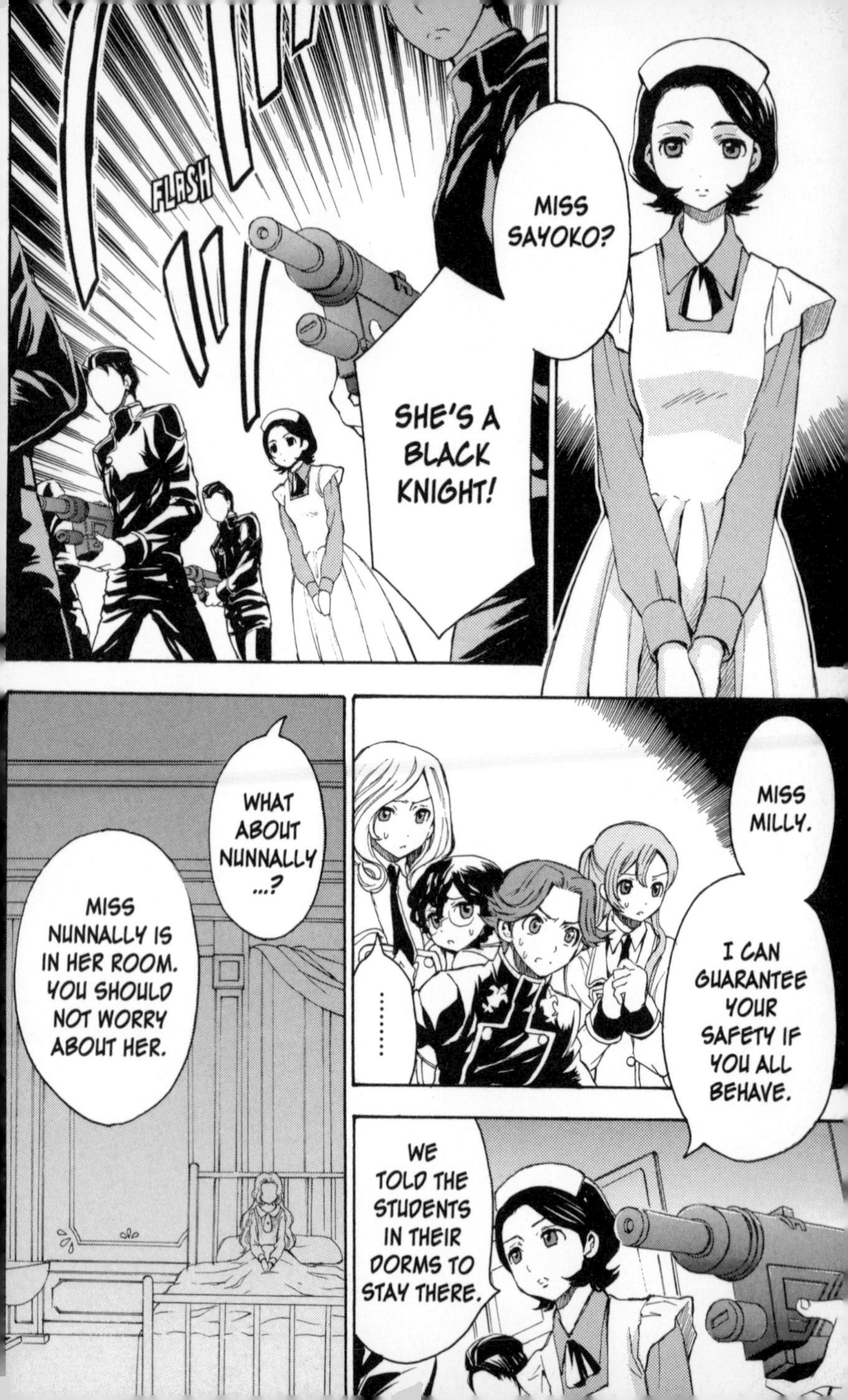
MISS SAYOKO?
FLASH
SHE'S A BLACK KNIGHT!
MISS MILLY.
....
I CAN GUARANTEE YOUR SAFETY IF YOU ALL BEHAVE.
WE TOLD THE STUDENTS IN THEIR DORMS TO STAY THERE.
WHAT ABOUT NUNNALLY ...?
MISS NUNNALLY IS IN HER ROOM. YOU SHOULD NOT WORRY ABOUT HER.

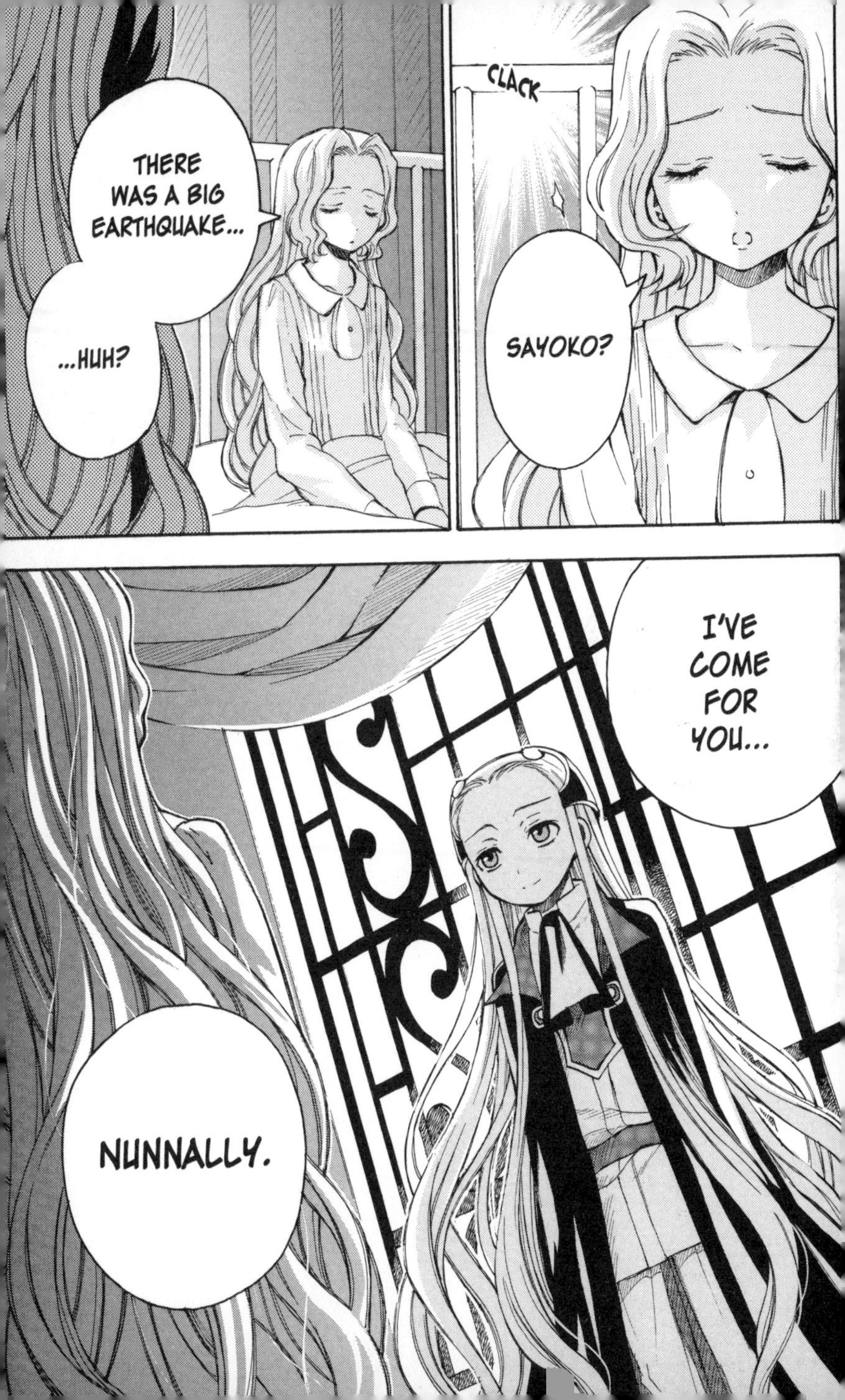
CLACK
SAYOKO?
THERE WAS A BIG EARTHQUAKE...
...HUH?
I'VE COME FOR YOU...
NUNNALLY.

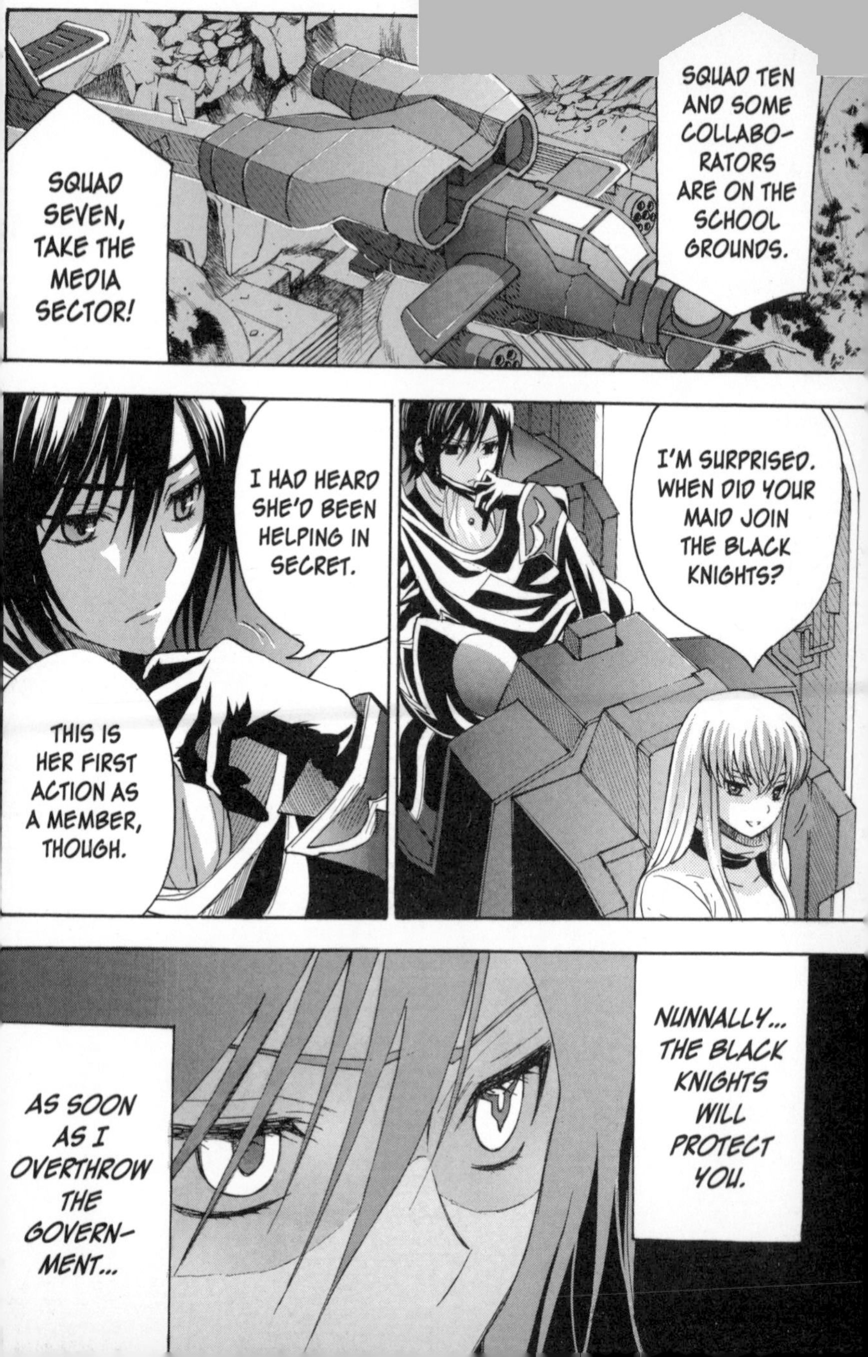
SQUAD TEN AND SOME COLLABO-RATORS ARE ON THE SCHOOL GROUNDS.
SQUAD SEVEN, TAKE THE MEDIA SECTOR!
I'M SURPRISED. WHEN DID YOUR MAID JOIN THE BLACK KNIGHTS?
I HAD HEARD SHE'D BEEN HELPING IN SECRET.
THIS IS HER FIRST ACTION AS A MEMBER, THOUGH.
NUNNALLY... THE BLACK KNIGHTS WILL PROTECT YOU.
AS SOON AS I OVERTHROW THE GOVERN-MENT...

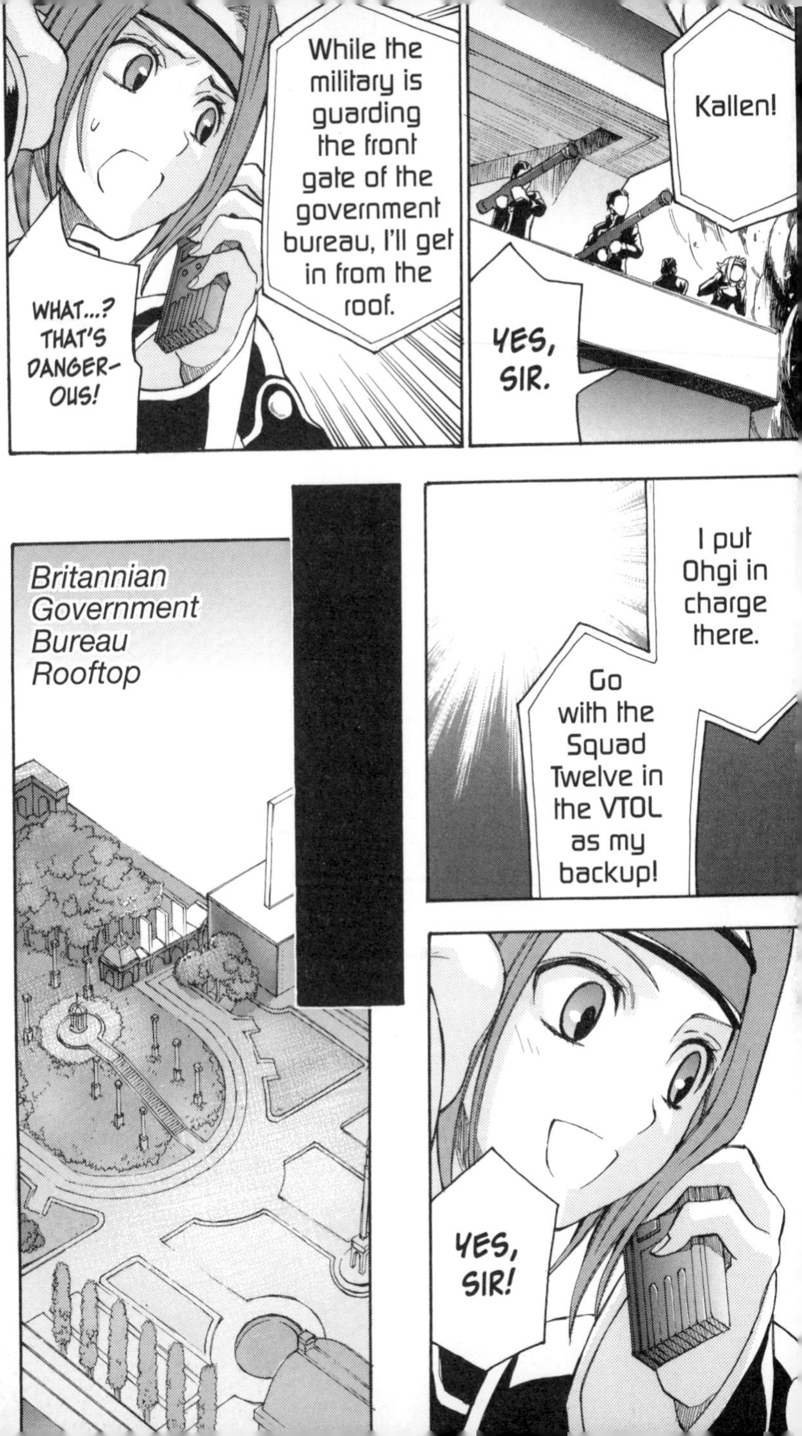
Kallen!
YES, SIR.
While the military is guarding the front gate of the government bureau, I'll get in from the roof.
WHAT...? THAT'S DANGER-OUS!
I put Ohgi in charge there.
Go with the Squad Twelve in the VTOL as my backup!
YES, SIR!
Britannian Government Bureau Rooftop

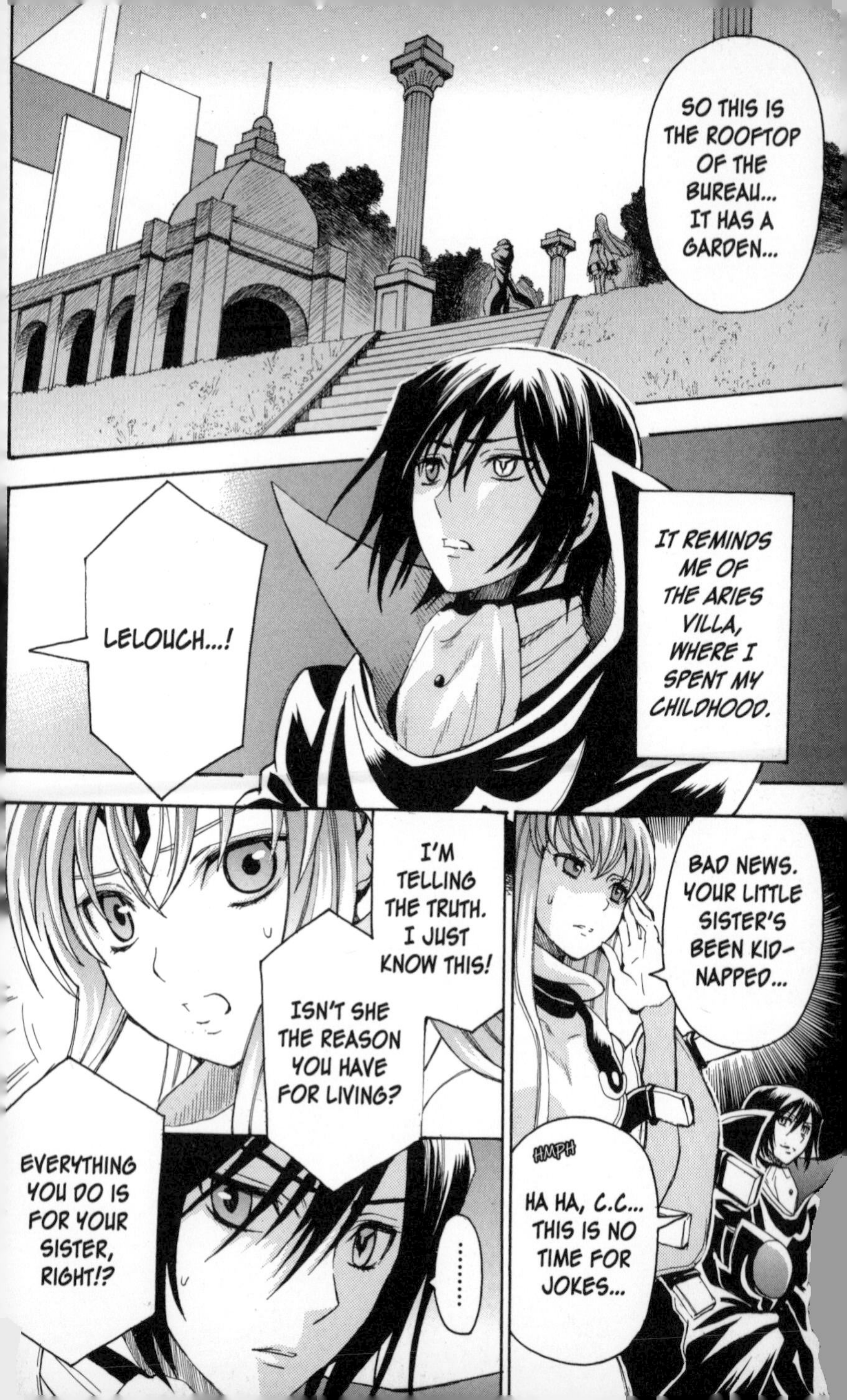
SO THIS IS THE ROOFTOP OF THE BUREAU... IT HAS A GARDEN...
IT REMINDS ME OF THE ARIES VILLA, WHERE I SPENT MY CHILDHOOD.
LELOUCH...!
BAD NEWS. YOUR LITTLE SISTER'S BEEN KID-NAPPED...
HMPH
HA HA, C.C... THIS IS NO TIME FOR JOKES...
I'M TELLING THE TRUTH. I JUST KNOW THIS!
ISN'T SHE THE REASON YOU HAVE FOR LIVING?
EVERYTHING YOU DO IS FOR YOUR SISTER, RIGHT!?
......

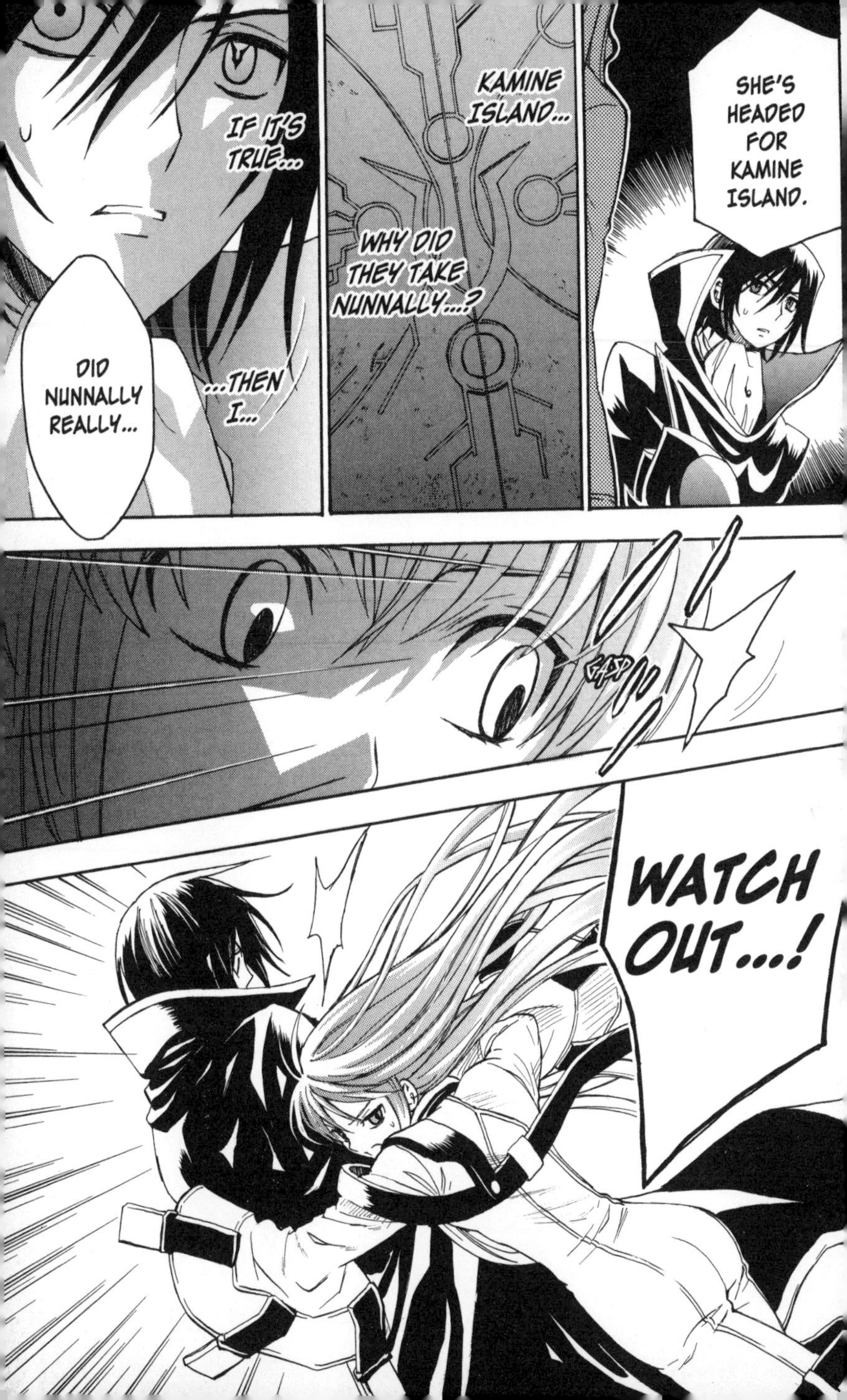
SHE'S HEADED FOR KAMINE ISLAND.
KAMINE ISLAND...
WHY DID THEY TAKE NUNNALLY...?
IF IT'S TRUE...
...THEN I...
DID NUNNALLY REALLY...
GASP
WATCH OUT...!

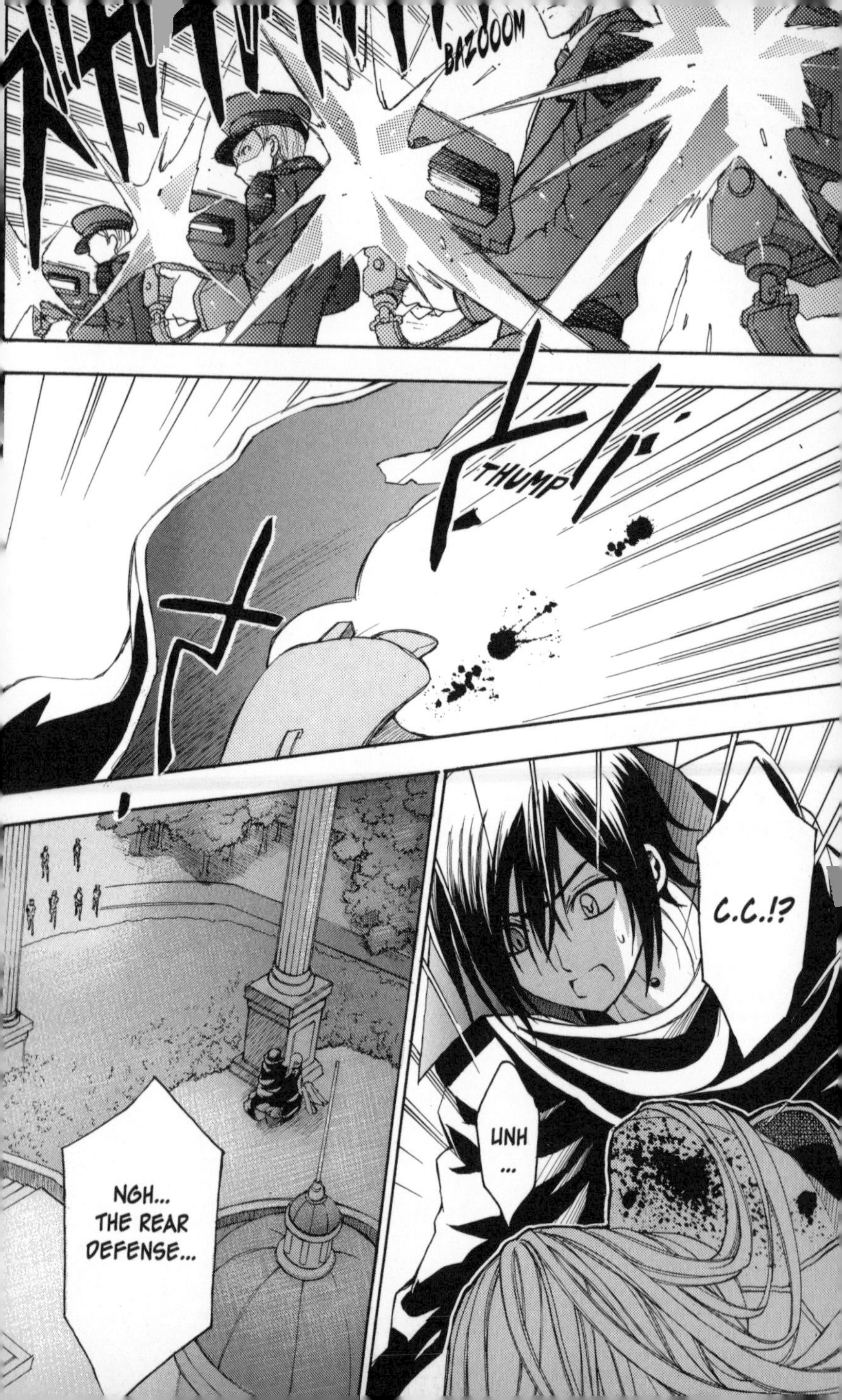
BAZOOOM
THUMP
C.C.!?
UNH...
NGH... THE REAR DEFENSE...

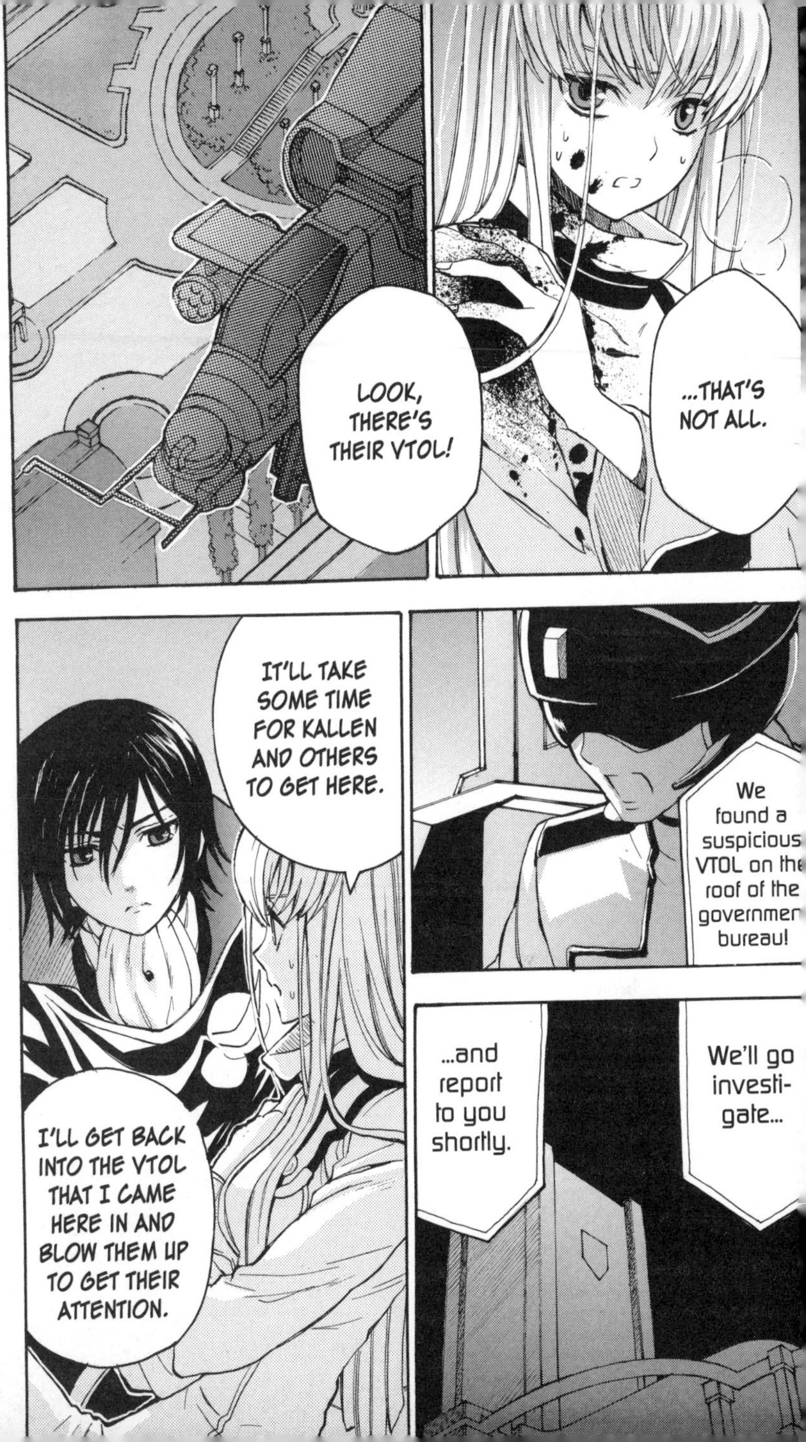
...THAT'S NOT ALL.
LOOK, THERE'S THEIR VTOL!
We found a suspicious VTOL on th roof of the governmen bureau!
We'll go investi-gate...
...and report to you shortly.
IT'LL TAKE SOME TIME FOR KALLEN AND OTHERS TO GET HERE.
I'LL GET BACK INTO THE VTOL THAT I CAME HERE IN AND BLOW THEM UP TO GET THEIR ATTENTION.

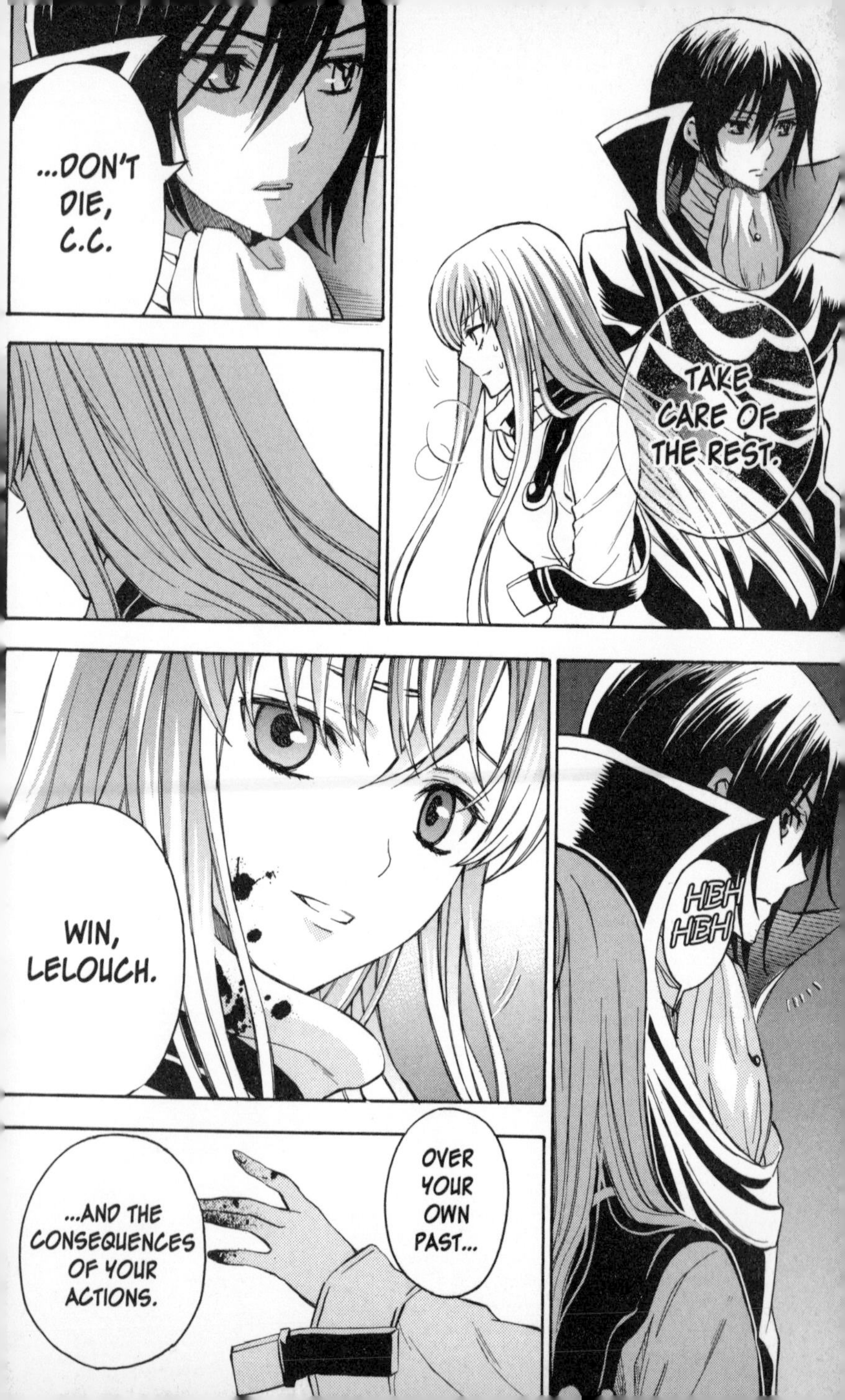
TAKE CARE OF THE REST.
...DON'T DIE, C.C.
HEH HEH
WIN, LELOUCH.
OVER YOUR OWN PAST...
...AND THE CONSEQUENCES OF YOUR ACTIONS.

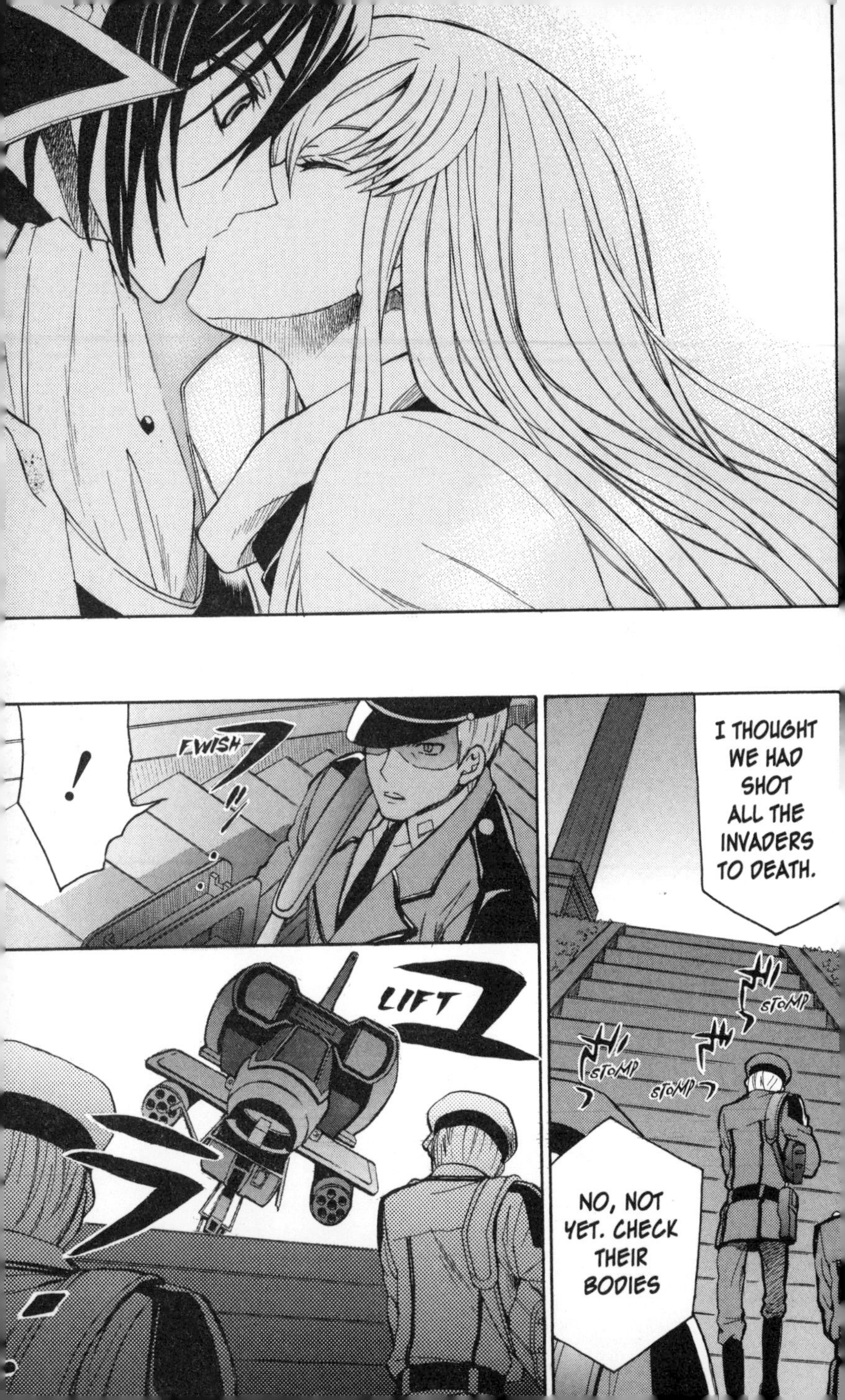
I THOUGHT WE HAD SHOT ALL THE INVADERS TO DEATH.
STOMP
STOMP
STOMP
NO, NOT YET. CHECK THEIR BODIES
FWISH
!
LIFT

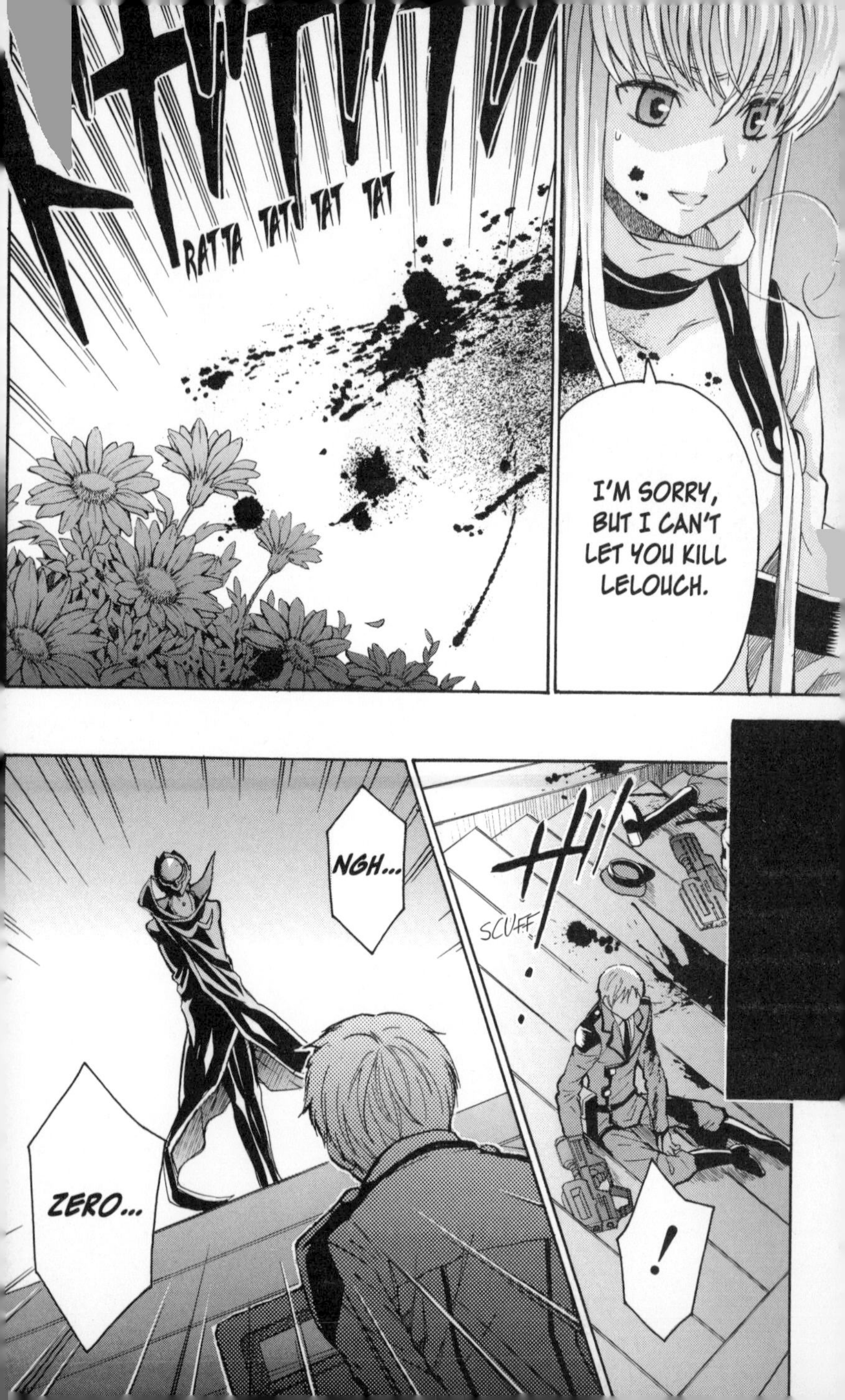
I'M SORRY, BUT I CAN'T LET YOU KILL LELOUCH.
RATTA TAT TAT TAT
SCUFF
!
NGH...
ZERO...

THUD

THUD

THUD

GLARE

YOU MUST...

DIE!

I'M SURPRISED...

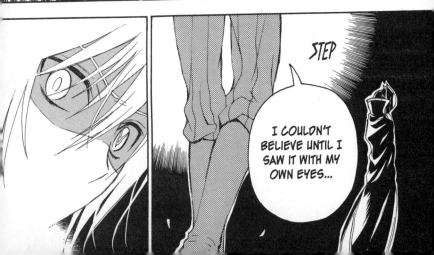

STEP

I COULDN'T BELIEVE UNTIL I SAW IT WITH MY OWN EYES...

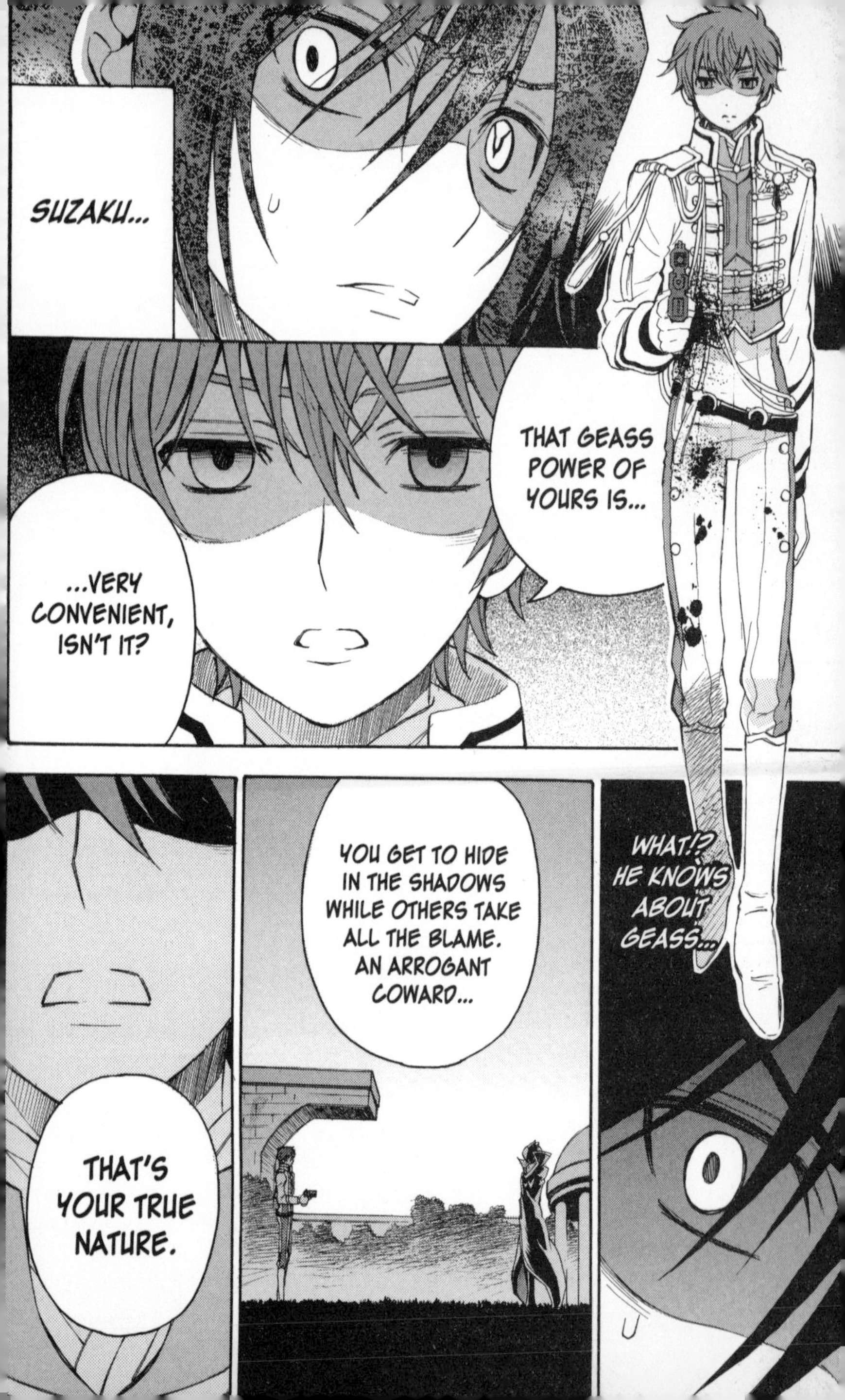
SUZAKU...
THAT GEASS POWER OF YOURS IS...
...VERY CONVENIENT, ISN'T IT?
WHAT!? HE KNOWS ABOUT GEASS...
YOU GET TO HIDE IN THE SHADOWS WHILE OTHERS TAKE ALL THE BLAME. AN ARROGANT COWARD...
THAT'S YOUR TRUE NATURE.

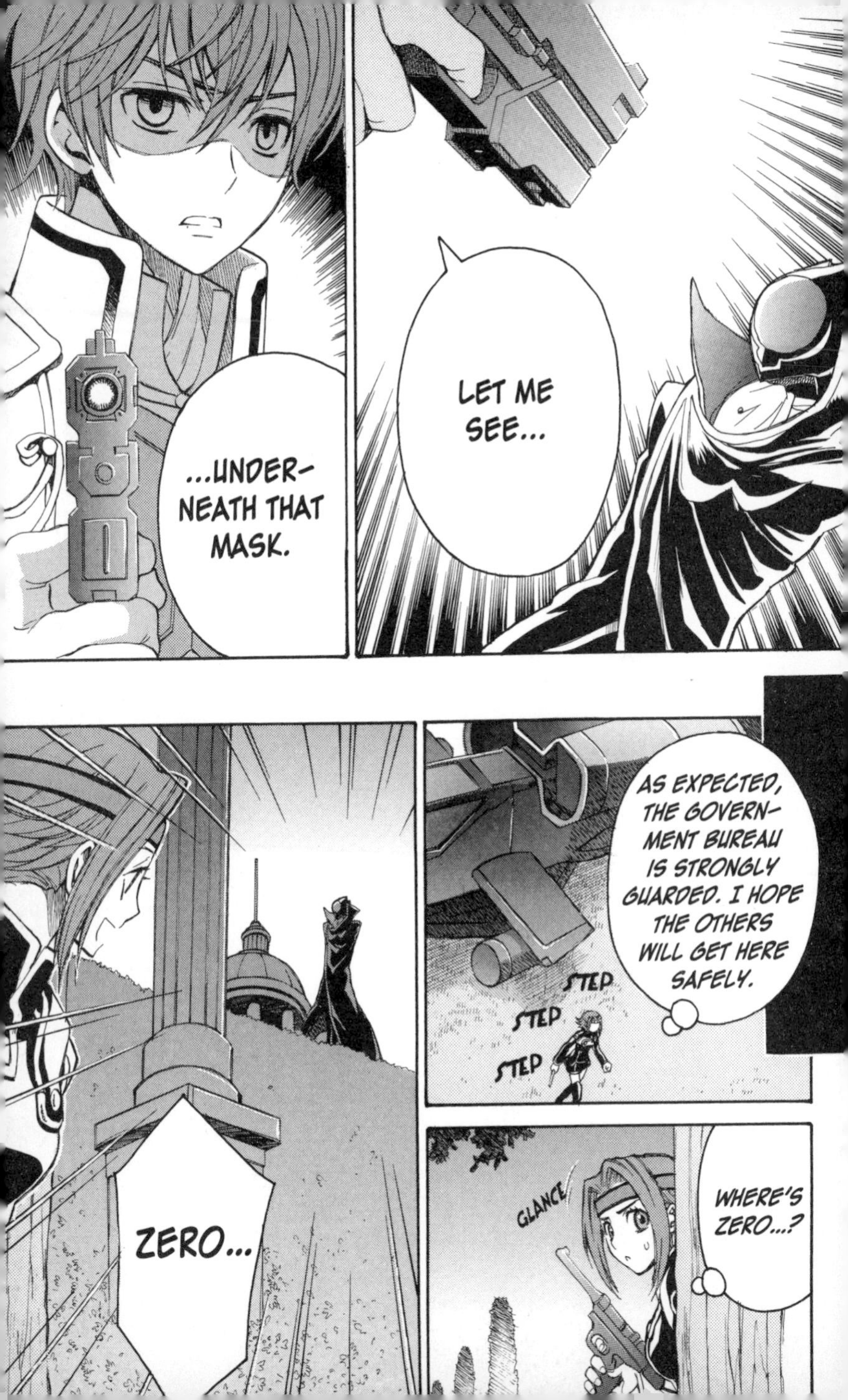
LET ME SEE...
...UNDER-NEATH THAT MASK.
AS EXPECTED, THE GOVERN-MENT BUREAU IS STRONGLY GUARDED. I HOPE THE OTHERS WILL GET HERE SAFELY.
STEP
STEP
STEP
WHERE'S ZERO...?
GLANCE
ZERO...

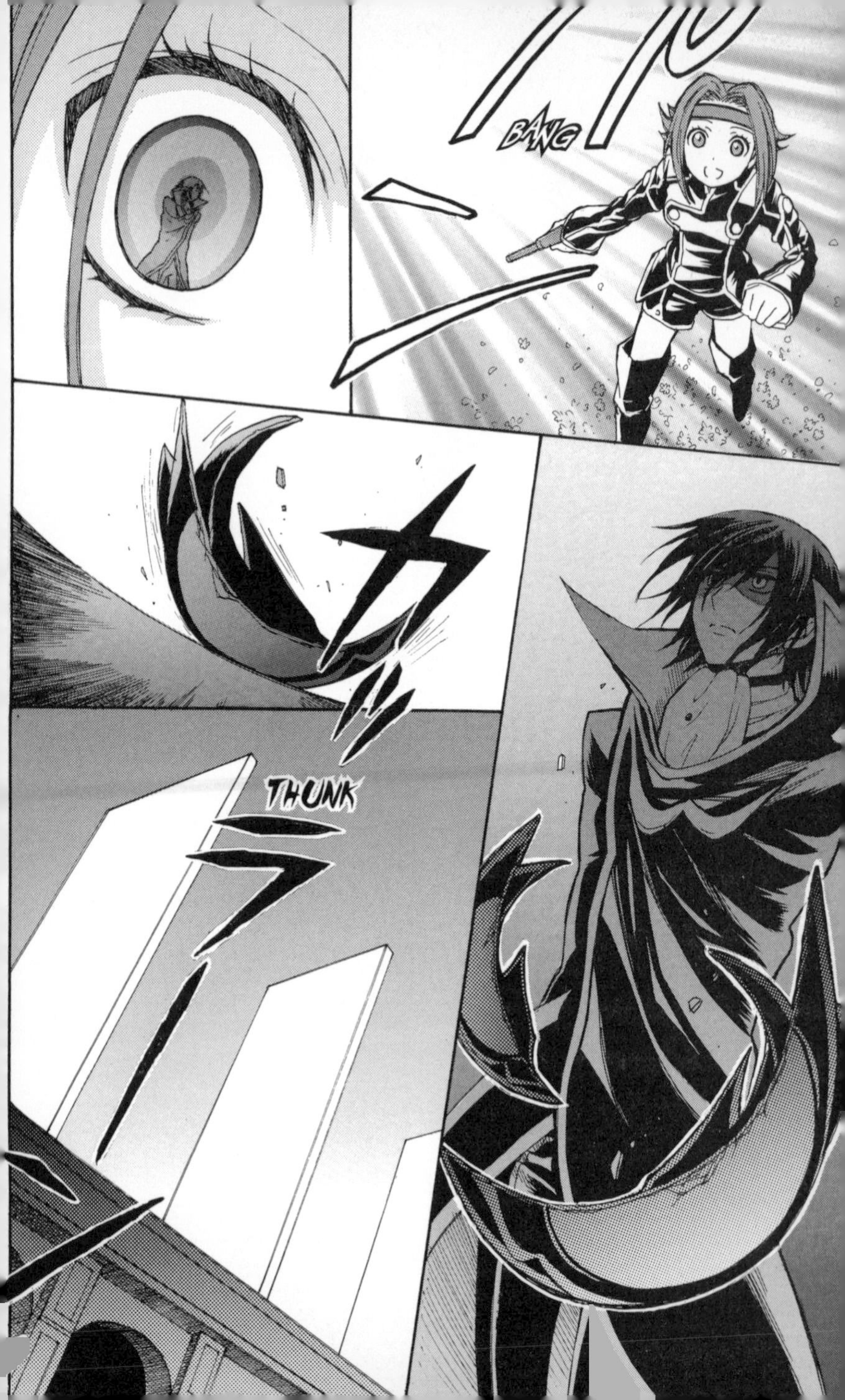
BANG
THUNK

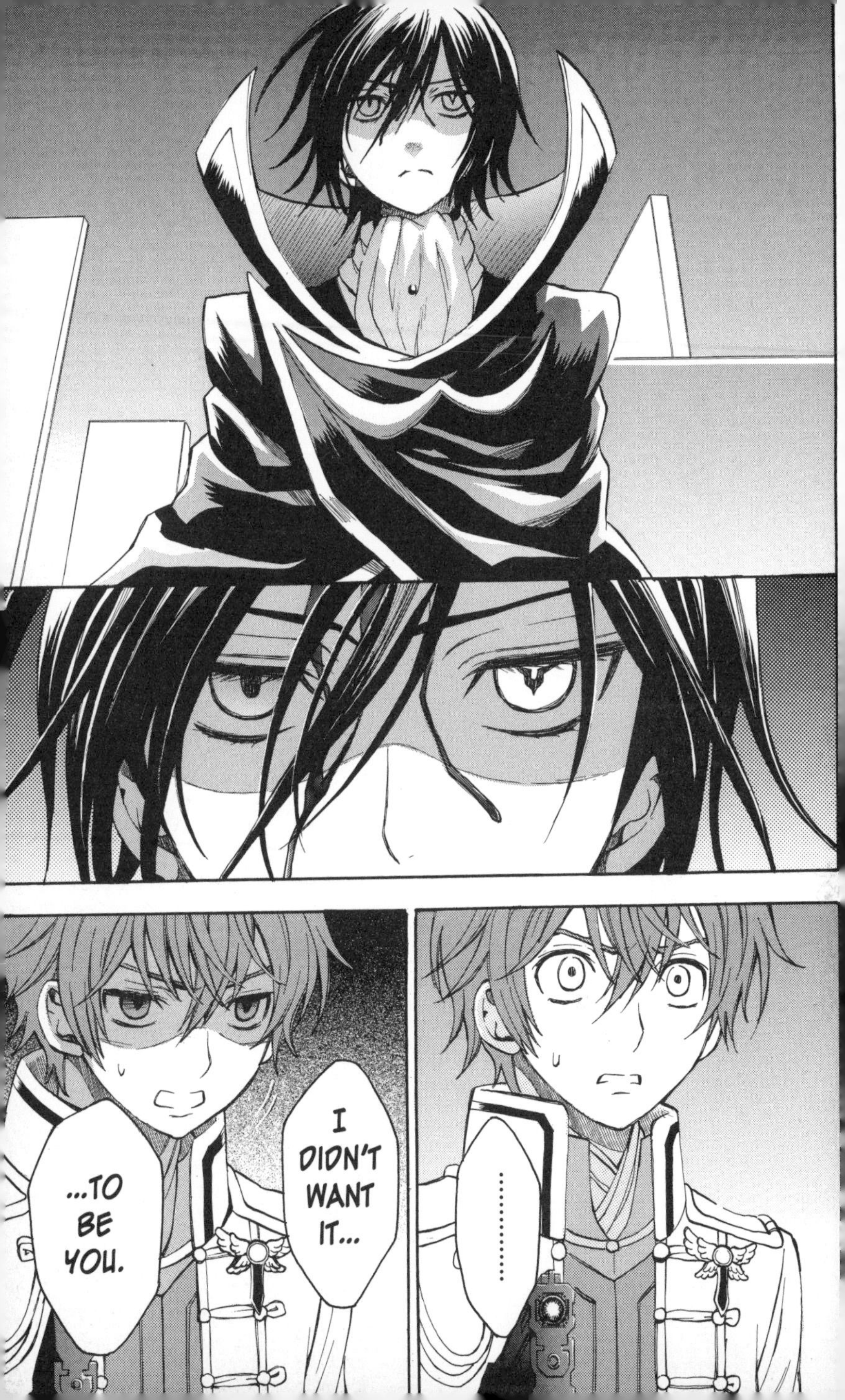
....
I DIDN'T WANT IT...
...TO BE YOU.

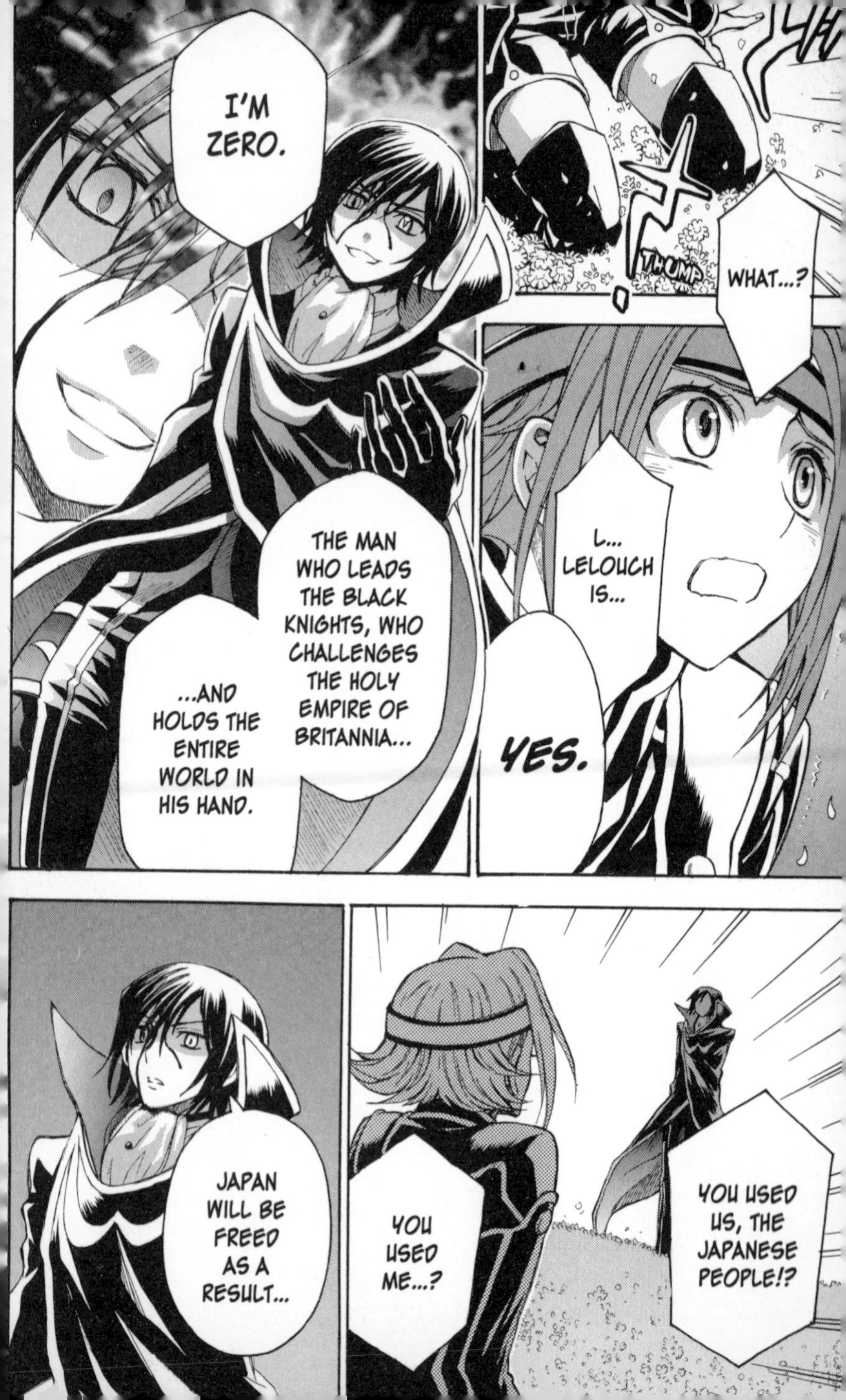
THUMP
WHAT...?
L... LELOUCH IS...
YES.
I'M ZERO.
THE MAN WHO LEADS THE BLACK KNIGHTS, WHO CHALLENGES THE HOLY EMPIRE OF BRITANNIA...
...AND HOLDS THE ENTIRE WORLD IN HIS HAND.
YOU USED US, THE JAPANESE PEOPLE!?
YOU USED ME...?
JAPAN WILL BE FREED AS A RESULT...

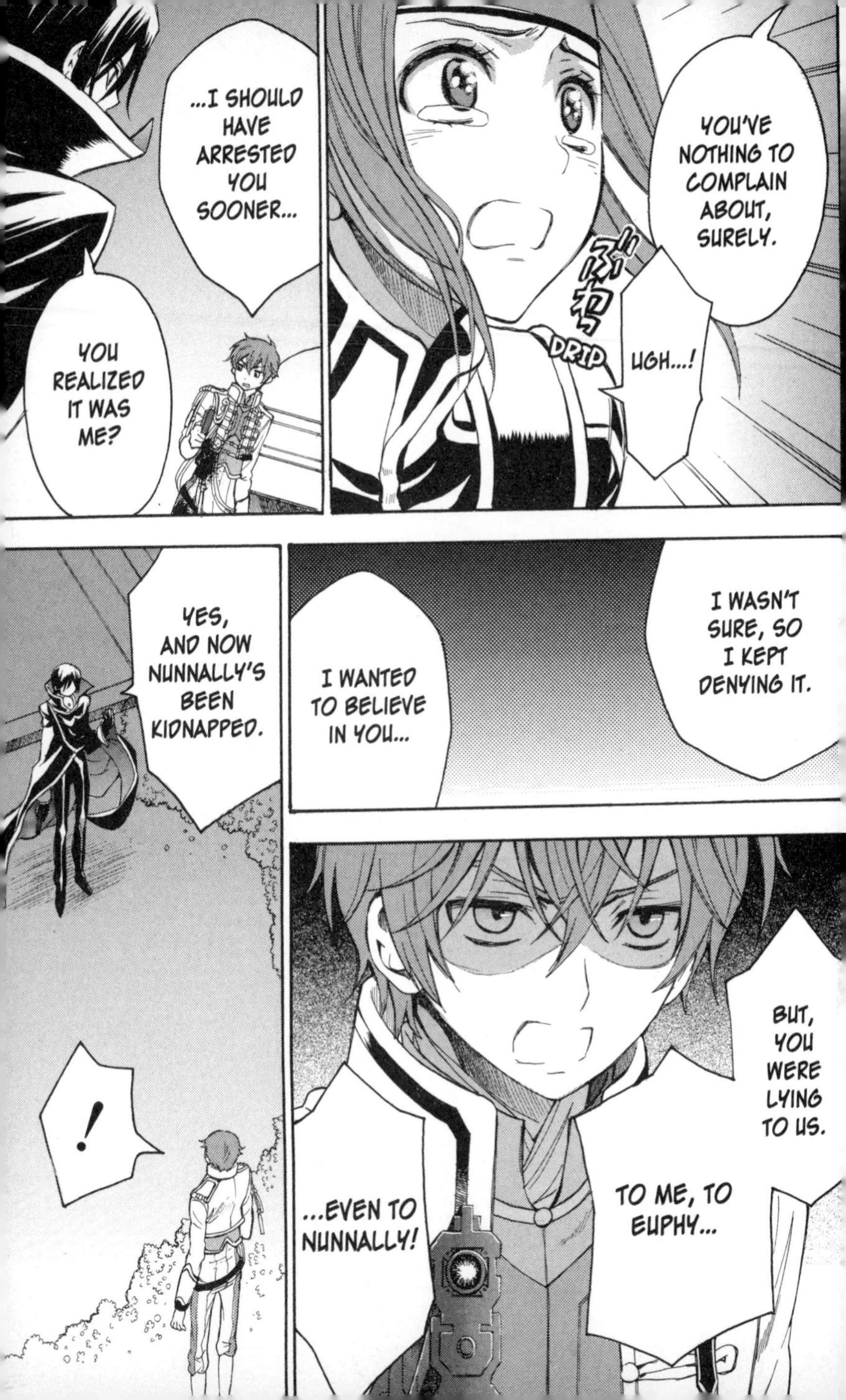
YOU'VE NOTHING TO COMPLAIN ABOUT, SURELY.
DRIP
UGH...!
...I SHOULD HAVE ARRESTED YOU SOONER...
YOU REALIZED IT WAS ME?
I WASN'T SURE, SO I KEPT DENYING IT.
I WANTED TO BELIEVE IN YOU...
BUT, YOU WERE LYING TO US.
TO ME, TO EUPHY...
...EVEN TO NUNNALLY!
YES, AND NOW NUNNALLY'S BEEN KIDNAPPED.
!

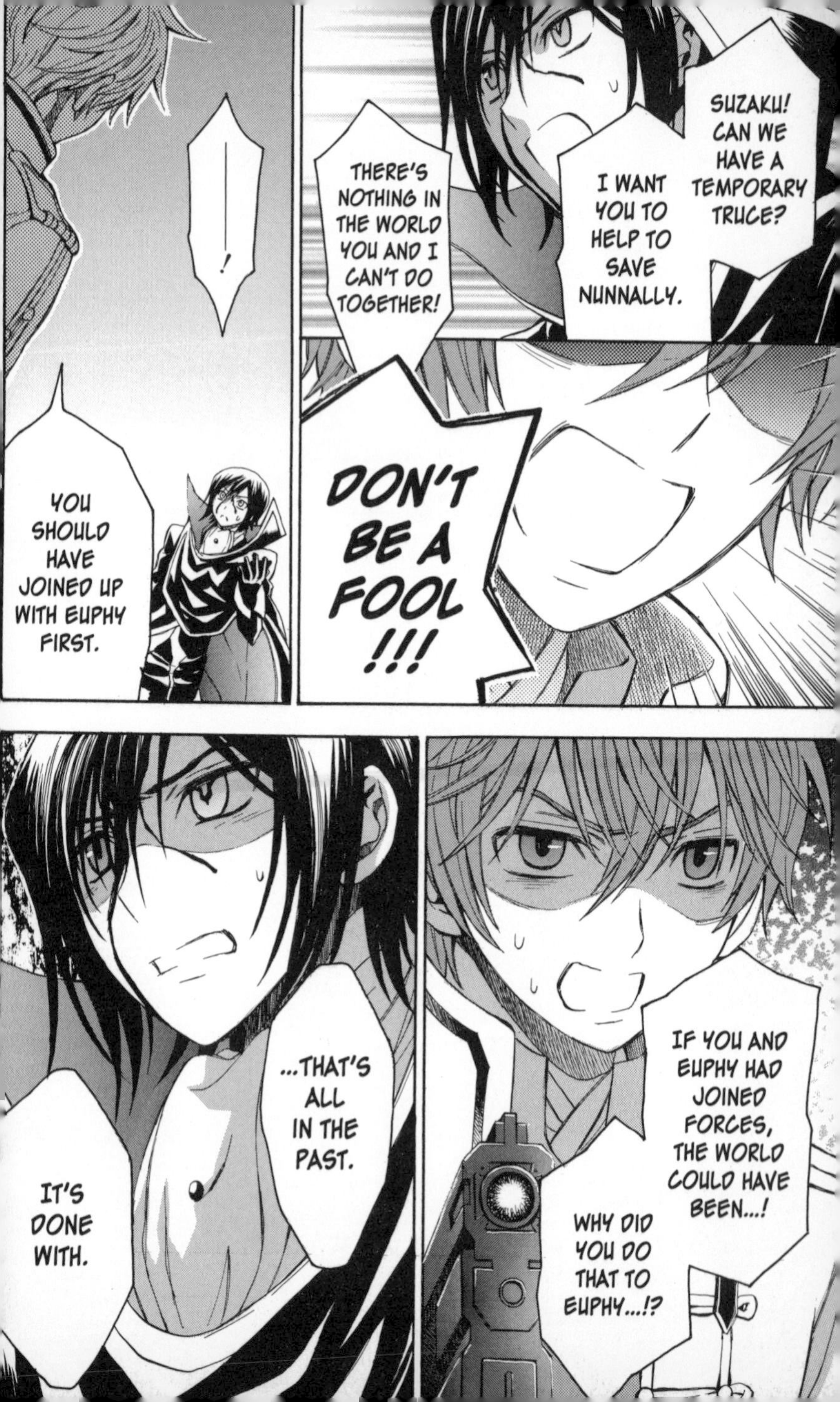
SUZAKU! CAN WE HAVE A TEMPORARY TRUCE?
I WANT YOU TO HELP TO SAVE NUNNALLY.
THERE'S NOTHING IN THE WORLD YOU AND I CAN'T DO TOGETHER!
DON'T BE A FOOL!!!
—!
YOU SHOULD HAVE JOINED UP WITH EUPHY FIRST.
IF YOU AND EUPHY HAD JOINED FORCES, THE WORLD COULD HAVE BEEN...!
WHY DID YOU DO THAT TO EUPHY...!?
...THAT'S ALL IN THE PAST.
IT'S DONE WITH.

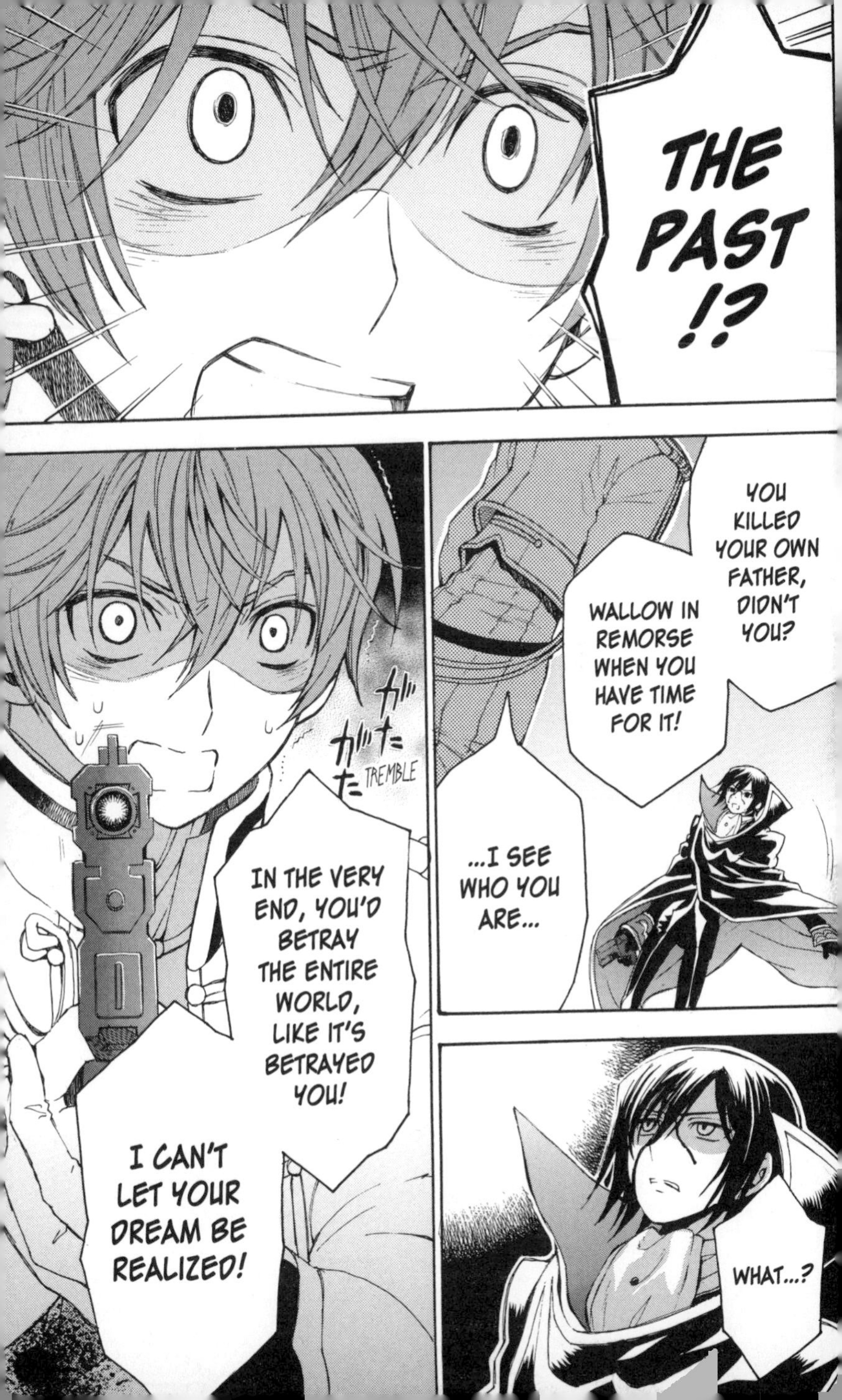
THE PAST!?
YOU KILLED YOUR OWN FATHER, DIDN'T YOU?
WALLOW IN REMORSE WHEN YOU HAVE TIME FOR IT!
...I SEE WHO YOU ARE...
WHAT...?
TREMBLE
IN THE VERY END, YOU'D BETRAY THE ENTIRE WORLD, LIKE IT'S BETRAYED YOU!
I CAN'T LET YOUR DREAM BE REALIZED!

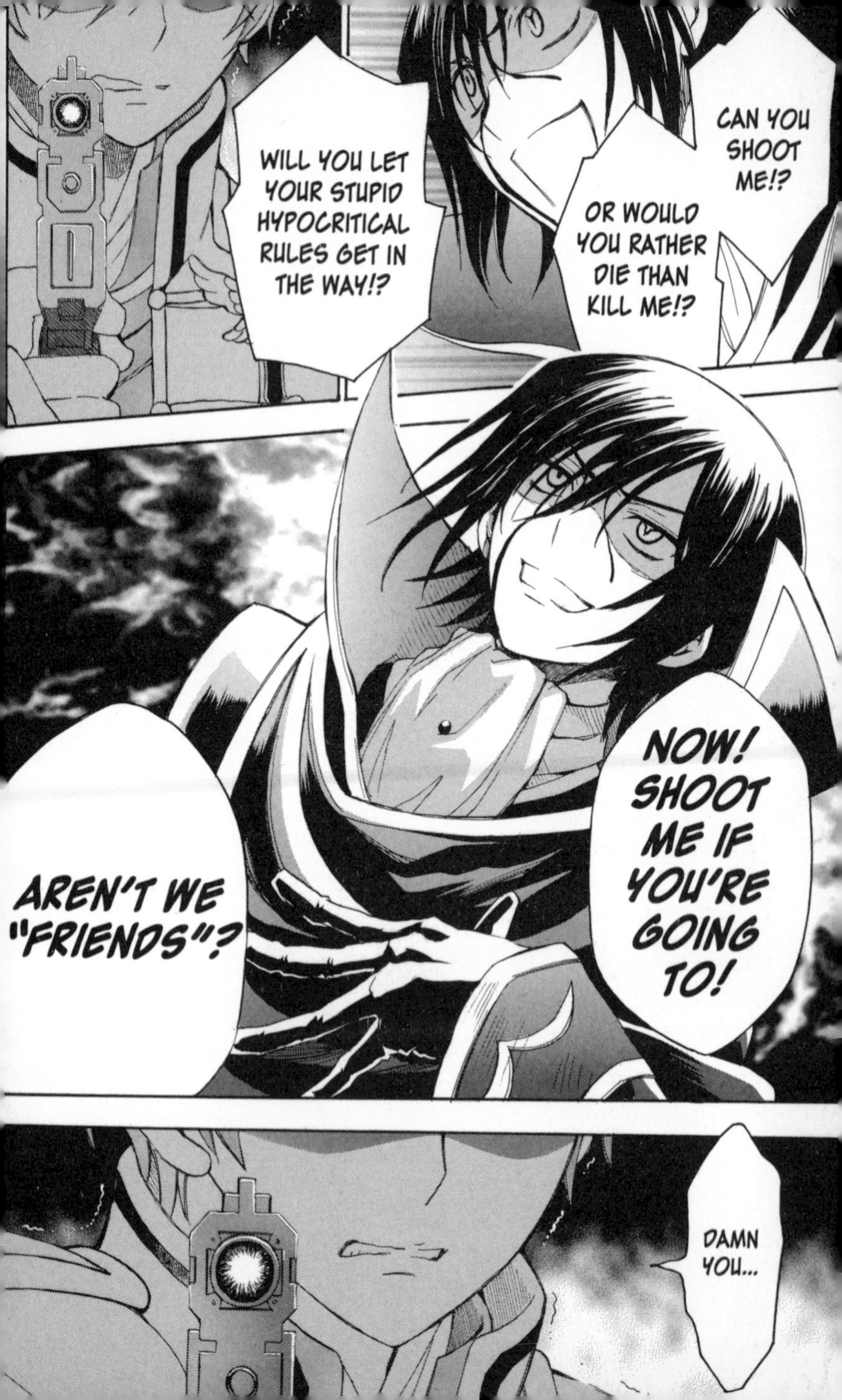
CAN YOU SHOOT ME!?
OR WOULD YOU RATHER DIE THAN KILL ME!?
WILL YOU LET YOUR STUPID HYPOCRITICAL RULES GET IN THE WAY!?
NOW! SHOOT ME IF YOU'RE GOING TO!
AREN'T WE "FRIENDS"?
DAMN YOU...

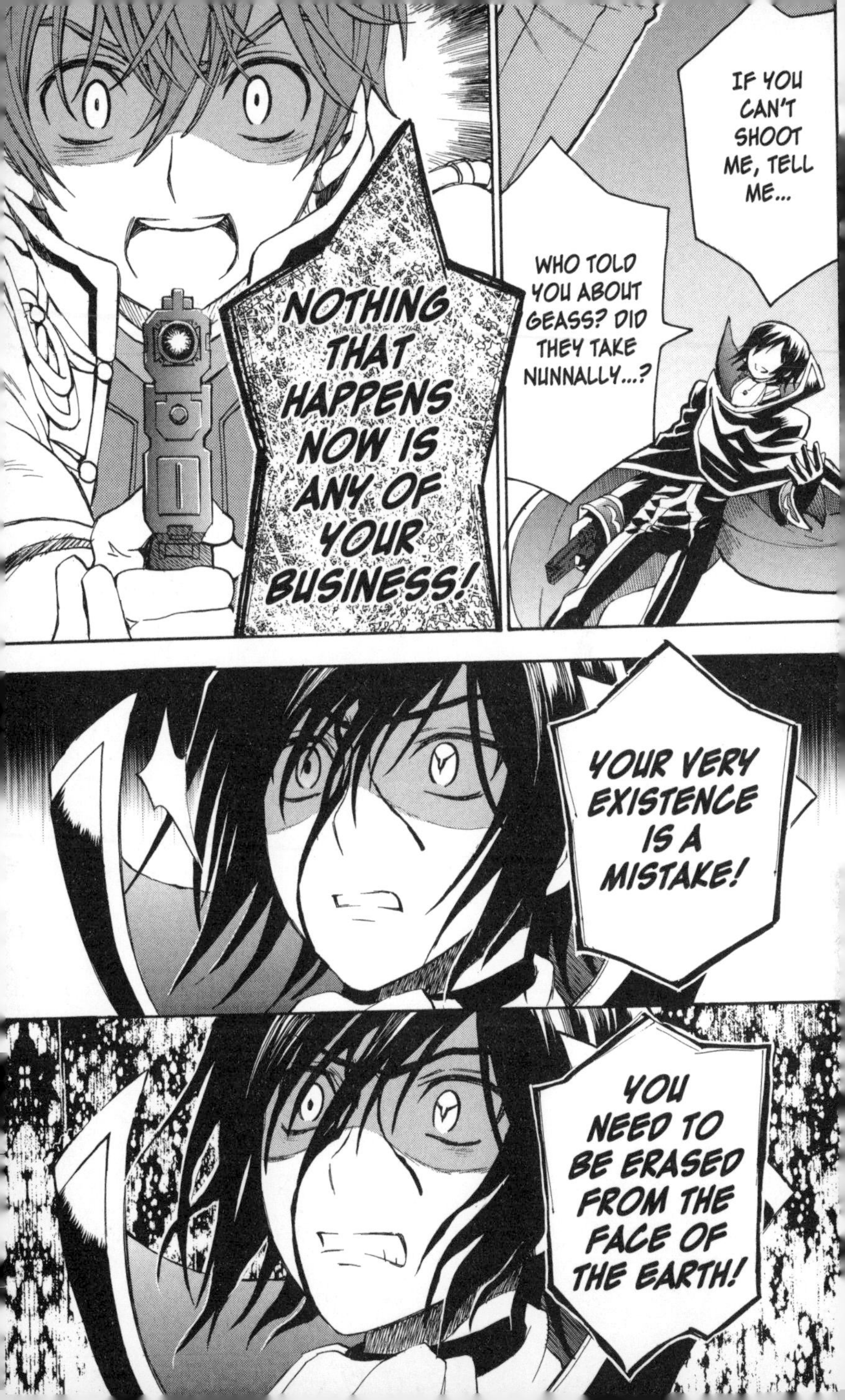
IF YOU CAN'T SHOOT ME, TELL ME...
WHO TOLD YOU ABOUT GEASS? DID THEY TAKE NUNNALLY...?
NOTHING THAT HAPPENS NOW IS ANY OF YOUR BUSINESS!
YOUR VERY EXISTENCE IS A MISTAKE!
YOU NEED TO BE ERASED FROM THE FACE OF THE EARTH!

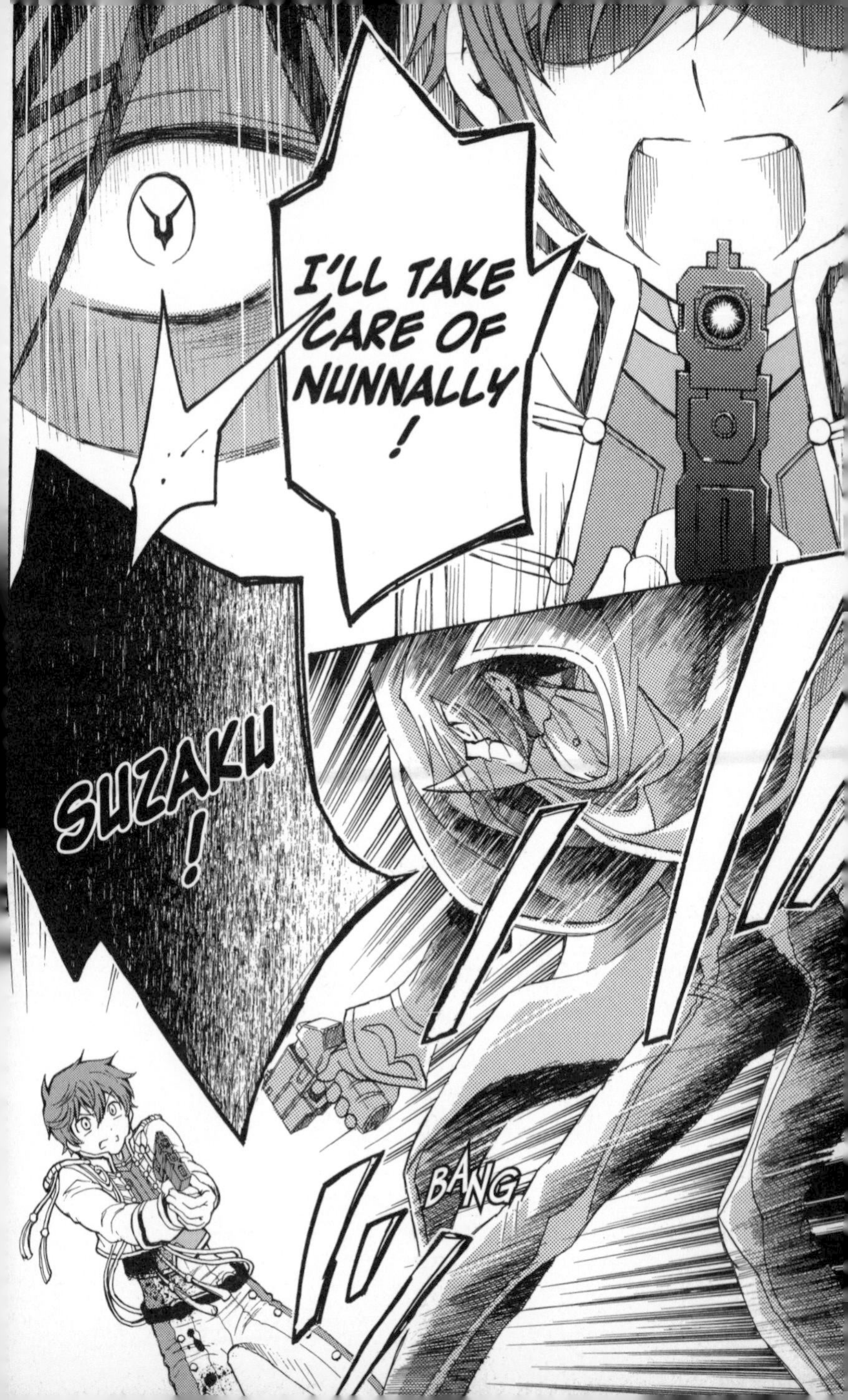
I'LL TAKE CARE OF NUNNALLY!
SUZAKU!
BANG

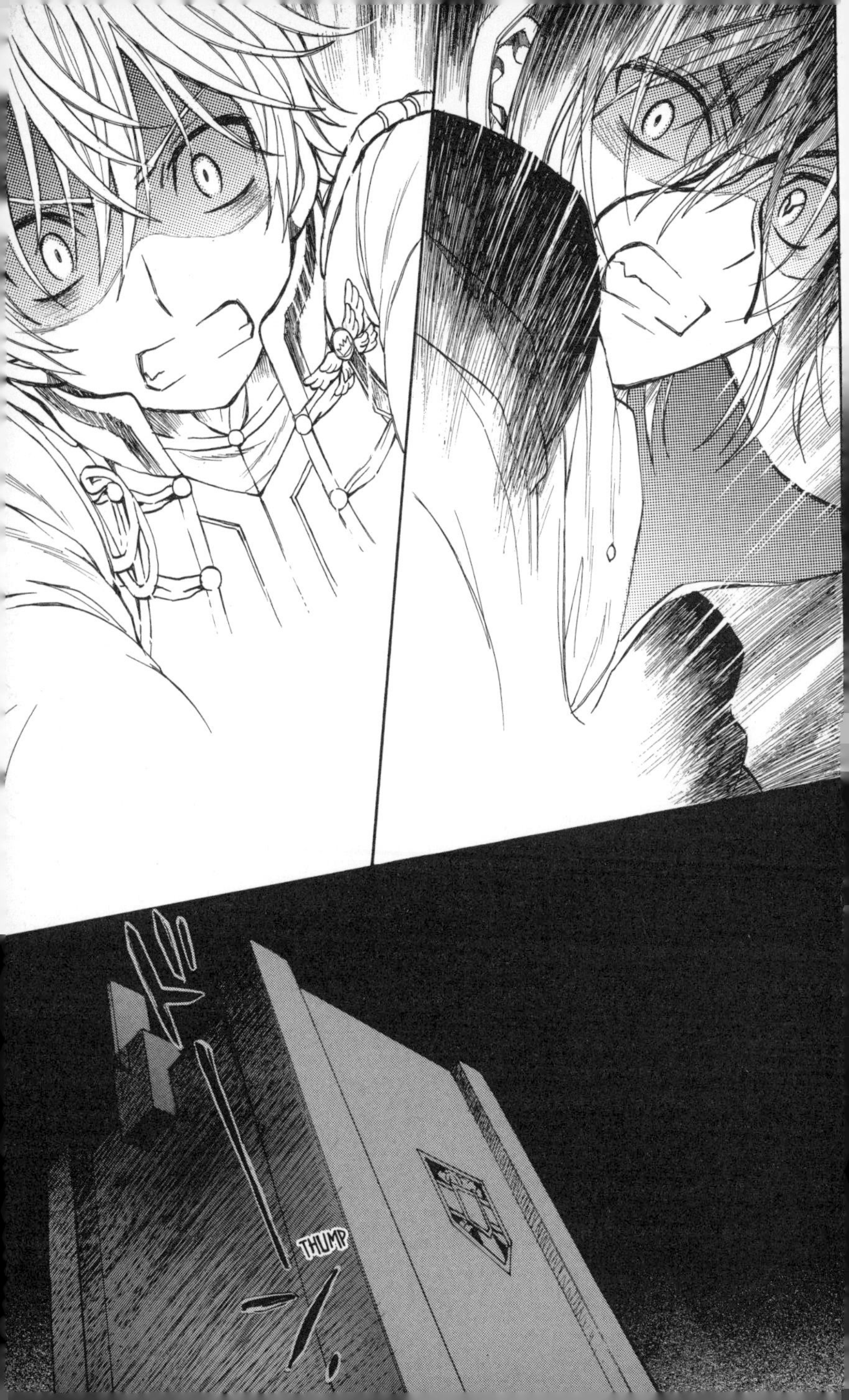
THUMP

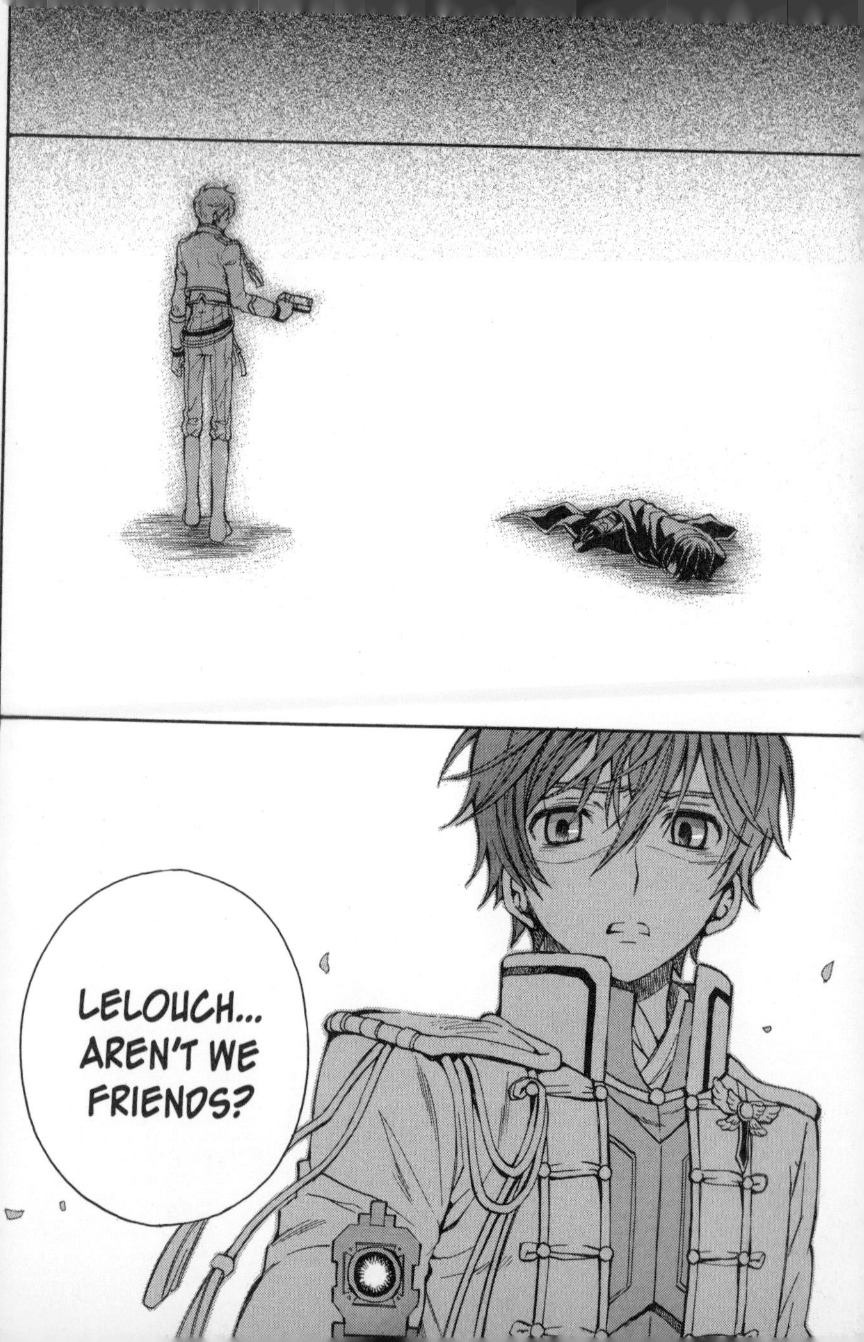
LELOUCH... AREN'T WE FRIENDS?

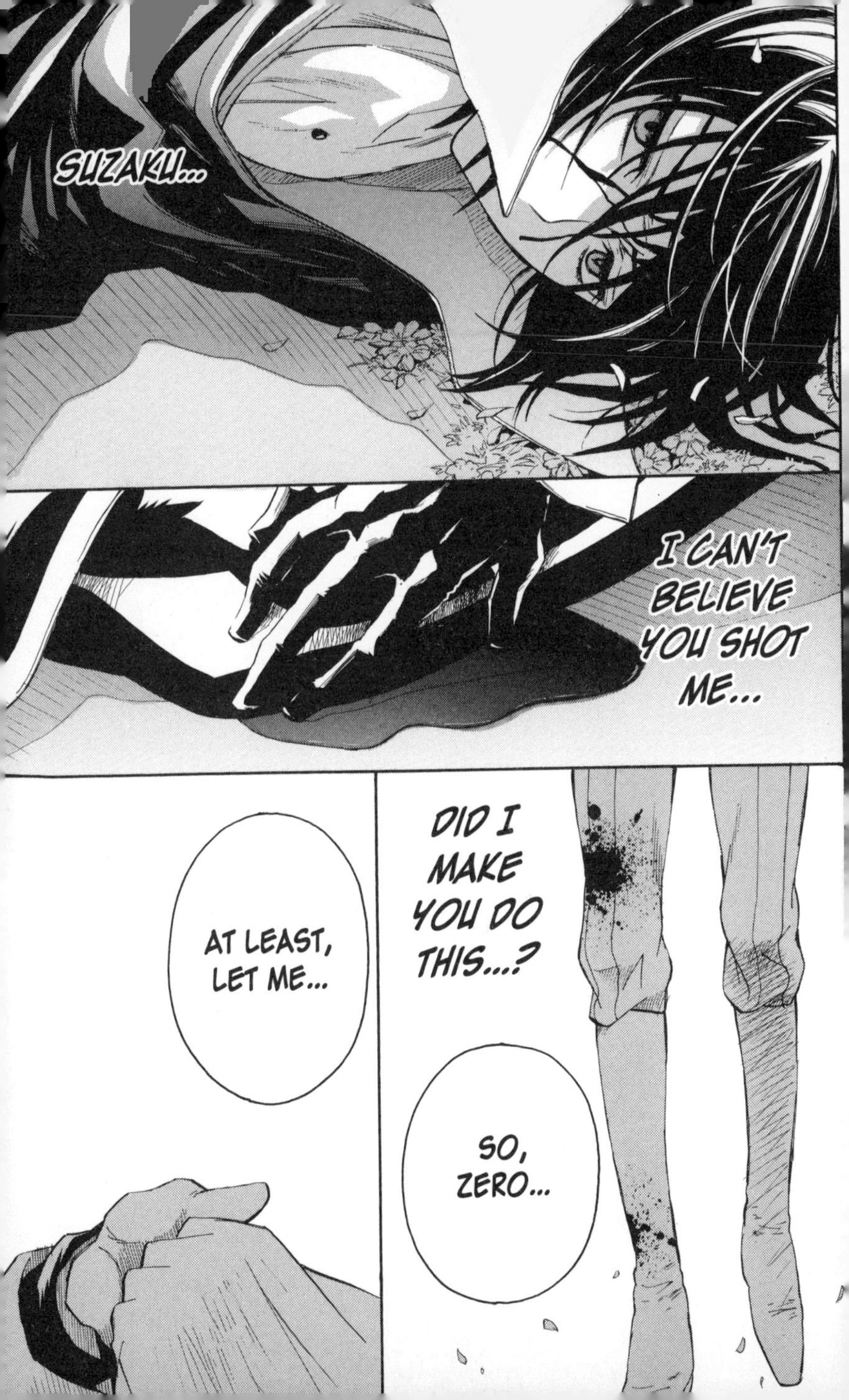
SUZAKU...
I CAN'T BELIEVE YOU SHOT ME...
DID I MAKE YOU DO THIS...?
SO, ZERO...
AT LEAST, LET ME...

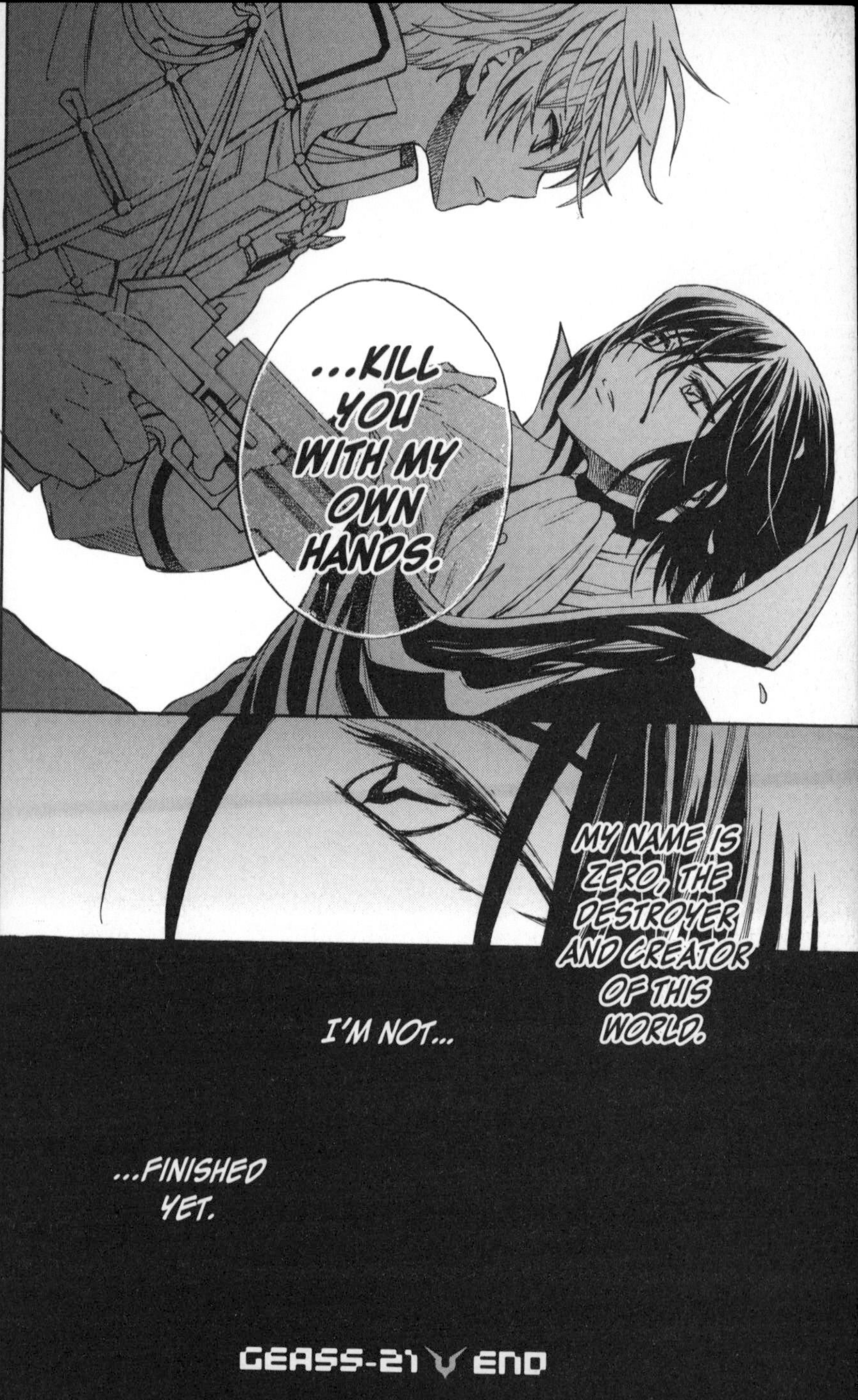
...KILL YOU WITH MY OWN HANDS.
MY NAME IS ZERO, THE DESTROYER AND CREATOR OF THIS WORLD.
I'M NOT...
...FINISHED YET.
GEASS-21 END

GEASS

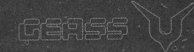

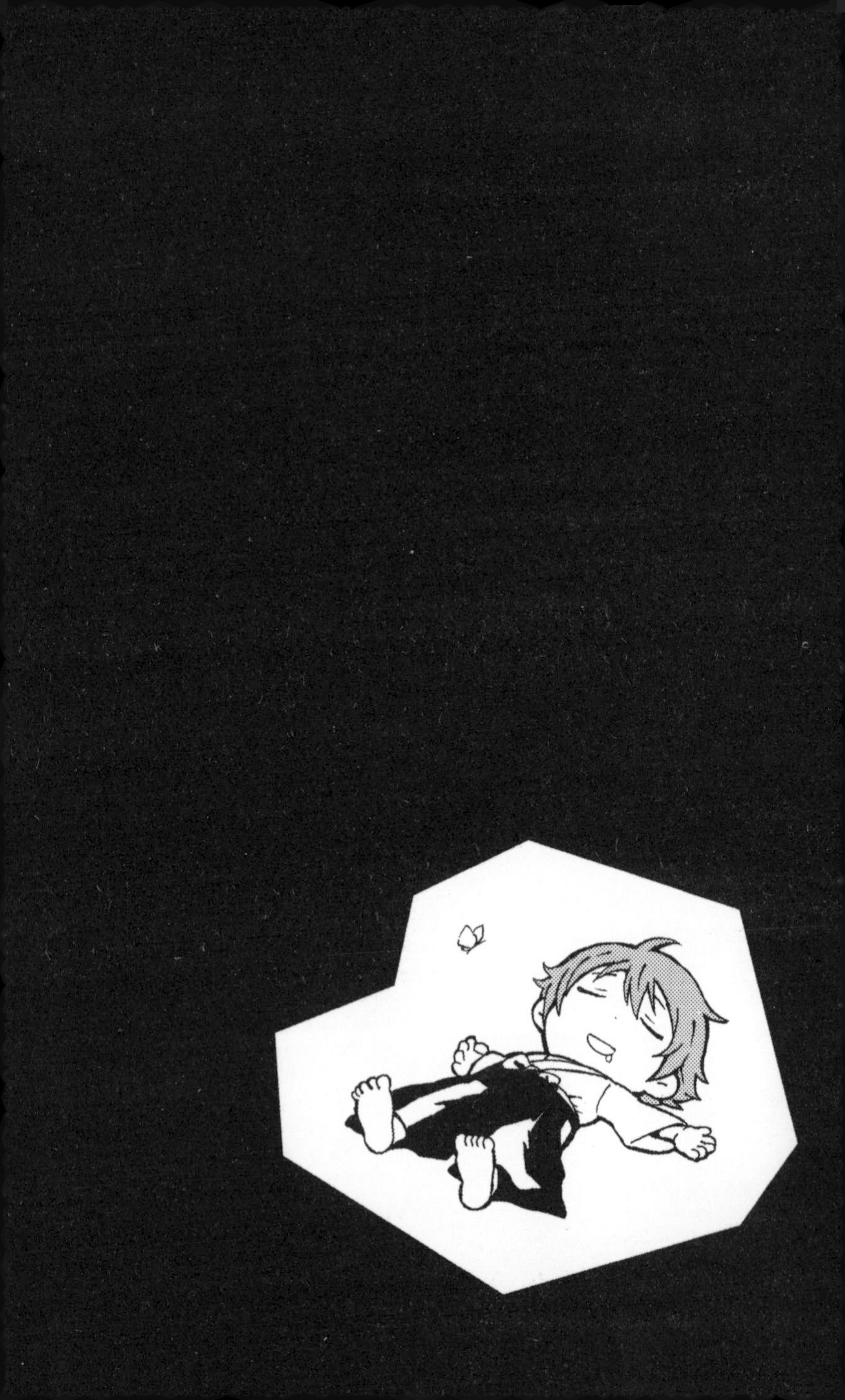

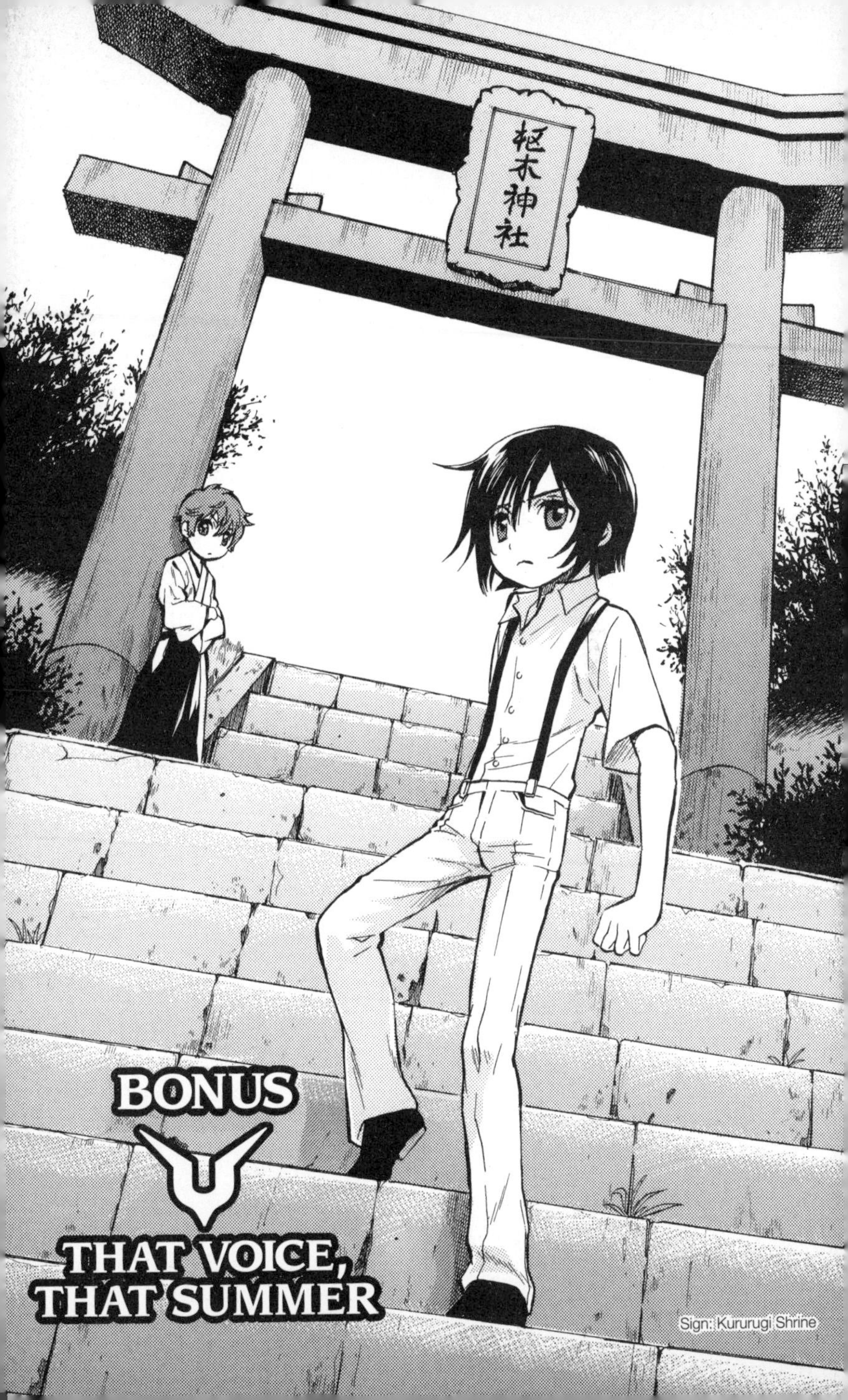
枢木神社
BONUS
THAT VOICE, THAT SUMMER
Sign: Kururugi Shrine

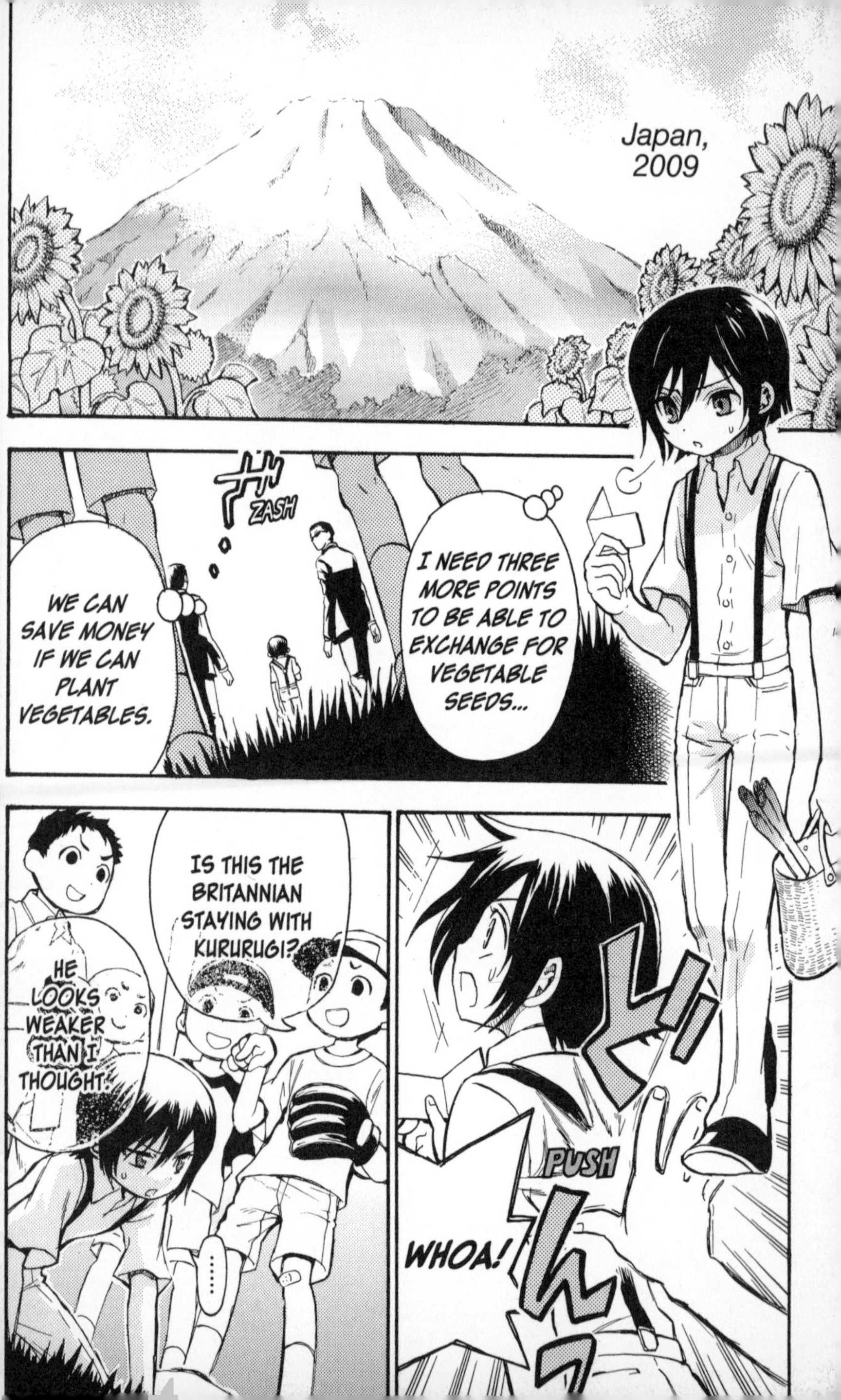
Japan, 2009
I NEED THREE MORE POINTS TO BE ABLE TO EXCHANGE FOR VEGETABLE SEEDS...
ZASH
WE CAN SAVE MONEY IF WE CAN PLANT VEGETABLES.
PUSH
WHOA!
IS THIS THE BRITANNIAN STAYING WITH KURURUGI?
HE LOOKS WEAKER THAN I THOUGHT.
......

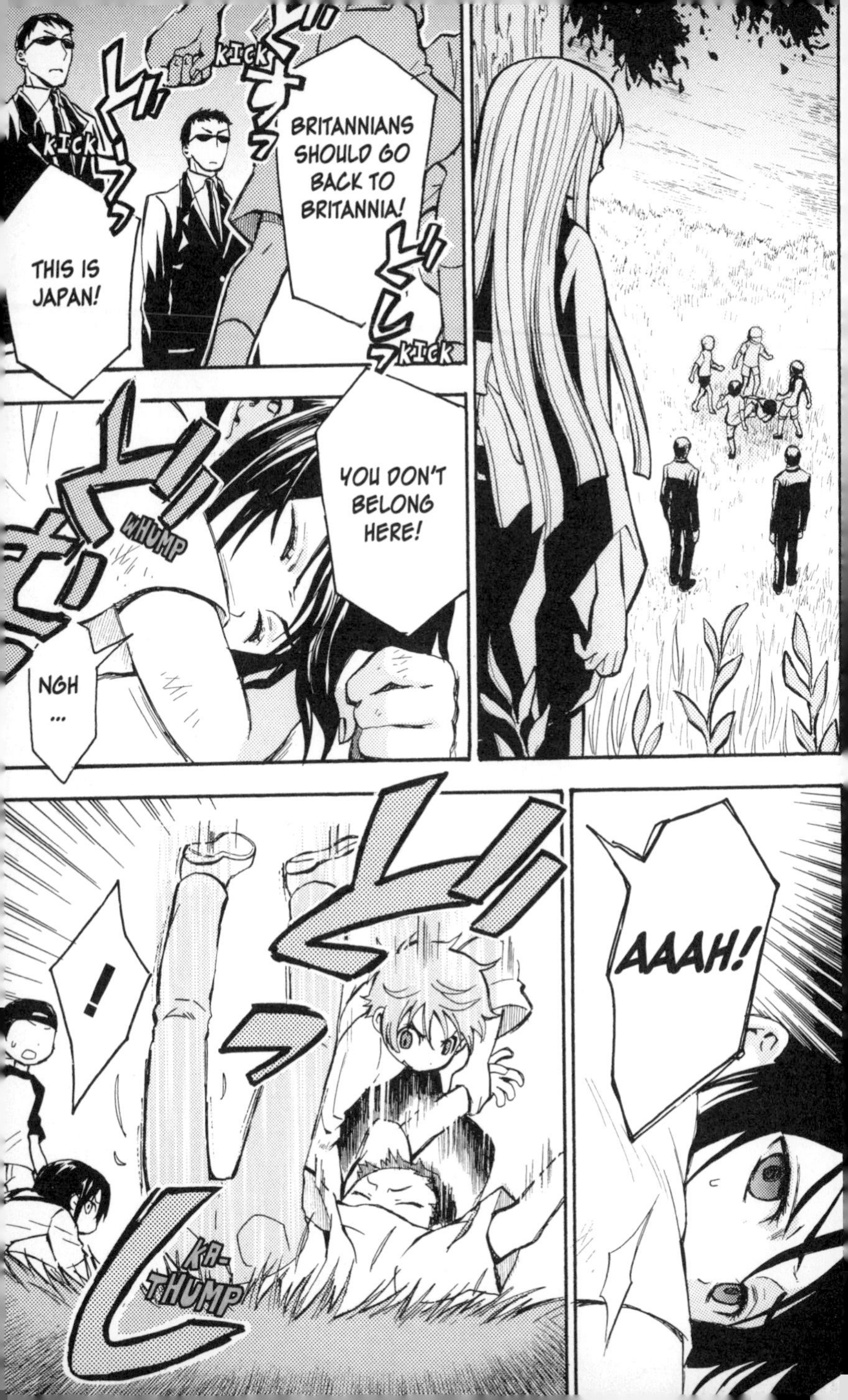
KICK
BRITANNIANS SHOULD GO BACK TO BRITANNIA!
KICK
KICK
THIS IS JAPAN!
YOU DON'T BELONG HERE!
WHUMP
NGH ...
AAAH!
!
KA-THUMP

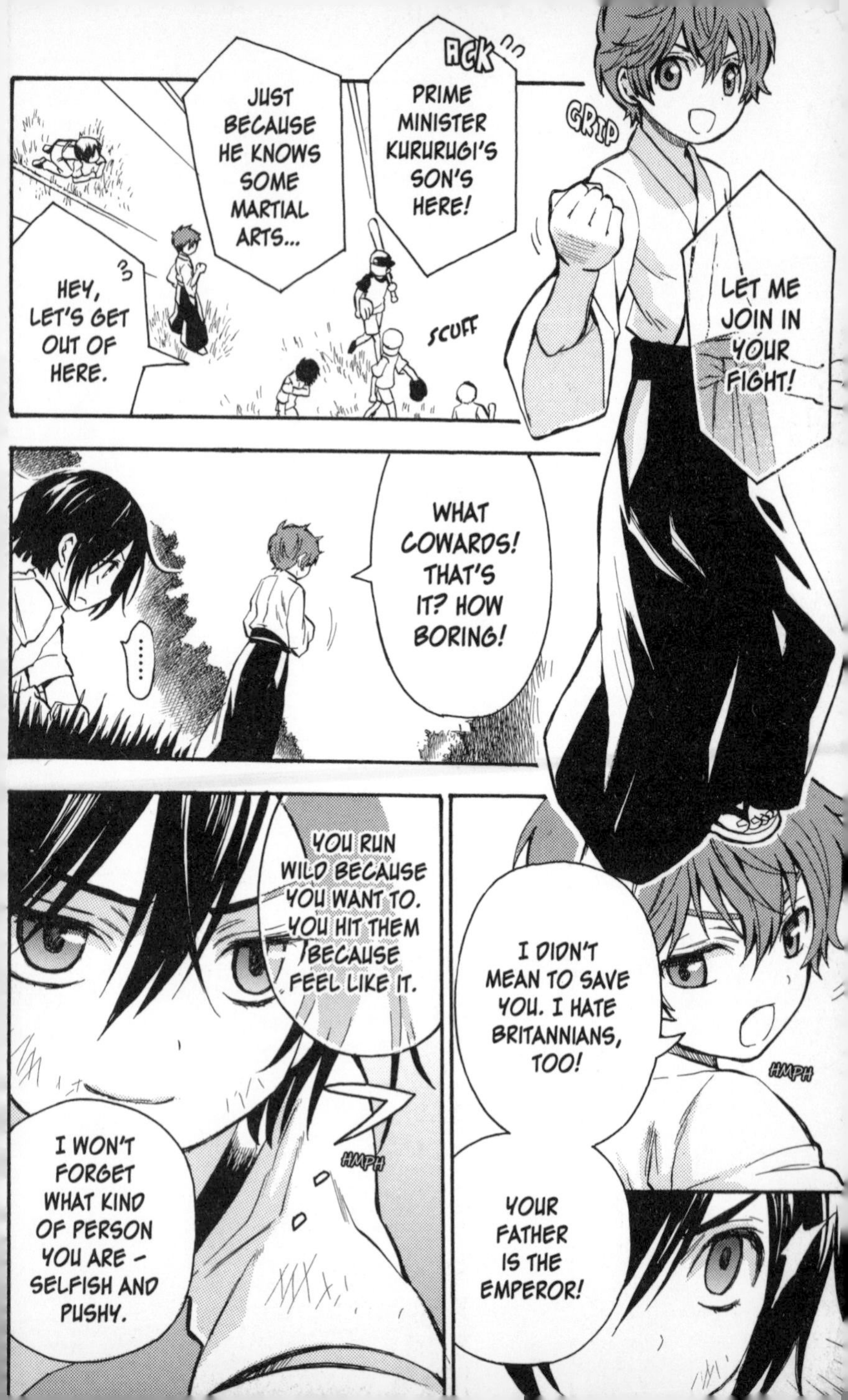
GRIP
LET ME JOIN IN YOUR FIGHT!
ACK
PRIME MINISTER KURURUGI'S SON'S HERE!
JUST BECAUSE HE KNOWS SOME MARTIAL ARTS...
HEY, LET'S GET OUT OF HERE.
SCUFF
WHAT COWARDS! THAT'S IT? HOW BORING!
......
I DIDN'T MEAN TO SAVE YOU. I HATE BRITANNIANS, TOO!
HMPH
YOUR FATHER IS THE EMPEROR!
YOU RUN WILD BECAUSE YOU WANT TO. YOU HIT THEM BECAUSE FEEL LIKE IT.
HMPH
I WON'T FORGET WHAT KIND OF PERSON YOU ARE - SELFISH AND PUSHY.

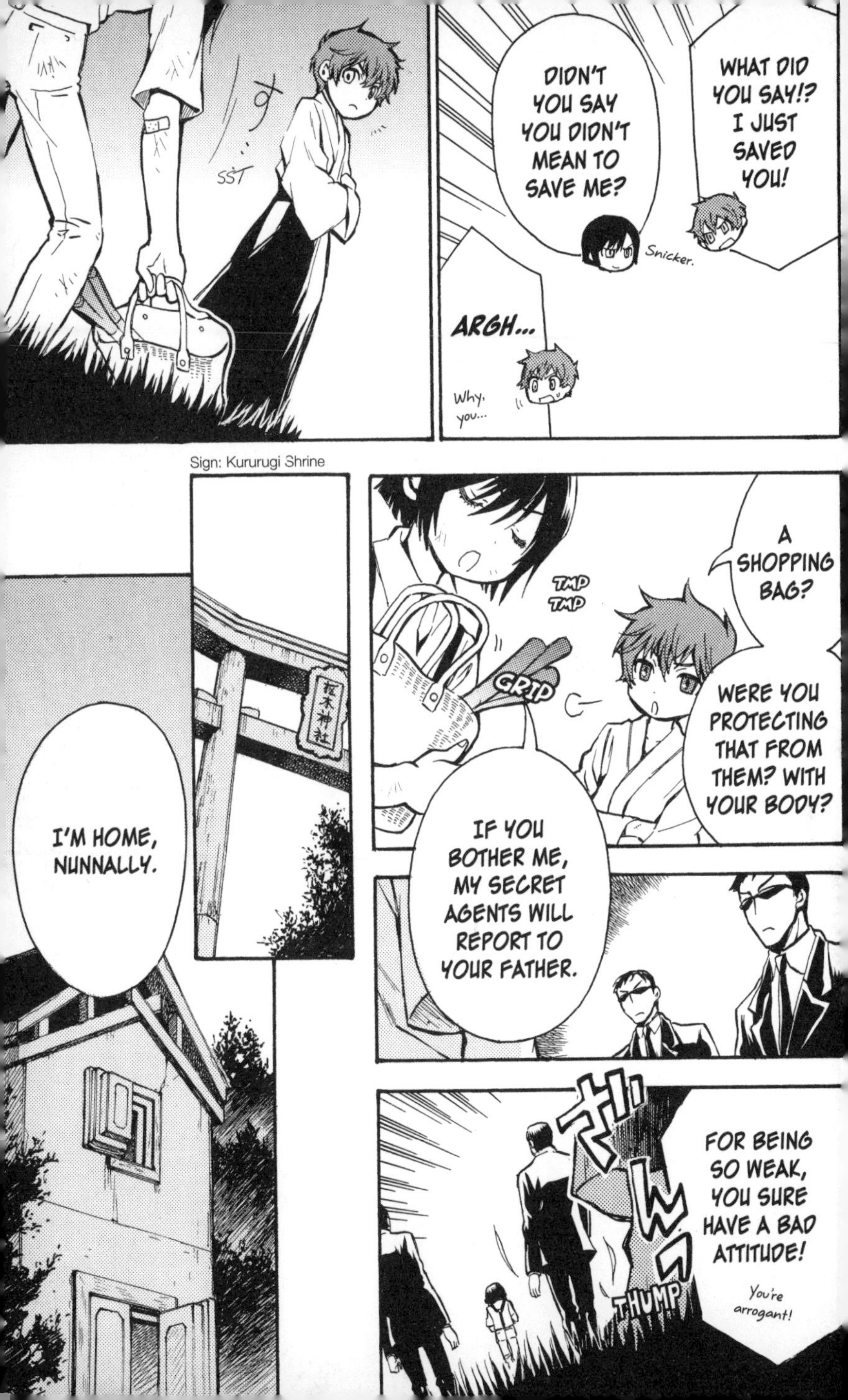
WHAT DID YOU SAY!? I JUST SAVED YOU!
DIDN'T YOU SAY YOU DIDN'T MEAN TO SAVE ME?
Snicker.
ARGH...
Why, you...
す
SST
A SHOPPING BAG?
TMP TMP
GRIP
WERE YOU PROTECTING THAT FROM THEM? WITH YOUR BODY?
IF YOU BOTHER ME, MY SECRET AGENTS WILL REPORT TO YOUR FATHER.
THUMP
FOR BEING SO WEAK, YOU SURE HAVE A BAD ATTITUDE!
You're arrogant!
Sign: Kururugi Shrine
I'M HOME, NUNNALLY.

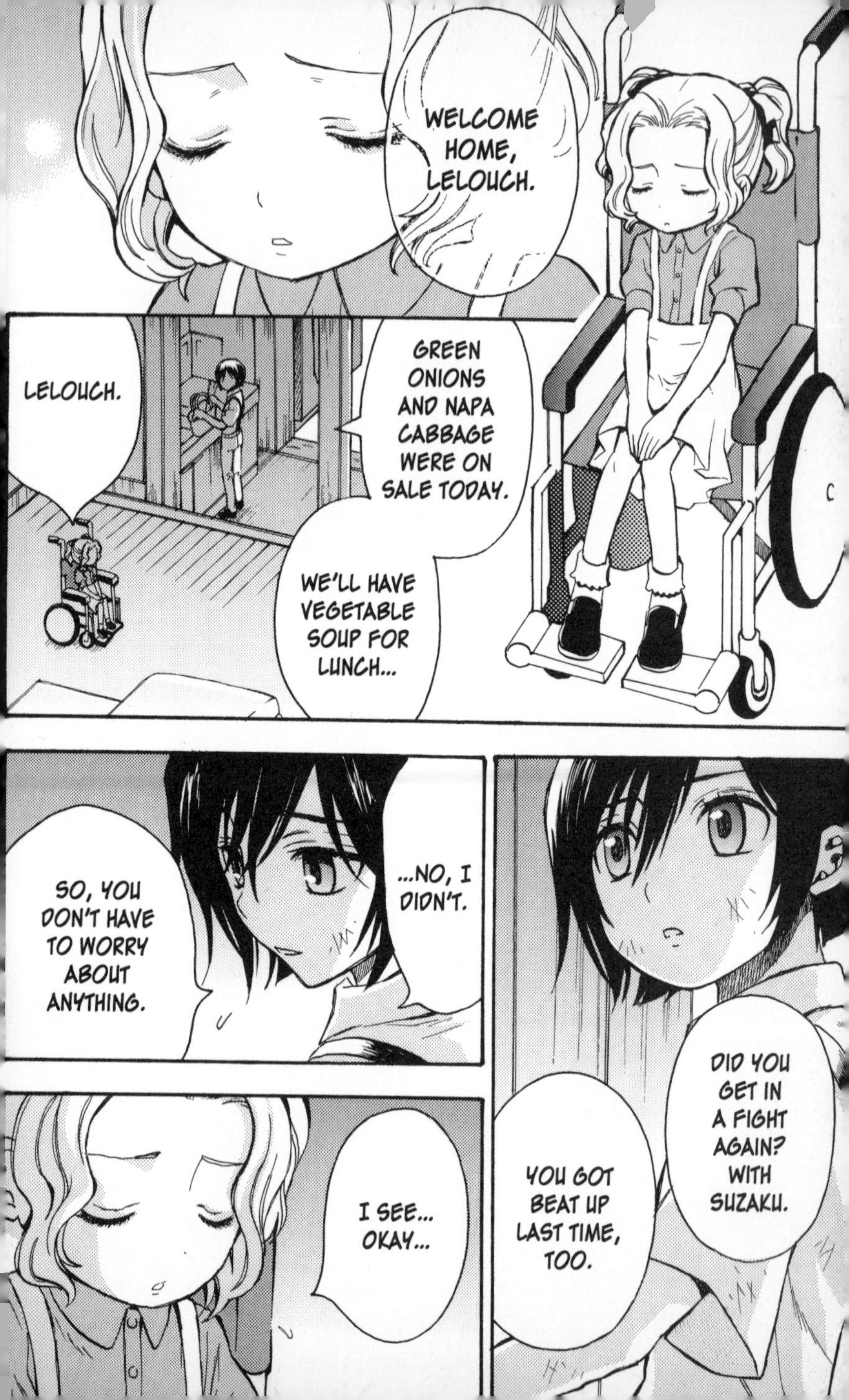
WELCOME HOME, LELOUCH.
GREEN ONIONS AND NAPA CABBAGE WERE ON SALE TODAY.
WE'LL HAVE VEGETABLE SOUP FOR LUNCH...
LELOUCH.
DID YOU GET IN A FIGHT AGAIN? WITH SUZAKU.
YOU GOT BEAT UP LAST TIME, TOO.
...NO, I DIDN'T.
SO, YOU DON'T HAVE TO WORRY ABOUT ANYTHING.
I SEE... OKAY...

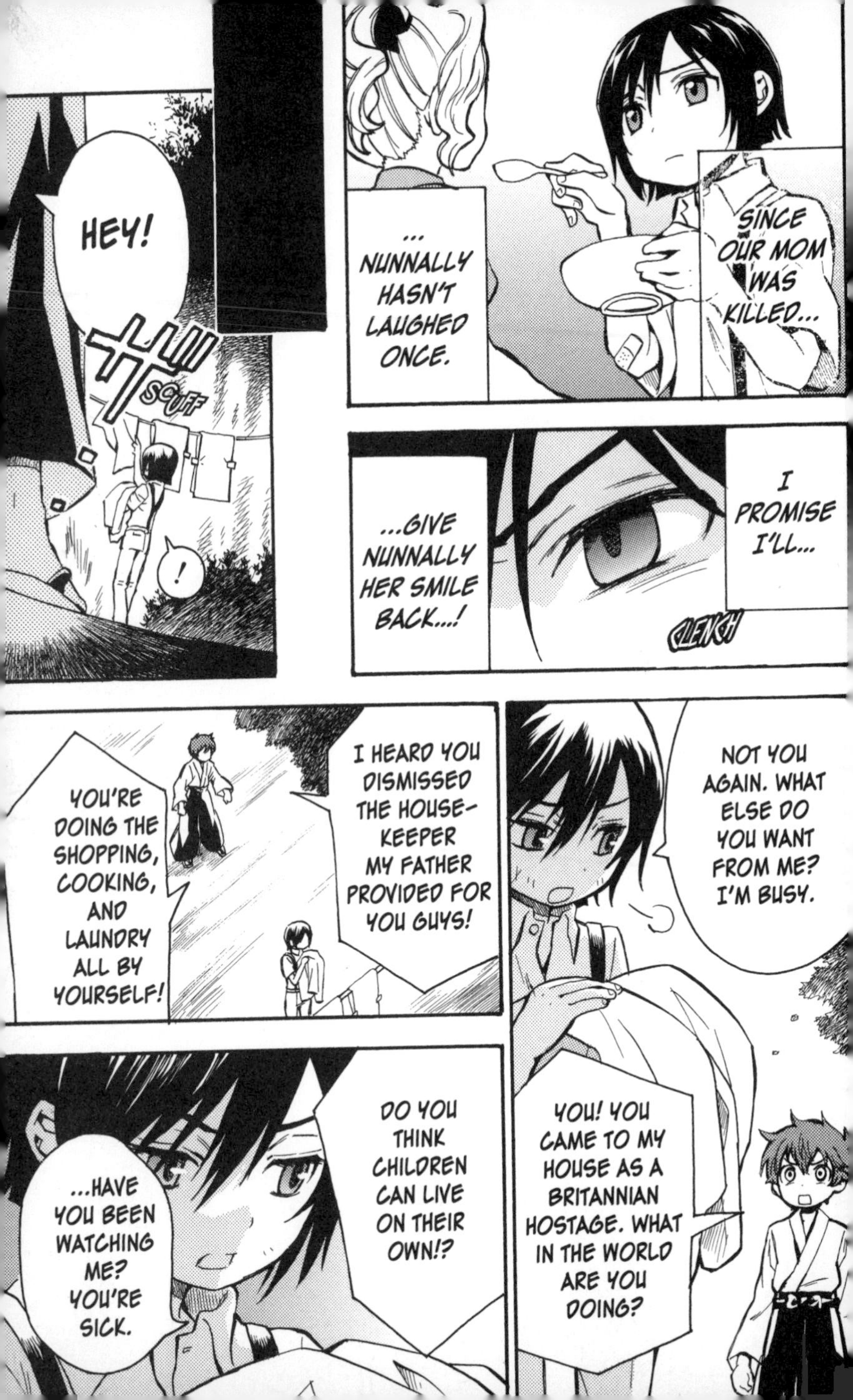
SINCE OUR MOM WAS KILLED...
...NUNNALLY HASN'T LAUGHED ONCE.
I PROMISE I'LL...
...GIVE NUNNALLY HER SMILE BACK...!
CLENCH
HEY!
SCUFF
!
NOT YOU AGAIN. WHAT ELSE DO YOU WANT FROM ME? I'M BUSY.
YOU! YOU CAME TO MY HOUSE AS A BRITANNIAN HOSTAGE. WHAT IN THE WORLD ARE YOU DOING?
I HEARD YOU DISMISSED THE HOUSE-KEEPER MY FATHER PROVIDED FOR YOU GUYS!
YOU'RE DOING THE SHOPPING, COOKING, AND LAUNDRY ALL BY YOURSELF!
DO YOU THINK CHILDREN CAN LIVE ON THEIR OWN!?
...HAVE YOU BEEN WATCHING ME? YOU'RE SICK.

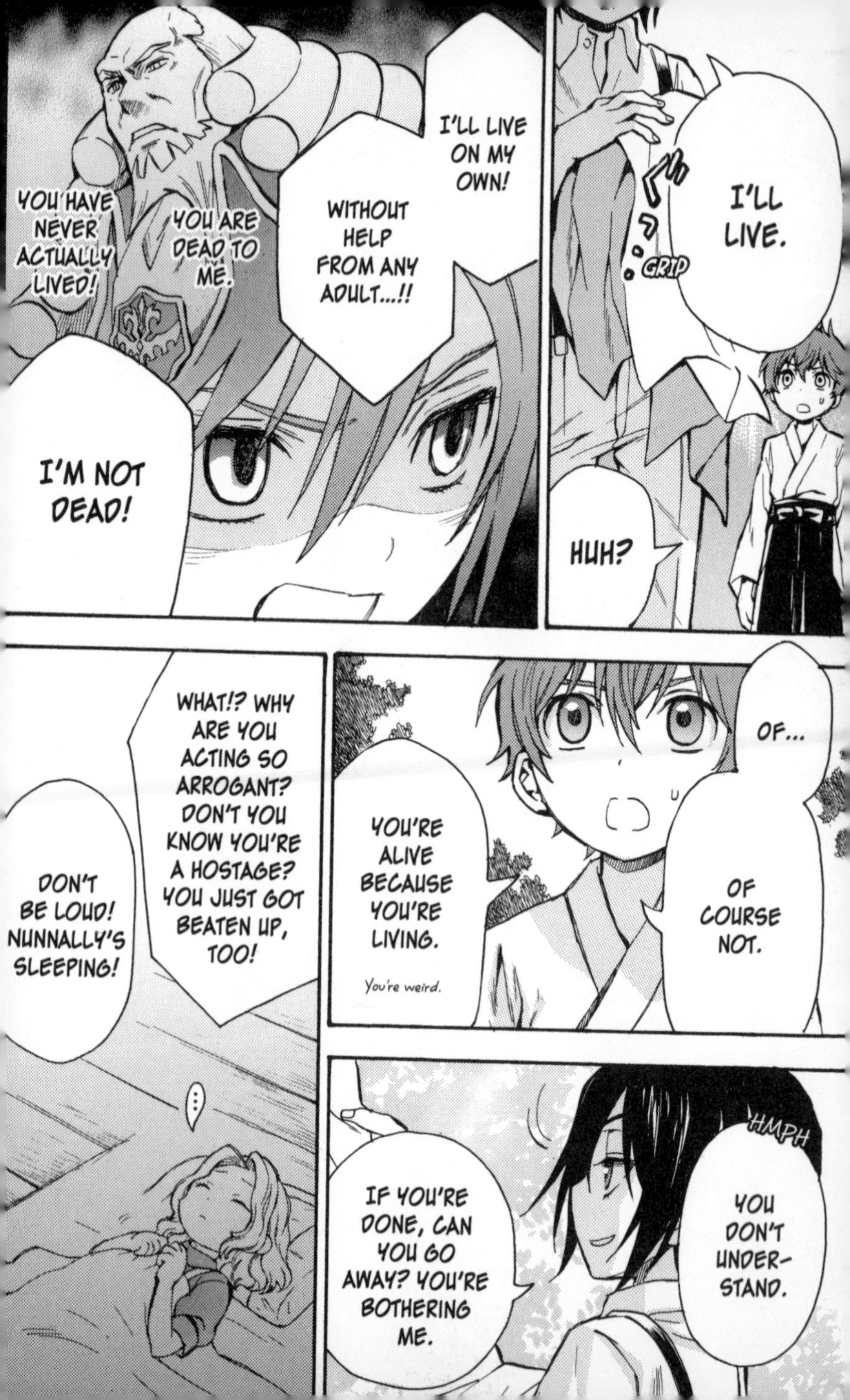

I'LL LIVE.
GRIP
HUH?
I'LL LIVE ON MY OWN!
WITHOUT HELP FROM ANY ADULT...!!
YOU ARE DEAD TO ME.
YOU HAVE NEVER ACTUALLY LIVED!
I'M NOT DEAD!
OF...
OF COURSE NOT.
YOU'RE ALIVE BECAUSE YOU'RE LIVING.
You're weird.
HMPH
YOU DON'T UNDER-STAND.
IF YOU'RE DONE, CAN YOU GO AWAY? YOU'RE BOTHERING ME.
WHAT!? WHY ARE YOU ACTING SO ARROGANT? DON'T YOU KNOW YOU'RE A HOSTAGE? YOU JUST GOT BEATEN UP, TOO!
DON'T BE LOUD! NUNNALLY'S SLEEPING!
...

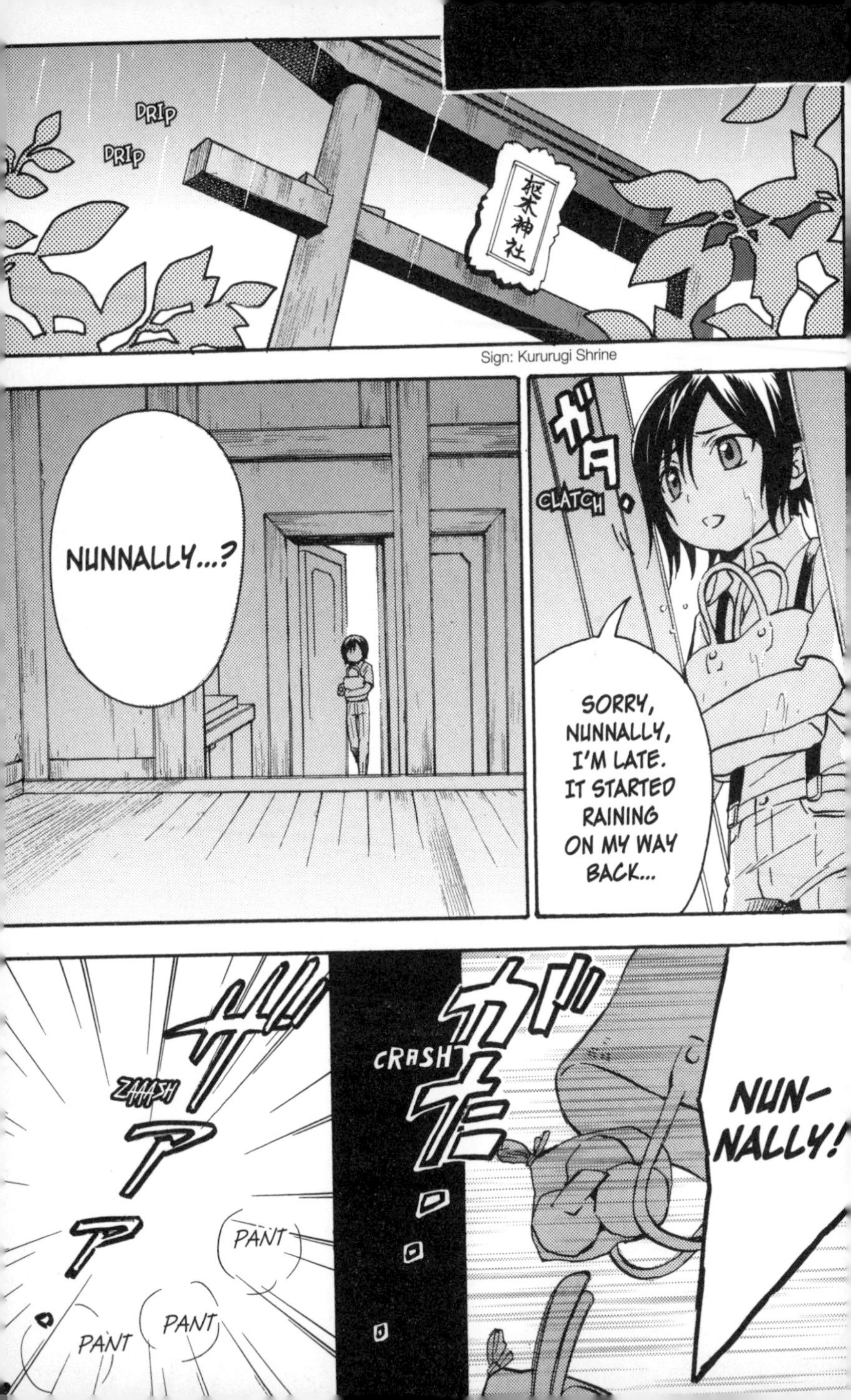
DRIP
DRIP
枢木神社
Sign: Kururugi Shrine
ガタ
CLATCH
SORRY, NUNNALLY, I'M LATE. IT STARTED RAINING ON MY WAY BACK...
NUNNALLY...?
NUN-NALLY!
CRASH
ザァァ
ZAAASH
PANT
PANT
PANT

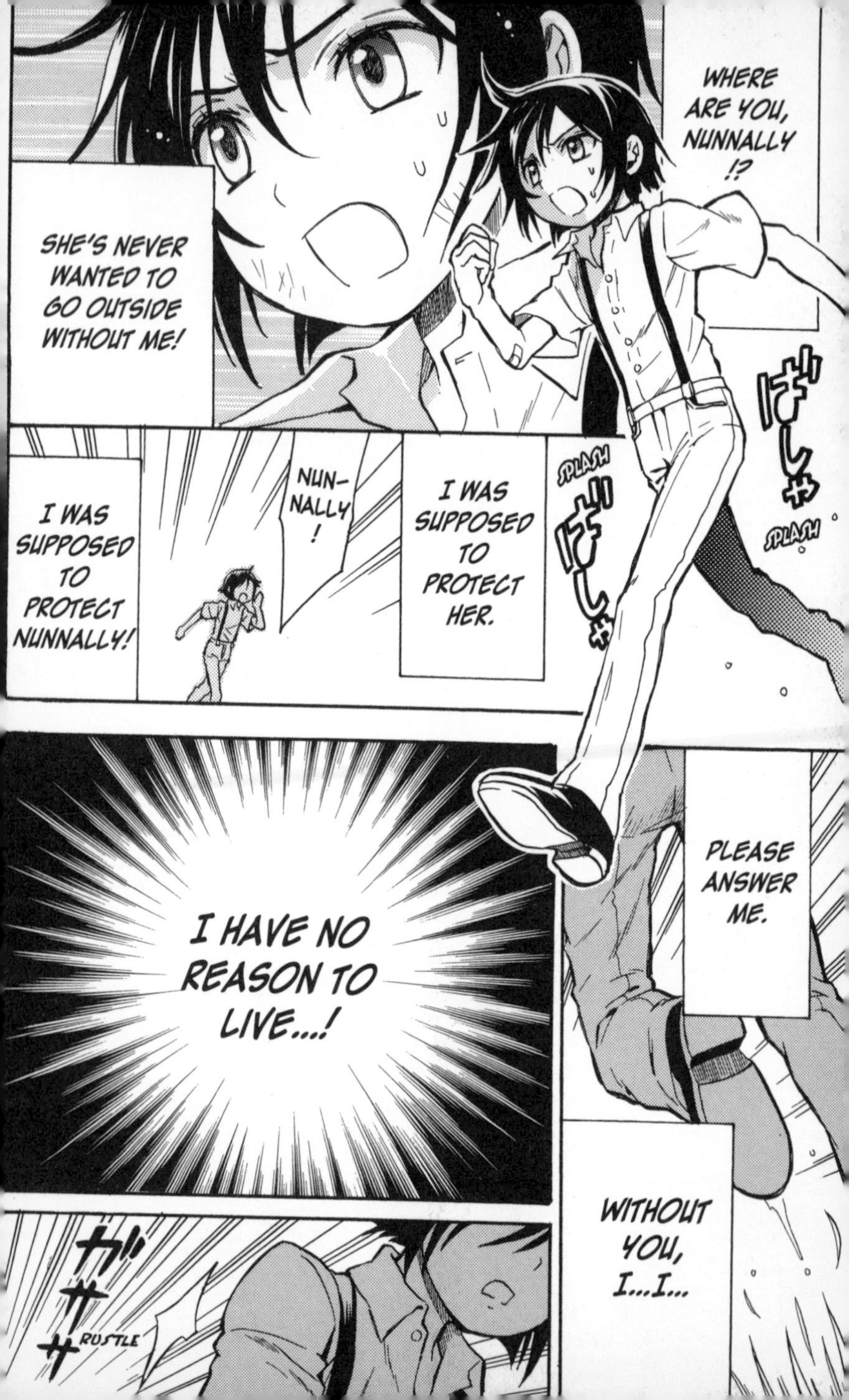

WHERE ARE YOU, NUNNALLY!?
SHE'S NEVER WANTED TO GO OUTSIDE WITHOUT ME!
ばしゃ
SPLASH
ばしゃ
SPLASH
I WAS SUPPOSED TO PROTECT HER.
NUN-NALLY!
I WAS SUPPOSED TO PROTECT NUNNALLY!
PLEASE ANSWER ME.
WITHOUT YOU, I...I...
I HAVE NO REASON TO LIVE...!
ガサ
RUSTLE

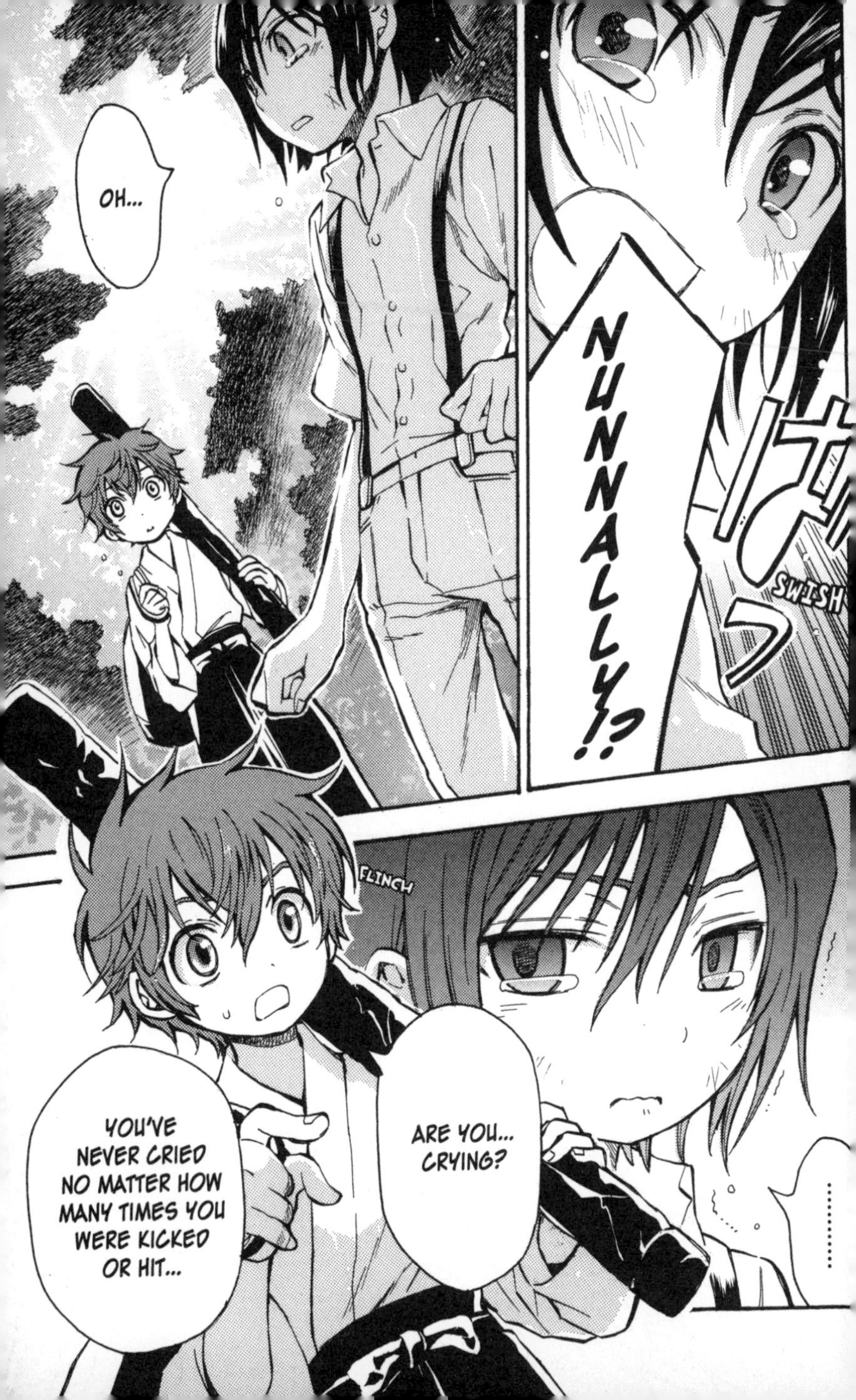
NUNNALLY!?
SWISH
OH...
......
FLINCH
ARE YOU... CRYING?
YOU'VE NEVER CRIED NO MATTER HOW MANY TIMES YOU WERE KICKED OR HIT...

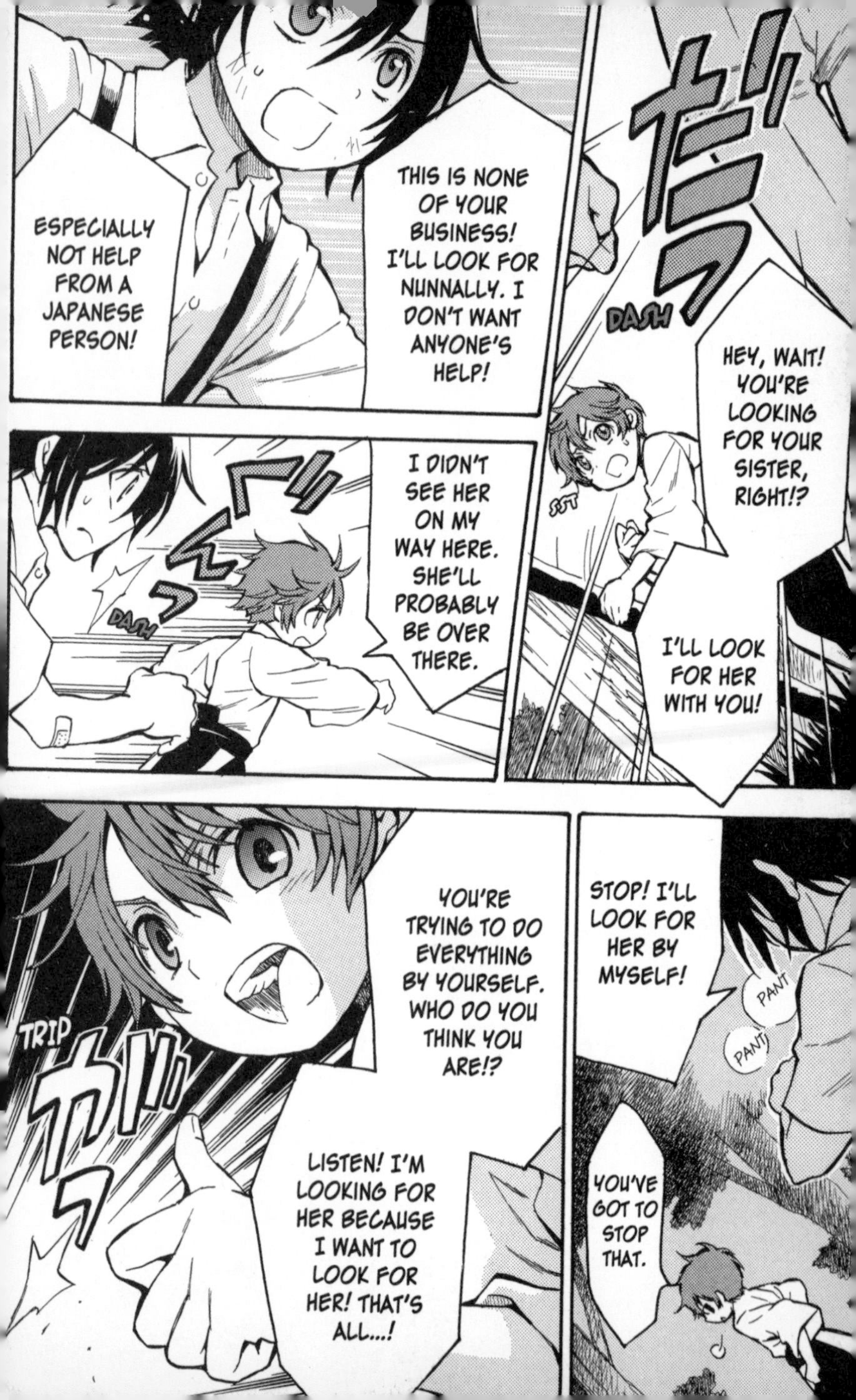
DASH
HEY, WAIT! YOU'RE LOOKING FOR YOUR SISTER, RIGHT!?
SST
I'LL LOOK FOR HER WITH YOU!
THIS IS NONE OF YOUR BUSINESS! I'LL LOOK FOR NUNNALLY. I DON'T WANT ANYONE'S HELP!
ESPECIALLY NOT HELP FROM A JAPANESE PERSON!
I DIDN'T SEE HER ON MY WAY HERE. SHE'LL PROBABLY BE OVER THERE.
DASH
STOP! I'LL LOOK FOR HER BY MYSELF!
PANT
PANT
YOU'VE GOT TO STOP THAT.
YOU'RE TRYING TO DO EVERYTHING BY YOURSELF. WHO DO YOU THINK YOU ARE!?
LISTEN! I'M LOOKING FOR HER BECAUSE I WANT TO LOOK FOR HER! THAT'S ALL...!
TRIP

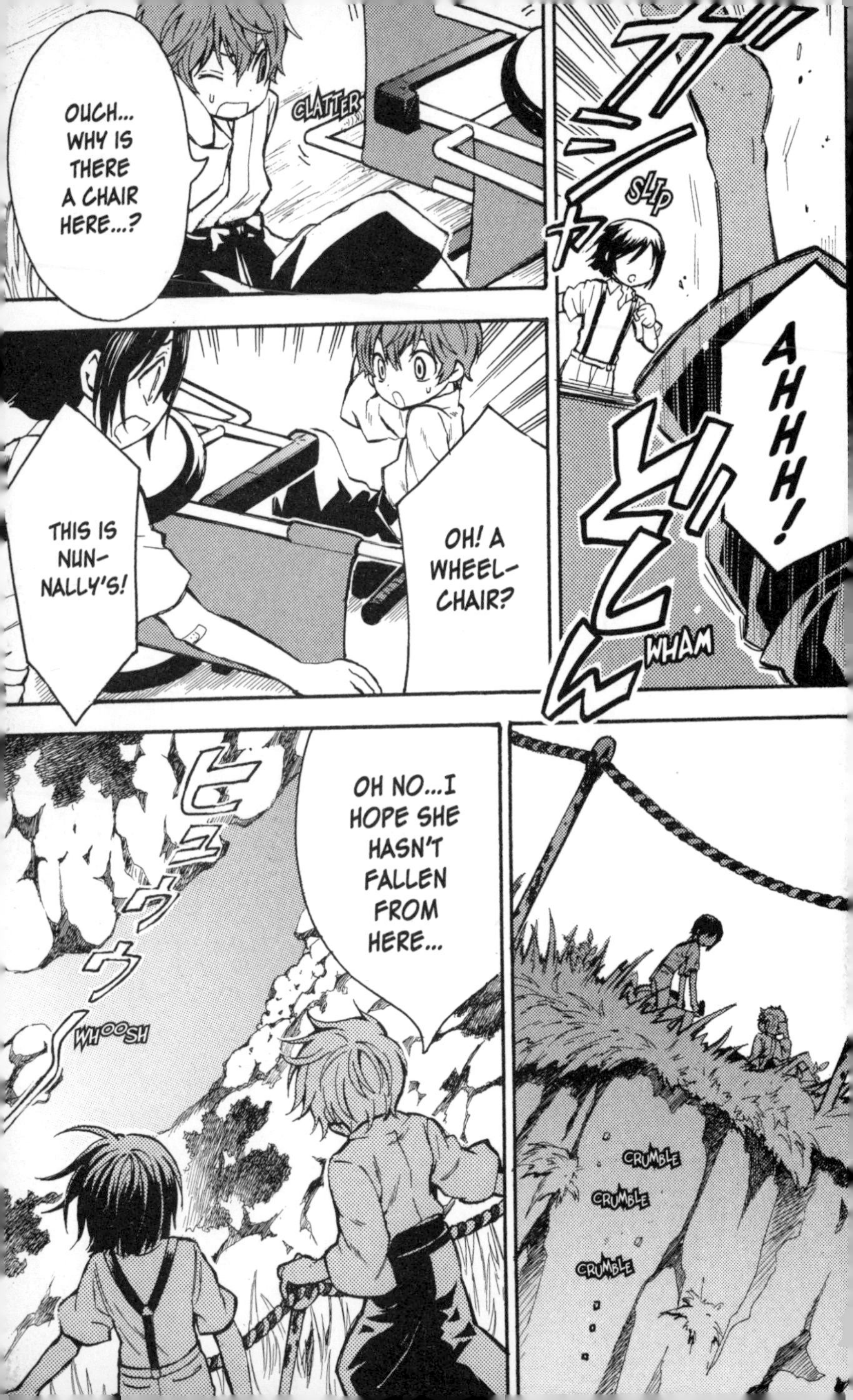
SLIP
AHHHH!
WHAM
CLATTER
OUCH... WHY IS THERE A CHAIR HERE...?
OH! A WHEEL-CHAIR?
THIS IS NUN-NALLY'S!
CRUMBLE
CRUMBLE
CRUMBLE
OH NO...I HOPE SHE HASN'T FALLEN FROM HERE...
WHOOSH

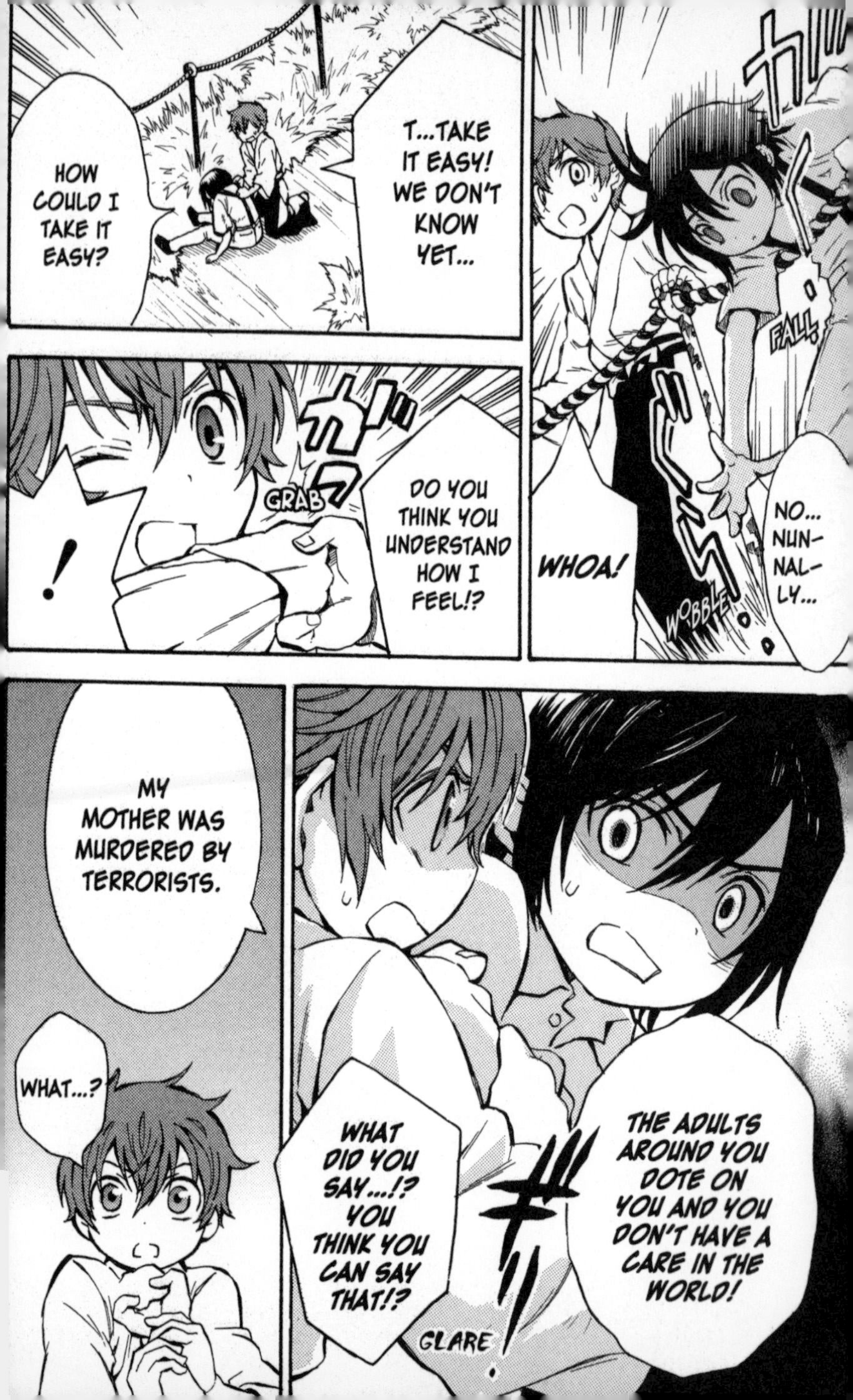
FALL
NO... NUNNALLY...
WHOA!
WOBBLE
T...TAKE IT EASY! WE DON'T KNOW YET...
HOW COULD I TAKE IT EASY?
GRAB
DO YOU THINK YOU UNDERSTAND HOW I FEEL!?
!
THE ADULTS AROUND YOU DOTE ON YOU AND YOU DON'T HAVE A CARE IN THE WORLD!
WHAT DID YOU SAY...!? YOU THINK YOU CAN SAY THAT!?
GLARE
MY MOTHER WAS MURDERED BY TERRORISTS.
WHAT...?

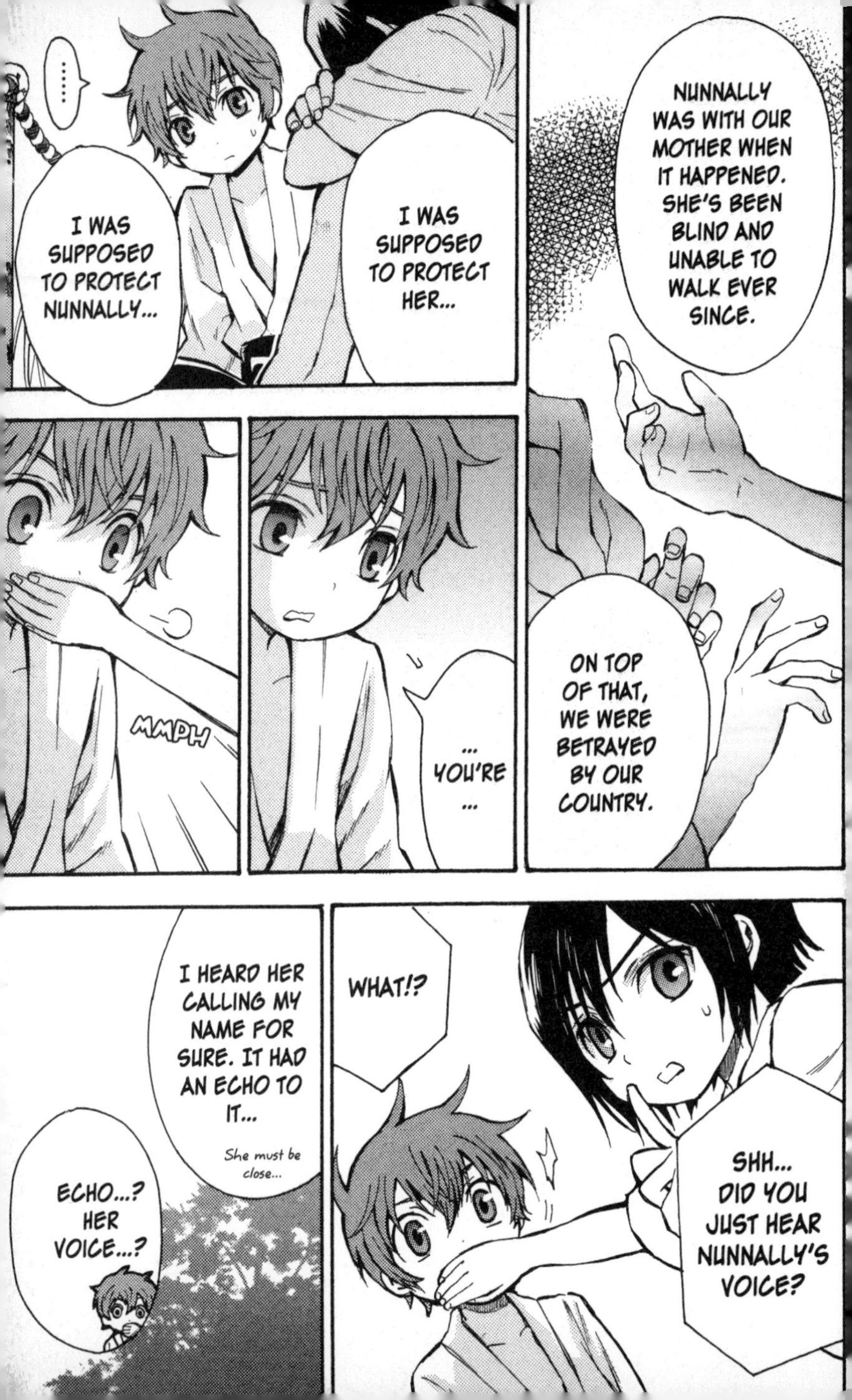
NUNNALLY WAS WITH OUR MOTHER WHEN IT HAPPENED. SHE'S BEEN BLIND AND UNABLE TO WALK EVER SINCE.
I WAS SUPPOSED TO PROTECT HER...
......
I WAS SUPPOSED TO PROTECT NUNNALLY...
ON TOP OF THAT, WE WERE BETRAYED BY OUR COUNTRY.
... YOU'RE ...
MMPH
SHH... DID YOU JUST HEAR NUNNALLY'S VOICE?
WHAT!?
I HEARD HER CALLING MY NAME FOR SURE. IT HAD AN ECHO TO IT...
She must be close...
ECHO...? HER VOICE...?

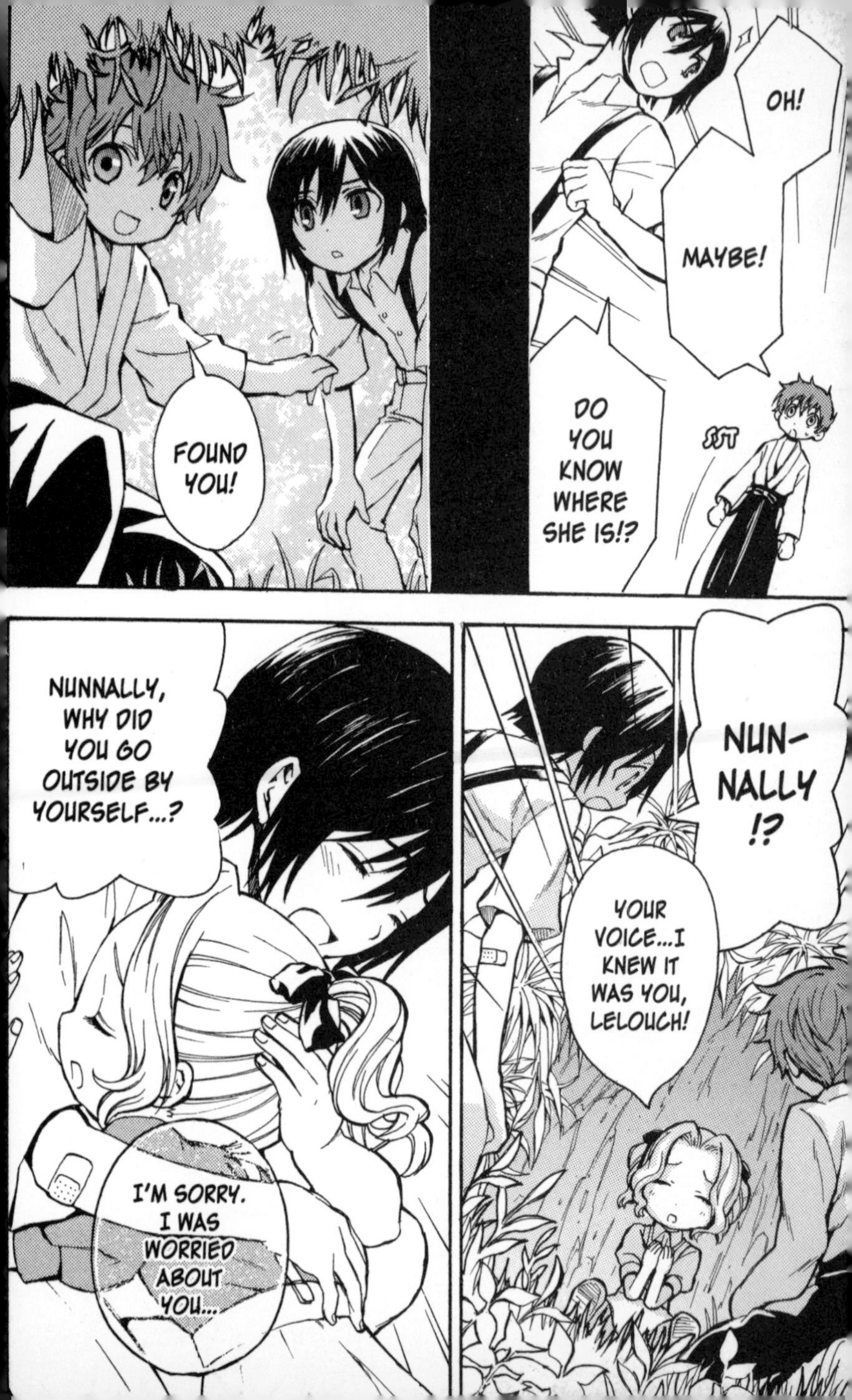
OH!
MAYBE!
DO YOU KNOW WHERE SHE IS!?
FOUND YOU!
NUN-NALLY!?
YOUR VOICE...I KNEW IT WAS YOU, LELOUCH!
NUNNALLY, WHY DID YOU GO OUTSIDE BY YOURSELF...?
I'M SORRY. I WAS WORRIED ABOUT YOU...

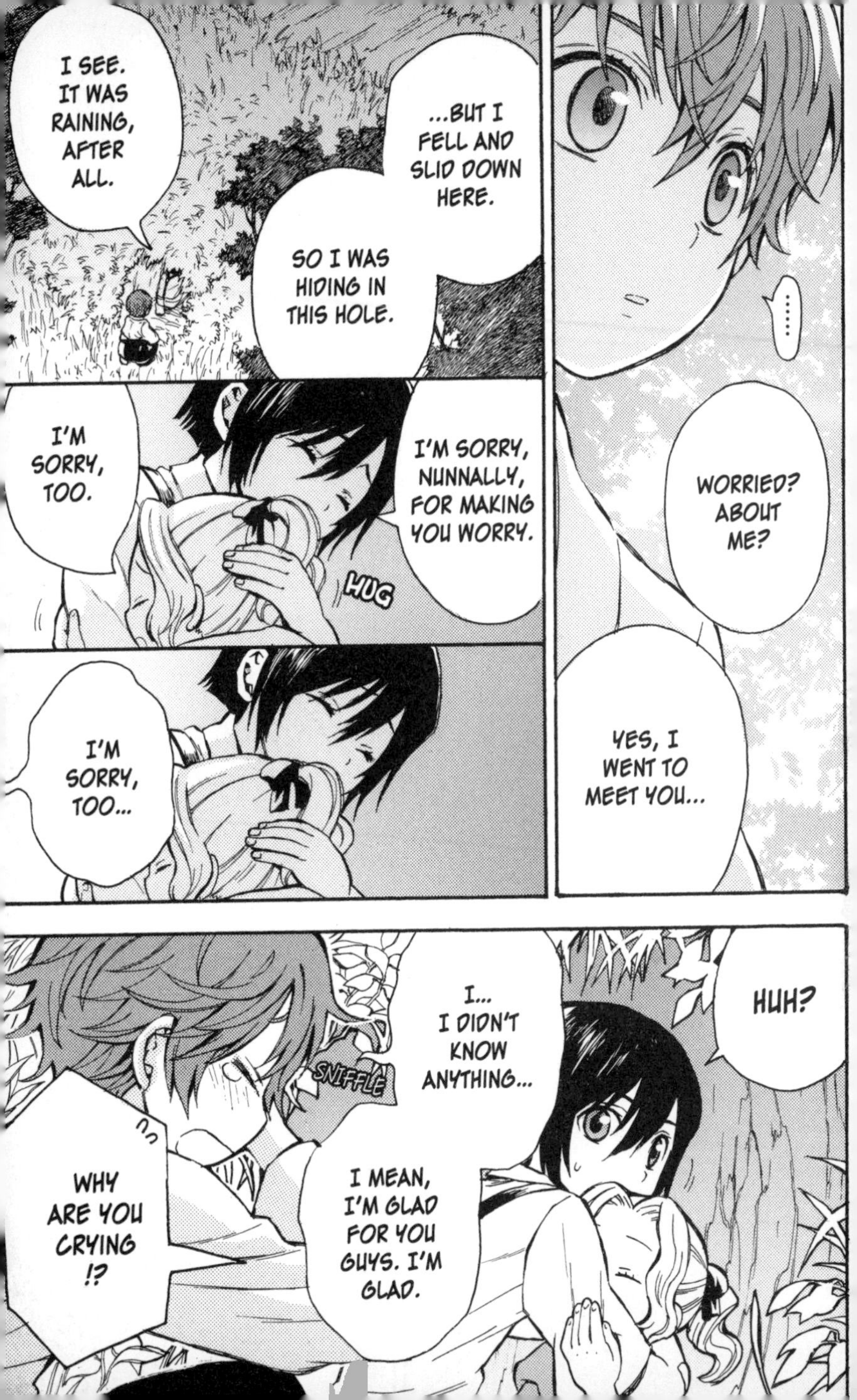
......
WORRIED? ABOUT ME?
YES, I WENT TO MEET YOU...
...BUT I FELL AND SLID DOWN HERE.
SO I WAS HIDING IN THIS HOLE.
I SEE. IT WAS RAINING, AFTER ALL.
I'M SORRY, NUNNALLY, FOR MAKING YOU WORRY.
HUG
I'M SORRY, TOO.
I'M SORRY, TOO...
HUH?
I... I DIDN'T KNOW ANYTHING...
I MEAN, I'M GLAD FOR YOU GUYS. I'M GLAD.
SNIFFLE
WHY ARE YOU CRYING !?

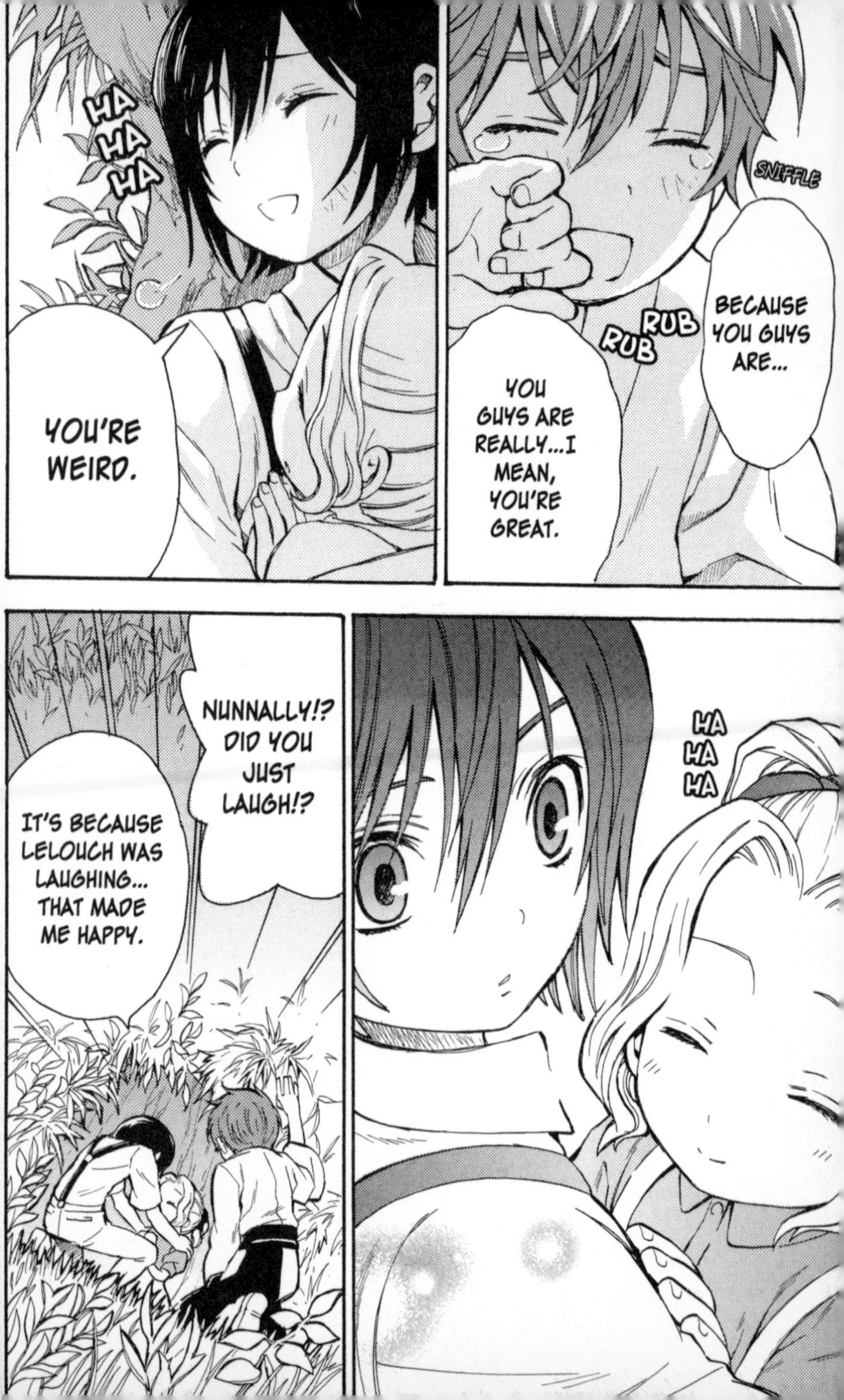
SNIFFLE
BECAUSE YOU GUYS ARE...
RUB RUB
YOU GUYS ARE REALLY...I MEAN, YOU'RE GREAT.
HA HA HA
YOU'RE WEIRD.
HA HA HA
NUNNALLY!? DID YOU JUST LAUGH!?
IT'S BECAUSE LELOUCH WAS LAUGHING... THAT MADE ME HAPPY.

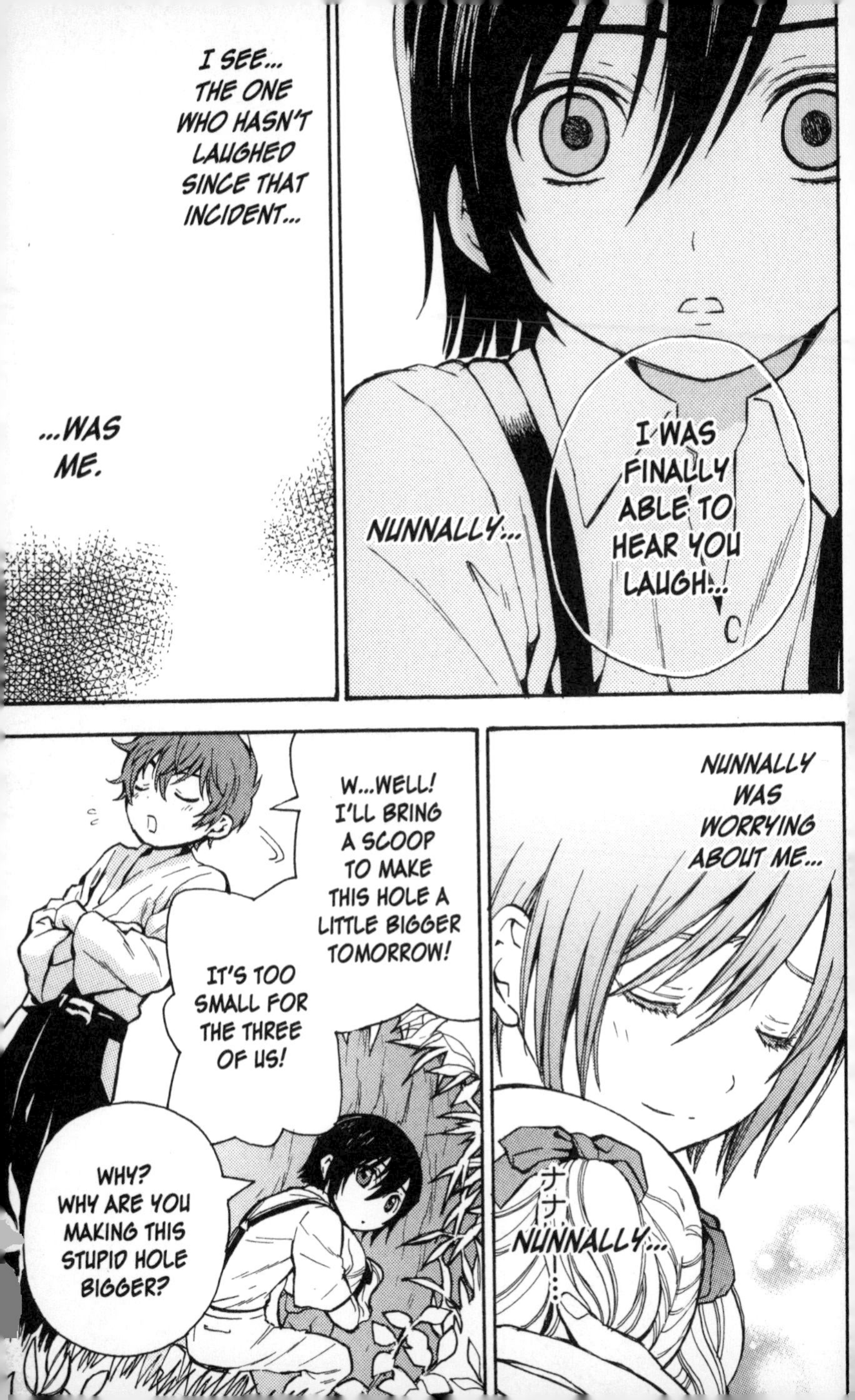
I WAS FINALLY ABLE TO HEAR YOU LAUGH...
NUNNALLY...
I SEE... THE ONE WHO HASN'T LAUGHED SINCE THAT INCIDENT...
...WAS ME.
NUNNALLY WAS WORRYING ABOUT ME...
ナナ
NUNNALLY...
W...WELL! I'LL BRING A SCOOP TO MAKE THIS HOLE A LITTLE BIGGER TOMORROW!
IT'S TOO SMALL FOR THE THREE OF US!
WHY? WHY ARE YOU MAKING THIS STUPID HOLE BIGGER?

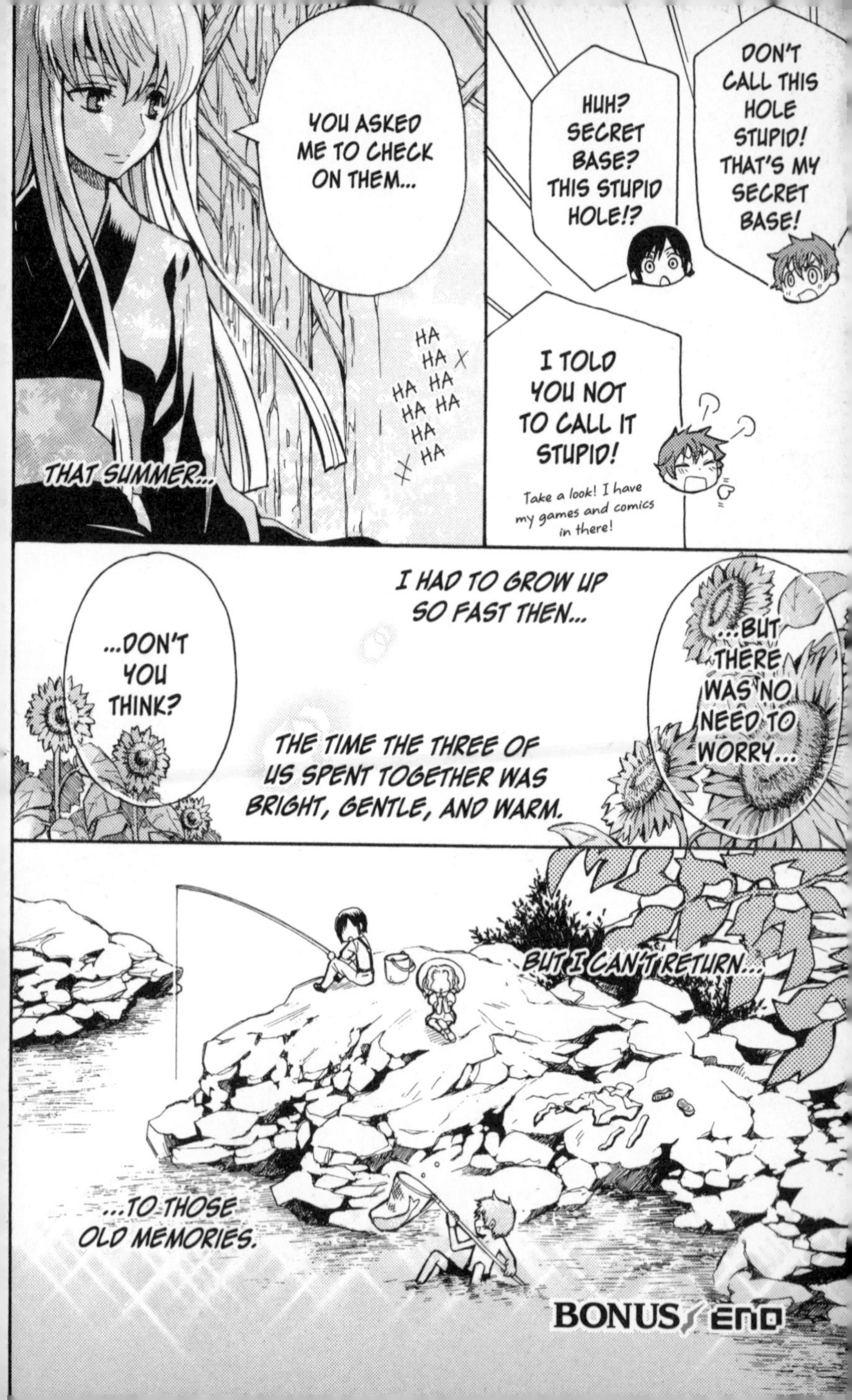
DON'T CALL THIS HOLE STUPID! THAT'S MY SECRET BASE!
HUH? SECRET BASE? THIS STUPID HOLE!?
I TOLD YOU NOT TO CALL IT STUPID!
Take a look! I have my games and comics in there!
HA HA HA HA HA HA HA HA
YOU ASKED ME TO CHECK ON THEM...
THAT SUMMER...
...BUT THERE WAS NO NEED TO WORRY...
I HAD TO GROW UP SO FAST THEN...
...DON'T YOU THINK?
THE TIME THE THREE OF US SPENT TOGETHER WAS BRIGHT, GENTLE, AND WARM.
BUT I CAN'T RETURN...
...TO THOSE OLD MEMORIES.
BONUS END

GEASS

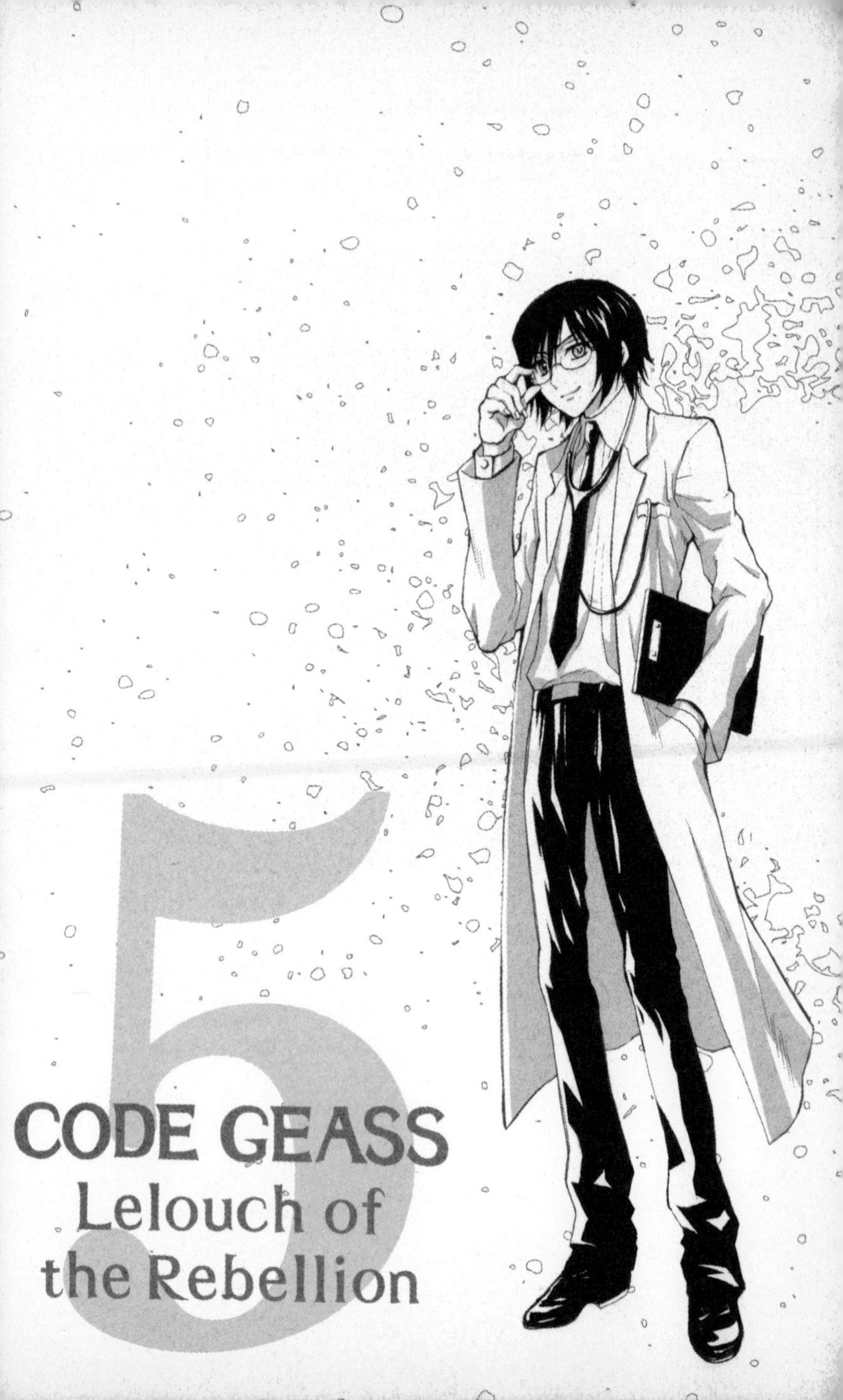
5
CODE GEASS
Lelouch of
the Rebellion

...of the first season of the anime conclude in this volume. If felt

...the past two years, every month was full of excitement. I felt that

...something in the months with 31 days, and I felt that I lost something

...hs with 30 days. I can't explain how I felt about February...

...at I couldn't have completed this manga on my own. I'm grateful for

...rt of my editors, assistants, sales, and readers. I also have to thank

...nd of course my friends and family, for their support. This is starting

...like the thank you note you'd write at the end of a series.

...ove it if you could support me for the next volume as well.

MAJIKO!

...you!

...rou Ohkouchi, Mr. Goro Taniguchi, Mr. Kawaguchi, Mr. S-mura,

...noto and Producer Mr. Kawaguchi

...ditor Mr. K-da

...STANTS:

...ase   Ueda

CODE GEASS
コードギアス
反逆のルルーシュ Lelouch
of the Rebellion

MANGA   Majiko!
ORIGINAL STORY   Ichirou Ohkouchi
                                          Goro Taniguchi

ENGLISH PRODUCTION CREDITS

TRANSLATION   KURO UZU
LETTERING   Keiran O'Leary
EDITOR   Robert Place Napton
PUBLISHER   Ken Iyadomi

Code Geass Lelouch of the Rebellion Vol. 5
©Majiko! 2008
©2006-2009 SUNRISE/PROJECT GEASS, MBS
Character Design ©2006 CLAMP

Originally published in Japan in 2008 by KADOKAWA SHOTEN PUBLISHING CO., LTD., Tokyo.
English translation published by Bandai Entertainment Inc. under the license from Sunrise Inc.

All rights reserved. No portion of this book may be reproduced or transmitted in any form or by any
means without written permission from the copyright holder. Code Geass is a work of fiction. Any
resemblance to actual events or locales or persons, living or dead, is entirely coincidental.

ISBN-13: 978-1-60496-159-1

Printed in Canada
First Bandai Printing: September 2009

10 9 8 7 6 5 4 3 2 1